"A Wind is Rising"

Eugene O'Neill, Shane O'Neill, and Agnes Boulton in Provincetown, around 1921. Yale Collection of American Literature, Beinecke Rare Book and Manuscript Library.

"A Wind is Rising"

The Correspondence of
Agnes Boulton and Eugene O'Neill

Edited by William Davies King

Madison • Teaneck
Fairleigh Dickinson University Press
London: Associated University Presses

Associated University Presses
440 Forsgate Drive
Cranbury, NJ 08512

Associated University Presses
16 Barter Street
London WC1A 2AH, England

Associated University Presses
P.O. Box 338, Port Credit
Mississauga, Ontario
Canada L5G 4L8

The paper used in this publication meets the requirements of the American National Standard for Permanence of Paper for Printed Library Materials Z39.48-1984

Library of Congress Cataloging-in-Publication Data

Boulton, Agnes, 1893–1968.
    A wind is rising : the correspondence of Agnes Boulton and Eugene O'Neill / edited by William Davies King.
        p.   cm.
    Includes bibliographical references and index.
    ISBN 0-8386-3808-2 (alk. paper)
    1. O'Neill, Eugene, 1888–1953—Marriage. 2. Boulton, Agnes, 1893–1968 Correspondence. 3. O'Neill, Eugene, 1888–1953 Correspondence. 4. Dramatists, American—20th century Correspondence. 5. Authors' spouses—United States—Correspondence. I. O'Neill, Eugene, 1888–1953. II. King, W. D. (W. Davies) III. Title.
PS3529.N5Z572   2000
812'.52—dc21
[B]   99-16532
                                                                     CIP

PRINTED IN THE UNITED STATES OF AMERICA

For my parents,
Janet McKown King and William Davies King
(still married after 55 years)

Contents

Introduction

Agnes Boulton and Eugene O'Neill married on April 12, 1918, and divorced on July 1, 1929. The decade of their marriage saw O'Neill rise from Greenwich Village's leading experimentalist in the one-act play to the foremost American dramatist and the first of international reputation. His work proceeded from nonprofit glory in the amateur "art theater" movement to commercial triumph on Broadway and beyond that to a nearly impossible level of theatricality, along the way defining the frontier of the American art theatre as well as gaining three of his eventual four Pulitzer Prizes. Even his worst plays of this period deserve close attention for the quest they were on, and his best made history. O'Neill himself went from relying on an allowance from his father to a state of patrician comfort, with a mansion in Bermuda, well-tailored suits, and investments solid enough to withstand the stock market collapse. His father, mother, and only brother died during these years, the latter from the effects of chronic alcoholism. O'Neill himself had, by the end of the 1920s, broken his own extreme dependence on drinking. Two children were born, Shane and Oona, and for a while the family was routinely pictured as an image of artistic aspiration in harmony with middle class comforts.

These were restless, exploratory years for O'Neill, a long series of moves from one "home" to another, half a dozen in ten years, with countless hotel rooms in between. His plays ventured far and wide as well. They were set in the West Indies, Palestine, China, Florida, and the North Atlantic, and even the plays set "at home" in New England were plays of departure, character studies of the will to be somewhere else and the damn good reason why. Style roamed far as well, discovering plays of realism, expressionism, symbolism, plays of classic form and plays of melodrama, satire, pure experiment, one-act, full-length, and twice-full-length. During this decade O'Neill became a focal point for journalistic speculation. From highbrow analyses to scandal sheet gossip, the O'Neill story came under public scrutiny. Persistently the writings about O'Neill returned, like O'Neill himself, to the circumstances of his life and the personality of the man. Even long before the explicitly autobiographical plays of his late career, journalists detected signs that this writer saw drama as a form for self-exploration. No American playwright has used the stage more ambitiously to explore the challenge of defining identity in the modern American state. O'Neill's

9

plays are always, on some level, about self-recognition. And so the journalists coaxed forth every detail they could from the life story of O'Neill, in the hope of resolving questions that were, for O'Neill, basically ontological. Was there some trauma from his past or present to account for the pervasive gloom of his plays? Face to face with these journalists, O'Neill was famously "taciturn." And yet in truth he saw his own life as an enormously complex drama. During the years 1918 to 1929 a leading character in that drama was his wife, Agnes Boulton.

The story of Agnes Boulton remains little known, narrated only as an adjunct to the story of O'Neill. Her involvement in his life came to a practical end just about the time a long string of biographers and critics began to integrate analysis of O'Neill's life with interpretation of his plays, and soon Boulton was regarded as just another of O'Neill's bitter memories. Furthermore, critical estimation of her work and character suffered under prejudices about popular culture, women's writing, and women's writing not specifically feminist. This book is a first effort to return to the subject of Agnes Boulton, who lies folded within these value systems and stubbornly resists them. O'Neill's later antipathy to her, which closed the book on her long ago, can be reopened now within a historical matrix. Certainly her letters appear in this volume because they provided the occasion for the private writings of an important figure of literary and theatrical history, but they also tell of another writer, successful in her way but not "great," who in her struggle to remain, as it were, on the same page with her husband, exemplifies the clash of aesthetic and social values in a significant moment of cultural history. This correspondence forms a drama of sorts in which the dialogue between two writers of vastly different sensibilities, bonded by an enormous passion, comes together in a fateful conflict, resulting in tragedy. This conflict stands forth here in more particular detail than even the most careful biographers have offered, and yet it is also representative—a text that reveals how a clash of identities, masculine and feminine, intersects with such other cultural categories as elite and popular, romantic and realist, public and private. Eugene O'Neill will probably always claim a place among the great writers, and this book will do nothing to challenge that, but the words of Agnes Boulton, which will never figure in any canon, also deserve close attention. They are, as it were, married to his words, and tell something about the way words bond, the way fictions are created, the way communication breaks down.

Agnes Boulton was a pulp story writer before the marriage, a single mother writing for a living, and she wrote well enough to have found a niche in the literary marketplace. The decade before World War I was a time of rapid growth for popular fiction in magazine format, a time when the notion of the disposable was becoming harnessed to American literature. The soft cover and pulp paper of the magazine were only the most obvious signs that the writing presented in this format did not ask to be retained. These magazines aimed to grab a reader's attention without ceremony and deliver a series of bold effects, like those of the gut-level advertisements which came to fill more and more of the layout. Anxiety about sagging chins, loose dentures, and wanted and unwanted hair accompanied the reader's drive into adventure and titillation. No invocation of the Muse, no courting of the critic, no nicety of style accompanied these quick and easy plunges into crime, sex, fashion, and foibles. And yet these magazines came to define an American voice that would soon be heard on the radio, in the movies, even on the Broadway stage, as an authentic vernacular, the true coin of American culture in a world market.

Boulton recalled publishing her first story of this sort by the age of seventeen. The earliest one I could locate was published in 1912, when she was eighteen, in *Cavalier.* "Tombstone Number Seven" tells of a tyrannical farm woman just married for the seventh time. She persists in comparing the new man, Jacob, a farm hand, to her previous six husbands, who are all dead and buried beneath headstones in the front yard. The narrator observes, "Jacob was in the position of many wives. . . . quite dependent." After a few months of submission, Jacob becomes terrified that he too is destined for an early grave. So he escapes, hiding in a nearby barn until his wife's search for him dies down. There he is surprised to find dirty magazines and liquor, unexpected traces of masculine liberty, and then one day overhears a rumor that his wife is saying he is sick in bed, dying of a contagious disease, and refusing to see a doctor. He realizes suddenly that the other husbands must have escaped as he has, that the tombstones are a pretense, and that his wife is a bigamist who cannot keep a man. Armed with these facts he returns to the house: "Jacob . . . was not the Jacob of old. He was no longer a weakling and dependent, but was on his way to become the head of the family, and the leader of the partnership."[1] There is nothing remarkable about the literary style of this story, but it defines an area of fascination which would extend throughout Boulton's career: the constantly shifting relations of power between men and women, especially within marriage. Some years later she would call August Strindberg her strongest literary influence, and even at eighteen, before it is likely she could have read his work, one might sense the affinity. Marriage as a battlefield struggle, unforeseen weakness within the dominator and fortitude within the underling, an ironic undermining of class and gender hierarchies: all these are as elemental to Boulton's "cheap" fictions as they are to Strindberg's precious works.

In her memoir she describes meeting Bob Davis, the editor of *Cavalier* (which later became *Argosy*), to discuss a story she had submitted, "Lanigan—Lineman." He wondered where this young woman had learned about linemen:

> He finally made me admit that my knowledge of them, or rather interest in them, came from seeing them climb poles along the road and thinking them very romantic men and even falling in love with one particular dark, bright-eyed one whom I never met, and whose only communication with me had been what they would now say was a wolf call from the top of a pole which I was passing on the way to high school, adding admiringly, "You for me when *you* develop!" which I pondered on, sometimes thinking he was fresh, but often thinking he meant something much more serious and wondering how we could meet.[2]

This sort of frank address of the world of men and especially the facts of sexual desire often figured into her stories, and ultimately came to define one important strain of pulp literature, a kind of dirtiness that depended not so much on voyeuristic descriptions of sex as on an unashamed and realistic depiction of the course of desire. Many of Agnes Boulton's stories were "dirty" in this latter sense.

The magazines in which she published played on that edge between modern manners and the scandalous. Their titles connote a liberated modernity, a licentious opportunity: *Breezy Stories*, *Snappy Stories*, or *Live Stories: A Magazine of Vitalized Fiction*. From the earliest years these "saucy pulps," as she called them, bore covers that toyed with the limits of propriety. In the thirties they and their descendants were the definers of the "torrid" or the "shocking," with covers that would be kept out of the sight of children. But in the late 1910s they published a range of stories: urban and rural, comic and serious, frightening and facetious, in a variety of literary styles. In the very early years one might find stories by Chekhov, Maupassant, and Pirandello alongside others by Rex Stout, Octavus Roy Cohen, or Clematis White. Soon though, the former dropped away and what remained were stories like "Why Not?" by Inez Thompson, advertised with the following teaser: "If a man were, in shameful secrecy, committing a revolting, monstrous and degrading wickedness, and in the very act he were exposed to the gaze of a jeering multitude, their scorn and contempt—that man could measure and understand the feelings of Selden Barris."[3] Boulton produced just that sort of "intimate" fiction in stories like "With Eyes of Flesh" and "The Prettiest Girl in the Show." Within this category the stories she wrote are quite diverse. Some are serious, some comical; some are urban, some rural; some are local, some exotic. She even published a handful of first-person monologues and dramatic sketches before she ever met O'Neill. It is true these pieces never seriously challenged received narrative form, in the way of high modernist fiction and drama. Still, the issue of how distinctive characters interpret the terms of modern life and define by their critical choices a new style of being forms a central area of concern in Boulton's work. The twist in her stories frequently comes from a shocking consequence of a character's breakage from convention, especially the conventions of sexual relations.

Of course, one whole strain of modernist literature would also trade on a non-euphemistic discussion of sex, and Eugene O'Neill would be counted among the boldest of American dramatists in this trend. O'Neill, too, would cite Strindberg as the writer who counted most in his development. Such works as *Desire Under the Elms* and *Strange Interlude* were accounted masterworks by some, salacious and despicable by others.[4] For many people O'Neill's entire career dealt entirely too much with the muck of life. Boulton's low modernism did little to disguise a fascination with that murky underside of life, but with no sense of critique or inquiry into the ultimate cause of either the murk or the fascination with it. Boulton reflected the sexy, electric, jittery, and jarring aspects of modern life while O'Neill was plumbing the soul.

Breezy Stories, founded in 1915, was typical of the magazines in which Boulton published her stories, and it was a venue for novelty and release, but not escape. The editor's statement in the first number promises contributors "whose work is stamped with pure realism; who write live wire stories of life as it is lived by the masses." The terms used in this statement are not much different from the ones that were being applied to O'Neill and the Provincetown Players:

Our tales have a tang of the sea; they are as strong as the wind blowing fresh from the ocean; they are vivid with deep emotion; they bristle with that subtle humor that is the very salt of life.

You will never find a dull line in our pages, even the seeming drab has a rose-colored lining, and there are glints of pure gold in the most tarnished settings.

Our novelettes are the clever output of master minds.

Our short stories are crisp with electric currents.

Our verse chants the love note to a modern accompaniment.[5]

Boulton's stories exactly suited this delight in the crisp and curious and concupiscent, the breezy, the snappy, the live, situated in the context of life as it is lived. Her stories offer an intimate experience of the private lives of modern people, just at those points where convention cannot fully dictate their destinies, where some capacity of art must enter in.[6] Her characters are often working-class, typically women for whom work among men, with all its danger, is inevitable. Sometimes the men discover, as Jacob did, that their leading women turn out to be predatory, and always they are at least practical and outspoken. They know quite well that life is no fairy tale. The endings are in fact often unhappy, always vaguely ironic, but "snappy"—modern.

And the point is, the stories sold. In my search through the crumbling bound volumes and reels of microfilm of eight pulp magazines of the period in the Library of Congress, I turned up forty-five of her published stories, sketches, and novelettes. No doubt there are more. At the time of the marriage, Boulton was a self-sufficient writer, living a life that one might find in her stories: a life of independence, adaptive strategy, unconventionality, a practical romanticism and an optimistic realism, and a taste for the *risqué*. These literary characteristics are just as reflective of her life as the sea plays of O'Neill are of his.

Agnes Boulton was born on September 19, 1893, in London. Her parents were visiting relatives at the time, but soon returned to their home in Philadelphia where her father, Edward W. Boulton, was a landscape painter, a student of Thomas Eakins. Cofounder and first president of the Philadelphia Art Students League, "Teddy" had helped Eakins make the death mask of Walt Whitman the year before Agnes was born. Her mother, Cecil Williams Boulton, came from a family with literary connections—her great aunt, Margery Williams Bianco, wrote the classic children's story *The Velveteen Rabbit* and many other books; her aunt, Pamela Bianco, was a multitalented artist and writer who was beloved by D'Annunzio; and her grandfather, Robert Williams, was a classics scholar, a Fellow of Merton College at Oxford. Agnes's mother was said to have adopted decidedly liberated ways—smoking, reading theosophy, marrying a painter, perhaps even taking a lover. She also wrote stories and planned a novel at one point. Agnes called her "the first free soul, one of the first emancipated women I knew." However, Agnes also remembered that her mother "wasn't very good to me" and even beat her with a razor strap.[7] Agnes attended a convent school in Philadelphia, but by the time she was an adolescent her family had moved to West Point Pleasant, New Jersey, and she had drifted away from the church. Linemen interested her.

She was still living at home when her stories began to sell, but she often made the short trip to New York City to talk with the editors. One of these was Courtland Young, who published *Young's Magazine* (thirteen of the stories I found were published in that magazine from 1913 through 1919) as well as some other magazines in which her work appeared. In 1915 a daughter was born to Agnes Boulton. In later years she told people that her first husband, Joseph L. Burton, also a writer, had died somewhere in Europe around the time of the birth. Little more is told about him. At the time of the 1929 divorce, O'Neill thought there might be something suspicious about the story of this marriage, something he might use in divorce court, and he asked his lawyer to investigate. Nothing was ever found to establish whether her story was true or false, no birth certificate or marriage record, but he probably found, as I did, in the courthouse of Litchfield County, Connecticut, that a farm which had once belonged to Courtland Young was signed over to Agnes Boulton in December 1915, just a few months after that child was born. Whatever the truth of the matter, it remains clear that Agnes Boulton was living at this time a "storied" life.

That story made the pages of the *New York Evening World* on October 7, 1916. The headline read:

> 'No Money in Milk Cows'
> Says Woman Dairy Farmer
> Who's Made a Brave Fight

Underneath her picture ran the subtitle, "'The More You Have, the More You Lose,' Asserts Mrs. Agnes Boulton Burton, Fiction Writer, Who Has Supported Herself, a Baby and a Herd of Cows by Her Pen." The occasion for the story was a strike of dairy farmers, and she was said to be in New York to bring out the facts about the hardships of the dairy business. She tells of having begun the business at the time of her husband's death and milking her first cow two weeks after the birth of her child. But the price for milk proved so low that making a profit was impossible, and what's more the local farmers looked dimly upon a woman in the business. Only in a story could this situation have a happy ending, she realized: "At first, you know, every time I got a check for a story I'd buy another cow. I thought that was investing the money. Now, whenever I can, I put the cows into a short story."[8]

This economy of a life subsumed into fiction repeats again and again through Agnes Boulton's life. There were moments when she tried to reverse the pattern— invest the stories in the cows—but most often what profit there was came from the stories she could tell—of the cows, of her marriage to Eugene O'Neill, of the ordeal of an independent woman and a life of much disappointment. That pattern of a life reused was true to an even greater extent for Eugene O'Neill, who thrived on the surplus value of a life's disappointments retold. For O'Neill, again, this self-consciousness could be read as a link to masterful high modernism, while for Agnes Boulton that self would appear as a figment of cheap fiction in the hands of an unreliable narrator—Boulton herself. The self, of course, is an elusive construct, whatever the cultural plateau of the work, but a whole army of critics has assembled to interpret

O'Neill's romantic self-representations, while the self of popular culture remains for the most part beneath notice—derivative, dispersed, and insubstantial. The whole of Agnes Boulton is not easy to reassemble. Partly it is the tradition of the short story form to evoke fragmentation, but in her case the effect is especially noticeable in the scattered array of stories she composed, especially when set in the midst of all the other detached, imperfect, skewed pieces of writing, published and unpublished, from her life. Her character flickers through these texts, always seeking something, always resisting easy definition.

In July 1917, four or five months before she met O'Neill, she published a story called "In Bohemia," which begins with a twenty-six-year-old woman sitting in a Greenwich Village cafe, staring into a mirror, and observing the first signs of age in her face. She's been around in this artistic milieu, and currently her lover is a middle-aged writer considered "mystical and *outré*." Also by her side is a younger writer, a man with smoldering eyes. But, the narrator tells us, "he could wait. At present she hated all men." She watches a conventional couple enter the cafe, and is surprised to discover that the man is someone she was engaged to once and the woman is also from her hometown. Suddenly she remembers once sitting under sweet honeysuckle with this man and longing for wedded bliss, and resolves to go home alone this evening, telling both of her companions: "I'm sick of you plaster-paris men! Free love—psycho-analysis—you're sickening, that's all. Why—you can't earn a decent living. I'm sick of it all." On her way out of the restaurant, however, she runs into the conventional man who has not recognized her at all. He took her staring at him for a sexual signal, so he gives her a false name and tells her he'll show her a good time. In a moment of epiphany she rejects the cad and all he represents and rushes into the cafe to tell the younger writer, "Come, let's go uptown to the rough-house ball!"[9] It is a sudden perception of the wrenching which is necessary to seize one's liberty, a turning of betrayal upon betrayal in a rough-house dance. This upward thrust beyond convention and beyond the conventions of the unconventional put Boulton on the same trajectory as O'Neill during those years. In their art they would engage with life in new and unrestrained ways, but without retreating into the cult of the avant-garde or bohemian revelry. In their lives, work and love (in uncertain order) would absorb all their energies.

At the time when this story was written, Boulton had several points of contact with the artistic underworld of New York City. She had known Harry Kemp, the vagabond poet and free spirit, from her hometown, and just that summer when "In Bohemia" was published he and his wife, Mary Pyne, had lived on her farm, sunbathing there in the nude. Both Kemp and Pyne had acted in Provincetown Players productions (Pyne played the sharp-tongued wife in O'Neill's Strindbergian experiment *Before Breakfast*, in which O'Neill himself played the silent, tormented husband). She had also known Christine Ell for some time, and Christine was the cook at Polly Holladay's restaurant alongside the theatre. Christine had once been a prostitute (the character of Anna Christie was probably based on her), and had a very hard life as a child growing up in New Jersey, not far from the Boulton family. But she had survived to become a beloved fixture in Village society. She would be the model for

O'Neill's Earth Mother character in *The Great God Brown*. Boulton remembered that it was while she was looking for Christine one day that she first met O'Neill, and soon she found herself drawn by his magnetism. In *Part of a Long Story*, the memoir she later wrote, she recalled her state of uncertainty about her life, expressed in terms that are woven together with the fiction that was her livelihood:

> I lay on the narrow bed, hearing the sounds of the city outside, and perhaps wondering what was going to happen to me. On a small table my typewriter stood with a half-typed sheet of paper in it. Looking at it I was unable to move; although all that was necessary was to add another, the finishing paragraph and the words *The End*. That was not bad. Finished, there would be a good chance of a check in two weeks from one of the pulp magazines. Not a large check, but it kept things going. But what kept me in a stupor on the bed was that *The End* was not the end. . . . Once this last page was removed from the typewriter another would have to be inserted with its blank carbon paper, name and address in the upper left-hand corner, number of words in the right. Then the thing turned down one third of a page to the left of center. New title—what? *She Never Knew Why* fourteen thousand words. A novelette. A hundred and fifty dollars—and it was not even started. "*She Never Knew Why.*" She never knew why *what*? And why not? I only knew that she had dark languishing hair, faint eyes—faint from pain or from too much sex? Or was she a blonde with hair like tabasco sauce and eyes like wine? Either way it was the body beautiful, very scantily clad, lying in bed probably, with silk sheets, with an eiderdown puff fallen to the floor, and the bed of sin on which she sold herself. She is waiting— for what? The telephone to ring? Or a knock on the door? Or perhaps this time instead of waiting she is thinking. But *could* she think? Is that why she never knew why?[10]

Eugene O'Neill, who had never by that time cashed a check for one hundred fifty dollars for his writing, who had had just about enough of free love and the roughhouse ball, and who was not exactly able to go back to the honeysuckle at home, came suddenly into her life, and she into his, and they offered to each other an unforeseen option. *The End* was not the end. They could marry and explore the possibilities of a committed love, they could continue to live beyond the conventional expectations of middle class society, they could continue to write and even cash some reasonably large checks but without the tedium of mindless formula. They could offer each other "the body beautiful," with its pleasures and excitements, but there would also be a definite sense of purpose between them, without prostitution of their talents or their souls. They could fulfill each other's needs. So the new story began.

Of course there should be no illusion that this uniting of purposes implied an equality or even equivalency between Boulton and O'Neill. The stupor that accompanies mechanized production, that collapses the writer into the typewriter, does not match the stupor of drunken nights in the Hell Hole and wrestling with the demons that haunt the human soul in the one-act play form. No more does the eiderdown puff fallen to the floor match the Merchant Seamen's card as a qualification for employment. The processes of thinking, and the obstructions to them, would be vastly different for these two partners, but in their joining came a sense of epiphany, a sudden knowing of why they must escape together.

Boulton continued writing and publishing sporadically during the marriage and for the rest of her life. After accepting a story of hers for the *Smart Set*, H. L. Mencken said, "I wish we had something of yours every month."[11] Her stories became harder-edged, more like the work of O'Neill, and she turned away from the short story form in search of a way to make a more extended statement, like a novel or a play. O'Neill encouraged and even assisted her in writing two full-length plays in the middle 1920s, both of which gained some attention from producers, but neither was produced. At the time of the divorce she turned again to stories and later to movie scenarios, but the market had changed, or she had changed, and nothing much got published. She did finally publish a novel in 1944, *The Road Is Before Us*, which earned several good reviews.

Then in 1959 she published *Part of a Long Story*. This, too, is a fragment, a memoir of just the first year and a half of Boulton's marriage to O'Neill. According to the original contract it was to have covered the whole marriage in three parts. The book that was published represented only a portion of what was to have been part one. The second section was to cover the successive deaths of three of O'Neill's family members in the early 1920s—father James O'Neill Sr. in 1920, mother Ella O'Neill in 1922, and brother James O'Neill Jr. in 1923. The third section, which would have been called "A Wind Is Rising," was to review the years 1923 to 1928, up to the divorce.[12] The same title had evidently been used for a novel she circulated among publishers in the early 1940s, but apparently never published.[13] The source for the phrase is probably Paul Valéry, "*Le vent se leve . . . il faut tenter de vivre*"[14] [The wind is rising . . . we must attempt to live]. This declaration of a will to live in the face of adverse circumstances seems to reflect Boulton's determination that some expression would survive the emotional violence which finally overwhelmed the marriage. Yes, a major playwright was "born," but much was also lost during those years—Agnes Boulton's romantic dream was shattered, the lives of their two children were scarred, and O'Neill himself began the process of retreat which would finally leave him nearly isolated from the world. But Boulton persisted with the attempt to live, and her *Part of a Long Story* is a strong expression of that.

Reviewers were either dismissive or guarded in their enthusiasm about the book, with many questioning its objectivity. It was the tone they tended to doubt, calling it "gushy," "garrulous," "over-written," "novelistic," "novelettish," "scribbled memories," "a parody of Victorian melodrama."[15] After all, there was so much of this other subject, this wife, intruding herself upon the topic, which, after all, must surely be O'Neill. Who would need or wish to read a book about her? What does she *know*? There are, to be sure, a number of minor factual problems in the book, and little is said there about any of O'Neill's plays. What the book does instead is clearly define the mythic elements of what was ultimately to prove an unrealistic and unreal sort of marriage, an intertextual cohabitation. The book, like the marriage, is a joining of fictions, stylistically fusing Boulton's pulp fiction with O'Neill's modern drama. It is the long-considered sequel to *She Never Knew Why*.

Agnes Boulton around 1960. Photographer unknown. Collection of the author.

The time for writing *Part of a Long Story* came after O'Neill's death in 1953, when his autobiographical plays were spurring renewed interest in the circumstances of his life. Half a dozen or more biographers were looking into O'Neill's life at this time including Croswell Bowen, Louis Sheaffer, Barbara and Arthur Gelb, Doris Alexander, and others who never completed their projects. On the edge of this group was a writer named Max Wylie, who took the suggestion of his editor at Doubleday and began to work on a novel based on the "tragic tale" of O'Neill's life that was beginning to emerge. With the highly acclaimed posthumous productions and publication of the late autobiographical plays, suddenly the O'Neill story was of compelling interest again. Wylie inquired of numerous people who had known O'Neill, looking for anecdotes, details, and characterizations he could use. He decided the person he most wanted to interview for the book was Agnes Boulton, but wondered if she was alive and where she could be found. Another writer who was then looking into the life of O'Neill, William Glover of the Associated Press, supplied him with an address. He wrote to her ("You seem to be the heroine of a novel I am writing") and was invited to her house.[16] Wylie recalls driving down to West Point Pleasant, New Jersey, on a foggy October day, to the same "Old House" where Agnes and Eugene had spent the winter of 1918–19, the house where Agnes wrote her first stories and wondered about the linemen. It looked uninhabited, with the yard overgrown and some of the porch boards rotted away. But the woman who answered the door impressed him with her vitality, lack of self-consciousness, and distinct traces of former beauty. She had just returned from a trip to Mexico with then-current husband Mac Kaufman, a fisherman. She took Wylie on a tour of the nearly empty house. As he later told it, nearly all the furniture had been sold during their trip by her son Shane, who was struggling with drug addiction and poverty, but Boulton later explicitly rejected this story as simply untrue. Here was an example of just that sort of narrative opportunity which a writer like Wylie could not refuse, an infusion of pulp fiction into history regardless of the painful consequences for members of the family.

Boulton herself would wrestle with the temptation to give a mythic shape to the facts of her marriage, but she, of course, had lived a part of that long story and had outlived O'Neill. For whatever reason, the house she lived in was bare enough to disclose in the corner of one guest bedroom a large heap of old documents—letters and manuscripts. When Wylie asked about these dusty papers he was told they were letters she and O'Neill had written to each other which had lain there since 1928. They each grabbed piles of the letters, took them into the kitchen, and began to read. Wylie says he realized at once "that many of them had immense literary interest and should somehow be preserved; that they represented a treasure of theatre lore, of deep character revelation, hardship, disappointment, bitterness, agony, triumph. Genius-at-work. . . . If laid out and studied, an entire decade of theatre history would almost surely be brightly, even intimately, illuminated." He understood that they needed to be preserved and protected—if only to keep them from being sold by Shane—and that they might provide some relief for what he saw in the house as "signs and symbols of something approaching destitution. . . . There was a Charles Addams spookiness about it all. And all about, intensified by the foghorns, a haunted feeling; a sense of

Max Wylie in the 1950s. Photographer unknown. Courtesy of The Special Collections, Boston University.

complete separation from the world; an atmosphere in which the cheerful Mrs. Kaufman seemed a striking anomaly."[17]

Some of the manuscripts (several early plays by O'Neill) and letters were eventually sold to Harvard, but only after Wylie had transcribed the latter.[18] He projected an edition of the correspondence as early as 1956.[19] In 1958 at a Pipe Night of the Players Club he told the story of uncovering the letters at Agnes's house and read a selection of them aloud.[20] He also wanted to use them as material for his novel *Trouble in the Flesh*, which was published in 1959 and is a sprawling and sensational work, transparently based on the Boulton-O'Neill marriage, as most reviewers pointed out. Its depiction of the principals makes for good reading, but there is nothing resembling historical accuracy in the arrangement of events. The portrayal of Eugene's brother Jamie is especially engrossing, but it is obviously drawn almost entirely from the imagination. Similarly, the character based on Carlotta Monterey, the woman who entered Eugene's life in the mid-1920s and became his third wife after the divorce in 1929, bears the marks of a classic character in fiction, the vampire. It is an entirely unflattering portrait. The actual Carlotta Monterey, widow of Eugene O'Neill, understandably might have taken offense at this depiction. In fact, she never stated that she had read or heard of Max Wylie's book, but the mere possibility that she might have would have deterred Wylie from approaching her about the letters. And yet she controlled most of O'Neill's literary estate and held the rights to all his unpublished writings. The letters written to Agnes by Eugene would legally be Agnes's property, but publication would require Carlotta's permission, which she never gave to Wylie or anyone else.

One need not look to Wylie as Carlotta Monterey's reason to withhold permission to publish the letters. The evidence clearly shows that Monterey, like O'Neill, bore an unmistakable malice for Agnes Boulton from the time of the divorce—for what were seen as her shortcomings as a wife, mother, and human being.[21] In retrospect Carlotta constructed the period of O'Neill's marriage to Boulton as a chaotic, disruptive, and even loveless time. The following years, from his remarriage to the time of his death, had not all been notably joyous ones, but they had at least been quieter and more ordered, and in that Carlotta Monterey took great pride. If she were to point to one source of turmoil during those years as the most troublesome, it would have to do with Agnes and her children. For these and other reasons Carlotta came to despise Agnes, and this did not lessen after Eugene's death.[22] The terms of the divorce agreement had stated that Boulton was not to write about the marriage, and she had done so. The agreement also stated that she was to return all manuscripts of Eugene O'Neill, and it was evident that she had not done so (the playscripts sold to Harvard). In Carlotta's opinion, the family had been treated with ample generosity, or at least justice, by Eugene. Although he had disinherited all his surviving children at the time of his death, certain rights to royalties from his plays had subsequently been assigned to the children. For Agnes there was a divorce settlement that had been renegotiated over the years, coming to an end with a final payment in the 1940s, by which time Agnes had remarried. Financially, Carlotta was comfortable, if not wealthy, so her share of whatever revenue might be generated from the letters would be unneeded.

Eugene O'Neill and Carlotta Monterey, 1928. Photographer unknown. Yale Collection of American Literature, Beinecke Rare Book and Manuscript Library.

Carlotta's main concern as executor of the O'Neill estate had been to maintain focus upon his plays and not let the petty details of a more or less unhappy life interfere. Probably she never read these letters, but she would know that some of them must have dealt with the messy intrigues of the affair and divorce. Thus, for any number of reasons, she would see no point in allowing this group of unpublished papers to be released.

Meanwhile, Wylie had run into another kind of resistance, from Agnes Boulton herself. As Wylie recalled it, it was he who suggested that she write her memoirs, and it was he who gave her the necessary impetus and advice to complete *Part of a Long Story*. Nevertheless, when she had a look at the manuscript of *Trouble in the Flesh* she required that all quotations from the letters be removed and even paraphrases from or references to them should be omitted.[23] When Wylie enlisted Ketti Frings, who had won the Pulitzer Prize for her adaptation of *Look Homeward, Angel*, to adapt his novel for the stage, their plans were suddenly halted by a letter from Boulton's lawyer which required them to obtain her permission, which she never gave. Wylie never saw her again. What went wrong? Was it a matter of proprietary interest, a market resistance? Was it a matter of propriety, a resistance to the invasion of private life? Or was there a marking here, in a different historical moment, of the boundary that had always been in play in this marriage, between what is story and what is history? It seems clear that Boulton felt that Wylie had invaded her life and laid hands upon a cherished property—the story of her marriage to O'Neill in all its dimensions. What came from that invasion is a confused mass of some of Wylie's worst and best writing, an amalgam of pulp fiction and modern drama quite like that which pervaded the marriage of Boulton and O'Neill.

Agnes Boulton died in 1968, Carlotta Monterey in 1970. In 1972, Max Wylie returned to the project of editing the letters. The rights to them had passed to Yale University, where the major collection of O'Neill papers was already housed. Presumably the personal grounds for withholding the rights would no longer apply, and a case could be made that the free market of ideas—the core ethic of scholarship—would require that these documents be made available for publication. Wylie directed his request to Donald Gallup, then curator of American Literature at the Beinecke Rare Book and Manuscript Library at Yale. Here he encountered, as he had expected, a different attitude—not a blank rejection but a demand that he show himself capable of preparing a scholarly volume. Gallup already knew a good deal about the history of these manuscripts; he had been at Yale when they came on the market and helped the university select certain items for purchase. There remained in his mind some doubts about the fact that these items had come to market at all, rather than reverting to O'Neill's possession at the time of the divorce. Perhaps, too, there was some doubt about the fact that Harvard had, by its purchase, established itself as a second, albeit minor, center for the study of O'Neill. The papers had been offered to Yale as well, but Carlotta Monterey might not have appreciated the consideration that would have been given to Agnes Boulton by this purchase. Gallup had close professional ties to Carlotta Monterey. He knew her attitudes and opinions well and would not risk offending her.

Gallup also knew something of Wylie, who had been an unofficial broker of the letters and manuscripts at the time of their sale. Gallup had read Wylie's novel and asked him about its depiction of the character evidently based on Carlotta. Wylie answered with a letter in which he contended that almost everything in the book, and that character in particular, was made up—a fiction. Wylie also contended that few readers had even recognized the connection between his novel and the life of Eugene O'Neill and others. This was not quite true, as a study of the book's reviews would show, since most had made the comparison. The fact is, Wylie had sought to play the O'Neill "story" both ways, drawing on the letters for the contrivance of his novel and then for a work of historical documentation. Literary invention runs through and through scholarly writing, of course. It is inescapable. Yet here there seemed grounds to question whether the "story" would be told in an impartial way, as free from pulp fiction as possible. So Gallup made a request of Wylie that he write an appropriate introduction to the volume and submit it for approval before the rights would be assigned.

Wylie complied, submitting in 1974 a sixty-seven-page introductory essay to a book he was now calling *A Wind Is Rising: The Private Letters of Eugene O'Neill and His Wife Agnes Boulton O'Neill*. The allusion in the title to Boulton's unpublished novel and the unwritten later portion of her memoir suggests accurately that this project rests uneasily on the blurred boundary line between fiction and history. The essay is a chatty and gossip-filled piece loaded with anecdotes of how he came to meet Agnes Boulton (including the previously mentioned tale of Shane having sold off the furniture) and stories about other people connected with O'Neill. For example, there are fully eight pages of reminiscences of O'Neill's oldest son, Eugene Jr., whom Wylie had met while working in broadcasting. These stories conclude with a detailed description of how the young man had committed suicide. A footnote informs the reader that the house in which the suicide occurred was owned by a brilliant editor who was also a Communist. And finally we learn where that man's widow now works. The only relevance of these digressive anecdotes would seem to be to establish an image of Wylie as an insider, and acquainted with grief. His discussion of the Boulton-O'Neill marriage is largely a rehash of the more lurid portions of *Part of a Long Story* or the letters themselves, laying strong emphasis on the material that reflected badly on O'Neill—his drinking, his habit of neglecting bills, his episodes of violence. Finally, he proposes his own theory about what might have led to such emotional turbulence in a man: congenital morphinism. At great length, he explains that the morphine addiction of O'Neill's mother had led to his being born into a condition of permanent withdrawal from "uterine ecstasy," in other words, the high of being a drugged fetus.[24] Desire to return to the womb would in his case resemble a drug fiend's craving. Wylie traces O'Neill's drinking to this supposed condition, and also his narcissism, his gloominess, and his inability to deal with Boulton. Along the way we read about Wylie's own alcoholism and that of his grandmother. Virtually nothing is said about the plays O'Neill happened to write, and little about the letters that were meant to accompany this introduction. The concluding paragraph deals with the unfortunate fate of Ketti Frings's adaptation of his novel. Clearly this was a ludicrously inappropriate way to introduce a volume of correspondence, and Yale turned him down. Wylie, who was suffering from cancer at the time, later took his own life.

Here then is a sad story about a man who took an interest, who knew that Agnes Boulton had something reasonably important to say about this marriage and found the time to listen, and who knew that, if nothing else, it would at least make a good book. But the clash of values that doomed the marriage of Boulton and O'Neill rose again to doom his book. Among the notes and fragments of Wylie's writing that came to Boston University after his death, one can find passages that convey a remarkable sense of language as a bond, a marriage of author and subject. At least sporadically, Boulton found—or created—a good writer in Wylie, and in those moments one can deduce something fundamental that was missing from the marriage to O'Neill:

> One day in Point Pleasant she told me that she suddenly stopped thinking of Eugene as a "public figure"; of herself as married to such, but instead, married to a man who was not only unlike all other men, but grossly deficient in every area (except sex) in which a normal woman can find trust, fulfillment, response, or secure companionship. She said there were times when she dreaded his returns to Bermuda, always buoyant with anticipated excitements that always after the first day (or the first night) reverted to his joyless moodiness, his habitual peevishness, his verbal abuse, monkish solitary rambles, ritual swimming, and silences so protracted she felt self-conscious when she had to trespass on them on domestic matters. . . .
>
> She was his lover, but never his wife. He didn't need or want a wife; didn't know what one was, didn't wish to know nor to think about it. She felt short-changed about everything; that the years of emotional attrition were beginning to disassemble *her*; that she could no longer envision a role for herself; that she had a strong sense of being a *person*, well-born, intelligent, and with abilities of her own that he never saw and never needed. She came one day to realize, while sitting with Shane at the fish pond, that however world-famous her husband had become (and she rejoiced in this, for him, from the earliest birth-agonies in the shacks and shanties that housed his early works, to the histrionic epiphanies that lighted theatres all over the world)— that this would never change. And one thing more: that most of the time, Eugene O'Neill was a hell of a bore. Petty, churlish, ungallant, unnoticing, self-immolated, and self-consuming.[25]

Lack of interest is fatal to romance, whether in the literary or interpersonal sense. The part of a long story that is "a hell of a bore" is likely not worth telling, and yet there is something fascinating that happens, literarily, in the final portion of this correspondence. It is an accident of literary history that few of Agnes Boulton's letters survive from the collapsing moments of the marriage, the moments when love turned into boredom. What survives are O'Neill's efforts to begin a new romance, telling the story of why the old love died and the new love was born. Agnes's few letters from this period suggest that she was also trying to get what she could—or at least what seemed fair—from the end of this old romance, *She Never Knew Why*.

Agnes Boulton found in Wylie a man—a writer—with whom she could construct a revised version of her marriage with O'Neill, and that version reflects not just the "facts" of the marriage but also, by the very sympathy with which he takes her part, a figure of the man O'Neill might have embodied in her romance. Wylie and Boulton reconfigure the marriage in the retelling. In this sense the marriage "story" never comes to *The End,* because the next sheet of paper, including the one I am writing on now, forms a new simulacrum of that marriage. In this volume, for the first time, the correspondence becomes public and represents yet another figment of the marriage, in which the bond changes shape *between* two writers. Of course, there is in fact nothing *between* the letters, except the apparatus of a scholarly edition, and in fact the marriage no longer exists and the parties are both long dead. But in the care with which we read these historical documents, we reconstruct upon the ruins some semblance of the marriage, give it form, make it a text. It is even possible, by sympathy, to ensure that the marriage figured here will not be "a hell of a bore," however petty, churlish, ungallant, unnoticing, self-immolated, and self-consuming *both* parties might have been at times. As Boulton wrote in a letter to O'Neill, "Love has its hellish phases" (#182), and even the worst of these "phases" works as an aperture to a story of two authors writing themselves into one "love story," though it was only a novelette in scale.

Late in the 1920s when O'Neill was writing her the final letters—long monologues like passages from *Strange Interlude,* with conscious and unconscious expressions equally voiced—Boulton faced her typewriter once again. Half a year after the divorce she sold a novelette to *Liberty* using her maiden name. A biographical sidebar puts the name in context ("whose marriage to Eugene O'Neill, famous playwright, interrupted a promising career as a writer, begun at seventeen, which she now resumes") for the story entitled "En Route," which tells of a woman on her way to Reno to divorce her famous husband. On the way to Chicago she makes the acquaintance of a charming, well-dressed man (who turns out to be a con man) who tries to set her up in a hotel room with a young man, "the Prince," a minor gangster, for purposes of extortion. What a surprise when the young man falls in love with her and turns the tables on his boss. And what a double surprise when the woman, too, turns out to be a con, impersonating the famous wife in order to fleece some sucker, in this case the con man who has fallen into her trap. In fact she's the wife of Honey ("Big Mac") Macomber, an underworld legend who's just run off to Europe with a floozy. But now, fifteen hundred bucks to the good, she and the Prince can catch that early morning train to Frisco: "We'll knock 'em dead there."[26] The story is nothing arresting, nothing more than the usual gesture romance makes to take the commonplace story of yet another marriage failed, yet another trip to Reno, into the realm of wish fulfillment.[27] The fact that it dovetails with the end of this book gives it another destiny, to help undo the "years of emotional attrition" which Max Wylie tells us "were beginning to disassemble *her.*" With this volume of letters I hope that process of reassembly continues—reassembly of Agnes Boulton, reassembly of a marriage, reassembly of a network of social and cultural contingencies through which happiness passed.

Forty-six of O'Neill's letters to Boulton were published in 1988, in *The Selected Letters of Eugene O'Neill,* edited by Travis Bogard and Jackson R. Bryer. Their selection gets at the main themes of the correspondence, professional and personal, and serves the world of O'Neill scholarship admirably well. Having the complete correspondence in print will bring to light numerous details not contained in their selection, giving for example the most complete record of O'Neill's changing attitudes toward Broadway professionalism around the time *Beyond the Horizon* opened. But it is in its portrayal of marriage itself, in particular the literary marriage with its interwoven mythology and rhetoric, that the correspondence stands out. What this edition makes accessible for the reader is a dialogue of sometimes astounding intensity. During their periods of separation, they called on each other to manufacture in a rush of posted language some simulacrum of their mutual passion. When the two voices of a correspondence come together again in an edition of letters, there is inevitably the effect of dramatic dialogue, often arranged around conflict with beginning, middle, and (in this case tragic) end. So once again the marriage of Boulton and O'Neill comes to be understood in terms of a literary invention. It is I think difficult to read these letters dispassionately, without feeling subtle shifts of empathy, traces of pity and fear leading to a catharsis. Literary invention, textuality, and self-dramatization lay within the fabric of the marriage itself. Wylie identified too closely with Boulton to be a proper dramaturge of this correspondence. He was too much the insider, seeing his own drinking, his own pulp story making, his own series of life tragedies as the equivalent of her own. But he was not wrong in the impulse that told him there was a "live wire" book here.

During those periods of separation, Aggie and 'Gene wrote sometimes as many as three letters a day, and if more than a day slipped by without a letter they quickly became bitter and accusatory. The sequence of these letters is occasionally hard to follow, since it was often the case that several letters were written between the time a given letter was sent and when it was answered. Since many of O'Neill's letters and most of Boulton's were undated, the task of arranging a sequence has been daunting. Wylie complicated the editor's task immensely by making marginal notations, offering spontaneous opinions, assigning tentative dates and his own sequence numbers. Since many of his dates were obviously wrong, I have ignored them and made only a few references to the inscribed comments. Most of the letters evidently remained with their envelopes over the years in Boulton's house, but many have been jumbled, so I have not given much weight to postmarks for assigning definite dates. The letters at Harvard were given inventory numbers by staff archivists and arranged in two rough sequences, one for O'Neill, one for Boulton. I have assigned new numbers in order to incorporate a number of letters found in other libraries and to convey the fact that the question of sequence has now been closely examined. I hope the result is that previously unobserved patterns of communication between the correspondents will be apparent—a textual correlative of the marriage itself with its underlying codes, its developing syntax, and its punctuation.

It is clear that this collection does not contain every letter ever written between these two correspondents. There are numerous examples of references to things said in letters that have evidently been lost. Then too there are long periods, especially in the middle years of the marriage, from which no letters survive. There are several possible reasons: their absences from each other were then fewer and more brief, they relied more on telephone calls, or perhaps they simply did not save the letters. What survives and is presented here is an effective tracing of those early years of passionate declaration and the late years of breaking apart, with the transitional years barely sketched. Biographers have addressed these intermediate years at length, and Doris Alexander's recent *Eugene O'Neill's Creative Struggle: The Decisive Decade, 1924–1933* is especially important for its treatment of the marriage and divorce. But again, these biographers, including the latter, tend to study these years in terms of their impact on a major playwright. In this volume I have supplied connective material in order to give these letters a historical background, but I have laid equal stress, or even more, on the less well-known story of Agnes Boulton. In the coming years I hope to write an extended study of Boulton in terms of how her story gets told and retold by biographers, critics, O'Neill, Carlotta Monterey, Max Wylie, and others, and in terms of how the literary traces of her life—her stories, plays, novel, memoir, letters, and so on—give outline to a phantom presence. I trust that readers who have picked up this book solely from an interest in O'Neill will accept it for what it is worth in that connection, but will also allow that other purposes might be served by it.

Travis Bogard read through my annotated transcript of this correspondence with his usual care and intelligence and offered very good counsel on its presentation. In this edition I have with his permission followed as best I could the format and editorial principles used by him and Jackson R. Bryer in the preparation of their volume of selected letters. That is, I have intended this edition for readers, not editors, offering texts that give as much as possible the experience of reading these letters without the distractions of an elaborate apparatus to record minor deletions or superscript emendations, irregularities in autograph format, misspelled proper names, Britishisms, or other incidental effects. I have tried to exercise caution in any situation where an irregularity might convey some meaning. So, for example, I have not regularized the punctuation because some sense of the implied phrasing might lie behind an oddly placed comma. The exceptions here are in a number of cases where there appear to be stray marks on the page and in the salutation and closing of the letters. I have also standardized periods in abbreviations and the positioning of quotation marks and have added apostrophes in contractions and possessives. Dashes have been typographically standardized. I have italicized titles, though both correspondents preferred to place titles in quotation marks. I have regularized A.M. and P.M. and the typography of ordinal numbers.

I have tried to assign at least a tentative date to every letter. In cases where some evidence allows for a confident dating, I have placed the date in brackets. The reader should approach even these dates with some caution. In fact, the dates placed on the letters by the correspondents themselves have several times proved incorrect; I have noted those occasions. In cases where a date can only be approximated, I have added a question mark after the date. Unfortunately, cases where there might be a date range of two or three days blur together with other cases where even the month or year is uncertain, but it seemed impractical to give a dating note to each undetermined letter.

Conjectural readings are in brackets in the text, with the more hypothetical ones indicated by a question mark. Most of these letters were handwritten and transcription problems arose frequently. This edition was prepared from the original manuscripts except, as noted, in those cases where only a copy survives. Attentive readers will note a few variations from the texts of those letters already published in the Bogard and Bryer edition. Undoubtedly other editors would arrive at slightly different texts from the ones given here. Fortunately, all the letters are housed in research libraries and available for further examination.

The following abbreviations have been used to categorize the physical form of each letter: AL (autograph letter unsigned); ALS (autograph letter signed); TL (typed letter unsigned); TLS (typed letter signed); WIRE (telegram); and COPY (transcribed copy of a letter, postcard, or telegram). The number of pages cited at the head of each item refers to the number of graphic pages—places where a writer continued writing at the top of a "page." Thus, in the case of a folded letter, two pages might appear next to each other on the same side of the folded paper, while one page covers the entire sheet on the other side. The correspondents occasionally numbered their pages using other systems (such as numbering each sheet of paper), but these have been ignored.

Notes

1. "Tombstone Number Seven," *Cavalier* 15, no. 3 (May 1912): 569–75.
2. Agnes Boulton, *Part of a Long Story* (New York: Doubleday, 1958), 24.
3. *Breezy Stories* 4, no. 6 (August 1917).
4. "The play itself will be hailed as realistic. No one will call it an entertainment, but at the slightest suggestion of its foulness, many will rise to exclaim: 'But that's life—that's real!' Sure. So is a sewer." Fred Niblo Jr., "New O'Neill Play Sinks to Depths," *New York Morning Telegraph*, November 12, 1924; reprinted in *Playwright's Progress: O'Neill and the Critics,* by Jordan Y. Miller (Chicago: Scott, Foresman, 1965), 40.
5. *Breezy Stories* 1, no. 1 (September 1915): 3.
6. Stanton Leeds's review of O'Neill's *Beyond the Horizon* in a 1920 issue of *Live Stories* helps bring the contrast into focus: "It is because of [O'Neill's] realism that he cannot help but fall short. A report of life as it is, if this report be well and thrillingly handled, is an excellent thing, but it is never real romance; for romance is always a visioning of something nearer the heart's desire than life itself, and so greater than life and more desirable—worth seeing, hearing, experiencing if only through report. For if art cannot bring something better than life, something to ease this strange existence, to make us forget, if it cannot bring us some new nepenthe, it is no better than a newspaper." "Plays and Players," *Live Stories* 22, no. 2 (June 1920): 118.
7. Louis Sheaffer interview of Agnes Boulton, July 15, 1959, Louis Sheaffer–Eugene O'Neill Collection, Special Collections, Charles E. Shain Library, Connecticut College (hereafter cited as Conn. College Collection).
8. See "clipping file," Eugene O'Neill Collection, Collection of American Literature, Beinecke Rare Book and Manuscript Library, Yale University (hereafter referred to as the Yale Collection).
9. *Breezy Stories* 4, no. 5 (July 1917): 53–55.
10. Boulton, *Part of a Long Story*, 13
11. I have seen photocopies of this letter at Yale and Boston University and from the Boulton family, but I have not been able to locate the original. It is dated April 6, probably in 1920.

12. Agnes Boulton, letter to Harold De Polo, August 13, 1958, Eugene O'Neill Collection, Alderman Library, University of Virginia (University of Virginia Collection).

13. Agnes Boulton, letter to Saxe Commins, September 27, 1941, papers of Saxe Commins, Princeton University (Princeton Papers).

14. From *Le Cimitière Marin* in *Charmes* (1922).

15. Rod Nordell, "A Wife's View of Eugene O'Neill," *Christian Science Monitor,* August 7, 1958, 11; Brooks Atkinson, "Life with a Dedicated Genius," *New York Times,* August 10, 1958, sec. VII, pp. 4, 17; "Tale of Two Masks," *Time* 72, no. 7 (18 August 1958): 85-86.

16. Max Wylie, letter to Agnes Boulton, October 9, 1956, Yale Collection.

17. Max Wylie, introduction to "A Wind Is Rising: The Private Letters of Eugene O'Neill and His Wife Agnes Boulton O'Neill," Max Wylie Papers, Mugar Memorial Library, Boston University (Boston University Collection), 34–35.

18. Other manuscripts were bought by Yale University, including several of O'Neill's early poems and O'Neill's annotated copy of Samuel Taylor Coleridge's "The Rime of the Ancient Mariner" (used in his dramatic adaptation). After Boulton's death, Yale also purchased O'Neill's "Scribbling Diary" of 1925 from her estate.

19. Max Wylie, letter to Philip Wylie, December 8, 1956 (Princeton Papers).

20. *Players Bulletin,* Winter 1958, 7.

21. See Louis Sheaffer's interviews of Carlotta Monterey and of other members of the family (Conn. College Collection). A softened version of these opinions can be read in the biographies of O'Neill by Sheaffer and the Gelbs, all of whom interviewed Carlotta.

22. One need only read a few of the letters Carlotta wrote to Harry Weinberger, the family attorney, for evidence of her feelings toward Agnes.

23. Max Wylie, letter to "Joyous Young Folks" [Philip and Ricky Wylie], February 1959, Princeton Papers.

24. Wylie, introduction to "A Wind Is Rising."

25. Max Wylie, note in the file of 1927 correspondence, Boston University Collection.

26. "En Route: The Story of a Game of Guile," *Liberty,* February 22, 1930, 56.

27. A few months after he had fled to France with Carlotta, Eugene advised Agnes: "Once they get it from your lips that we're definitely separated for good because we simply couldn't get along any longer, but that there's no question of any third party having anything to do with it, and that you've decided to go West and sue for a divorce, they'll lay off of us for good. There's no news value to a simple divorce without correspondent, as you know, no matter how notorious the people. Divorces are too common" (#290).

Note on Sources

The letters in this volume are housed in the following collections:

Boston University: Max Wylie Papers. Special Collections. Mugar Memorial Library. Boston University.

Connecticut College: Louis Sheaffer-Eugene O'Neill Collection. Special Collections. Charles E. Shain Library. Connecticut College.

Harvard University: Letters of Agnes Boulton and Eugene O'Neill. Harvard Theatre Collection. Houghton Library. Harvard University.

University of Virginia: Eugene O'Neill Collection. Clifton Waller Barrett Library of American Literature. Special Collections. Alderman Library. University of Virginia.

Yale University: Eugene O'Neill Collection. Collection of American Literature. Beinecke Rare Book and Manuscript Library. Yale University.

The name of the library has been given in the heading of each letter. I would like to thank the staffs of all these libraries for their assistance with this project, and especially Howard B. Gotlieb, Director of Special Collections, Mugar Memorial Library, Boston University; Jeanne T. Newlin, former Curator of the Harvard Theatre Collection, Harvard University; and Michael Plunkett, Curator of Manuscripts, Special Collections, Alderman Library, University of Virginia.

Brian Rogers, Special Collections Librarian of Connecticut College, was immensely helpful in guiding me through the maze of the Louis Sheaffer collection, which had only recently arrived at the college, and made it easier for me to make the most of its almost overwhelming resources. I am also grateful to Connie Dowell, Head Librarian at Connecticut College, for her assistance and hospitality.

I also appreciate the kind assistance of Patricia C. Willis, Curator of American Literature, Beinecke Rare Book and Manuscript Library, Yale University, and her excellent staff. Donald Gallup, the former Curator of American Literature at Beinecke Library, has generously offered excellent counsel on this project from its early years and helped clarify many questions about the manuscripts published here.

I have benefited greatly from research in numerous other collections, including the papers of Saxe Commins, George Tyler, and Philip Wylie at Princeton University. I am grateful to Mary Ann Jensen, Curator of the William Seymour Theatre Collection, and Don C. Skemer, Curator of Manuscripts at Princeton University, for their assistance. I also appreciate the assistance of Philip N. Cronenwett, Curator of Manuscripts and Chief of Special Collections, Dartmouth College, for supplying me with material from the Ralph Sanborn and Bella Landauer collections. Finally, I would like to thank the Special Collections Department, Van Pelt Library, University of Pennsylvania, for use of the Horace Liveright collection.

I spent many hours in the Library of Congress in connection with this project and wish to extend my thanks to the many staff members who assisted me, especially Gayle Harris. I am indebted to two local historians from northwestern Connecticut, where Agnes Boulton had her farm, for their assistance in locating the farm and relevant legal documents: Jeanne Majdalany of the Sharon Historical Society and Michael R. Gannett, President of the Cornwall Historical Society, Inc.

I am grateful to Yale University for permission to publish photographs from the Eugene O'Neill Collection and to Boston University for permission to publish the photograph of Max Wylie. One photograph of Agnes Boulton was generously given to me by Maura O'Neill Jones. For most of these photographs I have been unable to determine the name of the photographer. I am grateful to Mimi Muray-Levitt and the George Eastman House for their cooperation and assistance with the Muray photograph. I hope it will be clear to those who might hold copyright to these pictures that their use here is for purposes of historical documentation, not commercial exploitation.

Ellen Margolis worked as a research assistant on this project for some time, and her work proved invaluable. She transcribed many of the letters, carefully checked the transcripts against the originals, and offered her keen intelligence to questions of dating, doubtful readings, and the vagaries of human expression. Finally, she read much of this manuscript with her usual unusual wisdom and sensitivity. I have learned much from her and enjoyed our discussions of these letters. Christine Nipe also read the manuscript and improved it in countless ways by her smart suggestions. Beyond that, she saw right to the core of what is interesting about this subject and helped me make sense of its most important issues. She saw in this story a bright light.

My travels in connection with this project were generously supported by research funds supplied by the University of California, Santa Barbara, and the National Endowment for Humanities. Others who kindly gave me information, lent me advice or accommodations, or just listened patiently include: Geoffrey Aronow, Barbara Bosch, Jackson R. Bryer, Seth Fraden, Ellen Gainor, Randy Garr, Melinda Halpert, Laura Kalman, Stanley and Laura Kauffmann, Andrew King, Lois McDonald, Diane McKay, Mary Parnell, Joy Peetermans, Sarah Pogostin, Mark Ringer, John Stevenson, Richard Stoddard, James Rawlings Sydnor, Glenda Walther, and Frederick C. Wilkins.

For all their hard work and caretaking on this book I would like to thank Harry Keyishian and Louise Stahl of Fairleigh Dickinson University Press, Christine A. Retz, Melody Sadighi, and Julien Yoseloff of Associated University Presses, as well as the copyeditor, Dean Curtis, and the anonymous readers and editors.

Travis Bogard helped guide this project from the beginning, and there could be no better guide. I only wish he had lived to see it reach its destination. Arthur Gelb offered his strong opinions in an odd phone call one afternoon. Doris Alexander sent me a letter with useful information and advice. Louis Sheaffer curtly refused to help me in any way, but in the collection of his papers which came to be housed at Connecticut College I had the awe-inspiring experience of looking into the very workshop of a devoted biographer. Sheaffer gave the same steadfast attention to the topics of this book as he did to the hundreds of other topics pertaining to the life of Eugene O'Neill, which means he brought to it inexhaustible energy, a strong sense of fairness, a deep human sympathy, and great care. I feel an enormous debt of gratitude toward him.

Maura O'Neill Jones, granddaughter of Agnes Boulton and Eugene O'Neill, has helped me understand the role these documents play in the history of the family, and even more so in the present state of the family among the many descendants. Barbara Burton, too, has generously supplied me with answers to many questions and offered pertinent advice on the project. This book would not have come into being at all without their assistance, and I sincerely hope that they will take pride in a book which, I trust, reflects the example of frank understanding, sympathy, and pride which they set for me.

"A Wind is Rising"

Agnes Boulton in Provincetown, early 1920s. Photographer unknown. Yale Collection of American Literature, Beinecke Rare Book and Manuscript Library.

I.

1918–1920

On THE NIGHT OF SUNDAY, DECEMBER 30, 1917, THE TEMPERATURE IN NEW YORK CITY DROPPED to thirteen degrees below zero, the "coldest day in New York within the memory of man," said the *New York Times*.[1] Possibly this is the night remembered by Agnes Boulton in the first paragraph of her memoir as a night in late autumn, "one of the coldest nights in many years," when she first met Eugene O'Neill.[2] Wearing only a thin suit, he walked her back to her Greenwich Village hotel that evening and the last thing he said to her at the door was: "I want to spend every night of my life from now on with *you*. I mean this. *Every night of my life*." This extraordinary introduction was soon to be tested. By the end of January 1918 they were living together in a Provincetown flat, and three months later married at the house of the Reverend William Johnson with just one witness. "I wanted you alone," Boulton recalled O'Neill declaring to her, "in an aloneness broken by nothing."[3] Getting to that point of exclusive and total access to each other would be a constant struggle until the marriage ended.

Louise Bryant, whom Boulton was said to resemble and for whom O'Neill had possibly mistaken her on that first cold, drunken evening, was in Russia with her husband John Reed for most of the first two years of O'Neill's marriage. O'Neill's affair with Bryant was still on the minds of the Provincetown Players and their circle that first winter, and allegiances were more than usually strained as a result. Since Bryant's departure, O'Neill had drawn the ardent attention of Dorothy Day, then a journalist and social activist, later founder of the Catholic Workers Movement.[4] Other women, too, seemed to be attracted to him. Boulton later tried to define that quality, identifying it as "something about his appearance that started and held the attention. Was it intensity? No, perhaps a quality of romantic somberness. If there *was* intensity, it was that of being himself—an awareness on the part of others of his being always intensely aware of himself. Now I am getting at it, for this would account for his shyness or whatever it was—which was really an intense self-consciousness."[5] For some, this quality of his personality proved magnetic, and when combined with his sudden success in the winter of 1917–18 the power of his attraction increased noticeably. The move to Provincetown and the sudden determined fixation on Agnes freed Eugene from the woven textures of New York life. But Day did not let go easily, and Bryant soon returned to New York in pursuit of O'Neill, later sending word to

Provincetown, presumably that she was intent on resuming their affair. O'Neill's insistence on his absolute feelings for Boulton helped seal the door against such intrusions on his privacy. Through this first year of their relationship no letters survive; their separations, if any, were few and brief.

The main problem for O'Neill was to extricate himself from a world which suddenly so aggressively answered his needs (for love, for approval, for a community) and insistently demanded his attention and work in return. Despite a variety of intrusions during this period, the first year of their marriage was remarkably productive for him. He wrote as many as six one-act plays, all but two of which were produced, and his first full-length play to be produced, *Beyond the Horizon*, which Agnes would later refer to as "our" play because she felt so close to Eugene in its creation. He dedicated the play to her when it was published. O'Neill was already well known as the genius of the Provincetown Players, offering one-act plays that stood quite apart from the lazy circles of American drama. His plays and those of Susan Glaspell largely elevated the group to national attention and established the viability of a distinctively American art theatre, drawing from American sources. Already though, he found himself at odds with the declared amateurism of the group. For one thing, he was beginning to write full-length dramas, beyond the capacity of most amateur performers and out of step with the Players' usual bills of diverse short plays. As early as the spring of 1918, critics were saying he had a rare gift for dramatic invention and should apply it to a longer play.

The two Broadway producers with whom he began working closely—John D. Williams for *Beyond the Horizon* and George C. Tyler for *Chris Christophersen* and *The Straw*—came from a world of theatre more familiar to his father than to the Provincetown Players. Tyler in fact had worked as a manager and producer for James O'Neill. Their impulses were commercial, but in a competitive market—and 1919–20 was an especially rich season with its sudden rush of productions in the postwar moment—the outstanding seriousness of the young O'Neill seemed a reasonable bet. Although O'Neill was initially skeptical about the Broadway actors Williams was tapping for this series of special matinee performances, seeing in them little more than the usual show shop glamor, eventually he came to respect their talents and their professionalism. This respect would not last beyond his debut. Many would be his frustrations with the manners and practices of New York theatre professionals through the rest of his career, but for *Beyond the Horizon*, his first Broadway production, the mechanism worked quite well. Since Williams was drawing on the players from two prominent, if not successful, productions for his cast, the company he assembled was exceptionally good by Broadway standards. Richard Bennett, who played Robert Mayo, and Helen MacKellar, who played Ruth Atkins, were credible stars, but what surprised O'Neill was their willingness to look at the specific demands of his script. What is more, O'Neill had the heady experience of making many of the preliminary decisions about how his play should be cast and performed, without the complex collaborative negotiations of the Provincetown group.

As it turned out, O'Neill had solid enough instincts about what would work in the theatre that he could make confident choices about how the production should be arranged. (The lengthy stage directions in his scripts would loudly signal this confidence for the rest of his career.) Tyler and Williams were of the old school that thought a solid play with a good cast would find its way without the ministrations of a visionary director. Directing for them was a nuts and bolts matter of putting together the pieces. The point was to serve the play so that it would work to the maximum effect on an audience, not to advance some artistic or ideological mission. Tempered by the experience of these veteran Broadway producers, O'Neill's attitudes about theatrical production hardened into a professional method during this period, one that combined elements of the old showmanship with some of the experimental attitudes of the art theatre.[6]

Then, too, over the years the Provincetown Players had come to be associated in his mind with "effete Village stuff" (#34), which seems to have meant a mannered, artsy attitude vividly in contrast to the more hard-edged style O'Neill cultivated in his plays and in his social life. As he tested out the society of Broadway professionals in 1920, he discovered how much he preferred it to the Greenwich Village society, with the exception of those hard-drinking Hell Hole bums who had little or nothing to do with the theatre. Broadway offered him an access to power and a style of masculinity (in its business practices and personnel) which he preferred to the more egalitarian and effeminate climate downtown. Perhaps more than anything else this preference had to do with drinking, which, with the beginning of Prohibition in July 1919, had become another challenge to be faced. One immediate consequence was to raise the cost of maintaining a drinking habit. (In January 1920 O'Neill paid twelve dollars for a bottle of bourbon.) Suddenly the old amicable and nonremunerative arrangement with the Provincetown Players might have seemed less feasible to a dedicated alcoholic such as O'Neill, especially at the time when he was still living on an allowance of fifteen dollars a week from his father. When *In the Zone* earned him fifty dollars upon its acceptance for publication in *Seven Arts* magazine, and was then produced by the Washington Square Players and later presented on the Orpheum vaudeville circuit, earning him as much as fifty dollars a week, O'Neill had a glimpse of other marketplaces for his work.

This income started coming in just about the time of their wedding and surely helped to conform their marriage to the conventional pattern of a husband supporting a wife, but the material foundation for their marriage lay just as much in Boulton's career selling short stories. She published at least nine stories in 1918, mostly in *Young's Magazine* and *Breezy Stories*, receiving a minimum of fifty dollars for each one. This was well down from her output the previous year, when she published at least fourteen stories and novelettes (two to four times as long as a typical story). As the third letter in this collection shows, she saw herself as a person who could "support the family" by her writing: "I always can, when it really gets down to brass tacks" (#3). Her stories were already the main source of support for her parents and daughter, and now the popular market could underwrite her husband's art as well. Of course that would mean devising plots "of the cheap & easy kind," not the "more serious, or any way, attempted serious, style" (#3) she had been aiming for under the influence of Eugene. It is clear that their marriage involved a literary recognition of each other, and on Agnes's part an adaptation of her style to suit his. From Eugene, on the other hand, came increasing recognition of his plays as literary properties well-positioned in a growth market.

There was a cultivated amateurism about the Provincetown group, a proud resistance to the lures of the commercial theatre.[7] For many members of the group, this was an important balance to the commercial work (in magazines, novels, graphic arts, etc.) which sustained them. For O'Neill too, the Provincetown Players stood apart from the show shop theatre of his father, but amateurism in craft might easily prove inadequate to the demands of his dramas. The eager acceptance of his exploratory work in the one-act play was useful at first, but in his third season with the group O'Neill was starting to look beyond the Village. James O'Neill Sr. barely lived to see *Beyond the Horizon* open on Broadway, and the time of arranging for and rehearsing that play was, as Eugene recalled later, a time when they regained friendship and respect for each other. Eugene also gained during this time a certain amount of respect for the rigors of dealing with the commercial and popular potential of show business. And James presumably saw that the intensity and rhythm of his son's plays were not all that different from the qualities of the old melodramas, only with endings less fantastical than true. After the triumphant opening, James O'Neill could barely contain his tears of joy for his son, but offered this famous advice: "It's all right, if that's what you want to do, but people come to the theater to forget their troubles, not to be reminded of them. What are you trying to do—send them home to commit suicide?"[8]

The first small group of letters in this part of the correspondence is from a time when O'Neill was still very much involved with the Provincetown Players, overseeing their production of his *Moon of the Caribbees*. The second group, though, comes a year later, at a time when he along with other founders had broken ties with the emerging leadership of the group and clearly had begun to view them with contempt. In these letters he shares his experience of transforming into a professional with Boulton, who clearly characterizes herself as a professional too, but now one committed to her husband's art. In her eyes O'Neill was a successful writer who would, of course, refuse to make such a compromise. Nevertheless, it would prove gratifying to her (and to him) when he won a thousand dollars for the Pulitzer Prize for *Beyond the Horizon*. For a while in the early 1920s it seemed that the remarkable thing about O'Neill was that he could make a long string of critics think and not just exclaim, and still keep the box office busy.

The next group of letters, the largest continuous grouping of letters in this volume (about one hundred items from early January to early March 1920) offer O'Neill's private narration of his adjustment to that new role, but they also offer Boulton's adaptation of herself to the new role of mate. She tests a wide variety of voices in these letters in search of the right admixture of tonal and stylistic qualities to fit this particular experiment in marriage. At the time of their wedding they had declared to each other that theirs would be a marriage based solely on love and mutual need, that nothing else should interfere with the nearly religious passion they had for each other. They both struggle with a highly wrought, unrestrained romanticism, which was clearly the rhetorical mode of their love for each other but often awkward when written down. Their protestations about the futility of words go well beyond the usual poetic figure.

Bogard and Bryer comment that O'Neill's passionate phrases mimic his earlier love letters (1914–16) to Beatrice Ashe: "The echoes, however, were paler than their source in the Ashe letters, and before long the amorous tone became domesticated and a little matter-of-fact."[9] In fact, as this volume shows, the amorous declarations continued almost to the end of the correspondence, but there was always a great mass of practical concerns—professional and domestic—which they shared. The point is, the real world was always a matter of immediate concern to both of them because of its intrusions into the marriage, and literarily they were both equipped for realism. Though her literary talent extended not nearly so far as his, her capacity for handling practical matters in an independent way was substantial. After all, it was she who calculated and paid their federal income tax during the first year it was imposed (1919). She also arranged for nearly all the accommodations—apartments, houses, hotel rooms—they would require. In the bargain she got access to romance and he got access to the real. But that is also too simplistic a formula, because she also valued him for his definable qualities and capacities, and he located in her the possibility of transcendent love. Right from the beginning, the correspondence articulates these discontinuous but coexistent impulses.

The modernism of the marriage—its shunting aside of material values and patterns of dominance and relations with an extended family—is addressed at length in *Part of a Long Story*. That book ends with the birth of their first child together, Shane, which is construed by Boulton as a sacred act of creation, replacing her earlier, unholy literary acts of creation, her pulp literature. She portrays the birth as her equivalent of the titanic artistic expressions of O'Neill. Yet soon it proves true, as this correspondence shows, that the birth of a child is a commonplace event, food gets eaten, contracts get signed, and the oppressive details of even so sanctified a marriage as theirs and even so outstanding a career as his multiply from day to day. This correspondence picks up again in November 1919, just after that birth, and there are at once clear signs that the baby has altered their marriage. At one point he declares his eagerness to be back in her arms, to be her "other—and firstborn!—baby again!" (#12). The intense isolation of their life in Provincetown is interrupted by that new voice ("Shane the Loud," he whimsically dubs the child)[10] and also by the clamor of producers in New York who demand his participation in the business of Broadway. Agnes continues the effort to use their absence from each other to charge the marriage with spirit. Partly what is at risk is the uniqueness, the singularity, the extraordinariness of their "Holy of Holies," and so she takes responsibility for having introduced that aspect of the prosaic, the world beyond truth and beauty, a reality discordant with art:

Too often I found myself judging you by ordinary standards—the little cheap standards of the commonplace man—instead of remembering that you have that within
you which is *not* of them—for,—in spite of your superb knowledge of maliciousness!—your heart has that simpleness and fineness which is truth. In *my* meanness I
attributed to you motives—oh, in "little things" of course—that even at the time I
knew were not true. But that was mostly because I had lost hold of my real self, as I'd
forgotten yours—I was giving in to outside things, instead of being guided by my
own knowledge—for, *instinctively*, I don't ever, ever misjudge you. (#11)

Years later she remembered what the act of marrying meant for both of them, and it
was not an equivalency she saw, but a compensatory balance of two very different
"real" selves: "For me it was perhaps a confirmation and for Gene it was a new and
peaceful freedom—freedom to live, to become, to create. . . ."[11] Of course, by the
time she wrote those words he was dead. When Sheaffer interviewed people who had
known O'Neill and Boulton, several scoffed at Boulton's book, finding its romantic
effusions a bit much for the O'Neill they remembered. Indeed, to them *Part of a Long
Story* is another sort of pulp fiction, a romance novel. The letters in this correspondence show that the lines cannot be easily drawn between the real selves and the
romantic effusions. When Boulton tries to recollect the words that O'Neill used to
define what the marriage meant, they sound something like a passage in a pulp story—
or one of his windier plays: "Oh, love of my life, we need nothing, you and I, but
ourselves. I have found my work, my peace, my joy. No—let me say it this way—I
have found *myself*! I will not say to you, my love, as a poet once said, that I will pluck
the stars of heaven to hang them in your hair—I say to you there *are* no stars in
heaven, unless I *can* hang them in your hair." The next paragraph begins by saying
that "soon after that" he said he was going to open a joint checking account so that she
could "make out the checks and take care of all that—then I won't be bothered."[12]
This jamming together of romantic flight verging on cliché, creating O'Neill as the
Byronic lover, and mundane egotism in which the world caters to his needs is the
formula of many of these letters. Boulton subscribed to this formula; indeed she was
its cowriter. Occasionally, she inverted it, inscribing her own Byronic desires and
egotism.

The year that opened with O'Neill's first Broadway triumph soon took its ironic
turns. *Chris* developed as such an obvious disaster in O'Neill's eyes that he did not
even attend rehearsals, preferring to send Boulton instead. Not long after *Beyond the
Horizon* opened, his father's health took a sudden turn for the worse and it was re-
vealed that he would soon die of cancer. In fact, his mother and brother would also die
within the next three years, but only his father's death figures into this correspondence. The series of letters written from New London in July and August 1920 offers
a vivid sense of tragic irony. The man he once idolized, then grew to hate, and finally
in the last year came to love and understand more deeply now became the incarnation
of suffering. Other sources make it clear that this was a period in which O'Neill did
much drinking, along with his brother, and yet his letters specifically deny that. An

element of duplicity or convenient fiction runs through both sides of this correspondence; the letters create their own world and the personae who inhabit them. The letters from New London turn frequently to the subject of his own marriage. What he finds in the ghastly spectacle of his father's agony is a sense that the one fine thing that his father had was the love of his mother. He suggests to Agnes that this should be a reminder to them not to fight and hurt each other, which he calls "a crime against the spirit of [their] love" (#122). Instead, he says they should protect their love against themselves. Her response is resentment that he would say their marriage had been unhappy, as if he had forgotten all their "lovely moments": "It made you seem alien from 'us'" (#123). And yet it is inescapable that from a distance, a difference had been glimpsed.

   1. "13 Below Zero on Coldest Day, Worst Is Over," *New York Times,* December 31, 1917, 1.
   2. There are many contradictions in the sequence of events recounted by Boulton in *Part of a Long Story.* She recalls having seen *'Ile* and a play by Maxwell Bodenheim (52), even though those plays were on the second bill of the Provincetown Players' season, November 30 to December 6, 1917. There were other cold nights that autumn—it was a notably cold season—but her memory of the extreme cold on the night she met O'Neill seems to point to December 30, when the temperature broke by six degrees the old record set just the day before. This was a cold spell long remembered. Then, too, the detail about the extreme cold might have seemed just the narrative device with which to begin her "story." Probably her experiences among the Provincetown Players began late in November or early in December. On the 11th of December the thermometer registered nine degrees.
   3. Boulton, *Part of a Long Story,* 21, 68.
   4. Details of both these affairs, if such they were, remain sketchy, and in the case of Day questions have been raised about whether there had been a romantic relationship at all. See William D. Miller, *Dorothy Day: A Biography* (New York: Harper & Row, 1982), 103–19. But see the entry under Dorothy Day in Margaret Loftus Ranald's invaluable *The Eugene O'Neill Companion* (Westport, Conn.: Greenwood Press, 1984), 152–56. For the story of Louise Bryant see Virginia Gardner's *"Friend and Lover": The Life of Louise Bryant* (New York: Horizon Press, 1982).
   5. Boulton, *Part of a Long Story,* 30.
   6. The production history of O'Neill's plays during the middle period has been analyzed by Ronald Wainscott in *Staging O'Neill: The Experimental Years, 1920–1934* (New Haven: Yale University Press, 1988). It is notable, however, that little use was made of the Boulton-O'Neill correspondence, which offers considerable information about production details.
   7. Robert Károly Sarlós's *Jig Cook and the Provincetown Players: Theatre in Ferment* (n.p.: University of Massachusetts Press, 1982) develops this idea in detail.
   8. Quoted in Louis Sheaffer, *O'Neill: Son and Playwright* (Boston: Little, Brown, 1968), 473.
   9. Travis Bogard and Jackson R. Bryer, eds., *Selected Letters of Eugene O'Neill* (New Haven: Yale University Press, 1988), 76
   10. Boulton, *Part of a Long Story,* 330.
   11. Ibid., 110–11 (Boulton's ellipsis).
   12. Ibid., 111.

1. **AB to EO** ALS 2 pp. ([Old House, West Point Pleasant, N.J.]) [Harvard]

Tuesday noon / [December 17?, 1918][1]

Dearest— I wonder if you know how much I hope and pray there will be a letter from you this afternoon. There was just a letter for you from Scotty,[2] this A.M. Oh Gene, I am missing you so! *I didn't appreciate you.* The first hours after you left were simply torture—I felt like running down the street after you, and then there was a dreadful feeling of something frightful going to happen—to you, or us, just because you were away.

This is to catch the noon mail, so dearest goodby—I'll write a long letter this afternoon—even if I don't [hear?].[3] Your own Agnes

1. The correspondence begins with an uncertainty about how to date a letter. This problem will recur frequently. Sheaffer dates this letter in early January of 1920, at the time when Eugene O'Neill (hereafter abbreviated EO) was going off to prepare for the opening of his first Broadway production, *Beyond the Horizon*. But he misreads the letter as dated "Saturday" and assigns it tentatively to January 3. Considering that O'Neill's departure letter (#18) implies that he left on Sunday, this is dubious. Furthermore the letters written by Agnes Boulton (hereafter abbreviated AB) from late 1919 and early 1920 nearly always make reference to Shane O'Neill, and they also have a more practical aspect, although they are also often infused with passion. Therefore I am tentatively assigning this letter a much earlier date, half a year into their marriage, before the birth of a child, at a time when EO was traveling from AB's family home in New Jersey, where they had decided to spend the winter, to the opening of his *Moon of the Caribbees* at the Playwright's Theatre of the Provincetown Players.
2. William Stuart, a woodcarver and friend of EO, also acted in *Bound East for Cardiff* (1916) and *Moon of the Caribbees* (1918).
3. Or possibly "leave."

2. **AB to EO** ALS 2 pp. ([Old House, West Point Pleasant, N.J.]) [Harvard]

Thursday *morning* / [December 19?, 1918]

Dearest, I'm not coming up. Not unless you send me a wire when you get this (you ought to get it Friday A.M., early). There was a letter from Lewis & Gordon, and things seem doubtful, about *I.T.Z.*[1] So, much as I want to come, it's better to wait. I'll mail the story to Sonia (it's finished).[2] And you'll have to tell me about *The Moon*.[3] But dear dearest heart, come home Saturday. I won't be able to stand another day longer than that without you. It's such a thin, shadowy world, very still, just waiting—for you. All the reality is gone, and it's only when I shut my eyes and think about *us*, about *you*, that I'm with something real—something still too, but with the stillness of the stars—something deep, something *complete*. How futile words are!

Dear dearest, it's so silly to tell you that I love you (millionth time!) Do you mind? I just wanted to say it again. You've never forgotten to say it to me, heart of mine. You are so beautiful, dearest, all of *you*.

I wonder if I'll be able not to take that train? I'm *lonely!* Your very very own wife, Agnes.

1.   *In the Zone*, which was first produced by the Provincetown Players in 1917, played for thirty-four weeks on the Orpheum Circuit during 1918. Albert Lewis and Max Gordon produced this vaudeville version of the play. Their letter probably announced the end of the run and thus the loss of an important source of income for EO.

2.   Sonja Levien (1898–1960) was coeditor of *The Metropolitan* and later a successful Hollywood screenwriter.

3.   *Moon of the Caribbees* opened at the Provincetown Playhouse on December 20, 1918.

~⌒

3. **AB to EO** AL 4 pp. ([Old House, West Point Pleasant, N.J.]) [Harvard]

Same day. / [December 19?, 1918]

Dearest Gene— I just sent you a letter—and, now, it seems to me that it wasn't a very *practical* letter, and that you might want to know more definitely about L. & G. So—I'm enclosing theirs. I did intend not sending it or telling you what they had to say until you got back, as I was afraid it might give you the blues, but on thinking it over, perhaps you will want, while in town to 'phone him & find out some thing more definite. So here it is.

Don't be discouraged. Now I'm *here*, & not so worried about things. *I'm* going to support the family for a change. I have started a story, & know I can do a lot. I always can, when it really gets down to brass tacks. You said just about that a week or so ago, and it's true. Only you didn't say it in quite that flattering way. I will simply do Harold De Polo's stunt for a while—look over old copies of the magazine I'm writing for & dope out some plots of the cheap & easy kind.[1] The reason I haven't sold stuff this summer is as you know, I was getting in too much of the other, more serious or anyway, attempted serious, style.

Wrote the two letters for you. I'm getting a lot done while you're away—*have* to keep busy, so as not to miss you too much. Having stove put upstairs, etc. Finished [typing?] story. Under the circumstances, I ought to stay here, & get things started . . . stories, I mean. So please dearest, don't fail to be down. Come earlier Sat. if you can. By getting your mother to phone Information, Penn. Station you can get time of trains. Wire me if you take other train than the one leaving 3. something. I'll meet that one Sat. evening with jitney, as I have to do some shopping. Love to all.

Au revoir, my own dearest. If you write me, on getting this, I'll get letter Sat. A.M. or noon. Please do.

1.   Harold DePolo was a prolific short-story writer and friend of EO since 1915–16.

~~

4. **EO to AB** WIRE, addressed to West Point Pleasant, N.J. (New York) [Yale]

DEC 20TH 1918

COME ON IMMEDIATELY WILL NOT LEAVE UNTIL YOU COME[1] EUGENE

1. In *Part of a Long Story*, Boulton recalls this telegram differently: "I will not come home until you come up" (p. 263).

~~

5. **AB to EO** ALS 2 pp. ([Provincetown, Mass.]) [Harvard]

[August? 1919]

Dearest 'Gene— There was a telegram from mother today, saying she & M.[1] arrives tomorrow via Fall River[2]—so guess I better stay in[3]—& ride out with them—and the wash—I'll try to catch the life saver & send out bread & this—and mail. Only this from Madden[4] so far.—but this afternoon's hasn't come yet—I *wish* I wasn't going to stay in—it's dreadful—I feel so awfully lost. The doctor says I must be in by 10th— Francis[5] will let us have Happy Home for Sept. I went in, and it's very nice. Am sending out what *Times* Stella[6] has—

X X X X Kisses!

O O O O Hugs— Your own, *Agnes.*

Wednesday

1. Probably Margery, AB's sister.
2. The ferries from New York docked at Fall River, Massachusetts.
3. AB and EO were living at this time at the old Coast Guard station at Peaked Hill Bar, a building formerly owned by the wealthy arts patron Mabel Dodge and purchased for EO by his father. In 1931 the building washed into the sea.
4. Richard Madden (1880–1951), EO's agent and a partner in the American Play Company.
5. John Francis, a Provincetown grocer, rented EO a flat above his store on Commercial Street and later the house known as Happy Home, where Shane Rudraighe O'Neill was born on October 30, 1919.
6. Stella Commins Ballantine was the wife of Edward J. (Teddy) Ballantine, a New York actor, and sister of EO's dentist and later editor, Saxe Commins.

~~

6. **EO to AB** ALS 1 p. (*On the train* [from Provincetown, Mass. to New York]) [Harvard]

[November 30?, 1919]

Own Dearest: What ho! This is the time I fool you. You won't expect this one, will you, after what I said—with malice aforethought. I'm hoping it will make you happy and less lonely.

It's writing under difficulties, though. The train seems to give an extra jerk at every word.

We're only just past Truro[1] but I already feel that pang of a great emptiness which always gnaws way down at the roots of my soul as soon as I become sickeningly aware of the vacant spot by my side where you should be. I love you so, my Own! You must believe that and also that I need you, your help and sympathy and love, as I have never before needed you. You said you thought my need had grown less, but that is mistaken nonsense. (Nonsense!) It has grown day by day, hour by hour, as you crept into my inner life, my finer self, until now that part of me is your creation, the soul of me which is all you and yours. You are wife of all of me but mother of the best of me. So ignore my bad moods and my irresponsible tongue. They are the leopard's spots; and, after all, a leopard isn't such a bum creation, taking him all in all, and he wouldn't be a leopard if he were spotless.

The above is incoherent but you'll get me, I know. Kiss Shane[2] for me. I *do* love him—"in my fashion." My best to Mrs. Clark[3] and tell her I rely on her to fatten you up with early hours— and much "eats." A long kiss, Own Sweetheart! Gene

1. Cape Cod town adjacent to Provincetown.
2. Shane Rudraighe O'Neill (1919–77) was born in Provincetown on 30 October.
3. Fifine Clark, nicknamed Gaga, was the O'Neills' nurse-housekeeper.

7. **AB to EO** ALS 4 pp. ([Provincetown, Mass.]) [Harvard]

Sunday night— / [November 30?, 1919]

Well—I've taken a bath, and nursed the baby, and here I am in bed by ten o'clock like a good girl—writing to you! You're talking to Hutch,[1] I suppose—near Point Judith.[2] Perhaps you're thinking about us.

I miss you so.

After all, I don't want to *say* anything to you now, I just want you to be here, near me.— dear old sweetheart! so I won't write anything more tonight, I'll turn out the light and—pretend you're not gone.—

Monday, A.M.— / [December 1?, 1919]

Mrs. C. has been repeating, at intervals of an hour or so, how "swell" you looked when you went away—you seem to have made quite an impression on her feminine heart. She says if you were *hers*, she'd never let you travel alone, also, she'd make you wear a wedding ring—thinks you aren't safe from assault, apparently, without one!

I went to tea at Mrs. Ullman's[3] yesterday. She is *scandalous*! You should have heard her remarks about the Hapgood family. However, I'm going with her to see Bill Farnum[4] tonight, in spite of it. No doubt she will be confidentially telling someone next summer that my thinness is due to syphilis, caught from you, you having acquired the disease during your wild past! That she "fancies" is what is "wrong" with the Hapgood children—that, and the fact that Neith is a *terrible* drunkard who spends most of her time "on the drawing room floor." (Of course don't mention this to Hutch— she's simply a little off, that's all, and there is no use making her trouble.)

The paper this A.M. contains nothing but the removal of *The Defense*[5]—to the Morosco. What does that mean? Seats four weeks in advance.

The Williams MSS. did not arrive—of course. The black curse on that man!— No other mail.

As Hutch says, you can't face the truth except at intervals, and so I don't fully realize yet that you are so far away from me. It seems as if you must be upstairs, or in the bathroom, or somewhere. Only once in a while it comes with a dreadful sense of emptiness—the knowledge that no matter how much I want to see you, hear you, be with you, it's impossible.

Well—it can't be helped—

Terry[6] says now he's sorry he didn't go down with you.

Tell me *everything* when you write. I'll always keep your letters—and it will be fun to read them when we're both—*old*.

Goodby, my own, dearest. I can still see you as you said goodby yesterday and it's a consolation. *Agnes.*

(1) Rubbers?
(2) Malted Milk?

1. Hutchins Hapgood (1869–1944) was a New York journalist and "philosophical anarchist." He was married to the writer Neith Boyce (1872–1951). They had four children. See *Intimate Warriors: Portraits of a Modern Marriage, 1899–1944: Selected Works by Neith Boyce and Hutchins Hapgood*, ed. Ellen Kay Trimberger (New York: Feminist Press at City University of New York, 1991).

2. Town in Rhode Island.

3. Alice Woods Ullman, divorced from the artist Eugene P. Ullman, was a charming and sophisticated writer who had recently returned to the United States from Paris.

4. William Farnum (1876–1953) was a well-known stage and screen actor.

5. *For the Defense* was a play by Elmer Rice (1892–1967), produced by John D. Williams (1886?–1941), initially at The Playhouse, later moved to the Morosco. Williams, who also produced *Beyond the Horizon*, was planning to use some of the cast members, including its star, Richard Bennett, from the Rice play in a series of special matinee performances of *Beyond the Horizon.*

6. Terry Carlin, born Terence O'Carolan, was a Greenwich Village personality, a Nietzschean anarchist and experimentalist in radical styles of life, also a chronic alcoholic.

Carlin first became friends with EO in 1915–16 and later lived in a shack on the dunes near EO's house on Peaked Hill Bar.

∽

8. **EO to AB** ALS 3 pp. (Stationery headed: New England Steamship Lines) [Virginia]

10 P.M. / [November 30?, 1919]

Sweetheart: Abysmal gloom! There wasn't a stateroom to be had when we got on board. They held out a promise that some that had been reserved might not be called for but nothing doing! We are now past Newport and every room on the boat taken. The best we can now hope for is a bunk and if there are too many others before us on that, we'll have to pick out a soft chair. Such are the delights of travel! The trip sure starts inauspiciously. I have a headache already and think it will be a long hard night to get to the end of.

Had a fine dinner on board—fried scallops with tartar sauce.

Wrote a letter to you on the train which I hoped to mail in Middleboro and surprise you with it tomorrow. But no chance! There wasn't a stamp to be bought so I'll have to mail it in New York tomorrow at the same time I do this.

I've got to the end of all the reading matter I want to read. Will have to take out the rest of the night with dreams of you—(waking!) I'll go out now and do this properly by watching the sea—our sea—the same that laps the front yard of our Peaked Hill Bar.

I love you, My Own! I miss you! I wish to the devil I were back in Happy Home this minute—(not only for the sake of a place to flop!)

A long kiss, Sweetheart—and don't forget me! And kiss our White Hope for me! Your Gene

P.S. This is a punk attempt at a letter but a writing room full of silly, chattering imbeciles on a rocking boat is not my idea of any author's sanctum. Another kiss!

Another kiss!

∽

9. **EO to AB** ALS 4 pp. (Stationery headed: Prince George Hotel / Fifth Avenue & 28th Street / [New York]) [Harvard]

Monday—6 P.M. / [December 1?, 1919]

My Own: Well, we arrived! Yes, finally, we got here! It was some long night! About twelve the purser passed out bunk numbers to us and we went below to have a look. Jig[1] quit at the end of the look, but I resolved to have a try at it. I crawled into the bunk and tried to go to sleep; but too many people had taken off their shoes in the compartment. I and those nude feet simply couldn't live in the same world. So finally, in spite of my foc's'tle training, I had to throw up the sponge and join Jig on an uncomfortable chair in the salon. Jig was already uneasily asleep but I didn't get to that point until three A.M. In the meantime the night watchman took a fancy to me, sat beside me, and unfolded his family troubles—just why his wife and his sister couldn't live in the same house in Fall River. After I had condoled with him, a Jewish gentleman, who also had missed a stateroom, woke up long enough to feel of his feet and confess to me how he suffered from corns and, in detail, the different cures he had tried ineffectually.

Oh yes, be the trip what it might, I got one long kiss of "the bleeding lips of suffering humanity." On the outside I must certainly look to be a sympathetic soul— (and perhaps they're right(?)).

Jig and I had breakfast on the good ship at six A.M. and I've been home ever since we landed. Mama[2] and I have been shopping all afternoon. I got a tweed suit—65.00— and an overcoat—85.00—shirts—collars—all at Lord & Taylors. Hope you will like me when you see me again. I thought I might as well stick to L.&T. as Mama knows everyone there and there would be no chance of the double-cross. Also, on second thought, I decided that pure sport clothes were a luxury one couldn't afford before laying the foundation of a regular, bread-and-butter costume. After *Chris*[3] brings home the bacon will be time enough for me to exhibit my strange fancies. Not that the present clothes are the absolute usual. They have too much class for that.

Most of the P.M. has been spent in the P. G. chatting with the Old Governor & Mama who both appear extremely glad to see me—especially after the detective work at the greeting failed to discover my breath guilty. They are full of thous. questions concerning the baby and crazy to see him.

The hope of unlimited booze at the Old Homestead is another yen hok[4] gesture. Papa had only *one-quarter of one bottle* left of the treasure when I arrived—and that is now gone, need I add? *And he is at a loss where to get more!* Honestly! He still loves Wilson[5] but hates his native land—U.S.—and swears to beat it hence with all his gold to some country where gentlemen may still be ungentlemanly. I've talked Bermuda to him and he says he is willing to buy a place and settle down there. Perhaps the fact that I told him good Scotch sold in the British dominions for 10 shillings may have something to do with his eagerness. At any rate I have him interested—and Bermuda would be a good old winter home to go to. I speak interestedly.

Have had three drinks and that is all I am liable to get during my stay. The Garden[6] is dry as dry.

My clothes won't arrive until tomorrow P.M. so can't start on my round of calls till Thursday morning.

Feel terrifically done up by the awful night on the boat. I honestly needed the drink Papa was thoughtful enough to proffer when I arrived. I was all in.

There's lots more in the way of home gossip to relate but it's unimportant and will wait for my next.

I've been wishing so much today that you were here! I've felt so punk generally—although the jesting tone of this letter might lead you to believe differently. New York looks rotten to me, and I'll be giving a loud cheer when the train pulls in to P'town again. I'm not joking. There's nothing at all for me here now that Prohib. is in force. Of course, it did make me happy to see Paw 'n' Maw again, and I suspect I'll spend most of my time right under their wing. So don't worry about me! I'm a good, good boy!

A long kiss, Own Sweetheart of mine! And one for Shane! It won't be long now till—our honeymoon! Bye'bye for this time. Gene.

Write!

    1.   George Cram Cook (1873–1924), novelist and playwright, was one of the founders of the Provincetown Players and their spiritual and artistic leader.
    2.   Ella Quinlan O'Neill (1857–1922) and James O'Neill (1846–1920) lived in a suite at the Prince George Hotel, as well as in New London, Connecticut.
    3.   *Chris Christophersen* was the early and unsuccessful version of *"Anna Christie,"* produced by George C. Tyler in March of 1920.
    4.   Underworld slang associated with opium use, thus suggesting a pipe dream.
    5.   President Woodrow Wilson.
    6.   The Garden Hotel.

10. **AB to EO** AL 3 pp. ([Provincetown, Mass.]) [Harvard 9]

Monday / [December 1?, 1919]

Dearest— It certainly *was* a surprise! I couldn't imagine how you'd managed, until I saw you'd mailed it on the train. You beloved dear, I'm glad you *do* need me—still. The feeling of emptiness you speak of almost drove me crazy this afternoon—before I got your letter.

I wrote you last night and this morning, and posted the letter in the box before eleven, so you will get it Tuesday morning. What advantage is there in sending a letter before seven? Do you get it the next night, or not?

Fifine says that Timmy misses you, and I really believe he does. She says he went up stairs twice to your room, and refuses to eat, and stood sniffing at your coat.—

Chris has taken to going out o' nights—courting—[1]

Tues. A.M. / [December 2?, 1919]

The enclosed is what was happening out in the harbor Sunday A.M. while we were eating breakfast.

Terry has been down for dinners. Seems sorry he didn't go with you. Talks about the "16th."

Well, I went to see Wm. Farnum. He plays the part of the handsome hero—but looks a bit old for it when you get him out of a sombrero and chaps, into a business suit. He's the fine, hearty, sunshiney lover, who shakes his head with an ecstatic smile at the sight of a baby's shoe. In one part he did a mad scene well though, and I thought of *Gold*.[2] Do you know, there is something about him—in the pictures of course—that makes me wonder if he would really want to appear in a role where he'd come before his beloved public—who so loves his youth—that is, his gay, laughing, springing vitality—as an old man. Even for the sake of art! You feel that he's so darned *proud* of that easy youngness of his![3]

Shane is fine. Will send pictures. The Williams MSS. did *not* arrive. No other mail. A. Ullman[4] was sick, so went to movies alone.

Goodby, my own. I want to get this in the noon collection. Many kisses—dearest! You know how I'm missing you.

"Your own—"

My love to your folks, and will you tell your mother I am writing to her?

1.   Timmy was a dog, Chris (Anna Christie) a cat.
2.   EO's expanded version of *Where the Cross Is Made* (1918), which in turn was based on a scenario by AB. *Gold* was produced by John D. Williams in June of 1921.
3.   Farnum (1876–1953) was a major star of silent film Westerns and melodramas. George Tyler was trying to interest him in the role of Chris Christophersen.
4.   Alice Woods Ullman.

11. **AB to EO** ALS 4 pp. (Happy Home / [Provincetown, Mass.]) [Harvard 6]

Tuesday. / [December 2?, 1919]

My own dearest Gene. Three letters in this afternoon's mail! I hadn't dared dream that you would think of me so much. They were such beautiful letters, dearest. I've read them all twice, and tonight, before I turn the light out, I'll read them again, and then Shane and I will lie there together in the dark and *love* you. He loves you, too, the dear funny little thing, though he may not know it yet because that part of him which is me—*my* half of him—couldn't help loving you. When I close my eyes and think about you, it seems almost as though you were there, with me.

The letter you wrote on the train gave me a deep peace, a beautiful humility, a feeling that was a wordless prayer before our Holy of Holies. Our faith is the dream that *will* endure—it *must*. If together we can conquer the loneliness of the world, then together we can conquer the loneliness of oblivion—if that should be the Secret. You were right. We *were* getting too used to each other. Too often I found myself judging you by ordinary standards—the little cheap standards of the commonplace man—instead of remembering that you have that within you which is *not* of them—for,—in spite of your superb knowledge of maliciousness!—your heart has that simpleness and fineness which is truth. In *my* meanness I attributed to you motives—oh, in "little things" of course—that even at the time I knew were not true. But that was mostly because I had lost hold of my real self, as I'd forgotten yours—I was giving in to outside things, instead of being guided by my own knowledge—for, *instinctively*, I don't ever, ever misjudge you. Now I've confessed, so three times I beat myself on the breast and say "through my fault—my fault—my most grievous fault!" Forgive me, beloved.

Of course the watchman and the Jewish gentleman told you their troubles, nut! Everybody likes you that sees you! But it was awful spending the night like that. Susan[1] laughed so when I told her about "the bleeding lips of humanity." She misses Jig a lot—I can see that. The suit and coat sound fine—I'm dying to see them —& you in them!

I got the nicest letter from Jamie. It must be awfully lonely for him up there—he had the blues—

Shane has just begun to cry for his dinner—and there was so much more I wanted to say—but I'll write this evening. Goodby dearest,—*have a good time* do you understand! Love to your father and mother, Your loving Agnes

1. Susan Glaspell (1882–1948) was one of the founders of the Provincetown Players. A prolific author of short stories, novels, and plays, she was married to George Cram ("Jig") Cook.

12. **EO to AB** ALS 3 pp. (Stationery headed: Prince George Hotel / Fifth Avenue & 28th Street / [New York]) [Harvard]

Tuesday A.M. / [December 2?, 1919]

Own Wife: Last night about ten I made a voyage to the Hell Hole[1] to see how it had survived the dry spell. Lefty, Jim Martin, Joe Smith[2] and quite a populous mob of the old bunch were there along with a lot of new "guerrillas" to whom I was presented as "our old pal, Gene." There was no whiskey in the house and Joe Smith told me they couldn't get it more than two days a week now—and then it had to be stolen by some of the gang out of a storehouse, and sold to Tom Wallace[3] afterward. All hands were drinking sherry and I joined this comparatively harmless and cheap—20¢ per drink— debauch right willingly. There was just enough kick in the wine to make everyone feel jovial and that's all. Some "hard" ladies of the oldest profession, who seemed to know me, were in the back room along with a drunk. Where this latter got his jug, I don't know. He had a huge roll of money and was blowing the house. I suspected he was being "framed" for a "frisk" and kept my eyes to myself. To support this theory of mine, I noticed that several parties after visits to the rear, came back with money to purchase further drinks.

There was much talk of the bike race[4] and finally a party of about 20, in which I am included, arranged to go up and see it tomorrow night. This ought to prove real fun for me. They're going to have several quarts of sherry to pack on the hip and even that "ladies" booze is not to be sneezed at in the New York of today. Believe me, Prohibition is very much of a *fact*.

Scotty had told Lefty of the Josephine song[5] being in *Chris* and the latter is tremendously elated. Also, to my astonishment, he swears—(and I believe him)—that Josephine is his own stuff, a song he made up when he was singing in a tough Wop cabaret—"my own bull s—t," he explains proudly. That it is to be heard on Broadway is a great event in his life. He offers, as soon as rehearsals start, to go up for a couple of hours every morning to instruct Corrigan[6] how to sing it—without desiring pay for his services! All he wants is two seats to take his girl to surprise her with his song— on Broadway!

This little incident of the song seems to me quite touching in its way. Don't you think so? And quite characteristic. It sounds rock-bottom and I think all the hours seemingly wasted in the H.H. would be justified if they had resulted in only this.

Lefty and Joe Smith seem as delighted with Shane's arrival as if they were godparents. They urged me to send all their blessings to you—"the little girl."

It was quite an "old time" night down there—minus drunkenness—and I thoroughly enjoyed it. No Villager came to spoil the atmosphere, thanks be!, and the Hell Hole was itself again.

I'm wondering what you're doing today and all the time since I left. Expected a letter this morning but was disappointed. What about your promise to write? Oh Sweetheart, how I wish you were here with me! I sort of feel empty and hollow—a body without a soul—and, except for a few moments here and there, I've been fairly aching with loneliness. But in a few days I'll be back in your arms, My Own, and be your other—and firstborn!—baby again!

This afternoon, I'm slated to continue the shopping ordeal under Mama's guidance. Still need a hat, shoes before I start my business calls tomorrow.

Send me or Mama the size of your bean so she can get that hat.

Haven't been near the P.P. yet but expect to go down tonight long enough to submit my play, at any rate. And all dolled up in new store clothes—if they come in time.

A million kisses, Beautiful! And a gentle one for my son—so it won't wake him up. More later! Your Gene

1. Nickname of the Golden Swan saloon, a regular hangout for EO since 1915.
2. Lefty Louie, bartender of the "Hell Hole," James Joseph ("Slim") Martin, an Irish steelworker and ex-sailor, and Joseph Smith, an African American gambler, were "Hell Hole" regulars.
3. Owner of the "Hell Hole."
4. Six-day bicycle races were held at Madison Square Garden.
5. "My Yosephine [Josephine]" is a song sung by the title character in *Chris Christophersen*. Scotty is William Stuart.
6. Emmett Corrigan played the title role in *Chris Christophersen*.

13. **AB to EO** AL 8 pp. ([Provincetown, Mass.]) [Harvard]

Wednesday / [December 3?, 1919]

Dearest Gene— I've just discovered that there is no seven o'clock collection in the evening from this end of town! That may have made a difference in your getting my letters, as I've counted on that collection. You should have got one Tues. afternoon. Dearest, I hope you didn't think I hadn't written!

I can't tell you what fun it was to read about your visit at Hell Hole. I seemed to see the whole thing. It was as real—! And I'm so *darned glad* you met all the old crowd. They were the real people. 'Nuff said! The comedy in the back room must have made it exciting—gee, how different from when the village used to decorate it with their inanities—(is that spelled right?) I think that is the strangest thing about Lefty writing "My Josephine"—why his future's likely to be made as one future great song writer! That song is going to make a hit in *Chris.*—and oh, what a little press story for the Rev. [Tuehy?].[1] Can't you see it? Really, though, there *is* something touching about it.

Hurrah for the bike race! I can just see you there with that bunch hip-packed with sherry! It will be wonderful for you, all right, and a chance for some real fun. According to the *Times* the crowd must be making up in smoking what they lack in liquor. Be sure and cheer for Dupuy— remember, he was fine last year? I see he is with your favorite Egg. Hope Magin don't keep in front, as last year, but he doesn't seem to be getting much attention so far. I am getting quite excited about the race now myself, and oh, be sure and remember the songs! Although I don't believe there will ever be another as good as "Goodby Mule!"

I'll enclose Jamie's[2] letter—and today, I was astonished by getting another from him, in which he says he forgot to mention that he had a friend of yours and "Pips," named Cousin, said Cousin now located in Boston, with "a bear of a Cadillac and oodles of Jack"—and he may drop in on us in P'town. What is "Jack"—booze or money? I hope he doesn't come until you get back anyway. I'm writing J. tonight that you are in town. Wasn't it nice of him to write to me?

I'm dying to hear your dope on the P. Players.—what you heard and saw there. (Hope you had your "store-clothes"!) Susan heard from Jiggie today, and came up to get me to have a cup of tea with her. I saw that she had something on her mind. J.'s letter was pretty discouraging. He said the trouble between Ida and Jimmy was all about *Djuna!*[3] What does it mean? Ida, it seems, is not to act there any longer, and, Fitzie[4] leaving too, the entire thing will be in the hands of Jimmie & Sue (his wife)[5]— *but* Ida wishes it to be arranged so that she, you, Jig, & Susan will still be "in power," so that you can get control *next* season if you wish,—leaving it for the rest of this season in the hands of Jimmie & Sue. Jig hinted that there was "too much Millay"[6] in the acting part of the Players. We are wondering what on earth the fair but malicious Djuna has been up to. Are Ida and Jimmy rivals? (Of course Susan is no party to that evil thought.) But she seemed to think it likely that Jimmy had been ensnared—and also that Ida and Djuna were no longer on good terms. Don't say you heard any of this via Susan & me, by the way. What do you think of Edna Ferber heading the bill?[7]

But Susan wasn't really caring about Ida and Djuna or Jimmie. She was just terribly blue and hurt, by Jig's letter. I could hardly bear being with her, she was trying so hard to pretend *not* to mind—but she looked *sick*—she said: "Agnes, you know I think Ida's awfully selfish . . . without meaning to be so (kind Susan) . . . but she's so fond of Jig, in a friendly way . . . and now she wants him to stay down in New York and live in her apartment and *write*." And then she said: "She don't seem to consider how I feel about it at all." Susan tried to keep it all, of course, on a very *friendly* basis—said Ida *might* realize that she couldn't manage the stores alone, etc. I felt awfully sorry for her. Then she read me Jig's letter, in which he said he was all up in the air—didn't know what he wanted to do—and finally said "Ida thinks it would be best for me to stay down here, where I have a warm sunny room, if I want to write." Ida is a b——ch, is my opinion. She's just made up her mind to keep him down there—somehow. She's hit his weak spot, cleverly enough. Susan said his great objection was—the fixing of fires, & not being warm. Well, as a consequence Susan talked very seriously about not staying on here. She seems all up in the air. Said she felt now perhaps when it came to winter it would be too much, and said if Jig felt he needed the change of N.Y. and company, etc., she might try and go to Bermuda to visit Steeles,[8] or get a room there. Don't say a word of this to Jig of course— Likely enough he'll come back as planned,— not, however if Ida can keep him there!

Well, Fifine has taken it into her head that *I* need *feeding up*, and has been *feeding me up*— cup custard, soup, corn-bread etc.! Strict insistence that meals be taken at regular hours!— She is a kindly creature. I heard her telling Terry a long list of what she thought would be good for me to eat. Actually, I believe she is right. I go right ahead and eat all she gives me, and as a consequence, I find I am feeling *very much* stronger.

You surely have been "temperance" so far. But I suspect a visit to the P.P. may change this. Terry seems sure that Christine[9] can get all she wants, so perhaps they will stage you a real party. Hope you don't get into any *fights* over fair ladies this time! Terry seemed rather blue at your departure, which was a surprise to him.

If you have room, how about bringing up a few lbs of sugar—say 5—in your suit case? And my muff? Will you thank your mother very very much for planning to get me a hat, and, as I don't know headsize, and have no tape-measure over here, tell her the enclosed string is exact measure of head just above eyebrows—over my knots, of course.

I expect you will look most awfully grand when you arrive—and by the way, dearest, if you want to stay for finish of bike race, or business or other reasons, don't hesitate to stay a little longer, as a week isn't very long for all you have had to do— but be sure and let me *know*, so I won't be waiting and *no you*. Wire me, if you don't leave on the Saturday boat—will you be sure? Unless you [have] written to that effect. This letter should reach you Friday A.M.

Shane is getting dearer every day. He smiled three times this morning. Well, I hope he has *your* smile!

Dearest, thank you so very very much for writing every day. I can't begin to tell you how much they mean to me—a wonderful break in the loneliness—although I miss you more than ever, afterwards! But it won't be long now—will it?— Goodby, my own, my dearest. Your wife—

1. Possibly this is Boulton's misspelled and ironic reference to John Peter Toohey, press agent for George Tyler.
2. EO's brother, James O'Neill Jr. (1878–1923), was a washed-up actor at this time, living in New York.
3. Ida Rauh (1877–1970) acted and directed for the Provincetown Players and eventually became a codirector. She was married to the writer Max Eastman. James Light (1894–1964) directed many plays for the Provincetown Players and its successors, including several by EO. In October, he and Rauh had taken over from Susan Glaspell and Jig Cook as directors of the Provincetown Players and promised to present a so-called Season of Youth. Djuna Barnes (1892–1982), novelist and poet, wrote plays for the Provincetown Players in 1919–20, including *An Irish Triangle*, produced on the third bill in January 1920.
4. M. Eleanor Fitzgerald (1877–1955) was business manager and later director of the Provincetown Players.
5. Susan Jenkins (b. 1898), who performed a variety of different tasks for the Provincetown Players, married James Light in 1917.
6. Several plays by the poet and playwright Edna St. Vincent Millay (1892-1950) were presented by the Provincetown Players. She also acted in several productions, as did her sisters Norma and Kathleen. Floyd Dell has been quoted as saying that Edna "generally did not take direction" (Sarlós, *Jig Cook*, 85).
7. Ferber (1887–1968), later a famous novelist, had at this time most recently been a war correspondent. Her play *The Eldest* headed the third bill in January 1920.
8. Wilbur Daniel Steele (1886–1970) was a successful author of short stories and novels. He and his wife Margaret, a painter, were among the founders of the Provincetown Players.
9. Christine Ell, cook at the restaurant upstairs from the 133 Macdougal Street theatre which the Provincetown Players constructed when they moved to this building in 1918. She was married to Louis Ell, stagehand and sometimes actor with the Provincetown Players.

14. **AB to EO** ALS 3 pp. ([Provincetown, Mass.]) [Harvard]

Thursday Evening / Five o'clock / [December 4?, 1919?]

My own— You've spoiled me! I was so happy waiting for the mail—then, slump—everything blue and empty. Now I'm wondering how I'm going to wait till tomorrow . . . and wondering if it was a big party at Christine's, and if yesterday you felt too sick and shaky to write.

Dearest, I'm missing you so *terribly!*

Enclose letter. There was also some thing from the Everyman Theatre[1] London about doing your plays.—a large, printed thing, MSS. size, so am not enclosing—

I went [uptown?] today. It's been awfully cold here. Something queer happened to the plumbing—it rattled like a dishpan this morning.

My own dear big baby, please take care of yourself. And come back. I wish I didn't have this dreadful feeling of calamity, just because there was no letter from you today. Agnes—

I love you so much.

1. A theatre in Hampstead just outside London.

~~~

15. **EO to AB** WIRE, addressed to Happy Home Cottage, Provincetown, Mass. (New York) [Yale]

DEC 4 1919

LAZY MANS LETTER SIX DAY RACE ETC SAW MADDEN TYLER[1] TODAY AND YESTERDAY EVERYTHING SEEMS COMING ALONG OK WILL SURELY BE HOME SUNDAY MORE I WRITE LESS I HAVE TO TALK THEN EUGENE

1. George C. Tyler (1867–1946), prominent Broadway producer and a friend of James O'Neill Sr., produced *Chris Christophersen* (1920) and *The Straw* (1921).

~~~

16. **AB to EO** ALS 3 pp. ([Provincetown, Mass.]) [Harvard]

Friday, A.M. / [December 5?, 1919]

Dearest— Just got your wire— Thanks so much. *Terry is holding Shane*, who insisted on being held by some one—can you imagine—while I write this for noon mail. He does it like an expert too—

Will expect you Sunday then, unless I have a wire to the contrary. This will reach you Sat. A.M. So if you miss boat send wire, but *come* if you can, I am dying to see you again.

Terry says if you see Hutch or Hippolyte[1] tell them he'll be in town after Xmas.
Hope you got books—from Brentano's—
Much much love, dearest, Your Agnes—

Bring Jig if you can.
My best love to the folks.

1. Hippolyte Havel, radical anarchist, was chef and waiter at the Greenwich Village Inn

(known as "Polly's") at 137 Macdougal Street, in the basement of the Liberal Club. He was also a regular at the Hell Hole.

~~⌒

17. **EO to AB** WIRE, addressed to Provincetown, Mass. (New York) [Yale]

DEC 6TH 1919

HAD DATE WITH TYLER BOOTH TARKINGTON[1] AT THREE SO MISSED BOAT TOMORROW SURE. EUGENE

    1. Popular novelist and playwright (1869–1946) whose *Clarence* was being produced by George C. Tyler at this time.

~~⌒

18. **EO to AB** ALS 4 pp. (Stationery headed: Prince George Hotel / Fifth Avenue & 28th Street / [New York]) [Harvard]

Monday evening / [January 12?, 1920][1]

Heart's Desire: A busy day after a night of comparative comfort—(compared to my last cruise with Jig)—in which Hutch and I sat up in a deck stateroom and theorized the universe to sleep until about midnight. I have grown to love Hutch. He's a peach!

    My firebrand letter to John D. produced immediate results—a messenger boy to the P.G. this morning with a reply. He is stirred to the heart, it seems, and rather sore, I judge. I enclose his note to save quoting. He also phoned Madden saying "O'Neill didn't know how much he (W) had done for the play." He's a great joker, surely, is Mr. Williams. Madden and I are to see him tomorrow and get down to brass tacks. We have agreed that he must "show us" or give up the play.

    Went up to Tyler's at two. He is extremely anxious to get Tearle[2] for the part of "Chris." It seems from what I have heard on all sides that Tearle, even in a play that was a flat failure, has scored the knockout hit of the season as far as acting is concerned. All the managers are after him. Tearle told me he had read at least fifty American plays sent to him by Belasco,[3] etc. but none was artistic enough to make it worth his while staying in this country. He had his passage booked back to England—then read *Chris* and decided to stick around a while.

    He seems a corking chap—not a bit actory—about 35—tall and good looking. He claims it has always been his ambition to play a character part. The only reason he hesitates on the *Chris* matter is because he is afraid he may not realize my conception of the part. We had a long talk together. I convinced him it made no essential difference whether Chris was tall or short as long as he was Chris in spirit. He is taking the play to go over it again tonight and give a final decision to Tyler tomorrow. I hope he decides to do it, not only because I liked him personally but also because, on account of his great popularity in London, he would make an English production a certainty.

Tyler has a new scheme. His Helen Hayes, now in *Clarence*, is soon to be starred in a new play which is to go for a run in Boston in the spring[4]. Tyler wants her to put on one special matinee of *The Straw* in the city. The idea is to try her out and see if she can play the part. Tyler claims she is going to prove *the* great emotional actress of the future—(she is only 19 now)—and wants to see if she's up to doing *The Straw* this early. If she is, he argues, it will be a great asset, as he thinks the part requires *real* youth and not some old actress pretending to be young, to be effective. I agree with him in this, and think the whole scheme for a Boston matinee is a fine one. If she fails, one matinee in Boston will not hurt the value of the play, and if she succeeds it will mean that the play, with her, will come right to New York next year.

Had an hour's chat with Madden. He is strong for Tearle as "Chris" and also approves of my stand with Williams.

Here's a bit of news: Lord Dunsany[5] had read my book of plays and asked Hopkins[6] where he could read my long stuff. Hopkins phoned Tyler who in turn phoned Madden and Madden sent a script of *Chris* to H. to give to Lord Dunsany to read on his return voyage. His Lordship has promised to return same from England as soon as he has perused it. The Lord evidently has a better idea of me than I have of him. Folks tell me, however, that he's a charming person to meet.

Father has been pretty sick and looks bad but is getting better. Mama is O.K. I'm having dinner with the two of them up in the room shortly.

That's enough news for one day. Bye'bye for this time, Own Sweetheart, and a long kiss! I love you, love you, love you!!! I'll be back to you the first second I can skip away! A kiss for our Shane from me, and all the love of his grandparents who are crazy to see him.

More tomorrow, s'help me! Another Kiss! Gene

P.S. (To Mrs. Clark) Has Agnes gained a pound yet?

1. Dating the letters at the beginning of EO's trip to New York for rehearsals of *Beyond the Horizon* is problematic. In #90, dated with fair certainty by internal evidence February 23, 1920, AB declares that it has been seven weeks since he left. That would put his departure on Sunday, January 4. Bogard and Bryer and Sheaffer use this time frame. The problem with this is that it puts a strange hiatus between EO's departure letter and the beginning of the steady interchange of letters during the week of January 11–18. Those letters can be dated with relative certainty, either by EO's inclusion of a date or by references to the expected opening of *Beyond the Horizon* in three weeks. Also, those letters, especially AB's, still have the sound of someone trying to cope with the sudden absence of the other and trying to figure out how to use letters as a substitute for direct contact. (The only letter that could without contradiction be dated during the week of January 4–11 would be #20, which responds directly to #18, but this letter reads just as well, if not better, in the current sequence, i.e. as written on January 14 instead of January 7.) As late as January 17, AB inquires whether he has a room at the Prince George Hotel (meaning a room of his own, instead of just staying with his parents at the same hotel). The answer to this question, if it was ever given, is not extant, but it seems strange for

her to be asking such a question thirteen days after his departure, as opposed to six days. Of course, it is quite possible that some letters were lost, even from this period when as many as three letters written by AB in a single day survive. Still, it seems more reasonable to suppose that AB miscalculated her count of seven weeks and that EO's departure was on January 11, instead.

    2. Godfrey Tearle (1884–1953) was then starring in *Carnival*.

    3. David Belasco (1859–1931), eminent producer and director, would later produce EO's *Marco Millions* (1928).

    4. Hayes (1900–1993) was trying out the title role of *Bab*, Edward Childs's adaptation of the novel by Mary Roberts Rinehart. Ultimately, Margalo Gillmore played Eileen Carmody in EO's play.

    5. English playwright, poet, and short-story writer (1878–1957).

    6. Arthur Hopkins (1878–1950) produced *"Anna Christie"* (1921) and *The Hairy Ape* (1922) in a long Broadway career.

19. EO to AB ALS 3 pp. (Stationery headed: Prince George Hotel / Fifth Avenue & 28th Street / [New York]) [Harvard]

Tuesday night. / [January 13?, 1920]

Own Dearest: Just a few lines tonight and this is why: Have been up at Williams' office with Madden all afternoon. Had a terrific battle with him over *Beyond* but finally came to a compromise. The old contract is to be torn up and a new one more fair to me made. *Beyond* is due to go on at the Morosco three weeks from yesterday— one performance first at Stamford, I guess. The first week it is to go on at special matinees—four of them. Then it is to play regularly the latter half of each week on night performances. The idea of a preliminary week of special matinees is to get the finest cast possible by taking people out of different N.Y. shows. This way they can play in *Beyond* without conflicting with their regular engagements. Helen MacKellar and Strong of *The Storm*[1] are to play Ruth & Andrew in this first week. Afterwards, the regular Williams cast will go on for the split-week night run.

    It's a long story and I'm not going to try to tell it here. Tonight I've got to go over all the W. cuts and have the script back by noon tomorrow. Some work!

    So you'll forgive me for not writing more, won't you? As soon as I get time I'll write you fully about all this. I've a million things to tell you but simply have to get to work on the *Beyond* script if I don't want to stay up all night.

    Old Sweetheart, forgive me!—but you'll understand, won't you?

    Your letter reached me when I got back from W. It was a Godsend of peace and security after my hectic experience this afternoon. I love you, My Own Own!

    A million kisses for you to divide with Shane! I love you! Gene

    1. This melodrama by Langdon McCormack was produced by Williams. MacKellar played the role of Ruth Atkins when *Beyond the Horizon* opened on February 20, 1920. Strong has not been identified; Edward Arnold played the role of Andrew.

~~○

20. **AB to EO** ALS 4 pp. ([Provincetown, Mass.]) [Harvard]

Wednesday A.M. / [January 14?, 1920]

My dearest— Susan was just here (it's nearly eleven) and I had such a nice chat with her. She is much better, and has an idea for a new long play about which she says she is crazy.—a real *american* play (serious).[1] She heard from Lucy[2] that the P.P. bill was very good, including Djuna's play; also that Djuna is becoming intolerably conceited and treats all the cast abominably—Send any reviews of the bill, and I show them to Jig & Susan, and then put them in your scrap-book.

I was so glad to get your long letter and all the news. Isn't it fun about Dunsany? I wish he could have seen *Beyond* though. You must send him the book.

No mail—so far.

I have written quite a bit on the story, and am living a model life, per schedule, which was arranged by Fifine & me, and which hangs on the wall over the radiator as a reminder. Here it is.

Breakfast,	9.	
work.—	10–11.	
errands—or work—	11–12.	malted milk
play with baby.	12–1.	
Lunch—	1.	
nap.	1:30, to 3.	!!! malted milk
writing—	3 to 5.	
play with baby.	5 '' 6	
supper—	6—	
read or work—	7–9:30.	
go to bed.	9:30.	malted milk
sleep—	10:00	

Well, what do you think of that? I intend to follow it too.

Today I'm hoping to hear from you about Williams. Also Tearle. He sounds fine. I do hope it turns out. Mrs. Clark proficies (how *do* you spell it) that I will get a letter today or tomorrow with *good news!*

I saw the Doctor and told him about Shane. He looked very wise, and said "Hm-m. You're drinking too much milk, & eating too much meat. Cut down on your meals." And was about to dismiss it with that, after assuring me there wasn't any sense in analyzing the milk. I sat on him good and hard, said I couldn't eat less than I did, and intimated that I would go elsewhere unless he could give me some sort of satisfaction. He then, after some profound thought, ordered me to give Shane Horlick's *Food*, with water, alternating with nursing. That is, at the same time—nurse a little, suck the bottle a little—This it seems furnishes starch and softens the curds of protein. I'm to try it for a week, and I really think it will be O.K.

Mrs. C. is going out now, so I'll give her this to mail—goodby my own dearest love. Your Agnes.

I wish I *could tell* you how I miss you, but—you know.

1. Probably *The Inheritors*, produced by the Provincetown Players in 1921.
2. Lucy Huffaker and her husband Edward Goodman were among the founders of the Washington Square Players.

21. **EO to AB** COPY 5 pp. (Prince George [New York]) [Harvard]

Jan. 14, 1920

Own Sweetheart: Have just returned from a second interview with Williams. Saw the models for *Beyond* sets by Hewlett.[1] They are very fine and quite in the right spirit. Madden and I handed him the bad news—for him—the new contract which is exactly the same as my Tyler ones. It further has clauses which limit his option on my plays to two years, requires a decision within 30 days, and generally do away with all the faults of the old agreement—my royalty to be 5, 7 1/2, and 10 instead of the former 3, 5, and 6—a big difference! Also he is not to deduct any of the thousand advance until *Beyond* is running by itself in consecutive performances at night. This means I will get paid my part of the matinees, etc., at once.

Things in the *Beyond* matter are not so bad, taking it all in all. I was not strong for the matinee idea and am not; but good actors are scarcer and hard to get these days and the matinees will at least enable W. to cast the play for its opening in a way he could not do by any other scheme. Also he has already laid out a lot of money in the production and it would be a dirty trick to make him lose all of it by taking away the play, even if I had another buyer for it. And I don't want to wait longer for a hearing. As things now stand it's a compromise with both of us giving in a lot. Let's hope it will turn out right. The split-week idea can't be helped. We can't get another theatre. *For the Defense* is making money and without it W. would have no theatre at all.

I labored until 2 A.M. on the cuts. Finished up the first two acts. A great many made by W. are all right but some are very silly and I will not stand for them. He leaves that up to me, however. In spite of my grudge against him I can't help liking him personally and we shall probably end up as good friends.

The play has already been rehearsing a week. I'm to attend regularly as soon as my revisions of the cuts goes [*sic*] into effect—day after tomorrow, I guess. Tomorrow, I have a session with Williams to go over the entire script with him. *Beyond* will go on Monday P.M., Feb. 2nd.

Tyler has not yet heard finally from Tearle who is evidently giving himself a private try-out in the part before deciding. If he turns it down, Corrigan will be called in. I've been busy on that too, making plans for the scenes for the artist to go by. I'm also due to have a confab soon with Stanhope,[2] the director, to go over the play.

So you see I'm a busy little bee these days.

Dr. Aspell, the "high up" specialist who operated on Mama so successfully and who has been attending Papa (the old man has been very sick, so serious that Mama was going to summon the priest and wire for Jim and me at one time. Aspell pulled him through, and he's now much better and on his feet again)—came in and gave me a quick once-over. I told him of my nerves. He said "Keyed up tight as a string. You'll snap it if you don't take care. Let down! Don't worry! Forget your work and rest!" Good advice, maybe, but how the hell can I keep it at this stage of the game? I'm to go to him on Saturday for a complete physical examination. Perhaps, after that's over, he'll know if there's really any physical cause back of it all or whether it's all just mental. I've confidence in Aspell. He has a personality full of strength.

The night before last was a scream. Tyler and Will Connor[3] called on the old man. They were both well "boiled" when they arrived. The old man brought forth a jug from hiding—the first I knew about it—and they had more and I had four which made me quite "squiffy." Tyler and Connor had a brawl over whether *Ile* or *The Rope* was the best one-act play ever written, Tyler cheering for *The Rope* and Tyler and I "went to the mat" on what was or was not the matter with the American theatre. They never left till one A.M. It was quite fun. The old man didn't drink but the excitement cheered him up just the same. Tyler, in spite of his "bun," was astonished to find I could be talkative.

Tell Susan I spoke to Tyler about her play and that he is genuinely eager to have a look at it. He said he had seen three of her plays at different times at the P.P.— *Bernice*, *Woman's Honor* and one other.[4] He said "that *girl* has a real touch of genius"—(he evidently thinks Susan is about as old as Helen Hayes), and he added with a questioning misgiving: "If the damned Greenwich Village faddists didn't get her into the radical magazine publications class." I didn't disillusion him about Susan being 19 and at the mercy of the faddist world—it was too funny—but I did say she was married to a very sensible man. Upon which Tyler heaved a sigh of relief and ceased to "view with alarm."

The funny end of it aside, her play will be received with gratitude at the Tyler office and given a quick reading, I'm sure of that. She of course knows that she can submit a copy to every manager at the same time if she wants to. The magazine ethics in this regard don't apply here in the theatrical game. So she can try Hopkins, Tyler, etc., simultaneously and let the best man win. If she judges it would be any use, if she will send me the play (I'll like very much to read it myself, of course) I will put it in Tyler's hand myself and keep asking him if he's read it, to get action. I'll be seeing him every day pretty soon. You can at least assure her for me that Tyler, personally, is a fine straight guy—and that's a lot in this man's business!

And he sincerely wants—on the strength of her work he has seen and liked immensely—to get a chance to read her play. The outcome is in the lap of the gods of course.

Finish that comedy![5] I'll get it read immediately and I really believe it has a grand chance. Get busy, now!

We'll all have to go down to Boston and see that matinee of *The Straw* even if Mrs. Clark has to come along to take care of the baby. It'll happen in spring sometime.

Both *Clarence* companies are turning them away in N.Y. and Chicago and Tyler is clearing about two thousand a week profit on them.

Met Bill Farnum on Broadway for a few minutes this morning as I was heading for the W. office. He inquired about *Gold*, is anxious to read it. He said: "I've more money than I'll ever know what to do with and I want to get out of the movies and *act*. That's all life means to me now." He's now getting 8,000 a week from the movies, Tyler told me—52 weeks in the year! He's a damn nice quiet chap, as I've always told you.

This is a very newsy letter and sounds cheerful. However, I feel punk physically, as if a mine were about to go off inside me, but Aspell, I know, will see the way out of that. So don't worry. The disease that'll kill me hasn't been discovered yet.

I'm sorry poor old Timmy misses me. Ask him "Where's Gene?" and see what he does.

Mama is all in a sweat to see Shane's pictures. Hurry them up.

The old man was a headliner in the papers this A.M. I enclose the *Telegraph* clipping, quite a tribute from Reinold Wolf, showing that stage folk aren't all wrong.[6]

I'd like to lay my tired buzzing old head on its own old place, own little wife! When I'm lonely I close my eyes and feel your arms about me, and I *know* you're here!

A kiss on Shane's adorable grin, and a kiss for you! Gene

P.S. My best to Mrs. Clark

1. The program credits the design firm of Hewlett & Basing for the scenery, but Homer St. Gaudens directed and designed the production.
2. Frederick Stanhope, British-born director, staged many of George Tyler's productions.
3. William F. Connor, business manager and friend of James O'Neill Sr.
4. *Bernice* was presented in March 1919; *A Woman's Honor* in April 1918.
5. *Now I Ask You*, a three-act farce begun by EO and then abandoned. At his urging she made efforts to complete it or adapt it as a novel. See *Part of a Long Story*, 191–93.
6. *New York Telegraph* article reporting on the serious illness of James O'Neill Sr. and calling him "one of the American stage's most brilliant actors."

22. **AB to EO** ALS 4 pp. ([Provincetown, Mass.]) [Harvard]

Wednesday night— / [January 14?, 1920]

My own dear, Today I was so excited by your letter with the good news of *Beyond*. Dearest— to think it may really be on in three weeks! After all these months—almost, all these *years*! I love that play so much, it is nearer to me, somehow, than anything you have done, and I feel quite agitated by all the details of its "going on." It seems a strange arrangement to me that one set of actors play 4 performances, and then another set play thereafter. You didn't say if *Bennett*[1] plays the first week. Will you be rehearsing both lots of actors at once?

I'm dying to know everything about your talk with Williams, and when you come back, I will be asking you questions about things that will seem a million years old to you. Good for you for getting him to make a new contract! Be sure and tell B. & L.[2] to have the *Beyond* book ready.

Have you seen Winifred[3] yet, and what is she like? Very fascinating? Please be *sure* and tell me. By now, I suppose you know if Tearle is going to do Chris.— I'm hoping to hear tomorrow that he *is*. I saw a photo of Helen Hayes in *Vogue*. She looks serious, and as if she had brains—pretty too, but not as *dangerous* looking as Winifred. It will be splendid to have the Boston try-out of *The Straw*. I know how much it means to you to feel *The Straw* is going to have a chance so soon.

Am having lunch with Cooks tomorrow, and will read them about *Beyond*. Dearest, how I miss you! It's half-past nine now, and I must stop this, and get ready to go to bed (living up to the schedule, you see!) I'm all alone but Shane—oh, and Tim and Chris! I really don't let myself go when it comes to thinking about your not being here, because I would get too blue. And after all, I'm tremendously happy, really, that you are where you can be doing something for your plays. And everything is going awfully well here. I have the satisfaction of feeling that by following out the rules for regular hours, etc. I am getting some work done, and *gaining* in health and strength. I took quite a pagan delight in a walk in the wind today.

Darling child of mine, goodnight. How I should like to have your dear head on my shoulder tonight and sleep in your arms.

Thursday morning / [January 15?, 1920]

I have been sitting, pen in hand, waiting to start this again, while the fair Fifine, backed up against the wall, discussed the 64 days to spring, how "Emma's" radiator burst, went over three times what we are going to eat tomorrow, said Shane was getting to look just like you and why—lofty brow, it seems, although the likeness is most striking when he's about to howl!—and told the entire plot of the High School operetta, which occurred last night.

She is a dear kind creature just the same. Wants to come over to Peaked Hill with us this summer.

Do you know it was zero here this morning? But the house is warm as toast. I'll have a cold, but sunny walk up to Susan's.

Shane is better—fine, in fact. He's a happy baby, all right, when he isn't howling. How Chris hates to hear him howl! He gives Shane the most bored and disgusted looks.

I haven't opened a book since you left; am devoting all my (spare) time to writing. Have done quite a bit on the Egotist story,[4] and will finish first draft of that, then begin on play, and rewrite story—or polish up.—when it has been laid aside awhile.—

Goodby, onliest! A million kisses for *you*, my own! And *you* don't have to divide them, either! *Agnes.*

Much love to your mother and father. Is Jamie there?

1. Richard Bennett (1872–1944) was instrumental in getting *Beyond the Horizon* produced and had a hand in revising the script. He played Robert Mayo.
2. The Boni and Liveright edition of *Beyond the Horizon* came out in March 1920.
3. Possibly the actress Winifred Lenihan, who would later draw attention in the title role of George Bernard Shaw's *St. Joan.*
4. H. L. Mencken recommended that she change the title of a story she had submitted to "The Hater of Mediocrity." Probably it was this story that was published in the July 1920 *Smart Set.*

23. **EO to AB** ALS 3 pp. (Stationery headed: Prince George Hotel / Fifth Avenue & 28th Street / [New York]) [Harvard]

Jan. 15, 1920

Own Little Wife: Just a line this evening. I've been up to my ears in work all day— four hours with Bennett and Williams this afternoon going over the script, and have to meet Bennett again tonight in his dressing room at the Playhouse to finish the job when we go from there to his home. It means from eleven-thirty until God knows what hour in the morning. There's a lot still to be done and, with only a little over two weeks still to go, it must be done at once so as not to hold up rehearsals. Talk about earning your bread by the sweat of your brow—that's me, kid!

Tomorrow P.M., after the *Beyond* rehearsal, I have to meet Stanhope, who is to direct *Chris* and go all over the script with him and with the artist who is to do the scenes. It's a hectic life, divil a lie, and how I'm to keep both the plays separate in my mind and think clearly about each of them is a problem. However, I feel so keyed up I could work 24 hours a day without eating, I think.

No word from Godfrey Tearle yet. He's taking his time to make up his mind— and Tyler thinks it wiser not to hurry him.

Was to have gone to *Clarence* tonight but can't make it as I have to work on *Beyond* in preparation for my meeting with Bennett. W. and Bennett mixed up their cuts and, as a result, there's a hell of a mess to straighten out—and I'm the goat! Honestly, these people don't seem to use their heads at all. It's amazing!

Have seen no notice of P.P. anywhere. Don't know anything about them and care less. Haven't been ten feet south of 27th St. since my arrival. Of course Djuna is intolerably conceited. Put a beggar on horseback!—but she ought to bear in mind that the *Little Review*[1] is a gelding, and with the blind staggers to boot.

What d'yuh mean, notices for scrap books? There's no play of mine on, is there?

I'll write you long, full letters whenever I get a chance, believe that. I love to write to you—but you see how I'm fixed.

I wish I could board that F.R[2]. boat tonight. Split 50-50 with Shane on a million kisses. Eugene

P.S. I like Bennett very much. He seems to feel the spirit of the play very keenly—and that's the main asset.

1. A self-described "Magazine of Art and Revolution" (1914–29), founded in Chicago by Margaret Anderson.
2. Fall River.

~⌐

24. **AB to EO** ALS 4 pp. ([Provincetown, Mass.]) [Harvard]

Thursday night. / [January 15?, 1920]

Darling, Here's our child! The interior picture was nothing but darkness. They're not bad, do you think, for snapshots?

My, but it's cold here—a bitter north wind. We keep warm, though. And it's been lovely and sunny. Terry says now that if he can weather this he might as well stay on here. I don't believe he has any idea of going to New York!

I wonder if you have any idea of how *much* your letters mean to me? I read them over and over. It's so fine, too, to be getting real, satisfactory news at last. You are a busy person, all right! Glad you liked the sets for *Beyond*. Isn't it exciting—and rather bewildering—to have everything happen at once like this? I get a great deal of pleasure and excitement myself out of imagining you at all your interviews and appointments.

You must have had a grand time on those four drinks. Tyler, from all you say of him, surely sounds like a corking sort. The description of what he thought about Susan was so funny that I've asked her—by letter—to come down tomorrow, so I can read her your letter. (Mrs. C's day off you know, so I couldn't get up there) I told them—read them—about *Beyond* at lunch today, and they seemed to consider it a strange arrangement. I can't—nor they—understand the having *different* actors for matinees and the regular run. I mean—it looks as if Williams *didn't* feel the *Defense* cast really adequate, if he can't risk an opening with them; and if it makes a big hit with Helen MacKellar, etc., and then the regular run starts with new people, not as good, won't it be a very bad thing for the play? Also, won't it be terribly hard rehearsing both sets at once? Still, I suppose he feels the first reception of the play is what will determine its success, and that's why he is using other actors? Is that it? Susan says of late "special" matinees have had quite a vogue. My *God*, I hope it turns out well—that it gets a fine production, somehow! This [shifting?] around of the cast makes me nervous!

Good for you about getting such a fine contract! Honestly, you and Madden must have been brutal to do it! I bet you let *M.* do all the asking!

Now if only Tearle does Chris!

I'm so awfully glad you are going up to Doctor Aspell's. After it's all over, you *must* take a rest somehow, old love—a *real*, relaxing, lazy time. Don't you think you could? You've *got* to! While you are in New York, try and think of some plan that would enable you to do this.

Your hint about getting to work on *Now I Ask You* was a great stimulus, although I planned to do it soon, anyhow—as I said in a previous letter.

Friday A.M. / [January 16?, 1920]

Last night I was awake almost two hours—in the middle of the night—couldn't get to sleep—Thinking about *you.* How I love and appreciate the fine quality of you Gene! Goodby, my dear love— *Agnes*

I've written every day—mail them at eleven A.M. (in the box) always. Do you get them?

∼⌒

25. **EO to AB** ALS 4 pp. (Stationery headed: Prince George Hotel / Fifth Avenue & 28th Street / [New York]) [Harvard]

Jan. 17, 1919 [1920]

Dearest Own Wife: A million pardons for my not writing yesterday, but when you know the circumstances, I'm sure you'll forgive me. Thursday night I went to Williams' office at 11:30 to meet Bennett. He called in a taxi with his wife—Adrienne Morrison—and we went down to his house on Eighth St. between 5th and Macdougal. He's got a perfectly corking place, wonderfully and artistically fitted up. The servants being a-bed, Adrienne—(a quite charming woman, by the way, but an actress from toe to scalp) made scrambled eggs for us. They both know Felton Elkins[1] very well. He has praised me to the skies to them—also Nina Jones[2]—and so I was treated as one of the 400. When his wife left us to our labors in Bennett's study, he turned to me and said impressively: "Do you like absinthe?" I said yes but what good does a liking do me. There isn't any real Pernod in this country. Yes, there is, quoth Bennett; I have fifty cases. Jack Barrymore and I are the only people in the country who have any. Produce, I returned avidly, I knew I was going to like you from the first moment we met.

He dug down in the old oak chest and a quart of *real Pernod* was the result. He mixed frappies in large, tall glasses and we sipped them as we worked on the play line by line with Richard reading aloud. Don't think I'm going to describe an absinthe orgy. We had one frappie to an act. If we hadn't had it we couldn't have kept awake.

Do you know what time the work was finished? 7:30 A.M.! We were both dead, and I came home and slept all day and felt so rotten when I woke up that I didn't feel up to writing you.

So you will forgive me, won't you, Old Dear?

When I came home I was too tired to get to sleep—you know that feeling—and in addition my brain was full of subtle fireworks from the queer poison of absinthe. I sat down and wrote a prose poem.[3] I'll send it to you. Want to get it typed. When I wrote it the whole world was shot through with White Logic and I seemed to see through the whole game. Looking over it now, I think it's fine and nutty. Be sure and show it to Terry when you get it. He'll be interested in it as an absinthe product.

Am glad the *Beyond* script is now straightened out. Will start in attending rehearsals on Monday at the Playhouse.

Today I spent the P.M. with Stanhope. Like him immensely. He dragged me to the Standard theatre to see *The Whirlwind*[4] because they were considering the star of that play—Laura Walker[5]—for Chris' daughter.

Oh, boy! Of all the rotten plays! As I said to Stanhope when we left the theatre at the end of the second act, everything in the play is so rotten—acting, sets, directing, dialogue, plot—that it's really a perfect thing without a false moment in it. (This remark is due to travel all over Broadway as Stanhope nearly died laughing at it.)

Toohey has blood in his eyes these days and prowls around me with his press-agent nose sniffing the wind. Pretty soon he'll begin to bay—and then watch the papers for news of your dear husband. You'll probably read some startling lies.

I seem to have lost a lot of my self-consciousness. Wander about New York regardless, walking everywhere I have to go.

Mama is "nuts" about the pictures of Shane but wants one "with his eyes open." Of course, she thinks he looks like me.

Christine phoned me and asked me to come down to a farewell John Barleycorn party[6] at the P.P. after the show tonight. I'm going—couldn't very well get out of it, she was so nice—but I'm not going in for any orgy. I've been drinking almost every day but, outside of the 4 absinthes with Bennett, have done it all up in the room with Papa—four drinks or so a day. So don't worry about my making a fool of myself. I'm a wise guy—when I know it's necessary. But it would be silly for me not to drink. Everyone I'm associated with does—Tyler, Williams, Bennett, Stanhope, Toohey and they'd simply think me a prig if I didn't.

Bye-bye for this time—and all my love! I wish you were here, My Own—but you will be later on. I'm fixing that now. XX for Shane—and all of me to you! Gene

1. "Pinky" Elkins was EO's classmate in George Pierce Baker's playwriting course at Harvard.

2. Another young playwright, who was studying with Clayton Hamilton in the New London area.

3. Bogard and Bryer say this poem is "62" in Eugene O'Neill, *Poems, 1912–1944*, ed. Donald Gallup (New Haven: Ticknor & Fields, 1980), 92–94, where the date of composition is wrongly given as September 1919. Bogard and Bryer, eds., *Selected Letters of Eugene O'Neill*, 105.

4. Play by George C. Hazelton (1868?–1921) and Ritter Brown.

5. Walker had a brief career as an actress around 1920. Lynn Fontanne created the role of Anna in the production of *Chris Christophersen.*

6. The Volstead Act, known as Prohibition, went into effect in July 1919. Possibly this party had to do with coming to the end of the supply of whiskey.

26. **AB to EO** ALS 2 pp. ([Provincetown, Mass.]) [Harvard]

[January 17?, 1920]

Dearest— Tell me when you write again if you have a room at the P.G.—I do hope so, and that you are comfortable.

Susan came up yesterday. She was immensely pleased with your letter, and very happy over your saying you would give play to Tyler, as she "didn't quite know what to do with it"—she'll send it to you as soon as she gets it typed, and says she'd like to have you read it, and then, if *you* think T. would do it, or like it, pass it on to him. She sends many many thanks.

Dearest, this is a rush letter—I was busy yesterday, with Clarkie away.

Shane is *much* better—do you know *one* reason why? I bundle him up now, open all windows & door, so there is a current of fresh air and he sleeps like a top. His cheeks get *pink*! He sleeps much more, and is not so nervous. I'm feeling fine, too. Sunday night I weigh myself, and hope, after following such *strict rules*, to have gained—.

Thank God you *are* so busy Gene! It means things are happening.

A long hug and kiss, dearest. Please think of me before you go to sleep at night—
Agnes.

27. **AB to EO** ALS 2 pp. ([Provincetown, Mass.]) [Harvard]

[January 18?, 1920]

Dearest Gene, It's thawing here—the streets are all slush. Be careful this weather, won't you? And *wear rubbers.* How about your cough? Do you take malted milk, as you said you would? You know milk is excellent for the nerves.

Terry has taken to coming about three in the afternoon, and staying until I have gone to bed. I don't think he intends going to N.Y.—talks of running a still in the dunes next year. It makes me rather sick, because round supper time, or five o'clock, I usually take a few minutes to look at the paper—but he's always reading it—I got a *Little Review* from Susan, wanted to see the Richardson thing,[1] and I swear Terry's never put it down—I've hardly had a chance to see it. There is a quotation in it from

Charles-Louis Philippe,[2]—extraordinary! It makes me wish I knew French thoroughly—or that Chas Louis was translated.

The bay white with ice and mush, and the sky all day has been sodden. There was a big black tramp-steamer in. I tried to think of her with a sense of adventure, to imagine her in hot foreign ports, or in some terrific storm, but she refused to be anything but a still, black shape of a ship against a sullen sky.

I saw the old gray life-guard, and he tells me the sand is hollowing out all about *our* Peaked Hill. You know the little bungalow made by the man who made the [dock]? It burned up the other night, in a terrific wind. The man had been there that afternoon, and must have dropped a match somewhere.

Shane sends love to his daddy. I think he is too little to have half of your million kisses so I only gave him a quarter—the rest I kept for me! Your loving, Agnes.

1. *Interim*, a novel by Dorothy Richardson, was being serialized in the magazine.
2. An article in the magazine discussed the writings of this *poète maudit* (1874–1909).

28. **AB to EO** ALS 3 pp. (Provincetown, Mass.) [Harvard]

Sunday. / [January 18?, 1920]

Here's a flower for you—from Shane and me!

He is at present lying in the big red chair, near the radiator—nice and warm—shaking his rattle for all he is worth!

Clarkie says he looks more like you every day.

Well, what did you think of the pictures? What did the folks say about their grandson?

I walked up to the p.o. last evening, thinking that there might be a letter from *you*—and of course there wasn't. Do you know it's just a week today since you went away? I wonder how many more it will be before we see one another again? There are so many things I could say about it—but what's the use!

From your last letter, Tyler evidently intends to do *Chris* soon anyhow, Tearle or not. Is that so? I don't see how you *will* be able to keep the plays separate—oh, I think I must have the blues tonight, so I won't write any more. I can't write any of the things I'm feeling, anyhow, and what's the sense of just drooling on?

I'll kiss the little flower, and send it to you that way—the kiss I can't give you. *Agnes.*

29. **AB to EO** ALS 4 pp. ([Provincetown, Mass.]) [Harvard]

Monday night. / [January 19?, 1920]

Well, old dear, you *do* seem to be having a great time, with your absinthe (ye gods, forty cases!) and your P.P. parties, and your duties and all. I had to go up to Cooks, just to tell Jiggie about those forty cases; the poor man was in a particularly responsive mood—having been up all night with fires, and longing desperately for a drink. But I fear your description of the Bennett [seance?] only made him bluer than ever! As for Terry, he nearly collapsed.

Mary O'Brien[1] had written Susan, and wants her to go out and help with the strike—for two weeks.

I wonder what you're doing tonight? Here it is the same as ever, Chrissie trot-ting-horsing around the floor, Timmy snoring, Terry reading the *Nation*, and the old black clock striking off the hours.

Do you know we've had Zero weather here?

Be sure and tell me all about the party—all the dirt!

Mrs. Clark enquired anxiously every letter, what you had to say about the "sched-ule," or "rule of life"; finally, when your last letter came, and she asked again, I told her you were most awfully impressed; that you thought it very fine, and praised both her and me for concocting such a marvelous schedule; and she was satisfied!

I'm glad everything goes so well. Now if *Chris* starts rehearsing, everything will be fine.

No letter this afternoon, so I suppose you spent Sunday recovering.

Good night—(it's bed-time) and much love. A.

Don't forget to send the poem!

1. Mary Heaton Vorse (1881–1966) was a prominent writer and political activist who had lived in Provincetown since 1907. Her husband, Joseph O'Brien, died in 1915. Her *Time and the Town: A Provincetown Chronicle* includes reminiscences of the founding of the Provincetown Players and of the first public performances, given in a boathouse on her wharf.

30. **EO to AB** ALS 3 pp. (Stationery headed: Prince George Hotel / Fifth Avenue & 28th Street / [New York]) [Harvard]

Jan. 20, 1920

Own Dearest: Meant to write you yesterday but felt so "punk" that I gave up the attempt. The party down at the P.P. on Saturday night turned out to be a fizzle. All of them had been on a bust the night before and were too dead to repeat the session. So it finally ended up with Christine, Louis Ell and I in the Hell Hole. They left me finally and I camped there all night—went to bed up in Tom Wallace's room. I've been feeling rotten ever since—thanks to the quantity of "red ink" I put away (which must have been just that—*ink*!)

Have had no word from Bennett as to *Beyond* rehearsals—the where and the when. Suppose he will call me up, as he promised, as soon as the new parts with the cuts are memorized. He said he was going to demand that every member of the cast be letter perfect before he would call another regular rehearsal in the Playhouse or Morosco.

Rehearsals for *Chris* will begin next Monday. It is to open up, I believe, in Atlantic City the first week in March.

I'm told there was quite a write-up about me in Sunday's *Telegraph*. If you get it via Romeike,[1] let me know and send it on, as I didn't see it.

More tomorrow. My stomach is all upset and I feel "on the blink"—(so much for frankly confessing my sins to you)—and it's lucky I had no important business engagements to keep yesterday or today.

All my love to you and Shane. I wish you were here—oh, so damnably!—(not only because I feel so blue!)

Two letters today! Thank you, My Own, from the bottom of my heart! Gene

P.S. Impress upon Terry that I expect him to come to N.Y.—that he said he was going to and we have made plans depending on his keeping his word. Tell him that I insist on you and I having Peaked Hill Bar entirely to ourselves until August 1st at least and that no guest of any sort will be welcome until that date. Hutch has made all arrangements for Terry to have a room in town here. Show him what I'm writing here, if necessary. Even at the risk of offending him, I think it's up to Terry to have a little consideration for our feelings. He didn't use to be so insensitive. He must realize that you and I have a right to be alone as well as he.

1. Clipping service that provided reviews to EO.

31. **AB to EO** ALS 8 pp. ([Provincetown, Mass.]) [Harvard]

Wednesday morning. / [January 21?, 1920]

Dearest Gene— I'm writing this in bed, as I slept very badly last night, and am "resting up." Just to see how often I did wake, I turned on the light every time—one, two, three, four, four-thirty, five-thirty, and six.

I try awfully hard not to worry and be unhappy when I fail to get a letter from you, but it's absolutely no use—I have no control of my "inward" feelings at all, in that respect. You may smile: but I do actually get *sick*—a feeling as if my backbone had been removed, a deadly depression, combined with a nervous sensitiveness that becomes perfect torture. I cannot eat, and can hardly sleep. (This *does* sound medical—but it's true.) There's no reason in all this, I know— looked at reasonably it's pure silliness—but it happens.

You see, I haven't heard from you since you wrote Saturday. *You* know how it was when the old mailman used to pass us by. Well—this is a thousand times worse.

Your letter Saturday gave me a feeling of depression and uneasiness—because, I suppose, you spoke of the farewell J.B.[1] party at Christine's. The absinthe party at Bennett's sounded fine—but then, somehow, to think that only a couple of nights later, you were going deliberately to a party where you knew there'd be a lot of drinking; when it wasn't necessary, and even, according to what you've said, much *fun* to go; where, (also your own dope) the whole crowd is more or less envious and only too glad to drag you down somehow into the dirt—that belies your very remark about yourself— that you're a wise guy, and nobody's going to make a fool of you. You *weren't* a wise guy *when you went*—when you know, as well as I do, the shape you get into after much drinking! When you know how important it is you feel fit for these rehearsals!

A few drinks a day certainly ought to help you keep going—but once you'd had a lot, and your brain is lit up with alcohol, you've got to keep on having a lot, or feel wretched—unless you've changed. I feel surprised and hurt and depressed that you should deliberately put yourself in the way of this happening.

I know just the temptation—you wanted to see them, let *them* see how fine you looked, tell them all the dope about your plays going on, about Bennett and the absinthe etc.—very real temptations, I know, but at the same time, you should have had guts enough *not* to go, at this time when so *very* much hangs in the balance. *Afterwards*—that's a different thing—

This *is* a lecture—my first—but I feel it's coming to you, old love! I may be all wrong but— am I?

Do *please, please* write me, if only *one line*, every day. Will you? I'm trying awfully hard not to get too lonely, to do some work—(I almost finished my story last week—and like it very much) and to get in better shape during your absence, and one letter a day is the most helpful tonic in the whole world. Remember, Gene, it *is* a great disappointment to me to be up here, away from everything, while the "big event" for which we both waited so patiently for two years is coming off—it *is* a tremendous disappointment to me, although I've not said much about it. Your letters are absolutely the only connection I have with any of it—and I can keep up the bluff to myself that I don't care—as long as *they* come. A.

Got a *most amusing* letter this A.M. from Mary O'Brien.

1. John Barleycorn.

32. **EO to AB** ALS 3 pp. (Stationery headed: Prince George Hotel / Fifth Avenue & 28th Street / [New York]) [Harvard]

Jan. 21, 1920

Own Sweetheart: They left a notice of your wire under the door of my room on the fifth floor last evening. I didn't see it when I went downstairs last night—I was up here all day and evening—(have been all day today, too)—and so I never got it from the office until this noon. Of course, the damn fools should have phoned up here to find me but they didn't—and there you are.

What d'yuh mean, two desolate days? I wrote to you and mailed it Saturday night and you sure should have received it Monday A.M. I also wrote yesterday, Tuesday, so you would get it today.

I haven't kept up the daily writing because on the days I've failed I've felt too rotten. At present I am hugging the family hearth—haven't been out of the P.G. in two days now—and waiting for any important development. (Also waiting for my liver to resume operations.)

The only news today was a phone from Tyler for me to go over the scripts of *Chris* and *The Straw* for any cuts *I* want to make. As I want to make none, this is an easy job. I'm glad they're not calling on me these days. I'm far from fit.

The poem still remains untyped. Will send it as soon as Mama's friend here in the hotel returns it. She has a machine in her room—a Mrs. Franck. I don't know whether you met her or not.

Bye-bye for this time. I'm "too poo'ly" to do much writing. There's no news. I love you—and miss you—and I love Shane and miss even his howling—all of which, except missing the O'Neill freshman college cheer, is no news to you.

You must talk to Terry—seriously. All arrangements will be made for him down here by Hutch—and it's up to him to be considerate enough of us to come. God knows we've been considerate of him and his feelings. It would be an entirely different thing if he had no other place to go.

My best to Susan & Jig—and Mrs. Clark—and Chris & Timmy. Gene.

33. **AB to EO** AL 2 pp. (Provincetown, Mass.) [Harvard]

Thursday— / [January 22?, 1920]

My own. Your letter came this morning—thank God, for I was nearly crazy when the old post-man didn't stop again yesterday. Did you think I was very foolish to send that telegram? I sent it 4:30 Tuesday afternoon "Monday and Tues. desolate days. How about tomorrow. Much love. A." but in your letter you don't seem to have got it. Did you? I sent it to get rid of that awful feeling of it being impossible to get in touch with you, and immediately felt better.

Will you write Nina Jones right away? Yesterday a beautiful little engraved cup arrived for Shane from her, and I see she is writing you, so don't delay thanking her, as it's up to me if you *don't*, but I can't say I want to do it.

My darling, I wish you weren't feeling so badly. I just long to put my arms round you, poor darling sweetheart!

This is a hurry letter, beloved, as I want to catch the twelve collection. It's fine about *Chris*, but you never told me Tearle will play—I'm so curious to know that.

This late production means you'll be down till March, I suppose: do you think we can come down during Feb.? Let me know. Clark will come too, if we could have a place for her, and take care of Shane. She's an old dear.

Much love, dearest lover, and I'll write a longer letter this afternoon. I'll tell Terry what you said. *Your* own.

~‿〇

34. **EO to AB** ALS 3 pp. (Stationery headed: Prince George Hotel / Fifth Avenue & 28th Street / [New York]) [Harvard]

Jan. 22, 1920

My Own: Your "lecture" letter seems to me unkind and unreasonable. Those sort of letters are not the kind that do any good and in this case I see no justification whatever for it—especially as I have been home here without leaving the P.G. ever since Monday doing a severe penance for my crimson-ink sins of Sat. night and Sunday. I assure you my sojourn in the Village—with the exception of about 2 hours at the P.P., was entirely spent at the Hell Hole where no one is trying to "drag me down." The night I slept there Lefty, Leo, Chuck and I camped in one bed! Imagine! That was the only way we could keep warm in Tom's zero flat. Now what in hell is effete Village stuff— or "party"—in that? Rather it was good old healthy H.H. days back again and I had a good time—of that kind. The red ink, though, is poison. I cashed a check for twenty dollars—the only money I have drawn since my arrival—and sent out for a quart of real whiskey at twelve dollars per. As there were about ten of us present in the back room that meant 2 small drinks apiece for each of us; but it *was real* bonded Bourbon. As I had been drinking their wine up without any money for twelve hours it seemed to me the least I could do.

No more lecture letters, please! You never used to be a moralist, and I've never in my life stood for that stuff, even from my Mother. My ethics of life forbid that in any conduct based upon emotional reaction, even Christ or Buddha should tell the lowest slave what he should do. That slave has something actuating him that they can never understand.

As for letters, you should have received one Monday A.M. and another Wednesday P.M. Is that so bad? Have a heart, won't you, and don't expect too much, especially when I'm feeling punk.

There is no news, as I told you in my last. And be assured that what you evidently think is my feeble mind is not losing any golden opportunities. Business is slack and I'm waiting. Gene

~‿〇

35. **AB to EO** ALS 4 pp. ([Provincetown, Mass.]) [Harvard]

Jan. 22, [1920]

Dearest— I hope by now you are feeling *much* better. Also, that you've been to a rehearsal of *Beyond*, for I know you won't be satisfied until you actually *see* them getting under way.

What a short time now—ten days! I wonder if they *will* get it on by the second? You haven't said if the book is out yet. I'm dying to see it,—*my* play!

I told Terry about a room being there for him, etc., and that you expected he was coming down, and he looked sort of doubtful. Then I said, "You know I won't be here. I'm going down, after *Beyond* goes on,"—so then he said he'd wait and go down with me and help with the baby. What do you think? He said "I suppose you'll be going down about the first of Feb." And I, not thinking he would want to wait for me, said, "probably the first week."

After *Beyond* goes on, if it looks as if it might make some money, and *is* making some, then do you think I could come? By that time I would have the play "finished," and a story done; I imagine, from what you said of *Chris*'s production, you will have to stick around until the middle of March, for the N.Y. opening. (It seems a pity it goes on so late in the season). The baby is so *infinitely* much better, that I don't feel it such a task to take him—better as far as his howling goes, I mean.—I'm absolutely in the dark as to where or how we'd live, of course, that *you'd* have to dope out. As I said before, Clark would come along for what we paid her here and her car-fare. *That* would be a tremendous blessing, but is probably out of the question—it would all depend where we were staying, I suppose.

What were *your* ideas? Tell me exactly what you think about it.

This will amuse you: Today I was walking up to the village, when a refined, well-dressed woman of sixty or thereabouts, very sweet looking, crossed the street in front of me, and I got the impression that she was making some remarks to kids playing in the snow; but when I caught up behind her I discovered that she was talking, (in a loud, vigorous tone) to herself. Imagine my surprise when she suddenly came out with: "The god damned f——ing (your pet word) son of a bitch, I show him. To hell with him!" I followed behind in utter amazement, the dear old lady, meantime, giving vent to a stream of *obscenities* and curses worthy of any sailor in his fo'castle. No one seemed to pay any attention to her. I went into the ice-cream place and said "Miss Livingston, *who* is that woman going up the street? Something is the matter with her!" I really thought it was some one gone suddenly mad—or drunk. "Why, that's poor Mrs. Cook," says Miss L. "She ain't crazy, but she has these "spells," and then she goes on like that. She's a perfect housekeeper, too . . . she used to come in here last summer when she got that way, and sit at one of my tables, and talk so terrible and so nasty that women would get up and leave. But I couldn't say nothing to her, because she always was a *beautiful* woman, Mis' O'Neill, one of the sweetest an' best *I* know. She got that way up in the Arctic, when they was froze in."[1]

Good night, my own, dear dearest; it makes me so happy to get your letters. Remember I *love love love* and miss you so I can hardly stand it.   A.

1. Probably AB has associated the woman in this anecdote with the character of Mrs. Keeney in EO's one-act play *Ile* (1916–17).

~◡

36. **EO to AB** ALS 6 pp. (Stationery headed: Prince George Hotel, / Fifth Ave. & 28th Street New York) [Harvard]

Jan. 23, 1920

Own Sweetheart: Your letter of Thursday arrived this A.M. Thanks for it! It gladdened my heart wonderfully. Own Little Wife of Mine, I miss you so!

No more of the lecture letters! And forgive my own of yesterday in answer to it. I didn't mean to be so harsh—but I wrote mine on the spur of the moment. I felt so sick when your letter arrived—and so it seemed more inconsiderate than it really was.

No more of that stuff—between you and me. Remember we're "pals"—first of all!

To tell you the truth I've been sick from more than the after-throes of "red-ink." I've had a bad cold. They thought for a time it was the "Flu." I must have caught it that night at Tom Wallace's—sleeping with overcoats over us and no bed clothes on the bed. I didn't want to write you about it with the return of the "Flu" headlined in the newspapers.[1] Now you needn't worry. I'm much better.

I had a letter from Adele Holladay[2]—special—yesterday. She wanted to borrow $25 *immediately*. "Fancy that, Hedda!" Such is fame! If I really believed she needed it I'd give it to her in spite of her poisonous tongue which has had no good word for you or me or Jim[3] since her last Provincetown stay. But I think she and her coterie of "fairies" are on a spree, and I'm not supplying them with booze in these dry days. Outside of her being Louis' mother, she has no claim on me. So I've decided to pay no attention to her letter.

Madden is out of town until Monday. So is Tyler. Tried to get either Williams or Bennett on the phone today—no use. The Doc. says I can't go out of the P.G. until Monday, with the danger of "Flu" in the air. I still feel pretty bum and I'm not sorry to lay off although I'd like to get a start at the *Beyond* stuff. Still I'll have a week of it— and that's about all an author ought to have to stand of rehearsals. After all, once the script is in shape, he's a mere figurehead—and God knows Bennett and I worked hard enough on that.

I'm sick of *Beyond* and convinced that I must forget it. In my judgment there won't be an ounce of Fame or a cent of money in it for us. All I want to do is get done with it and throw the script into "the deep blue sea." I'd never go near a rehearsal if I didn't have to—and I'll certainly never see a performance. Those people will never— can never—be my Robert, Ruth, and Andy—and what would be the use of my watching another lot of actors perform—after all these years of watching them?

Perhaps this is the pessimism of sickness—"Quién sabe?"

Tearle decided not to do *Chris*. Held the script for four days and then brought it to me, not to Tyler. Said: "I've gone over the part ten times—gone down to the waterfront to try and get the lingo. I'd be a failure, Mr. O'Neill—and I don't want to spoil the only real artistic play I've ever read or seen by an American, in his own country, at that." He's a fine chap—and sincere—is Tearle. He's sailing for England in a week—asked me very cordially to be sure and look him up when I came to London.

I thought I'd written you all this before. I have a distinct recollection of writing a letter just about Tearle's refusal. Either I or the U.S. Mail has missed a step.

Corrigan is to play *Chris*. Perhaps it's better. Tearle would have been a gamble (in this part, I mean) while C. is sure fire.

I enclose Nina's[4] letter. Read it and you will like her for what she is—a naive, childish- simple soul and a lady of real breeding combined. I think it would be more perfect courtesy—and please her more—if you wrote a few lines first. Do it, won't you? If we ever decide to go to So. California, she would be a willing slave at looking up a place, making all arrangements, etc. The place they live—Montecito—is the most beautiful town in all California, Mother says—and that's saying something! But these practical considerations are nothing! She's one of the few genuine ones—(it's so easy to make fun of them)—and I think you'd find you'd like her, and that she'd prove one of the best friends you ever had.

Bye'bye, Sweetheart! This is a long letter for an "unwell" gentleman. A long kiss for you and Shane! Gene

P.S. About your coming down—all depends on *Beyond*—What can I talk with now?

1. More than 20 million people were killed throughout the world in the 1918 influenza epidemic.
2. Mother of Paula (Polly) Holladay, proprietor of the Greenwich Village Inn, and Louis Holladay, EO's friend, who committed suicide in January 1918.
3. James O'Neill Jr.
4. Nina Jones, whom EO had met in New London around 1915, when she was visiting from California to study playwriting with Clayton Hamilton.

37. **EO to AB** ALS 3 pp. (Stationery headed: Prince George Hotel, / Fifth Ave. & 28th Street New York) [Harvard]

Jan. 24, 1920

Own Dearest: Your daily letter is the most tremendous comfort to me, especially now when I am marooned up in the family rooms or my room. They're both dull enough, and the weather outside is the worst ever with rain and hail—and muck. The "Flu" is raging as a consequence, with headlines in all the papers. So don't speak any more of coming down to this plague spot until the present epidemic is over.

Isn't it the curse of the Gods, that, just as the "Flu" starts to rage again my first play is to go on! It will put an awful crimp in theatre attendance, you know, and place the final touch on the fiasco which will be *Beyond the Horizon*.

I try to be cheerful—but it's almost too much!

Will be allowed out Monday, I guess, and can go to *Beyond* rehearsal. Will not take the chance, however, unless the weather changes.

I'm too gloomy to oppress you with any more of my Schopenhauer musings.

There's only one bright spot in the world, my Own—you and Shane! Take care of yourselves for me.

All my love to both of you!   Gene

P.S. No news anyway—just a phone from Bennett saying *Beyond* was coming along nicely.

38. **AB to EO** ALS 4 pp. ([Provincetown, Mass.]) [Harvard]

Saturday— / [Jan. 24?, 1920]

Dearest Gene— Your long letter reached me about an hour ago, and I appreciate it so much—In the meantime, I'd answered yours of yesterday—which *was* harsh—with one in much the same tone. Tear it up and forget it. I was really hurt by your letter, and wrote to try and justify my "lecture" letter. I did feel that you'd taken it differently from the way I meant it.

So, if I mail this now, you ought to get them both at the same time—Monday. Finis!

Dearest heart, do you know how *badly* I feel that you're sick like this? You must be very, very careful of yourself, not to take more cold. You are probably rehearsing today, but try and rest whenever you can.

Won't it seem dear and wonderful when we can see one another again? I miss you so very much, Gene—But I'm trying to get a lot done while you're away, and to get in to fine physical shape for this summer. I gained 2 lbs the first week, and tomorrow night I'll weigh myself again. I want to be beautiful for *you*! Your own, *Agnes*.

Did you know Alice Macdougal died of Caesarian operation? I'll write to Nina—

This isn't a *letter*—it's just so you won't get mad at what I said in the other, and stop writing.

39. **EO to AB** ALS 3 pp. (Stationery headed: Prince George Hotel, / Fifth Ave. & 28th Street New York) [Harvard]

Sunday / [January 25?, 1920]

My Own: Your letter of Friday received when I got up this morning.[1] Perhaps a lot of the points you make in it are true enough—from your standpoint—But, Oh God!, My Own, the tragedy which overwhelms me in all our bickering is this: If you and I, who love each other so much, who have been through so many fundamental life experiences successfully together; if, at this so crucial moment of our union, we cannot keep petty hate from creeping into our souls like the condemned couples in a Strindberg play; if our letters are to become an added torture to our hearts already tortured by separation and by the mishaps of outside chance; if we cannot stand back to back to face failure or the equally fatal possibilities contained in success; if the morale at home cannot reinforce the morale at the front when that falters, and vice-versa—then we are lost; and my only remaining hope is that the "Flu," or some other natural cause, will speedily save me the decision which would inevitably have to come at my own instance. If you and I are but another dream that passes, then I desire nothing further from the Great Sickness but release.

I am supposed to make some little cuts on the first scene of *Chris* today. Your letter has put over the K.O. I'm "out" temporarily—until I get another letter from you and, let us hope, a kinder one. You don't have to be hypocritical to be kind, do you? Your letter may have been true; but, where love is concerned, isn't kindness greater than truth? And do you think that greater kindness is a product of—a "flat surface wife"? There may be depths—of love—in that—

As for my letter to you which drove you to the response you made, if you had written your good advice first and the way you felt last, I would have remembered only the last. As it was—vice versa—I wrote on the spur of the moment remembering only the good advice—(which we all hate!). You might have known all this—if you knew me.

The "Flu" has already caused an official regulation of theatre opening hours. You can imagine what it is doing to the attendance. Ah well, there has been all through history a curse which, after minor victories, through no fault of their own, always smites the O'Neills at the wrong moment. The Curse of the Red Hand of Ulster![2]

But all this is puerile—and aside. Your letter was gall when I prayed for wine. You always have kicked me when I was down,—do you realize that?—you did not mean to, of course, but you always have. Gene

1. No letter from AB written on Friday, January 23, has been found. Possibly it answered his letter of January 22, in which he rejected her "lecture."
2. EO recalls the legend of the ancient O'Neill who first came to Ulster. The story was that the first who touched land would be greatly rewarded. So the legendary O'Neill cut off his hand and threw it onto the shore before the boat was beached.

∽

40. **EO to AB** ALS 3 pp. (Stationery headed: Prince George Hotel, / Fifth Ave. & 28th Street New York) [Harvard]

Jan. 26, 1920.

Own Sweetheart: I didn't get your two letters together this morning. You forget they deliver to hotels on Sunday, so I received the angry one yesterday and you'll get my reply to it today—you ought to, anyway. I wasn't mad when I wrote—only deeply hurt.

No, I'm not going to *Beyond* rehearsal today. The Doc says I better stay in another day at least with all this "Flu" flying about. It's a bum day for it, too—cold and cloudy.

Besides, Williams and I are not yet settled on a fixed basis. He is still "beefing" over the clause in the contract relative to the immediate payment of royalties, ignoring the advance. I'm going to insist that I get paid at once for the special matinees. Talked with Madden a few minutes ago. He is to see W. this afternoon. Of course, I have W. on the hip and he has to do what I say. He is only "appealing to my fairness!" Fancy that—from him!

They assemble the cast for *Chris* today to read the play, I believe. I doubt if real rehearsals will start until next Monday. That will be a full five weeks before the opening date and Tyler desires to give the play the extra week beyond the usual four.

It's my own opinion that there is a good chance of *Beyond* being postponed on account of the "Flu." This is only a hunch of mine, mind! I have no reason to think so.

Things do drag out hellishly, what?

As soon as I get definite dope on all this I'm going to arrange to come back to P'town and You at the first possible moment. There's no need of my being at many of the *Chris* rehearsals. I can trust Stanhope, with his four years' experience before the mast, to do it—and me—justice.

Lynn Fontanne,[1] the English actress, is to play the daughter, I believe, and be co-starred or co-featured in it with Corrigan.

If you have missed me, you can imagine how I've missed you during the week just past. It's damn lonely in a hotel room, not able to go out, electric light all the time, etc.

Papa has not been permitted to go out either so we've played companions in misery.

Today I feel much better mentally and physically and, although there's no new development to make me optimistic, still I have a strong inward hope for the ultimate outcome.

I love you, My Own Little Wife. A long kiss for you and Shane. I'll be home to you as soon as God will let me. I can't stand being away much longer. I'll try and make it sometime next week after *Beyond* has gone on.

I love you, Own Girl of Mine! Gene.

1. Fontanne (1889?–1983) first acted in New York in 1910. She later married and appeared together with Alfred Lunt in many prominent productions. In 1928 she created the role of Nina Leeds in *Strange Interlude*.

41. **AB to EO** ALS 3 pp. (Provincetown, Mass.) [Harvard]

Monday, [January 26?, 1920]

Dearest Love— Wednesday or Thursday you should receive a box, express. When you see that it is marked "Rush!" "Perishable—handle with care!"—and—"This side up!"—don't imagine you're going to open it and find Shane inside. It is *from* Shane! It is a surprise for you! I am sending it *COD* because I really believe they send them quicker when they haven't already been paid—so tell them at the desk you are expecting it, and to pay the charges and send to your room if you are not there.

Your letter written Sat. sounded so lonely and blue, dearest! But I can fully understand that—it is certainly *hell*—about *Beyond* and the "flu"—it seems as if some evil fate were pursuing that poor play! But, do you know, Gene, I *do believe* that once the play is on it will simply sweep ahead and conquer in spite of everything. Susan feels the same about it. It has *power*—an emotional power that will send people home in a new, higher key than they've experienced before; and this will amaze and thrill them, and they'll tell others, who will come to get the same thing. After all, people like to be *moved*—when you can give them a drama with the reality and truth of life in it, and, by dramatic genius, make that truth and reality so vivid and powerful that they will get as much excitement and thrill from it as if they were attending their favorite melodrama, why *then you've got the old public on its knees!*

Enclosed some clippings—only one worth sending. The *Telegraph* one never came.

The Theatre Guild, via Ida, telegraphed Susan to send them her new comedy, as *The Power of D.*,[1] although artistically a success, wouldn't last so long, and they wanted a comedy!—

Dearest, I'm so worried about you and the flu—do for God's sake, take care of yourself, and don't take any chances. Remember, after this cold, you will be particularly susceptible so it's a case of keeping up your resisting power.

About Adele,[2] you did right in not answering I think, but if she *says* anything to you about it, I'd tell her you didn't get the letter, or that you were too sick, and didn't have the money anyhow. There's no sense in making needless enemies, do you think? She is an old grafter,—but you'll get lots of that stuff once your long plays are on.

No—you never told me about Tearle. He'll give you a big boost in London now. Did you get your *photo* taken?

Au revoir my dear beloved boy—I wish I could put my arms around you and look into your dear dark eyes! I get *such an emptiness* for you sometimes—But it will be finer than ever when you come back to me—and Provincetown. A.

Send your poem and I'll type it.

1. *The Power of Darkness* (1886) by Leo Tolstoy.
2. Adele Holladay.

42. **EO to AB** ALS 3 pp. (Stationery headed: Prince George Hotel, / Fifth Ave. & 28th Street New York) [Harvard]

Jan. 27, 1920

Dearest Own: Your letter with the clippings arrived this P.M.—greeted me on my return from *Beyond* rehearsal at 4 P.M. Yes, I went up this morning at eleven and saw the massacre. They all have the possibilities of being very good and they all just miss it. Things, according to the usual Williams' formula, are very much disorganized. The characters don't seem to hang together. They all appealed to me to dope out for them the real meaning of what they were trying to do. I tried my best, and I'm no director, God knows, and whether my talking will result in any improvement I don't know. Tomorrow's rehearsal will tell.

Helen MacKellar—a charmingly pretty little blond—has all the stuff in her to be tremendous—if she can turn it loose. She is a very intelligent person, at any rate. Andrew will be all right; and Bennett—well, he's either going to rise to it or he isn't. The rest of the cast are all right—the father, and sea-captain, and invalid mother, especially good.

I suppose my feeling of disappointment is my usual one at all rehearsals. God blast 'em, how I hate to see a play in that stage of development!

They open—Flu be damned, says Bennett—for a preliminary out-of-town performance on Monday afternoon, Tuesday matinees at the Morosco in New York. So a week from today will be the show-down—and Gawd help us! Williams is doing no advertising and I don't know how people are to know about it. That is his dope on how to get a select, intelligent audience for the first performances. But I'm tired of kicking at his methods. He can "[shoot the piece?]" and I'll be damned glad when it's all over one way or the other. He'll never get another play of mine, you can bet your life on that.

Rehearsals for *Chris* are still uncertain as to next Monday or a week from Monday— depending on whether he decides it needs four weeks or five.

Madden tells me over the phone that their London agent is now in touch with the Everyman Theatre man and results are expected soon.

I feel like a limp rag after this rehearsal business. Hope I'll get used to it in time or the strain would be too much and you'd have a young wreck on your hands.

All my love, Own Sweetheart, and a kiss for you and Shane. Will be home to you both the first chance I get. Will look forward to the package arriving. What is it, I wonder?

I love you!   Gene.

43. **AB to EO** ALS 2 pp. (Provincetown, Mass.) [Harvard]

Wednesday—28th Jan. [1920]

Dearest— I've *just* finished my story! Aren't you proud of your hard-working wife? I'm really pleased with it. Now it has to be gone over and typed, but I will "lay it by" for a week, so as to get somewhat of a fresh angle. Now for *Now I Ask You*! You know, there isn't so much to do on that now. I did a lot this summer.

You should get the box this A.M. Did you?

Why the double-hell doesn't Williams give out some announcements of *Beyond*? How will people know about it? I'm waiting in the greatest excitement to get a letter *after* you've seen a rehearsal, telling me what you think of it. You are surely right in insisting on money from these performances. Tell W. you have a wife and baby!

I'm glad you are being careful, and evidently under the Doctor's orders.

It would be wonderful if you would come back but listen—*don't take the trip if the Dr. thinks you would be liable to get the flu on the way*, as I'm afraid it would go badly with *you*. What do you think? It is breaking out in Boston now, and there are 2 cases here. I think I can't stand not seeing you much longer, but if it was a case of your getting sick and maybe *dying*, I'd rather stand it than take a chance.

This is just a hurry note, beloved. I haven't any time for more if I want to catch the mail. More, and more interesting tonight.—

—A thousand kisses, dearest. — A

Enclose letter. I opened it. Did you get one I forwarded from a McClucken?

෴

44. **AB to EO** ALS[1] 3 pp. ([Provincetown, Mass.]) [Harvard]

[January 28?, 1920]

Well, my dear love, at last you've been to a rehearsal! It all sounded horribly discouraging to me—but perhaps it *is* just because you hate rehearsals so. At least you say they have the *possibilities* of being very good, and perhaps when they really get before an audience, they will live up to them. What I think is, that *you* are the person they need to direct them. For God's sake, don't give up in despair, but drum it into them what to do.

As for Williams, I'd like to have him here. I'd tear him limb from limb! What an idiot and fool he must be! Not even an *announcement*; who does he think will go to see *Beyond*—a lot of actors and actresses, who aren't playing on those days? Why it just seems to me that everything is being done by him to make the play a failure. There are dozens and dozens of people in New York who would be *anxious* to see your first long play, and they won't know it's going on! Oh, there is no use raving, but I feel sick about it. There is one consolation, however, and that is, that *Beyond* is a great play, and this won't be by any means the only time it will go on.

Will you explain this to me when you write again? Is the *regular* cast, the cast that plays *after* the four special matinees, rehearsing? Or has Williams made up his mind that there will be *only* the special performances? I don't get that part of it at all, so be sure and explain—*if* you've time!

I'll be in a state of excitement now, till Tuesday. Only six more days! One thing more I can't understand is why the author wasn't called until the last week of rehearsal!

The enclosed came from Deem.[2] *What* do you think of Nathan publishing your letter! (Or had you seen it?) Won't the Theatre Guild love you now! I'll drop Deem a line and let him know you are in town.

I dreamed last night you had gone back to Catholicism, and were about to go to communion; you were treating me in a very chaste and aloof manner, which I much resented!

How did you like the box?

Much love, dearest!   A.

Shane is wonderfully well and happy.

He's lucky he is not old enough to miss you the way *I* do! but as if he ever could!

1.   Possibly this is an addendum to another letter, or the beginning is missing.
2.   Charles Demuth (1883–1935), famous watercolor painter and poet. His name was pronounced Dee-muth, with accent on the first syllable, and his friends called him Deem. Emily Farnham, *Charles Demuth: Behind a Laughing Mask* (Norman: University of Oklahoma Press, 1971), 82.

45. **EO to AB** ALS 6 pp. (Stationery headed: Prince George Hotel, / Fifth Ave. & 28th Street New York) [Harvard]

Jan. 28, 1920.

Dearest Sweetheart: Have just returned from my second *Beyond* rehearsal. It was a stormy session. Bennett and I "went to the mat" with a loud bang at the close of Act II Scene I. He had his own idea of what he should do—(Williams, the damn idiot, had inspired it)—but I rebelled and insisted on the directions for reading the lines as per the text. He tried to get away with some learned remarks as to the true nature of the hero in tragedy. This was a bad mistake for him because I know more about that than he ever dreamed of and I showed him up before the whole company, who were now assembled at the ringside to see the scrap. He was stung, and resorted to sarcasm anent my inexperience in Broadway productions. But no one can beat me at that game and I came back with a remark about his inexperience in playwrighting. Finally, furious, he yelled: "Will you be responsible for the failure of this scene if we play it your way?" And I said yes, I'd be responsible for its artistic success and that was all I cared about. Then they went over it and he played Robert faithfully—(I'll hand him that)—

as I wanted. After it was done he turned to me enthusiastically and said "By God, you're right! Let's have a few more fights and this play'll pick up 100%." So it all ended in the most friendly manner. He's sincerely fighting for the play as much as I am and so, no matter what tiffs we have, we'll remain friends; and he's as frank to acknowledge when he's wrong as I am.

For two days now I have occupied that position so unattainable to most play-wrights—the only man in the auditorium, director of my own play! And I don't think I've made such a fizzle of it either! They all showed a noticeable improvement today, and also a marked improvement in their respect for me. At the end of each scene Bennett calls "Suggestions!" and every member of the cast who has been in that scene lines up at the foot lights while I—a lone figure in a vast auditorium—go from one to one, praising or panning, and not excepting Bennett himself.

Can you imagine! No, you can't—or any one of the P.P. either. For at every one of their rehearsals I was "pickled" and not myself. You can bet that doesn't happen nowadays.

Tomorrow Williams is due to be present and there may be fireworks between him and me. But he, too, sincerely loves the play and any brawls will be forgotten if *Beyond* profits thereby. He has been down at Atlantic City putting on the Brieux-Lionel Barrymore play—*The Letter of the Law*.[1]

I am getting to be great friends—now don't be jealous!—with Helen MacKellar. She read *The Straw* when the script was in Williams' office and liked it immensely—(so she says!). She is the best person in the play—excluding Bennett—and I think will do Ruth quite well. She sure is one ambitious hustler, playing in one play and rehearsing in another at the same time—which means 11 in the A.M. to 11 P.M., and after, with few intermissions. She isn't more than 25, I should judge.

Altogether *Beyond* is not so very bad off. Things might be worse. It has a splen-did cast— from a Broadway standpoint, at any rate—and I have no cause for com-plaint on that score. They are not my ideals but they are good.

You would miss a lot of the text in the play. Nothing has been written in or substituted but it sure has been cut. That had to be. It was over half an hour—30 theatrical pages—too long. That was my fault. However I'm sure that by my supervi-sion of the cutting, the meaning of the play has not suffered by consequence. It seems to me to benefit by it, rather. You know I always knew *Beyond* was too long. At least the cutting makes it much more thrilling.

All this about *Beyond*! Well, *Beyond* takes up all my time these days—and will. Tomorrow rehearsal with sets for the first time—all day—next day, ditto—Satur-day—half-day with the rest devoted to going over *Chris* with Stanhope. Sunday, dress rehearsal of *Beyond* from 3 P.M. until 3 A.M. (I guess, knowing dress rehearsals) and Monday, first performance in Yonkers—Tuesday, first N.Y. showing at the Morosco.

There you have it! I'm a busy bee. Just as soon as *Beyond* gets on I'm going to Tyler and arrange to get away for a time—back to you! God, how I need you and want you! The whole thing is without meaning without you! Talk about missing my arms at nights—God, if I haven't wanted yours in my dingy cell on the Prince George court where eternal twilight is a fact! And my bad, bad dreams—but they were all of you,

My Own, showing that the Nightingale[2] has not forgotten. He sends his love to Her and asks Her not to forget him but to just wait and He will soon—Ah, My Own, how much I want you!

Kiss our Shane for me. And to you—All of me! Gene

1. Play by Eugène Brieux (1858–1932).
2. EO's pet sexual term.

46. **EO to AB** ALS 6 pp. (Stationery headed: Prince George Hotel, / Fifth Ave. & 28th Street New York) [Harvard]

Jan. 29, 1920

My Dearest: This is just a few lines. I've this minute finished dinner here in the room with Papa after putting in from 11 A.M. to 5.30 P.M. at the Morosco Theatre with *Beyond*—not an interval for lunch, even, for me who had to be there every moment of the time. Today we rehearsed in the gents smoking room downstairs while they were rehearsing the sets on the stage above. I had to be on one floor one minute, and on the other the next, to give my opinion. After it was all over—(I thought)—about 4:30, Bennett takes it into his head to take me into his drawing room and go over the whole part of Robert speech by speech. I arrived home in a taxi at 6 P.M.—*Dead Tired!*

To make matters at this epoch still worse, as an after effect of the grippe—or, I guess, of my being in the house so long—I have the most terrible insomnia. I simply can't sleep any more. Every night I stay religiously with the family—have only been away from home one night since I got down here—play "rummy" with the "old man," have two or three drinks of rum, and go to bed about 11:30. I try to sleep, pitch and toss, and finally do sleep about 5 or 6 A.M. It's frightful! I've never had it before. And I have to be up, bright and smiling, at 8:30! For the past week I've averaged about 4 hours per night. Last night I took Veronal—with the only result that I didn't get to sleep till 6:30 this A.M.! Got up at 8:30—at theatre at 10:45—and then an all-day grind. The funniest thing about it is that I don't feel bad, only a bit woozy.

Listen now! The following is important, *very*, and I rely on you to get action and let me know at the very earliest moment. Williams asked me today if I could suggest any names to him of people to whom *Beyond* might appeal, to use in advertising—that is, to send personal announcements of the special matinees to. I didn't think of any at the time but since then it has occurred to me that if I could get the list of P.P. subscribers, it might help a lot. He wants a selected audience for the matinees and for the first performances generally—people who can appreciate the play. He thinks they will speak about it to their friends and thus be the best ad in the world. Now I'm not especially friendly with the[1] queer gang—except Jimmy—who are at present pervading the P.P. I want to go down for that list with authority at my back. So tell this to Jig and Susan. I want their consent to it. Furthermore, they have read the play and know they are not backing any unknown quantity. It seems to me only fair that I should have the benefit of the list which my plays, on 14 out of 28 bills, have done their part to build up. Ask Jig, as President, to write a letter to the Secretary to that effect—and *immediately!* And you let me know what Jig & Susan say—also *immediately!*

After all, it is only a question of getting the address of people to send a card of announcement to.

Ads for *Beyond* will begin in all N.Y. papers Saturday.

Rehearsals look better. I think the play has a good chance for artistic success—beyond that, hope nothing!

All my love, Own Sweetheart! The N. sends his last gasp to Miss P.[2]

Only a little while now, Own Little Wife! Gene.

P.S. (later) Just opened the box. A ton of hungry gratitude from all the family! Mother loves the jelly & cakes, Father craves the cold bird, and I—all! And we're all so grateful for and proud of the pictures of Shane! The Old Man bubbles over! And I—you both look so beautiful, My Own, that I'm afraid you can't be mine, I feel so unworthy.

I want to get back to you and see—and prove my claim. Tell Shane his poor Daddy is as busy these days as a centipede with St. Vitus dance but as soon as he gets one [hook?] free for a reflective hour, he'll certainly answer that letter. In the meantime tell him my advice as one Sinn Fein to another: Never trust a woman, or depend on her, especially—as Shane the Proud will be sure to whisper out of the subconscious—a woman born in London, surely![3]

1. The word "bums" has been crossed out here.
2. AB recalled that the term Nightingale came from *The Decameron*, Miss Pussy from the vernacular (Louis Sheaffer interview, November 1962).
3. AB was born in London.

～◯

47. **EO to AB** ALS 3 pp. (Stationery headed: Prince George Hotel, / Fifth Ave. & 28th Street New York) [Harvard]

Jan. 29, 1920[1]

My Own: Never got through rehearsals until 6:30 tonight. We were going over the play at the Playhouse while they were setting up the outdoor sets at the Morosco. So Williams, Bennett, and I were dodging from one theatre to another all day. The outdoor sets, done with a cyclorama, are very punk up to present writing. Let's hope they'll improve before the opening on Tuesday.

They've started advertizing the play, as you'll see by the *Times*. Also there's a big spread in front of the Morosco—"Eugene O'Neill's first long play." That's the feature. Bennett isn't starred in this, you know—only mentioned at the head of the cast.

I'm tired to death—and nothing but work in sight.

No brawls with W. today. On the contrary, he turned out to be a director after my own heart.

Phew! That notice of Nathan's—(he had no right to print it without asking my permission, by the way)—will certainly earn me a few enemies. Well, what the hell! They have always panned me behind my back, anyway, and are no friends of mine. Also what I said in that letter has been proved by the failure of *Silas Lapham* in every way, and by their being forced to snatch at Reicher and his son to try and save their artistic skins.[2] So it's just as well for them to know I had their number.

As friend, Maître François Rabelais would exclaim: if they don't like what I have said

A TURD FOR THEM!

Took some of the chicken up in sandwiches for lunch today. It was great! Mother & the Governor say so, too. They're tickled to death with the contents of that box!

All my love to you & Shane! Mr. N. wants to make a date with Miss P. for—well, he'll let you know in a few days, now. Tell her to expect him. Your own, Gene.

1. EO's dating of this letter is probably wrong by a day and should be January 30.

2. *The Rise of Silas Lapham*, adapted by Lillian Sabine from the novel by George Eliot, was presented by the Theatre Guild on November 25, 1919, starring James K. Hackett. It was an expensive failure. The Guild turned to Emanuel Reicher, former director of the *Volksbühne*, to direct Tolstoy's *The Power of Darkness*. His son, Frank Reicher, was also a director and actor in Guild productions.

48. **AB to EO** COPY 2 pp. ([Provincetown, Mass.]) [Harvard]

Friday evening. / [January 31, 1920]

Dearest Gene: This afternoon when your letter came I was alone in the house with the baby—it being Friday. I thought I would have to wait till Terry came, and then go up to Cooks about the list. However, Susan dropped in, fortunately. She seemed a bit confused about your request, and went to some trouble to explain that lists were very sacred things—*secret* things! For instance, the Washington Sq. Players[1] would not let the P.P. see *their* list, and so on. She said that managers resorted to all sorts of deception and trickery to get one another's lists; which was all news to me, as you may know. However she said she thought you surely had a right to use it personally, *if* you could do so without letting any outsiders see it. It all seemed very mixed up, but I impressed on her that you wanted to know right away, and asked her to have Jig write a telegram to the Secretary; and tonight, after Terry came and Shane was asleep, I walked up there. Susan said "Jig feels just as I do—that Gene should have the use of the list, but it should not be let out of the office." She then gave me Jig's telegram, which was to Jimmy.[2] You may have seen it. It told Jimmy to let you copy list but not to let it go out of office, etc. Then I went up to office and sent off both night-letters. I thought it better to wire, as the time is so short now, and [by] wiring you hear Saturday morning. There—wasn't I quick in "getting action"?

The above seems like a lot of words to tell a simple matter, but I wanted you to understand just what happened.

I'm terribly worried about your having insomnia. Perhaps if you tried sitting up till one or half past, reading, until you felt yourself getting sleepy, you could get to sleep easier. I'm afraid to think of the condition you'll be in when it is all over! But you'll never know how glad I'll be to get you back again—just so you are alive!

The influenza situation, according to today's paper, threatens to be worse than last year. Our luck! I wonder how things *will* turn out for us? Sometimes I have a dreadful feeling that when the inevitable success does come there will be something to spoil it all for us.

Saturday. It is zero weather here today—*awful*. I am just bound out to do some shopping, and I dread it. Have been going to the dentist—did I tell you? And this afternoon Alice Ullman wants me to go with her up to see Whiskey Bill and his wife—otherwise, the Nobles. They have a most exciting story, according to her. I imagine that Whiskey is a fine sort, from what I hear—I saw him once and was much impressed by his big breezy western type made unique by the unmistakable stamp of dissipation and brains. I don't know that I will care much for her—she seemed rather affected. They have a baby a week older than Shane—and his name is *Tawanda!*

Dearest, I miss you so! A thousand kisses! Agnes.

It is so wonderful to get your letters, and know that you miss me and need me, too.

1. Washington Square Players, founded in 1914, were a Little Theatre group, committed to investigating the plays of European experimentalists, in contrast to the American playwriting focus of the Provincetown Players. Members of the group later founded the Theatre Guild.

2. James Light.

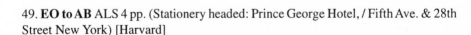

49. **EO to AB** ALS 4 pp. (Stationery headed: Prince George Hotel, / Fifth Ave. & 28th Street New York) [Harvard]

Jan. 31, 1920

My Own: Never got home this P.M. until seven. Rehearsal at the Morosco, 11 to 1:30, 2 to 6:30 at the Lambs' Club going over the script of *Chris* with Stanhope. At that we only got through the first two acts—one still to do, the third. Stanhope left it absolutely up to me and I found many cuts to make. I'm a lot wiser now than when I first went to *Beyond* rehearsals. Honestly, I've learned a tremendous lot that I wouldn't miss for worlds—knowledge that will be of *real* worth to me hereafter. I don't mean knowledge of the technique à la Broadway—*Beyond* isn't being put on like that—but *real* stuff as to the theatrical medium. Bennett is really a liberal education all in himself. He has brains and he uses them every second and, outside of some misconceptions, he has really been a great help to the play. And even from his mistakes, I have learned a hell of a lot. I'm a better playwright already; I feel it. This whole experience has been invaluable to me as an artist who ought to know his medium from top to bottom. And Bennett represents the best there is in this country. He, at least, knows all the plays of all countries and is far from the type of usual ignorant, egotistical star.

I got your wire about the list of P.P. subscribers on my return. When I see Williams tomorrow I'll tell him Susan's suggestion about sending down an addresser. John, with all his faults, is a gentleman and I know he would take no unfair advantage of any favor granted him.

Thank you for being so prompt in attending to my request. You're a peach, Little Sweetheart!

You won't mind if I don't write tomorrow, will you? I don't see how I'll ever get the time. The dress rehearsal starts at one and it is their intention to run that through and then start another trial performance at 8 P.M. Now I know something of dress rehearsals, and if I get out of that theatre before 3 A.M. Monday, I'll be a surprised prophet. But I will write at length after I get back from Yonkers Monday.

It doesn't look as if I'd be able to get back to you as soon as I expected. I thought I'd be able to get out of the *Chris* preliminaries and first rehearsals, but Stanhope says he'd much rather have me at first and let me off for the middle week or ten days.

The N. droops and languishes at this news. He has been pestering me to death at every thought of you. He's a very vexatious fellow when he has his mind set on something. But he sends word to Her that he's damn well going to make up for all this lost time when he finally does see her—and you can tell her that's a promise!

My dearest love to our Shane. I'm so glad to know he's flourishing and full of smiles. Kiss him for me.

Dear Wife of Mine, how I wish you were here! I'll be back the first second I possibly can, My Own, I swear to you; but I don't want to go and then get a wire to come back at the end of 24 hours. I want to be sure of ample time for a real, wee honeymoon with you. You understand, don't you, Dear? Your Gene

50. **AB to EO** ALS 1 p. ([Provincetown, Mass.]) [Harvard]

Sunday. / [February 1, 1920]

Dearest: You won't have time to read any long letter *today*—I know that! So just a line to send my love—and our Shane's.

You'll be in Yonkers tonight, of course. . . . Will you be at the Morosco Tuesday night—tomorrow? I don't see you sitting out in front, but imagine you might be behind the scenes—sweating blood.

Take care of your dear precious self, my own! In the excitement of the next two days, don't get *cold* again, or the *"flu."*

I'm thinking of you all the time. Your lonely, *A.*

~~◡

51. **AB to EO** ALS 4 pp. (Provincetown, Mass.) [Harvard]

Monday—Feb. 2nd [1920]

Dearest Love— You'll get this by the morning of the Great Day—although I've no doubt you are feeling sick and disgusted with everything, and wish you'd never heard the word play in all your life!—and so refuse to consider it a great day at all. Lord a-mighty, how I wish I was going to be with you! But I will be—in spirit.

Cheers, old dearest, and be brave! The play will win! There's never a doubt of that—in *my* mind.

I feel that when the curtain goes down on the last act, those people in the audience will have seen the soul of *you*—all the hope, the despair, the beauty—of *you*, my own! It is a strange feeling—I cannot quite explain it—but perhaps you will understand.

Somehow, as if the you I love were being *shared*—(no, not *all* of you, dearest!) And it makes me very, very happy—

I love you so! *Agnes.*

Think of me this afternoon!

~~◡

52. **EO to AB** ALS 2 pp. (Stationery headed: Prince George Hotel, / Fifth Ave. & 28th Street New York) [Harvard]

Feb. 2, 1920

Own Sweetheart: Your two letters greeted me this morning and did a lot to buck me up in the depression which followed the dress rehearsal of yesterday. One in the P.M. to one this morning, that's how long we were at it without leaving the theatre! No intermission for dinner, only sandwiches sent in. Toward the end I was so tired and deathly sick of hearing and seeing *Beyond* that I wished it were in hell! It all seemed false and rotten and I wondered why the devil I'd ever written it. The sets for the outdoor scenes especially get my goat. To my eye they are the last word in everything they shouldn't be. And—well—what the hell—all dress rehearsals give everyone concerned the same feeling, so they all say.

Helen MacKellar as "Ruth" is going to make the hit of the play, I think. She is really corking, the real "Ruth" of the play as written. Bennett, being an old fox at the acting game, is probably holding a lot back to display at the N.Y. opening.

I couldn't endure the idea of suffering through the Yonkers performance so I made the excuse that I had to work on *Chris* and so got out of it. Today I'll stay home and rest.

In regard to the P.P. list, I told W. yesterday that the only way he could make use of it would be for him to send someone down with envelopes and address them down there. No copy of the list would be allowed. He agreed gladly, acknowledging that they would be fools to let anyone have their list although he disclaimed any intention outside of *Beyond* and reminded me that it was my suggestion, not his. I'll go down with whoever he sends.

Well, Wednesday morning will tell the tale: I don't think there's a chance in the world of the play being a financial success, although W., Bennett and other people seem to think there is, but I do hope it will add something to my rep.

Good bye for this time, My Own. I'm too much on pins and needles to write much. Don't worry about my insomnia. It's all gone now and I feel pretty fit—only *some* nervous!

A long kiss for you and Shane. Your Gene.

53. **AB to EO** ALS 2 pp. ([Provincetown, Mass.]) [Harvard]

Monday / [February 3, 1920]

Dearest— When you get this the ordeal will be over. God, I hope last night brought you all you deserved!

I got your letter an hour or so ago, and am awfully sorry you'll have to *wait* before coming back. But I do think it's very much better for you to be at the first and last rehearsals—infinitely better.

Frankly—you don't mind my being frank, do you?—it is *hell* for me that you are not coming—that you are not here now. You speak about the "N."! Well—! *We have lived together too long to be separated like this*! It was different—for me, anyhow,— when I was having Shane. It seems as if I couldn't *stand* it, I want to *love* you so! There—do you hate me for being so frank? Gene—your little Miss P. is meowing, and howling and behaving like a perfect devil. Oh, Gene, it is *hell* for you to be so far away! I've almost a mind to get on the train and come to *you*, and let the devil take care of what happens! I'm in such a funny, vibrating physical state, it almost frightens me. This experience shows you must *never, never* go away and leave me for long—or I away from you.—oh, well, not till we're both *sixty*, at least.

I don't know that I ought to send you this letter. But you've told me that something like this is happening with you, too. The nightingale is luckier than his pen friend—he at least can dream of her and be a little happier— A.—

Tear this letter up!

54. **AB to EO** ALS 2 pp. (Provincetown, Mass.) [Harvard]

Feb. 3rd [1920]

Dearest Gene— It's after eight o'clock—and I'm feeling so depressed and blue. I wonder so much what happened in New York this afternoon and I don't know—and maybe *won't* know for a couple of days.

Wednesday's *Times*, of course, won't come tomorrow!

Were you at the theatre? Did you get my telegram?

I thought perhaps you would wire me tonight how things went—

This afternoon I was lying down in your room upstairs. It was nearly three o'clock. There I was, staring at the silly, stupid wall paper, and two hundred miles away, *Beyond* was having its premiere. Well—if a year ago, when we were down in Pt. P. someone had told me I'd be in that room—in Provincetown—alone—and you and *Beyond* in N.Y.—I suppose I should have rebelled! Certainly, I'd never have believed it—I'd have said—"I'll get there *somehow*"!

Now I don't suppose I'll *ever* see the play—and I can only shrug my shoulders! What's the use? Certainly, the chance is gone for seeing the "big event"—the first performance of your first play. Hours ago it was all over, and I don't even know what the audience thought of it—

Well, guess I'll go to bed—don't feel like reading. Too late for a wire from you now—but tomorrow maybe there'll be a long letter telling all the good news— Much love, A.

55. **AB to EO** WIRE, addressed to Morosco Theatre, West 46 St., New York (Provincetown, Mass.) [Yale]

FEB 3 1920

THREE CHEERS FOR YOU AND BEYOND AND MUCH LOVE   AGNES

56. **EO to AB** ALS 3 pp. (Stationery headed: Prince George Hotel, / Fifth Ave. & 28th Street New York) [Harvard]

Wednesday / [February 3, 1920] / 11:30 P.M.[1]

My Own: This is the very first second I've had in which to draw a free breath— and not so damn free either because I *have* to go see *Clarence* tonight. It's the last night Helen Hayes is to be in the cast and Tyler insists on my giving her the once over.

Have been up at the *Beyond* matinee all the P.M. We made some further cuts and rehearsed them this A.M.—meaning that I have been at the Morosco since 10:30 this A.M. until my arrival home a few minutes ago.

I explain all this to show you that my negligence in writing is not my fault. I think of you—oh, I swear to you, all the time! but I hate to sit down unless I have time to write you at least a pretense of a real letter.

The first performance was hell! I sat through it as I couldn't shake Williams and he planted me beside him. I suffered tortures. The waits were terrible and the show never ended until ten of six. I went out convinced that *Beyond* was a flivver artistically and every other way. That's why I didn't write you last night—I was too depressed. I dreaded to see this day's papers. When I did—lo and behold, in spite of all the handicaps of a rotten first performance, *Beyond* had won. You never saw such notices! There was not a single dissenting voice—so far, at any rate. Even old Towse, who has always panned my plays to a frazzle, came to life in the *Evening Post* with a big boost.[2] Woollcott is to run a special on Sunday with quotes from the script in the *Times* and photos of the play.[3]

Today the play went great—not a whisper in the house from start to finish, but many in tears. Ida was there, and Jimmy Light, and Grace Potter and Rob Parker.[4] They all liked it. Ida even kissed me in the lobby in her enthusiasm. Lewisohn of the *Nation* was there. He liked it immensely, Jimmy told me.[5]

I'd send you notices but you'll get them all from Romeike before you get this, I suppose.

There are a million other things to tell you. Will try to do it all in a long letter tomorrow.

I got yours from Miss P. this A.M. Oh, Sweetheart Wife, I want you so! It's a torture of longing at night when I'm in bed alone—result, insomnia. I'll be home to you, and the N. to Her, very, very soon now—the very first second I can. Believe that won't you? A kiss to Shane, and you—and Her!   Gene

1. This letter was probably written late February 3 (Tuesday) and finished in the early hours of February 4 (Wednesday).
2. J. Ranken Towse, "Beyond the Horizon," *New York Post*, February 4, 1920, p. 11.
3. Alexander Woollcott, "The Coming of Eugene O'Neill," *New York Times*, February 8, 1920, sec. 8, p. 2.
4. Ida Rauh, Grace Potter, and Robert Parker were members of the Provincetown Players.
5. See Ludwig Lewisohn, "An American Tragedy," *Nation* 110 (February 21, 1920): 241–42.

57. EO to AB WIRE, addressed to Provincetown, Mass. (New York) [Yale]

4 FEB 1920

HAVE WRITTEN BUT THIS IS JUST A LINE SO YOU WILL NOT WORRY *BE-YOND* IS A TRIUMPH ALL I EXPECTED WILL BE HOME TO YOU FIRST SEC-OND I CAN VERY SOON NOW ALL MY LONELY LOVE TO YOU AND SHANE EUGENE

~⌒)

58. **EO to AB** WIRE, addressed to Provincetown, Mass. (New York) [Yale]

FEB 4TH 1920

PLAY BIG ARTISTIC SUCCESS GREAT NOTICES ALL PAPERS AM WRITING LOVE. EUGENE.

~⌒)

59. **AB to EO** WIRE, addressed to Prince George Hotel, New York (Provincetown, Mass.) [Yale]

FEB 4, [19]20

CONGRATULATIONS SO GLAD FOR WIRE WAS AWFULLY BLUE NOT KNOWING   AGNES

~⌒)

60. **EO to AB** ALS 6 pp. (Stationery headed: Prince George Hotel, / Fifth Ave. & 28th Street New York) [Harvard]

Feb. 4, 1920 / 11:30 P.M.

My Ownest Own: Have just returned from *Clarence* with Mother and now that I am in my dark hole-on-the-court room, the voice of Mr. N. becomes insistent and he demands that he be put into instant communication with Miss P., or at least, poor lonely bird that he is!, that he send a message by me to her which you are to tell her in the still hour before you fall asleep. So here goes—my own Fuzzy-Wuzzy, he says, if you find it *hell* to be away from me then I find it triple- plated *HELL* not to have you beside me in the long, lonely nights! But *wait*, only *WAIT*, my little Sweetheart, and in a few days now I will be back to you. For my master is going to tell Mr. Tyler that he simply must get away as near immediately as he can be dispensed with. And then your mistress and he, and you and I, what a sweet honeymoon we'll all have! Be patient, Own P., for just a wee while longer. The reunion will be all the more intense for the enforced wait.

   That's what he says, the poor forlorn nightingale!

Oh My Own, My Darling Agnes, My Own Little Wife, I want you, and need you, and love you so! It's been *hell*, I've been so lonely. My family are all right, and as kind as kind can be, but they are not You—beautiful, adorable, lovely wife of mine! I've been tempted to send for you, to wire, a thousand times I've never mentioned to you. It was only the thought of the Flu danger to you and Shane which kept me level-headed. And, after all, it's better for us to reunite in our own home, with our own dear child, where we can be alone—and not in a rotten hotel room.

I swear to you I'll be back to you the first moment I can! I know you wouldn't want me to play coward—(it takes courage to stay!)—to Us, Our future, *Chris*, and Tyler; and my experience with *Beyond* has convinced me that there are certain things an author must see to right at the start or they'll never be done right—notably the sets. Stanhope wants me to go with him and the artist to visit tramp steamers at the Bush docks in Brooklyn and barges in Erie Basin. Also we have the last act of the script still to go over. Also Corrigan has to be taught the Yosephine song. These three things I simply *have* to attend to personally before I leave. I want to go back to you with a mind free from the worry that things such as cropped up in the *Beyond* production are not going on behind my back. I want to have You—and my happiness which is You!—without a disturbing thought. Believe me, Own Sweetheart, it is from a standpoint of our happiness—Us Three—that I make all decisions. God, it has been hell not to have you with me in this hour of consummation. You remember what I used to tell you in the old days when realization of each other was first peeping through our love—that paraphrase of a line of Louis XV in *DuBarry*[1]—"The stars are only stars, Sweetheart, when I can hang them in your hair!" Well, I still feel the same—only more so!

You'll see what a knockout *Beyond* was when you get the Romeike clippings. It's positively stunning! Whatever it may or may not do in a financial way, it has done all I ever expected of it already—and more. It's useless to prophesy the money end. It'll take a week yet to get any dope on that.

And it's a tremendous ad for *Chris*.

I'll not tell you any more news in *this* letter, My Own. It isn't meant to be newsy. It's a letter from the soul of me—the soul and heart of a lover—which will always be the first of me to spring to your love, even should we both be in our nineties. Your lover, always to the end of time—that's me!

A long kiss, My Darling, and be patient—(and Miss. P. too!)—I'll be back soon. You know what Robert says in *Beyond*—"It's hard to stay—and harder to go, some-times."

You are my life!   Gene

1.   Play (1901) by David Belasco.

⚭

61. **EO to AB** ALS 2 pp. (Stationery headed: Prince George Hotel, / Fifth Ave. & 28th Street New York) [Harvard]

Feb. 5, 1920. / 6.30 P.M.

My Own: This is just a line. Have been at it since 10:30 this A.M. with Bennett first, then Stanhope at the Lambs, then the scenic artist for *Chris*, then Tyler. Tyler says I may leave for P'town & You the middle of next week. Oh My Own, how I wish it were that now and how long the days are going to seem! But, at that, it's sooner than I expected and that's a happiness. Tyler also says if *Chris* is the success he hopes he'll run a bill of my one-act plays from the book at special matinees. "Fancy that, Hedda!"

The good notices—*good*, no I mean super-good notices of *Beyond* continue— there was a fine one by Burns Mantle in the *Eve. Mail*, in the *Call*, this A.M., and in the *Evening Sun*.[1]

My Own, I have made them take my work—and like it! That's no egotistical lie!

But all this is beside the mark. I'm sick of praise—and of hard work of a kind I'm not keen about—the Lambs and Broadway theatres from 11 A.M. to 6 P.M.—and not a drink in sight. Even Papa is no longer an oasis as he is reduced to port wine without a trace of a kick.

I want to get back to You! I must or I'll be worm-eaten with that gnawing long-ing. I want to rest on your breast again and tell you all my troubles and hang my poor little stars in your hair. For it is to you I owe everything I am or can ever become.

I love you so! Good-night. Gene.

P.S. I don't like to boast of being a model husband for you to have faith in—*but*— only one night (I except last night at *Clarence* with Mother) have I been out since my arrival. I'm getting to be a "rummy" fiend. Mama, Papa, and I play every night.

1. Burns Mantle, "A Fine Performance of a Fine Play," *New York Mail,* February 5, 1920; "Eugene O'Neill's Beyond the Horizon is One of the Great Plays of the Modern Ameri-can Stage," *New York Call,* February 5, 1920; "A 'Worthwhile' Drama," *New York Sun,* Febru-ary 5, 1920.

62. **AB to EO** ALS 2 pp. ([Provincetown, Mass.]) [Yale]

[February 5?, 1920]

Dearest Gene,   Still snowing! Still no train! An isolated world, grey and wind-swept, pierced only by the cry of the gulls!

Enclose a poem—which you may like—being one of the race who so often stand— with a sword drawn "against a deathless sky!" It's written by an Irishman, of course.

To turn from the poetical to the practical—don't you want to send old lady Clark a New York post card? She's done such a lot for me since you've gone—and is so *intensely* interested in you and your plays. Mention the good things in the box. Wish you *would* do this—.

Much, much love, my own,   A.

Can hardly wait to get your letter and know when you're coming up.

63. **EO to AB** ALS 3 pp. (Stationery headed: Prince George Hotel, / Fifth Ave. & 28th Street New York) [Harvard]

Feb. 6, 1920.

Own Dearest: No word from you today but I suppose the blizzard has held up the mail as it has everything else. I hope it hasn't delayed my letters to you—two the day before yesterday and one yesterday.

New York is a mess. Snow piled in the streets, the surface cars running, no L, not a taxi to be had without begging. And now comes rain and the streets are a mass of slush, ankle-deep.

In view of this impossible condition for theatre goers—with the Flu scare at its height—I am astoundedly delighted to report that our matinee was the biggest we have had. The orchestra was almost completely filled—and not with "dead-heads" either. This is a very promising sign that next week, if the Flu dies down and good weather returns, we ought to sell out! At any rate, *Beyond* is now the big talk. Already I've been asked for two photographs—for *Current Opinion* and by Louis De Foe of the *World*. I sent De Foe a snap shot. Don't know whether he'll use it on Sunday or not. You know I haven't a single photo and will have to have some taken just to save trouble, I guess.

I've not said anything to you in previous letters about the work you are doing— the story you finished and the completing of *Now I Ask You*. Don't mistake this as indifference on my part. It isn't; but I've been so sure of being back with you in the near future to talk over everything which concerns both of us that I've thought it best to wait till then. My mind is in such a topsy-turvy. You couldn't pry an idea out of it that would be worth reading. So please don't think it's been indifference, will you, Dear?

Only a few days more! That's what my heart keeps singing to me now! Only they're going to be long, long days. Oh, Sweetheart, I want so much to be with you again. You're right. After this experience we must never again be separated for so long a time—and, by God, we won't be!   Gene.

P.S. Thank Mrs. Ullman, Jig & Susan for their wires.
P.S. I'll let you know exactly what day next week I'll be back to you and Shane just as soon as I can find out myself. And I'll rely on you to shoo Mrs. Clark away for that day and tell Terry you won't be there—(any stall to keep him from coming)—We want that day and night to be just our very own, don't we? And you'll just have to lie so that it will be!

All my heart to you & Shane! I love you both so and I miss—yes, even his Irish battle cry!

P.S. (again) I've been asked to speak at a dinner at the Biltmore—some high-brow organization or other—John Drinkwater[1] spoke at their last session. I refused, of course. If that's fame they can leave me out.

1.   English playwright and poet (1882–1937), best known for his chronicle plays including *Abraham Lincoln* (1918) and *Robert E. Lee* (1923).

64. **AB to EO** WIRE, addressed to Prince George Hotel, New York (Provincetown, Mass.) [Yale]

FEB 6 1920

ISOLATED SINCE WEDNESDAY BUT TRAIN TONIGHT ALL OUR LOVE AGNES

65. **AB to EO** ALS 2 pp. ([Provincetown, Mass.]) [Harvard]

Friday— / [February 6?, 1920]

Dearest Gene— We are in the middle of a howling storm here—and yesterday's noon train—which has your letter! I suppose—is not in yet.

Well—isn't it exciting? Even here I get an echo of the "glory and the honor" that you must be enjoying, as shown by the following telegrams.

"Eugene's play great success. Hope you and baby can come to share joy and honor—Ida Rauh, Grace Potter, other friends."

And this to Jig—

"Just saw Gene's play, a great great play. I am wildly excited, dawn of a new day. Superb acting audience enthusiastic, hurrah. Jim Light!"

Wasn't that dear of Ida, etc.? I certainly appreciated it—it's nice to realize that one's friends—although not such very close friends, at that—are thinking of you. And I've no doubt that if one of them had the room, they'd try and arrange it so I *could* come. Well, it's my own bad luck that I don't have folks in N.Y. who *can* ask me and Shane down for a week. Poor Stella[1] remains my only invitation!

Your telegram surely meant much to me. Thanks, old dear! The only criticism I've seen so far was the *Times*—read it a dozen times. Jim L. must have *loved Beyond*!

Well, you're probably being interviewed and photographed, besides *Chris* rehearsals, and haven't much time to read long letters; and besides, there isn't much to tell. Things go on the same as ever here—only that at present we are snow-bound—

So a thousand kisses and a big hug—and a smile from Shane— Aggie

I'm so happy over your success, but at the same time I feel at a loss how to speak of it—And it doesn't come as any surprise to me—you know that—I've thought over and over all it must, and will mean to you that *Beyond* is recognized as such a great play, and I've really "thanked God."—a state of mind, of course, rather than a prayer—for it.

1. Stella Ballantine was the sister of EO's close friend (and later editor) Saxe Commins and married to Edward J. Ballantine, actor and director with the Provincetown Players.

66. **AB to EO** AL 4 pp. ([Provincetown, Mass.]) [Harvard]

Friday night / [February 6, 1920]

Dearest— I think of you so much, and then when it comes to writing a letter . . . I've written you *two* letters and mailed them. But all the time I was hating myself for not somehow putting down, so you could know, all I was feeling. They seemed almost abrupt when I read them over. But I *couldn't* write more.

What I feel about you, all I want to tell you now that you have your great success—*our* great success!—should be told close, *close* to one another—hardly in words at all. I wouldn't need words, for you would understand. But there I sat, and there was the pen and the paper—and you miles away. It seemed impossible. I'd say to myself—oh, I must somehow let him know! And I'd start—write a few stupid words. Then a curious rage—resentment, something that—yes, really!—made me *tremble*, would overcome me. Against all the circumstances that keep us apart now, just when we should be together! . . . For, oh Beloved, I have been with you when you were suffering, when despair and loneliness were upon you, and I needed to be with you triumphant! I wanted to give you my silent love, and my faith, which is *your* faith,—as I did in those old days in the studio, when together we dared our own ghosts—you, a phantom of the past, and I a sickening phantom of the future. Before the joy of your moment of triumph had faded—(with the dear images of a wistful, waiting You close to my heart!) I wanted to see you happy, proud, elated, secretly *intoxicated* with this success, which so soon—for such are *you*!—I'll see you drop as an empty bauble.

Together, without saying very much, I wanted to know that we were remembering—happily now, dearest—the hard things, the funny things, the wonderings and doubtings of the past two years; to have you look at me, and know you would tell me that you had only plucked a star to place it in my hair! (Do you remember, when we lay close together once, you whispered that you'd change those words—that there were *no* stars, unless *you* could gather them—for *me*?)

All this—but most of all, it was *my love* I wanted to give you—and there was pen and ink and paper—and you two hundred miles away. The mockery of it! As if I could *tell* you—*write* you—what I was feeling! Do you remember that poem of Blake's—? see if *I* can remember it

> Never seek to tell thy love
> Love that never told can be,
> . . . . . That moves
> Silently, invisibly—"[1]

Something like that, isn't it? It's true.

So forgive my stiff letters . . . —and try and understand how happy I am about *Beyond*. This afternoon I was thinking about you, and I suddenly saw that those letters weren't quite fair—that I should try somehow to let you know a little of what I felt. So I'm writing this—to wish you happiness—*There*—do you see how I blunder! There's no use trying! I'll be offering you "cordial congratulations" next! Wait till I see you!

I *love* you. *Yours*.

Shane is so dear, too.

1. First stanza of untitled poem from Blake's notebook, with variant—"seek" for "pain." *The Poetry and Prose of William Blake*, ed. David V. Erdman (New York: Doubleday, 1965), 458.

~⌒

67. **EO to AB** ALS 3 pp. (Stationery headed: Prince George Hotel, / Fifth Ave. & 28th Street New York) [Harvard]

Feb. 6, 1920. / 11.30 P.M.

My Own: This is just another lonely note at bedtime to tell you again how I am longing for you and how happy I am that another cross on the calendar can now mark off a dead day which brings me nearer to you. Not long now, My Own, not long! I'll fight to get away at the very earliest possible moment, you can bet your soul on that!

Am to see Stanhope early tomorrow and my forecast is that I'll have a long hard day of it—with a trip to the Brooklyn waterfront a probability.

Corrigan is down at Atlantic City studying the part already.

Our psychic friend, [Libbins?], was at the matinee today—also Helen Westley,[1] who either has not read the *Smart Set* letter[2] or chooses to ignore it—at least she was very generous with her praise.

Also met Metcalfe, the critic on *Life*, who said a few kind words. As he is an inveterate "panner," this is worth mention. He's the only critic I've met so far.[3]

But to the devil with all of that. Without you, what does it mean? It's less than the dust of a dream. I want You! You!! You!!! My whole body and soul are calling to you! I'll never be away like this again, I promise you!

Only a few more days, Dear Heart, and then—Oh, how I long for the feel of your arms around me again, to hear your voice, to kiss your dear lips again!

Good night! I love you more than life!   Gene.

1. Actress (1879–1942), member of the Provincetown Players and one of the founders of the Theatre Guild.
2. The letter quoted in Nathan's article, mentioned by EO in #44.
3. See J. S. Metcalfe, "Beyond the Horizon," *Life* 75 (February 19, 1920): 332.

68. **AB to EO** ALS 3 pp. (Provincetown, Mass.) [Harvard]

Late Saturday night— / [February 7, 1920]

My own, my darling, my sweetheart! The train just arrived, and I went up and got your three blessed letters. Oh, my own, dear love, they made me want you so that I can hardly bear it. But they made me happy—so beautifully happy. *Every single day* I love you *more, more*—though it doesn't seem possible. I just can't *believe* that God has been so good to me, to give me the wonderful, blessed gift of your love. What you mean to me I can never put into words, but with my love, the knowledge of what you *are* (—how can I explain it—all the *wonder*, the *fineness* of you—?) blends into some eternal and beautiful and *peaceful* current that flows always beneath my consciousness. I want no other religion, no other belief—it is all there—in *you*—in us.

And Miss P. loves her N. as I love you—poor little wretched separated dears! *She* was so glad to get her message from *Him*! She says to tell Him the nights seem long and lonely to her, too! But she'll *wait*—'till *then*.

Before the train came in tonight I wrote you a telegram, and gave it to the messenger boy to send tomorrow morning, so you'll get it Sunday—the office was closed tonight. I thought you might be worrying, not hearing, so don't think I am extravagant.

Beyond dearest, must have made a terrific hit. I have seen so far only the *Times* crit. and tonight from Romeike, an *Evening Telegram*, and *Post* review—that was all. I am dying and hungry to see all the others—particularly the *Tribune*—The *Telegram* and *Post* aren't so important, and Woollcott is not one of our highest intelligences—although he seems to have gotten remarkably well what you were doing. Broun, Lewisohn, Clayton Hamilton—*those* I want to see.[1] From the three received, though, I can see what an absolute knockout *Beyond* gave them. But Gene, I want so to know what they intend doing now—they *mustn't* close! What a hell, *hell* of a shame it didn't open regularly, evenings, etc.! It would have played all season. This god-*damned* nonsense about the play not appealing to the public is a disgusting piece of stupidity, just in line with Williams's former doubts; it is an outrage and a shame if the play is to be kept for the "elect," and labelled and treated so that the average man—or woman—will be scared off. Listen—*Beyond* would find a response in the everyday, common audience and 99 out of a hundred won't get seats for it. They are being *cheated*.

And W. is *cheating* people who have little enough of beauty and real emotion in their lives, in adopting this attitude. I *know* it—I *know* it—once they see it. But those people are scared of the word *tragedy*—and *"special matinees—"* They see the boosts in the paper—interested by them, perhaps—then the thought inevitably comes to their minds "oh—high-brow stuff."—and even though the story, as told by the reviewers, seems simple to them, they become inoculated with the fear of something beyond them—something that might *bore* them—

The idea of one admirer telling another, and so advertising the play is very good—but it seems to me in this case it fails of its purpose—because a special performance audience is bound to be more or less interrelated—surely you see that—and so it becomes sort of a "vicious circle."

I think the play should have been—or *be* advertised as a *drama*—not *tragedy*. It contains the drama—in essence—of *most* lives, *Beyond* does—and is no more *tragic* than most of them. But most people never admit that their lives are tragedies. That word means, to them, something unusual, horrible, dreadful—*gloomy*. They're *scared* of it! (After all, the destiny of human life is either pathetic or ridiculous—one or the other—which-ever you choose! and so all real plays should be divided into Tragedy or Farce.—if you're going to be *particular*!) So if *I* were producing *Beyond*, Drama, not Tragedy would be used in the advertisements—not from a box-office point of view, but because the public deserves to see the play, and I'm convinced that by *our* public the word Tragedy is misunderstood—for them, A Drama would be nearer the truth of the play.

For Susan's *Bernice*[2] Williams's methods would be ideal. Its appeal *is* limited by its subtlety, although it has much of truth and fineness, but *your* plays, it seems to me, are tremendous in their power of breaking down the barriers to the emotions universal to almost everyone, (that isn't very clear, but you'll get what I mean). Take some *ordinary* folks—well, from what I've heard of them, the Rippins, where you boarded in New London.[3] The old lady and the girls would see *Bernice* and they'd wonder what the devil it was all about: but they'd see *Beyond*, and they'd be tremendously stirred, and absorbed—they'd think it was sad, but it would *get* them.— although they might not get all of *it*!

I don't often get stirred up by anything, but I'm convinced I'm right about this,—perhaps it all seems a bit incoherent to you, but try and see what I mean, and see if I am not right. I feel very deeply about *Beyond*, and from your letters, and the notices I have seen, there seems no sureness that it will do more than these matinees—

Sunday afternoon. / [February 8, 1920]

Dearest: I started this letter Sat. night—wrote all that about *Beyond* this morning, after getting into quite a state about it all by my lonesome; and now here's more. I got your telegram—but had already sent you one, as you know. Today is glorious—clear, sunny. I'm going up to Susan's for supper. Read her play. It's awfully amusing.

Later—Susan and Jig are joyous over *Beyond*. Did you get their telegram?

Dearest love, how happy your three letters made me last night. They were the first I'd gotten from you, you know, since *Beyond* went on. And there must be more coming, from what your telegram says.

And in your letter, you mentioned the very thing I'd written to you—about the stars. After I'd written that, I thought—maybe he *won't* remember that he ever said it and he'll think I'm silly. But you did dearest! How happy and—yes—*thrilled*—I was when I realized it.

Maybe your next letter will say when you are coming—oh, dearest, soon I hope. Goodby, my love. *Agnes.*

1. Heywood Broun, "Beyond the Horizon by O'Neill a Notable Play," *New York Tribune,* February 4, 1920; Clayton Hamilton, "Seen on the Stage," *Vogue,* April 1, 1920.

2. Glaspell's first full-length play (1918), initially produced by the Provincetown Players.

3. James and Helen Rippin ran a boarding house on the same street as the O'Neill house in New London. EO roomed there during the winter of 1913–14 and befriended several of their seven children.

69. **EO to AB** ALS 2 pp. (Stationery headed: Prince George Hotel, / Fifth Ave. & 28th Street New York) [Harvard]

Sat. Feb. 7, 1920. / 4 P.M.

Own Dearest: I was much disappointed and a bit hurt to find there was no letter for me today. However, I suppose it is no fault of yours but just that rotten blizzard which has delayed the mails. You are probably in the same boat—wondering why I've been so unkind as not to let you know about all the "big doings." If you felt this way, it will heap coals of fire on your head when you find out that this is the sixth letter I've written you since Wednesday A.M. The last time I've heard from you was your Wednesday wire in answer to mine. And I feel lonely and out of your heart, somehow.

I also feel sick physically and had to break my date with Stanhope today. He assured me over the phone that my presence wasn't imperative, so that doesn't matter much. The Doc. has ordered me to stay in the house today & tomorrow, with medicine every two hours. This is the way of it: Mother got wet feet—no taxis to be had— the night we went to *Clarence.* She got a bad cough and obstinately refused to see a doctor until last night, by which time she was really very bad. The Doc. said he found a trace of pneumonia in one lung which would have proved a very serious matter if allowed to develop further. As it is, she is in bed with a fever and will probably not be permitted out for a week or so.

I must have caught it from her for I woke up in the middle of the night in a sweat and with a rotten cough. The Doc. came to me in bed this A.M. and said I had caught it just in time—that if I'd stay in and take the medicine, I'd be all O.K. again by Monday.

So there you are. You can bet I'll obey instructions to the letter. I won't take any chance that will further delay my return—*home*!

Have just finished Kenneth Macgowan's criticism in the *Eve. Globe* which he saved for his Saturday spread.[1] Like all the rest without exception it toasts *Beyond* to the skies.

I have a headache and my ears are buzzing—must be quinine in my medicine. So bye'bye, Own Little Wife. I'm longing so for a letter from you! Yours is the only voice I haven't heard in all this ballyhoo of praise—and yours is the only one I give a damn about. I feel fearfully depressed—as if I'd lost you. Gene.

1. Kenneth Macgowan, "Eugene O'Neill Writes a Fine, Long Play," *New York Globe,* February 7, 1920.

∽

70. **AB to EO** ALS 4 pp. ([Provincetown, Mass.]) [Harvard]

Tuesday / [February 10, 1920]

Onliest! I'm worried *sick* since your letter, arriving yesterday afternoon, saying you weren't well. I have a dreadful feeling now that I won't see you soon. Oh, Gene, if you know how I want you here—or to be *there*, with you!

I've arranged with Clarkie to beat it the day you arrive—we'll be all to ourselves once again—I'll fix Terry, somehow, never fear. Little Shane doesn't nurse now at two—goes from ten at night to six in the A.M.—so we can sleep together again—up in your room. I'll slip down at six, and nurse him, and then—come back to you. Mrs. Clark has been staying here nights, in the little room off the kitchen, but when you are here I am going to have her sleep in my room and see to Shane—and she gives him his bath in the morning, too. But for your first day we'll be *all*, all alone.

Darling, beloved, *don't* let anything happen so you can't come.

And let me know *in time*—also, wire *when you leave*—because I'll have to know *sure*, in order to make these arrangements.

I'm so awfully sorry about your mother—give her my love—and maybe the photos of her angel grandson will cheer her up. Isn't he *dear*? I wrote her—not knowing of course she was ill.

Your letter sounded so blue dearest: you understand, don't you, that from Wednesday to late Sat. night, we were entirely cut off from the world.—A freight train went off the track at Yarmouth, and lay square across both tracks—this, *besides* the snow. Wires were all down—no telegraph—your wire Wed. day—was the last word from you until late Sat. night—no papers, either—But *I* wasn't blaming you—I knew it was just a case of be patient. Also I wired *you*, before I got your Sunday wire—and was so glad then that I had.

There'll be so much to talk over when you come!

You dear, of course I didn't think you were indifferent when you didn't mention the story, etc. Believe me, I have not given them a thought this week either—you & *Beyond* take all my time—Last night I dreamed I was at a performance of *Beyond*, which was completely spoiled because all the characters were in evening clothes, and a trained cat occupied the center of the stage, doing a turkey-trot all the time to jazz music somewhere off stage. It was a scream—and clear as day. You were there too—but you seemed very busy and hadn't much time for me!

You don't know how anxiously I am waiting for the mail today, hoping a letter from you will say you are better. I am so worried.

Till then, my own—all my love—and loneliness,   A.

P.S. Of course, Sunday's *Times* hasn't come yet—Tues.! The mailman left Susan's Sunday *Trib* here yesterday, by mistake.

71. **EO to AB** ALS 3 pp. (Stationery headed: Prince George Hotel, / Fifth Ave. & 28th Street New York) [Harvard]

Tuesday / [February 10, 1920]

Dearest Heart: Just a line written from bed. Feel weak and shaky but the Doc says the disease is running its course naturally and all's well. This is not such cheerful news when your temp is still 102, your stomach sick, and you feel generally as if Fate had carried the joke a bit too far. I can't sleep much, either, the cough prevents that. It's a mean business—this Flu—and seems to hit you in every part at the same time.

I wish to hell I were on my feet again and going back to you. Predictions on just when that will be will have to await events, God damn it! Of course, just having the Flu is no such unique affliction that it justifies blasphemy. All New York has it, it seems. I was really lucky to see *Beyond* through its opening week before it "got" me.

But to have it happen now just when I intended to return to you!—Damn it, I'm sore and sick of everything!

As soon as I get my head out of the racking, buzzing class, I'll write a long sensible letter in answer to all of yours of yesterday and today. They were awfully sweet, My Own, and they mean so much to me—alone and miserable—you can imagine.

We must both be brave, Sweetheart, and bear this cross with resignation. Let's hope it will only postpone things a few days. All my love to Shane and you.   Gene

P.S. Tell Susan Eddie[1] phoned. The old man got it. I don't believe he said anything about her script. I haven't been allowed to get out of bed to answer any call. They are all sent to 850.[2] At any rate, no script has arrived of her play. As soon as I'm up and about I'll get after the matter. At present, I'm helpless to do anything.

1. Possibly Edward Fisk, a painter and friend of Charles Demuth since they had been students together at the Pennsylvania Academy of Fine Arts (where AB's father had earlier worked), later married AB's sister Cecil.
2. EO's mother and father lived in Suite 850 at the Prince George Hotel.

~~⌒

72. **AB to EO** WIRE, addressed to Prince George Hotel, New York (Providencetown [*sic*], Mass.) [Yale]

FEB 11 1920

JUST TO SAY HOWDY AS MAILS STILL DELAYED GOT YOUR FRIDAYS LETTER TODAY DONT TAKE COLD AFTER GETTING UP MOST DANGEROUS TIME REMEMBER HUTCH[1] DONT RISK TRIP HERE NOW OR WATERFRONTS ETC WISH COULD BE WITH YOU IF WORSE WIRE WILL COME THIS IMPORTANT WORRIED TO DEATH MUCH LOVE   AGNES.

1. Charles "Hutch" Collins, whom EO had known since his days in New London and who had acted in several of his plays for the Provincetown Players, died of influenza in January 1919.

~~⌒

73. **AB to EO** ALS 6 pp. ([Provincetown, Mass.]) [Harvard]

Wednesday, *A.M.* / [February 11, 1920]

My own— After a night of despair,—I *knew* something was wrong—I got your letter this morning, a few minutes ago. Thank god, dearest, you are better—When I saw—that you had the flu—well, you know how I must have felt. But I'd been imagining such dreadful things—that it was, in a way, a relief to know some thing definite, and that you were better—but oh, Gene, I don't know what to do—I can't come to you—and the thought of you *alone*—in that room—not your mother, even to be with you— I am overcome—and helpless. For God's sake—Gene—*insist on a nurse*. You shouldn't be alone—

Just this second your telegram came, and thank God—and you—for it—I'm so glad you sent a night-letter—tell you why— yesterday afternoon, after I'd given him the telegram for you, I said "send it now, I expect an answer tonight" he said "You won't get it tonight, anyway, we close at six and don't open again—new rules." So I wouldn't have had a wire till now. After this, any wires that would come after 5:30, or six, send night-letter—might as well.

Dearest—you say you are better. *Listen* read *carefully. The great danger in flu is after you get better, getting pneumonia.* Death after death occurred in young people, right in this town, this way. Remember Hutch. NOW YOU MUST NOT DO ANYTHING TO GET COLD AFTER YOU ARE BETTER. Gene, I beg and plead with you not to take any chances, for my sake, and poor Shane's, for I swear if anything happens to you I will not live in this world without you—I simply *couldn't*. Don't start for Provincetown—you nearly always get cold on the train. We will just have to wait a little longer. You must not take that chance—another thing, the situation here is this: We have just exactly enough coal to last *3 days* more—*none in town*. Freights all stalled, with no idea of when they get in—Mrs. Clark has nearly a ton of small coal she will let us have if worst comes to worst, but I don't know how long that will last. I nearly died when Baker told me we were so short. We will just have to let the furnace out, I suppose, and live in the kitchen. However, I'm going to save Clark's coal—not use it—so if you *should* come—it will be warm.

About my letters—dearest, you should have had three, Monday A.M. Two silly ones, stupid ones, and one explaining them—a long one. Then, Tuesday, two more, and a batch of photos—But the mails are so rotten. Do you know we never got Sunday's *Times*—and I was so anxious to see it.

   Well, dear baby Gene, I must go uptown with this—there is much more I must say later—My own, own love.   Agnes.

   It almost kills me to think of you alone—sick—in that room—
   —P.S. give my love to your mother. Mrs. C. sends her love to you, and says she wishes she could make you some nice cup-custards.

74. **AB to EO** ALS 3 pp. ([Provincetown, Mass.]) [Harvard]

Wednesday night. / [February 11, 1920]

My own— Sent you a night letter tonight—The thought of you alone in that room nearly drives me wild, and it maybe pleased you to get a wire—to break the monotony. Also, mails are so rotten. There was a letter from you this afternoon—only one—and imagine my consternation when I read about a date with Stanhope, and Brooklyn waterfronts! I saw you dead from pneumonia, sure! *Then* I saw the date— Friday, the 6th—nearly a week ago. And no Sunday *Times* yet—
   Sweetest, you do know how I love you, don't you? Oh, Gene I so much want us to be living together again—our dear home life. It seems to me now that I would be so different—so much nicer—so much more *understanding*—than I have been. I suppose it is silly, but I feel that no woman in the world has as *perfect* a husband-lover as I have, and I want a chance to show I appreciate it now. I want to make our home the most beautiful place in this world—in a spiritual sense—for you.
   It seems to me now that I have been so hateful during much of the past. Dearest, won't you forgive me?
   I wish so that there was something I could do for you. Dear God Almighty, I hope we are never so far away from one another as this again! It seems as if once it got us

separated, some fate were diabolically working to prevent us being together again. My baby, my own, my dearest, to think you are there all alone, sick, without me. I can't bear it!

Good night! across all these miles! I would give the world to bend over you—slip my arm under your dear, dear neck,—kiss you—your eyes, your hair, your dear prickly moustache—your lips. My own!

Thursday A.M. / [February 12, 1920]

A letter from you—and the *Times*, with Woollcott's review. Wasn't it nice—rather amusing about your lonesome life on the bleak [span?] of the Atlantic. You can imagine what a sensation of absolute "know-nothing-ness" about *Beyond* I got when I read that the second act had been "telescoped" into one scene—the first I knew of it—Well, there's just no use my trying to keep in touch—I guess—with the plays—I give it up! Tried to imagine what the second act was like—suppose it means it's all played in the kitchen, not on the hill. Quite a radical change—

Will you be careful about pneumonia after getting out? That is the *great* danger, my own—remember that—

Must close now, to catch the mail—Did you like the photos?

Goodby, dear heart of mine *Agnes*

⟨⟩

75. **EO to AB** ALS 3 pp. (Stationery headed: Prince George Hotel, / Fifth Ave. & 28th Street New York) [Harvard]

Thursday. / [February 12, 1920]

Own Dearest: Felt too all in to write yesterday. Tried getting up as an experiment but I nearly fainted from weakness on the way up to 850. It's surprising how Flu takes the starch out of you in a few days. I had to go back to bed. This awful cough is the worst ever. I'm sure I average a bark every other minute, both day and night. My stomach and sides hurt like hell from the muscular exertion. As for eating, I can't stand anything but milk. Everything tastes funny and my "tummy" is out of order. Can't smoke—cigarettes taste like Chinese incense.

Today I feel better in as much as I believe from the way I feel that my temp. is down to normal again. That is a definite step of right progress.

I'd have wired for you to come down only—it's a Flu infested household at present. How about Shane? You better wait until the pest has left us. I'll have to apply for rooms here two weeks in advance at least. They have a long waiting list. It was considered a stroke of *marvelous good luck* when I got this hole in the wall after two days.

And yet I'd love to have you here so much! I miss you so damnably! I'm so lonely! What a cursed situation to be in!

Williams wrote me today—sympathy for sickness. He ended up "The Town is yours."

They can keep it. Success has meant to me the meaningless futility I always knew it would—only more so. All my love   Eugene

Eddie brought Susan's play today, I believe. Everything goes through 850 and I'm incommunicado—otherwise I'd be jumping from bed to phone every minute. Tell Susan that I expect Stanhope to pay me a call tomorrow and I'll give him the script to take right up to Tyler. That'll be the best and quickest way, under the circumstances, and be the same as if Tyler got it out of my own hands.

P.S. Mama brought down the pictures. They're corking, aren't they, especially the one where he's lying down.

‌ ‌

76. **AB to EO** ALS 2 pp. ([Provincetown, Mass.]) [Harvard]

Friday. / [February 13, 1920]

Dearest Heart—   I'm writing this letter in an agony of despair and helplessness. No letter this A.M.—no letter yesterday afternoon—the last word from you one written Tuesday—three days ago—today's *Friday*. Can you imagine how I feel when I don't know what has happened to you since *Tues.*—when you wrote —don't know if you're better or worse—maybe delirious, and can't write—when every time I pick up a paper, I see somebody has just died—from flu—when I know so well how in just *one* day or *two*, a person sick with flu can develop into pneumonia.—I have imagined so many terrible things that I'm in a state of numbness from it all—the most dreadful part of it is that if you *should* get—*be*—worse—how can I get to you? God, why didn't we go to Pt. Pleasant—

If I don't get a letter this afternoon I'll wire again. A dozen times I've made up my mind to come, anyway. Then the thought of Shane stops me—what *can* I do? Dr. Hiebert[1] said it would be crazy to go down with him now—unless you were "seriously" sick. But I don't know if you *are* seriously sick or not—all my family had it last year, remember, and it wasn't bad—but so often it *is* bad.—Oh, I've gone over the whole thing again and again and again, and don't know what to do—

Have you a dressing gown? Have your father order one sent from L & T's,[2] if you haven't won't you? *It is important you don't get a worse cold sitting round the room.* I was going to send yours, but express is so delayed.

This letter system is sickening in cases of illness like this—you won't get *this* probably, till Sunday. The only thing is to send me a night-letter every afternoon, until you are all right—even if it does cost more—it's only 40 cents—would you want to wait two days if *I* was sick—not to know till Thursday morning how I was *Tuesday?*

This is a crazy, silly letter, I know, and doesn't begin to tell you how I feel, but I can't do better now—If I don't hear that you are much better before noon tomorrow (Sat.), Shane and I will take the 2:40 train for N.Y. and be in N.Y. Sunday—to hell with what happens to us. I'll be with you anyhow. Your own— *Agnes*—

1. Provincetown doctor whom EO had known since his days at Harvard.
2. Lord & Taylor.

77. **AB to EO** ALS 6 pp. ([Provincetown, Mass.]) [Harvard]

Friday / [February 13, 1920]

My own love,   This is the *third* letter I have written you today. I'm really ashamed of the other two—which I mailed at noon—and realize they were probably hysterical and silly—and not the sort of letters for an invalid to receive. But you'll forgive me, won't you? I won't try again to tell you how worried I was. Wait till I see you, and I'll try and explain then.

Yours of yesterday cheered me up beautifully,—although I know you are still feeling rotten, you say you've no fever—that's the great thing. I know for our sake you will try and be careful about not getting worse cold—and pneumonia.

Is your mother better? Give her my love—and Shane's.

You didn't say anything about coming up—and I suppose you won't be able to make it at all now, as it would be at *least* ten days before you could safely try the trip, and by that time you would be needed at rehearsals. Is that the situation?

Wish you'd write in full, if you feel well enough, and tell me.

Really, I don't think we should be away from one another much longer, do you? For many reasons.

Susan and I were talking about my going down, and all the difficulties of it. What do you think of this plan? Of course, it is only an idea. But, if there is any idea of my coming, wish you would talk this over with your mother, and see what she thinks.

Locate a decent, clean rooming house, somewhere right near the P.G.—there are lots in that neighborhood—and get a large, sunny room, if possible with running water and a "gas-ring"—the sort of room they rent for light housekeeping. In same house, same floor, (if possible) get a hall-bedroom. Then Shane, I, and Mrs. Clark come down; she have [*sic*] the hall-bedroom to sleep in, and Shane and I the big room. You keep on at P.G. With this arrangement I would have someone to be with Shane, and he could come "visit" at the P.G.—and I could spend a lot of time with you; Mrs. C. and Shane being in the big room—I don't mind leaving him with her a bit—

The meal proposition would be an easy one. Mrs. C. seems to exist on nothing— she could get most of her meals over a gas-ring, or even a Sterno outfit. Her wages would be the same as here—$12 for two weeks—and Lord knows that is cheap enough to have a baby practically taken off your hands! And she could do a lot of sewing for me at the same time.

This would give us a chance to be *alone* together a lot, dearest, and also, it would give me a chance to see *Beyond*, and some *Chris* rehearsals. Your folks—and you—could see all they wanted to of Shane. Also it would be a lot less expensive than just Shane and me being at the P.G.—there we'd surely have to pay $3.00 a day—$21. a week. A big room such as I mean cost about five or six dollars a week three years ago. You ought to get one now for ten. The hall-bed room would be about another $3.00—$17.00 a week. As I said Mrs. C's meals would cost very little—And if I didn't take her, we would have to keep paying her here, anyway,—that is unless we want to let her go altogether—and you know she has promised to go to the outside this summer—"for little Shane!"

You know dearest, we couldn't have a room together, even if I stayed at the P.G.—it wouldn't do for you to be sleeping in the same room as Shane, because your rest would be broken, and that would make *me* nervous—and this way we really *can* be *all to ourselves* a lot.—There'd be no reason why I couldn't spend every evening at the P.G. with you, till eleven or twelve o'clock.—if we wanted to, down in your room—or some of the evenings, anyway!—Perhaps I could even stay all *night* sometimes,—if they didn't put you out for having a woman in your room!

What do you think of this? It strikes me as the best possible plan. Will you ask your mother? Just for a couple of weeks, anyway—

And let me know "right off." Say I would come around the 23rd—{deleted: or 21st}. My clothes are O.K.—I had the suit fixed by the tailor, and it fits all right—{deleted: all I'd need is some gloves}.

Does this seem a solution to you? You wrote as if you wanted me to come—that's why I'm suggesting this—The "flu" seems on the decrease, and by the 23rd, there wouldn't be any danger of getting it from you, would there?

I'll mail this now—to get the early Sat. train—And let me know—won't you?

Good-by, ownest own—I'm dying to be with you soon. And Miss P. sends the dear old N. her *love*—and a very special message to him that she hopes *he* didn't have the "flu" too!

Your "lonely wife" *Agnes*.

It might be possible to get a couple of rooms in a private apartment—you can, sometimes.

78. **EO to AB** ALS 2 pp. (Stationery headed: Prince George Hotel, / Fifth Ave. & 28th Street New York) [Harvard]

Feb. 13, 1920

My Own: Just a few words, My Own. I feel too punk to write more. Am still running a temp over 101 and not able to eat. Even the mere idea of food makes me sick to my stomach. Except for a glass of milk taken under protest now and again, haven't had anything to eat at all in a week now.

Won't be able to get out of bed until this temp breaks up and I get some strength back.

I feel so miserable. You don't know how lucky you are to have escaped it. The weather is vile, too.

All my love! Excuse pessimism but I can't help it. At least you and Shane keep well and keep the balance 2 to one.   Gene.

～つ

79. **EO to AB** WIRE, addressed to Provincetown, Mass. (New York) [Yale]

FEB 14TH 1920

MUCH BETTER TODAY TEMPERATURE NORMAL AGAIN FOR FIRST TIME DON'T WORRY LOVE.   EUGENE

～つ

80. **EO to AB** ALS 2 pp. (Stationery headed: Prince George Hotel, / Fifth Ave. & 28th Street New York) [Harvard]

Saturday eve. / [February 14, 1920]

My Own: Sent you a wire this P.M. which I hope you got O.K. It's funny about your not receiving my notes. I managed to scribble a few lines every day this week except last Sunday. It's just cursed luck if they were lost, and have kept you so worried by failing to appear.

I'm much better today. The Doc. found my temp had sunk back to normal—no fever for the first time—and I've been able to take a little nourishment. I'm very weak and plagued now by those sweats whenever I drop off to sleep—can't blame it on booze this time! My face looks as if I'd been dug out of the grave by mistake, the past week has taken it out of me so completely.

I'm so weak I can't attempt to make these notes more than just "I love you" messages. Don't worry, I'll pick up in a rush from now on. Expect to be allowed to get up for a while on Monday. All my love,   Gene.

P.S. Mama is much better.

~~~

81. **EO to AB** ALS 2 pp. (Stationery headed: Prince George Hotel, / Fifth Ave. & 28th Street New York) [Harvard]

Sunday. / [February 15, 1920]

My Own: Your long letter about your N.Y. scheme arrived this noon. It listens well enough—if the rooms of that kind can be found in N.Y. this winter which I very much doubt. Just at present there's no one in this family to go looking. Mama is tied down and I won't be out of doors until the latter part of the week, I guess, even with luck my way. I'm not even out of bed yet. Nor is my mind in any condition to pass judgment. But cheer up! There'll be some way to beat the game and we'll find it. It would all be so simple if Shane were not in our midst, or if you only had him weaned.

At any rate I wouldn't consider taking action on any plans before the first of next month, if I were you. It's still possible, depending on my getting well soon, that I'll be able to get to Provincetown as I expected—for a week, at least—and we could then go over everything. The Doc says I must have rest—fresh air, etc.

Still feel very weak and am so thin I could go with a circus; but, in spite of appearances, am really much better and enjoying food again. All my love,   Eugene.

~~~

82. **AB to EO** ALS 3 pp. ([Provincetown, Mass.]) [Harvard]

Monday, A.M.— / [February 16, 1920]

My dear— I didn't write Saturday or yesterday, as I had one of those dreadful head-aches—I haven't had one since you've known me—when the only thing is to stay on the bed, as the slightest movement causes terrific pain and dizziness. Am O.K. now, though.

Thanks for your wire Saturday—particularly as I didn't get a letter—Friday's came this A.M. Poor dear sick darling. I'm so, so sorry for you! Wish I could be there to cheer you up.—Also, a bunch of clippings—fine, all of them—a column and a half in the *Boston Transcript* of Feb 5th, headed "O'Neill Ascends"—and *very* flattering— with N.Y. papers all quoted—Then another col. and 1/2 in the *Christian Science Monitor*. You are surely "it" these days. Next it will be the *Nation* and F.H. I suppose. Listen—get a *good* picture taken. Pirie MacDonald[1] does nice ones of men.

Well, I have a hunch we do not see one another for three weeks or so—just a hunch.

Shane is the dearest, jolliest, *lovingest*, little kid. You won't know him when you see him. I'm giving him one nursing of [Klimo?], now—

What did you think of Susan's play?[2] My impression was this—it's a corking idea, and has all her fine characterization, and delightful, ironic fun-making—some delicious comedy and witty lines—all the people would *play* well, and get the audience's interest.—and at the same time I get the feeling from it that she doesn't know her stage *technique* yet—(not in a long play, anyhow) that it isn't constructed as well as it should be—that it ought to be pulled apart, and put together again. Do you feel that? And *cut* a lot, too. I had to read it so hurriedly that perhaps this isn't a fair criticism.

It makes me sick to hear from outsiders that you are going to be "up" Monday, that you haven't the flu, just the grip, and so on—(Eddie wrote Susan). It's almost as bad as seeing for the first time in the newspapers what had been done to *Beyond*'s 2nd Act. I just feel as if I don't really know anything about you or your plays any more. Oceans of love. A.

[postscript across top of first page:] Remember—this cold weather how *very* important it is that you do not get cold! After being sick *PNEUMONIA!*

    1. MacDonald was exclusively a portrait photographer for men.
    2. Probably *The Inheritors*.

~⁀◯

83. **EO to AB** ALS 3 pp. (Stationery headed: Prince George Hotel, / Fifth Ave. & 28th Street New York) [Harvard 157]

Monday / [February 16, 1920]

Sweetheart: I have nothing to report except more physical trouble so this shall be brief. Expected to go to *Chris* rehearsal today. Woke up at 4 A.M. with the most terrible pain in my side, just over my heart. I thought first: "this is cases," and afterwards "it's pleurisy." The pain was so fierce whenever I moved that I couldn't get out of bed to the phone to call up Mama. I had to lie there until 11 A.M. when the chamber maid opened the door and I got her to go to Mama's room—about fifty feet away—and sound the S.O.S.

Well, it was a case of Doctor again, and he found that I didn't have pleurisy—only neuralgia of some nerve connected with the heart. This was cheering, but doesn't alter the fact that the pain was among the worst I've ever bumped into. It will return off and on for some time, he blandly confesses, unless I take an electric massage treatment.

I seem to be reaping the whirlwind of I know not what wind—unless it be the long nervous tension of this fall and early winter. At any rate both King and Aspell[1] unite in declaring that I am worn down to the last notch, without resisting power, open hospitably to all ills. Stripped, I look like a medical student's chart, every muscle outlined and every bone and bit of sinew. I weigh about 125, I estimate.

And I feel—well, only a drink makes me feel alive at all and drinks come about one every other day. Even the Old Man is "dry" as a bone these days—not even port wine any more.

I hate to write you these pathological letters, but what can I do? Life with me now consists in wondering: "What new ill is going to hit me tomorrow?"

Just think! I haven't been out of this hotel since the Friday after *Beyond* opened! And all "the honor and glory" passes by in the street below. And I haven't even the comfort of your presence! Life is a sweet thing, is it not?

But I've gotten to that stage now where nothing can hurt or anger me. Like the Old Woman in *Riders to the Sea*[2] I feel I've won to that spent calm where neither joy nor sorrow over anything exist.

Don't mind the above, Agnes. I'm sick, that's all. I want you—need you—and yet, with Shane, what is the use of my heart crying. It's all so impossible. I love you! Gene

1. Thomas Armstrong King and John Aspell, New York physicians.
2. Play (1904) by John Millington Synge; EO had seen this play performed by the Irish Players of Dublin's Abbey Theatre during their 1911 American tour.

84. **AB to EO** ALS 2 pp. ([Provincetown, Mass.]) [Harvard]

Tuesday afternoon— / [February 17, 1920]

Dearest Gene— I couldn't get a letter off this A.M. as I had an appointment with the dentist at 10:30. He ground out all that broken front tooth without killing the nerve—but nearly killing *me*— and is going to fill it tomorrow; of which I'll be mighty glad.

Thanks for letting me know about my N.Y. suggestions so soon.

It's cold as the very devil here—and last night the furnace went out—we nearly froze. Today is windy but nice.—I guess I don't really mind the cold as much as you do—

How is your mother? In one letter you said she had a touch of pneumonia, but later you speak of her coming down to your room. Give her my love.

Saw in Sunday's *Times* that *For the Defense* plays last seven times—and *Beyond* moves to the Criterion.[1] I'd awfully appreciate—if it isn't too much trouble—if you could let me know the latest dope on *Beyond*—and has the book been published yet?

You are being careful, and taking care of yourself, aren't you? Please *do*—for us! Shane and I send all our love— *Agnes*.

1. *Beyond the Horizon* moved to the Criterion Theatre and began evening performances on February 23, 1920.

85. **AB to EO** ALS 2 pp. ([Provincetown, Mass.]) [Harvard]

Wed. A.M. / [February 18, 1920]

Dearest Own— Your letter about the pain in your heart came this A.M.—in spite of a howling nor'easter. I am just worried sick about you. Would or *wouldn't* I be any help, if I were there?

Take the electric massage. But the most important thing of all, in your present condition, is to see that you don't get *worse cold and pneumonia*, when at *rehearsals*. You will be very, very careful, heart of mine, won't you!

Isn't it just as you always said it would be, though? Here you have this tremendous success—and can only be miserable! I don't wonder that you are a pessimist. Damn it, so am *I*!

My own, own dear baby, I long so to be with you! But it won't be so very long now.

I saw in the *Times* that *Chris* opens March 8th at Atlantic City. Do you have to be there for the opening? Will you let me know this in your next letter? *I* particularly want to know—

Shane is fine. By the way, will you ask your mother if she ever got a letter I wrote her? I suppose she is much better now, as you don't say anything to the contrary. Give her—and your father—my best love.

The idea of you lying, suffering and helpless in that room from 4 to 11 o'clock haunts me like a dreadful dream. Now dearest, do drop me a line every day, or get your mother to, otherwise I will be crazy. You cannot realize what a strain it is to have someone you love sick, so far away—I feel so helpless!

Goodby for the present, my love—I send you a long, long kiss. *Agnes.*

Mrs. Clark wishes me to send you her best wishes.

~⌒

86. **EO to AB** ALS 3 pp. (Stationery headed: Prince George Hotel, / Fifth Ave. & 28th Street New York) [Harvard]

Thursday. / [February 19, 1920]

My Own: You want all the dope on *Beyond*, eh? Well, the only reason I haven't written much about it is that all I have heard have been the bubble rumors of the Williams' office, one per day, soap bubbles which explode and mean nothing on the morrow. Williams applied to the Shuberts for a theatre for my play for a night run and Jake or Lee switched his cigar from one corner of his mouth to the other and said: "Nothin' doin'! It's got great notices but nix on the tragedy stuff until you show us the old box-office returns." That was a week ago. Since that time even the S. Bros are beginning to listen to reason. *Beyond* is really the talk of New York and is doing a wonderful matinee business. Williams has decided to [dish?] *For the Defense* for good. He is engaging a company for night performances and now hopes to get the Little Theatre, (Winthrop Ames' theatre), for *Beyond*.[1] Don't rely on this, however. It may only be another dream. Williams is putting up an awful battle and, with *Beyond* nearing the thousand mark per matinee, he ought to be able to force the Jews to give him a theatre.

As for interviews, I've been dodging them from all sides. I'm pinned down tomorrow: to the *Tribune* and *Theatre* magazine. I wish them luck! I feel so stupid and weak they will sure find me a prize bonehead.

Endless invitations to speak at dinners, this society and that society, Hunter College girls—all the silly rout. I get about twenty letters per mail—praise, sickening, deadening—but I feel so punk I couldn't be egotistic if I wanted to. And I feel too punk to attempt to answer the letters.

Mama and I have been combing the papers looking for some ad. for a place suitable for you to come down to. It's awful hard—you have no idea. It seems as if there's nothing worth while under 200 a month. Well, we'll find something!

I'm not convalescing very well. Can't eat or sleep and have terrible cough that tears me to pieces. Haven't been out of hotel yet. Doc. won't allow me to go to *Chris* rehearsals. I'm really in awfully bad shape—and can't seem to pick up.

I hope you'll want to go to Arizona or New Mexico. I'm liable to have to live out a more bitter ironic tragedy than I ever put in a play.[2]

But don't believe this! I'm morbid, I guess, these days and unhealthily prone to grabbing at the hopeless conclusion.

All my love to you and Shane! As soon as we can fix it, you'll come down, won't you? Gene.

1. *Beyond the Horizon* moved on March 9 from the Criterion to the Little Theatre, which was owned by Ames (1870–1937), a New York producer.
2. EO seems to be anticipating rehabilitation in the Southwest as a treatment for pulmonary disease, no doubt recalling his earlier stay in a sanitarium for tuberculosis in 1913, which is also the subject of *The Straw*.

87. **AB to EO** ALS 2 pp. ([Provincetown, Mass.]) [Harvard]

Thursday—and Friday— / [February 19–20, 1920]

My dearest Just a line. It's snowing—flakes, really, big as butter plates. *Damn* these continual blizzards!

And not a letter from you—or anyone—to cheer me up! The postman just passed provokingly by.

Wasn't that a nice note from Nina Jones? Which of Shane's photos do you think would be nicest to send her?

Did you know I had made a *dress*? Out of that brown corduroy. It looks pretty—rather medieval in effect, with a cord round the waist and a quaint neck.

Also, I had the suit fixed—or did I tell you. And a little dressmaker has come here for four afternoons—$1.00 an afternoon—during which time she has helped me fix over the dresses and the black satin [suit] that your mother gave me. Thought I might as well get them done when you were away.

How would it be to send you another box of stuff to eat. *Let me know*!!!

Poor darling. I hope so that you are feeling better. You don't know how I sympathize with you.—I don't *dare* hope you'll really get back. I was so disappointed before.

Give my love to your folks—and remember me to any of the old crowd you see. And all the love in the world to you—from Shane Rudraighe and me—

Your $\left\{ \begin{array}{l} \text{loving} \\ \text{lonely} \end{array} \right.$ *Agnes*.

Now would be a good time to drink lots of malted milk. Won't you?

∽

88. **AB to EO** ALS 2 pp. ([Provincetown, Mass.]) [Harvard]

Saturday / [February 21, 1920]
. . . After the postman has gone by.

No letter! You remember, don't you, how *we* used to watch for mail? An amusing little game. . . . And I've just seen his blue uniform—weighed down with such a heavy mail-bag, too—go by, on up the street.

You only write every other day now?—have, all week. Well, I suppose it does become tiresome. And of course, it doesn't make *any* difference to me—not the *slightest!* Especially now that you've been sick I'm *so* much easier when I don't hear!

And Saturday's such a nice day not to get a letter, too—makes Sunday all the more pleasant! *Agnes*

∽

89. **EO to AB** ALS 4 pp. (Stationery headed: Prince George Hotel, / Fifth Ave. & 28th Street New York) [Harvard]

Saturday. / [February 21, 1920]

My Own: My cough continues bad although Aspell, after an extensive examination, has assured me it is a bronchial after-gift of the Flu and has nothing to do with my lungs. But it sure makes me feel rotten, nevertheless. However, no matter what, I've got to get out to *Chris* rehearsal on Monday—and will.

Tremendous snow storm here today and last night. Wrote you note yesterday but suppose you won't get it until after this. No word from you today. The P'town mail ought to be investigated. I can't understand why you say: "haven't heard in two days". There's only been one day in the past seven I haven't written. I wrote at length regarding *Beyond* two days ago. The royalties are the only thing I didn't mention. As they only amount to about a hundred a week for now it will take seven weeks more on a matinee basis before I get a cent. So why mention? My only hopes for a quick return is a night run.

Deem & Fisk[1] visited me last night for an hour or so—after which they went off to "see the [News] of Neurasthenia." They had nothing new to tell. Fisk has had the Flu, too, and looks as pale and drawn as I do.

I'm afraid to come home to you—I look such a skinny wreck!

Yesterday was interviewed by Madell[2] of *The Tribune*. You'll see it in tomorrow's paper, via Susan. I hope I won't sound as stupid and sick as I felt.

Today a lady came from *The Theatre Magazine*. I had to see her as she's been pestering me for weeks. I felt punk and pessimistic and she insisted on my divulging my philosophy of life. I gave it to her as bitter and poisonous as I could. You'll laugh when you see it. I probably said ten million things I'll be sorry for, but I thought if she was looking for ["pep"?] I'd sure give it to her. She took leave of me by saying she was so afraid she would find me a disappointment to look at after reading my plays. "But I'm not! They're all there—in your eyes" she remarked enthusiastically. So be prepared to read of "my great, sad eyes." Toward the end they must have been great pools of grief—I was wondering when in hell she was going away and leave me to cough in peace![3]

Had a very nice note of praise from St. John Ervine last night.[4] He was "proud to know the one distinctive American playwright was of Irish blood". It was really a corking little note and damn nice of him to write it. He went to see *Beyond* on Wednesday.

Wait till the movie rights of *Beyond* sell—then we'll have some cash!

I'm still marooned in the house, must get out Monday. Will try and get to P'town some time next week. If I hadn't lost this time—! It's up to Tyler.

Bye bye for this time and all my love to you and Shane. I'm so lonely and sick I'm tired of mentioning it.   Gene.

P.S. Tell Susan Tyler has been out of town all last week with the Hayes show in Boston and Arliss[5] in a new Tarkington play somewhere else. He's expected back tomorrow and I'll bring her script to him Monday. I like her play tremendously and think it has fine chance with him—or any one else.

1. Charles Demuth and Edward Fisk.
2. Probably EO's error for Philip Mindil, whose "Behind the Scenes" was published in the *New York Tribune* on February 22, 1920. It is reprinted in *Conversations with Eugene O'Neill*, ed. Mark W. Estrin (Jackson: University Press of Mississippi, 1990), 3–5.
3. See Alta M. Coleman, "Personality Portraits: No. 3, Eugene O'Neill," *Theatre Magazine,* April 1920.
4. Irish playwright (1883–1971), associated with the Abbey Theatre.
5. George Arliss (1868–1946), prominent English actor, appeared in Tarkington's *Poledkin.*

~~)

90. **AB to EO** ALS 2 pp. (Provincetown, Mass.) [Harvard]

Monday— / [February 23, 1920]

My own Beloved— Your letter this A.M. sounded more like *you*—dearest. As if you
were feeling better.

I laughed so at your description of the Lady Interviewer! And then Susan came in
and brought your *Trib.* interview—and I had to laugh at myself. I got into such a rage
at him describing you as a tall—sad eyed—delicate—person! Wish he could see you
swimming! I was raving around in the most indignant way. And then Susan said
"Now I'm going to make you *jealous*!" —and produced a page of Blonde Beauties,
whereon were most ravishing portraits of Misses MacKellar and Hayes. She *is* pretty!
(Helen Mac), and Miss Hayes also.—and of course the green-eyed demon began
gnawing, while I visualized Miss MacK. coming to cheer you up in your lonely sick
room, and so on. Then I read Susan the part of your letter describing how you gloomed
to the Lady Interviewer and I got madder than ever. "The idea! Why, Susan, all these
women will imagine Gene is a poor, sad creature, with a dreadful home life, and
they'll all be dying to make his lot more easy. Dammit!" It was funny!

Susan is writing a one-act play about a *bed-bug!* (Jig, it seems, found one.)

I never got any letter written Friday. *Did* you write one? Do you know what I do?
I write you long long letters, and put them away under the blotting paper, and the next
day I tear them up! I never think I'm going to tear them up when I write them of course,
but just before it's time to mail them I get a curious feeling—a sort of Yogi feeling—
"Oh! What *is* the sense!" And into the fire they go! *(I don't mean they are horrid!)*

Heart's beloved, I'm hoping so you can come back this week. I'll take good care
of you. It will do you good to see Shane. He is the most perfect, adorable bunch of
small humanity imaginable.

Lovingly yours *Agnes.*

Do you know it's seven *(7)* weeks yesterday!

~~)

91. **AB to EO** ALS 2 pp. ([Provincetown, Mass.]) [Harvard]

Tuesday. / [February 24, 1920]

Dearest— There have been a great many clippings about *Beyond* from all over the
country. —do you want them, or will you wait until you get back? We will need at
least *two* scrap-books!

The *Nation* this week—(Feb. 21st) has a fine review of *Beyond*—the best yet.

Did you read it? One could hardly ask more than the opening sentence, and then, I particularly liked the ending—where he [takes?] up the bum scenery—

Wonder if the *New Republic* has anything?[1] Haven't seen it for two weeks.

It was fine about St. John Ervine. He must be a decent sort.

I think you could get a good photo taken here. [Stitt?] only charged $6.00 for twelve of those of Shane & me (4 different poses). Don't you think that is cheap? In this last *Vanity Fair*— or is it *Vogue*?—there is a photo on the "Their Leisure Hours" page of Dunsany and a very homely wife. Did you see it? If they want yours, and they will, if you haven't a decent one of yourself, give them this one of both of us (in bathing suits) for that page— *Don't* give them a *bum* one of yourself!

Goodby, sweetheart   Your own wife,   *Agnes.*

1. Lola Ridge considered the play good but not great in her *New Republic* review, January 5, 1921, pp. 173–74.

92. **AB to EO** ALS 3 pp. (Provincetown, Mass.) [Harvard]

Tuesday evening— / [February 24, 1920]

My own—   This afternoon I got a letter from you written *Saturday*—after getting one yesterday, written Sunday! The mails must be topsy-turvy still. Thanks, angel, for writing so faithfully when you were ill.

Are you about yet? Wish you could "convales[ce]" up here—I'd feed you up, all right!

Up at Jig 'n Susan's this afternoon—and S. and I were much excited over the interview with Mr. John D. Williams—in the *Trib*. We have decided that he is a most intriguing and handsome young man! Susan wants *him* to see her play! And I am quite looking forward to some day meeting him.—the mixture of Irish and Puritan sounds amusing!

Seriously, I do believe that Susan's play would stand a better chance with Williams than with Tyler. The play struck me as being just a bit "cluttered" at present, and the ideas and dialogue that clutter it would prove good fun to Williams, while with Tyler they might prove a serious stumbling-block to seeing the real merits of the play. I perhaps influenced Susan into thinking W. would be even better than T.—and perhaps I shouldn't have done so—but—*some*how— I have me doubts about T. caring much about it.

Well, *you* are quite dragging Williams into the lime lights, aren't you? Of course they interviewed him because he produced *Beyond*. And on the next page—Louise Closser Hale,[1] in *Beyond*, gives *her* views. *When* are they going to interview *you*?

Do be a dear angel, and tell me all the dope about *Beyond*. I'm just dying to know, and you've never told me beans—well I don't believe you read my letters anyhow, you never say anything about anything I say in them. I guess I write them too long, don't I?

Wednesday A.M. / [February 25, 1920]

No letter, so guess you didn't write Monday,—don't blame you if it was your first day up! But if you are writing, hope I get 'em all, as they mean so much.

I'm tackling *another* story—I just love to work. I think my "Egotist" story is pretty good— for me![2]

Love to your father and mother, and a million kisses and hugs to you, darling one. *Agnes.*

1. Louise Closser Hale (1872–1933), who played Mrs. Atkins in *Beyond the Horizon,* was a well-known actress and wrote novels about theatrical life.
2. Her story, retitled as "The Snob," was published in the June 1921 issue of *Smart Set.*

93. **EO to AB** ALS 6 pp. (Stationery headed: Prince George Hotel, / Fifth Ave. & 28th Street / New York) [Harvard]

Wednesday / [February 25, 1920]

Own Sweetheart: Forgive me for not writing yesterday. One reason for my not doing so was the neuralgia in my chest would start in raising hell every so often and, besides, although I'm still tied down to the room there's always something over the phone to keep me on the hop.

Stanhope had me on the wire for a long talk, principally about Scotty. To come down to cases, Scotty is to be fired! No, not for drinking or any sort of misbehavior but just because he hasn't made good. He hasn't the instinct for the stage, so Stanhope says. They've given him every chance to pick up but he just simply can't make it. In his scene with Corrigan at the end of Scene One—very important, if you'll remember—Scotty has failed absolutely to "hold up." Corrigan, of course, is wild as he can't carry the whole burden of the two parts himself.

The damnable part of the whole business is that they've been afraid to fire Scotty on account of his being my choice, as they thought. On the other hand, Scotty has lost his old job and is very much up against it and was relying on this to save his life. But there is more than that to it. He's been so proud of playing the part, he's had such a genuine enthusiasm and confidence in himself, that this throw down is due to break him all up. There isn't even a smaller part for him as all the cast is engaged and each one has made good.

But you see what I mean by its getting me in wrong, can't you? The management cursing me for foisting a bum actor on them, Scotty probably thinking by now that I could save his skin if I wanted to—Well, never again! No more of that friendship game in business!

Williams has picked Helen Freeman[1] to play Ruth when *Beyond* goes on at nights. As I've never seen her work, I pass judgment until I do. It's very hard to get any one at this stage of the season. The receipts for three matinees week before last were $2,600. As the capacity of the Morosco is $1,700 for one performance at 3.50 prices and as *Beyond* is playing 2.75 you'll see that's pretty fine. Friday matinees for the past two weeks have been well over $1,000—which means practically capacity. What it will do when it goes on regularly, the devil alone knows.

Worry not and gnash not your teeth over the "blond beauties." They come not, no, not one, to sit beside my couch. Helen MacK. has written me several letters of commiseration over my illness, but that is all. As in private life she is Mrs. MacQuarrie, and I know her husband[2]—a corking big fine chap that I don't blame her for being so much in love with, I hardly think her kind letters can be regarded jealously—even by one as green-eyed as Agnes O'Neill. (You will remember I spoke of meeting MacQuarrie at rehearsals and of how much I liked him. At that time I suspicioned that he was Helen's lover, or, more conventionally, her intended; but it turned out that the two Canadian Scots were quite prosaically married, even as you and I.)

If you saw me now you'd believe the interviewer's "sad-eyed & delicate." I look like a ghost who is all eyes. The Flu simply knocked hell out of me.

I wouldn't worry about their believing I'm sad because of an unhappy home life. They're much more liable to guess the truth—that it's being away from my home that makes me sad.

Tell Susan her script is now at Tyler's office awaiting his first breathing spell. It's a bad time for quick action from him. He's made three new productions in the last ten days—Phil Moeller's play[3] among them—and is busy as a bird dog with fleas. If she had sent it to me two weeks before she did—

Helen Hayes in *Bab*[4] in Boston seems to have made a big hit. Rehearsals for *The Straw* are to start up there very shortly.

Did you see Lewisohn's criticism in *The Nation*? A corker, the best I have received.

The book of *Beyond* is held up by trouble with the printers. Liveright is tearing his hair but hopes to have it out within a week.

Am reading *Jurgen*[5]—a wonderful, beautiful book! The boneheads who suppressed it ought to be hung! The Lady Interviewer of the *Theatre Magazine* loaned it to me—said that Cabell and I had the same feeling behind our writing. At any rate, I'm "nuts" about *Jurgen*. It doesn't sound American a bit—reads more like Anatole France than any one. I wish you could read it but it can't be got anymore except at $25.00 a copy when you buy it on the sly, like booze.

The L.I. also loaned me another book—short stories of the Malays—by some Englishman who died unsung,[6] the book being now out of print. It is called *The Further Side of Silence*. Some title, eh? I haven't read them yet.

Well, this is some letter for you! Bye'bye, My Own, and a long kiss! The date of my return now depends first on the old Doc. The neuralgia still gives me hell at night when I lie down but my cough seems much better. Well, cheer up, pretty soon I'll have had every thing and then I'll have to get well.

All my love to you & Shane! Be patient with me! I'm doing my best to get well and back to you. I'm so lonely and unhappy here! Gene

1. Freeman, who later acted in the *S.S. Glencairn* plays (1924), was on the original managerial board of the Theatre Guild.
2. George D. MacQuarrie was a successful Broadway actor.
3. *Sophie*, which opened on March 2, 1920.
4. Play by Edward Childs Carpenter (1872–1950).
5. Novel (1919) by James Branch Cabell (1879–1958).
6. Book (1916) by Sir Hugh Charles Clifford (1866–1941).

94. **AB to EO** ALS 4 pp. ([Provincetown, Mass.]) [Harvard]

Thursday, Feb. 26th [1920]

Dear Gene— Waited until this morning to write, thinking, as no letter came from you yesterday, there might be one on the morning mail. But "nothing doing!" Suppose you didn't bother to write Tuesday—well, honestly, I think—oh, what's the use of what I think! You say you have attained the spent calm of the old woman in *Riders to the Sea*—Well, I have sensed that in your letters for some time—and your absence of them. What is the matter? Has Louise[1] been writing you—congratulations?

At all events, it is very obvious that your feeling toward me has changed. I was reading over some of your old letters last night, and comparing them to the ones you write now. *Quite* a difference! Well, I knew success would do *something*! Your sickness, if you really cared, would make you need and want me more, instead [of], as seems to have happened, less. Well, don't bother—I certainly don't intend to hang round your neck. Reproaches are odious things, and this is the last letter in which I shall touch upon anything so out of date as our feelings for one another—like you, I shall stereotype a beginning and farewell—"Dearest Gene—" and "All my love!" And the content shall be of the least romantic—in fact, the Income Tax will, I surmise, be the subject of my next!

Had Dr. Hiebert yesterday, as I was sick—had been feeling rotten for a couple of days, and finally gave in. He gave me medicine and is coming today—Mrs. Clark has put a couch in the front room, and I lie there, instead of going to bed in the back room where Shane sleeps. He seems to think perhaps I am going to be unwell.—anyhow, I have a good deal of pain, and nausea. From the taste, ergot is what he is giving me.

As soon as I am all right, I'm going to pay a visit at Pt. P. and if I am all right, may leave about the 3rd of March—so if you are not in Atlantic City, will have an hour or so's visit. Mother is anxious to have me come, and I believe a change would do me good—I don't see that there can be any chance of your coming up, with *Chris* going on, and I no longer have the inner serenity that your letters used to give me—the serenity that made solitude beautiful.

Well, old dear, au revoir—and don't be too unhappy about life—there's still the South Seas! And I have—not even that! With a kiss— *Agnes.*

I asked Hiebert about your pain. He says that almost *invariably* occurs after influenza cases. So don't worry.

1. Louise Bryant (1890–1936), novelist, short-story writer, and member of the Provincetown Players, had an affair with EO in 1918, just before EO met AB. She was married to writer and political activist John Reed (1887–1920).

∽∘

95. **AB to EO** ALS 3 pp. ([Provincetown, Mass.]) [Harvard]

Friday / [February 27, 1920]

Dearest Gene— The Dr. was here yesterday—gave me more pills—nothing has happened yet, and now he says it *may* be a light "flu" attack. I can't see how he thinks it though. —I have no sign of a cold in my head or chest. But awful pain in my arms and legs—more like nerve-pains, not in the joints. But this A.M. I am feeling all O.K. again. Mrs. Clark has gone off to her Friday work, and am alone here.

The Dr. also gave me much dope on the income tax. He sent in for a copy for me. I'll have to try and dope it out from the book where you have our "income"—What your father gave you don't count; also, any expences, (business), etc. are to be deducted, so I will deduct trips to N.Y. to see managers, they are expences. (*Two* last spring!)—And $250 off for every child. It all has to be in by Monday, or $5.00 a day fine.

I hope *you* are much better. I haven't had *one word* from you since a letter written *Monday*—and it's Friday! Thought sure there would be something this A.M.!

Much much love *Agnes.* xxxxx *(kisses!)* ooooo (Hugs!)

∽∘

96. **EO to AB** ALS 3 pp. (Stationery headed: Prince George Hotel, / Fifth Ave. & 28th Street New York) [Virginia]

Feb. 27, 1920

My Own: Failed to write you yesterday because, to tell the truth, I was too "pickled" to write anyone. Whereon hangs a tale, and this is it. Wednesday night I was frightfully nervous. Life cooped up in these hotel rooms, feeling rotten anyway, has been steadily getting my goat and I was due to crack. Well, Wednesday night the two female pests of the Western World, my cousins,[1] called. I had no chance to get out of the way. Well, after an hour of them I felt that I must shriek, go mad, jump out of the window—or get out of the hotel. I grabbed my hat and coat and set out for the Hell Hole where I found a big "bust" of the "rough-necks" just starting. I was welcomed as a brother. They had whiskey—of a kind!—and I was soon as full as a tick. I spent the night as a bed-mate of the First Division doughboy, Chuck, and returned home last night.

The funniest part of all is that on this jamboree I lost my neuralgia and also my cough. I feel 100% better—except for my nerves which are somewhat tattered as an after effect. But what would any doctor say was the cause of my being cured of my cough and the pain in my chest, I wonder, after all medicines had failed. Alcoholic Christian Science is my only dope!

Am going to *Chris* rehearsal tomorrow. The Flu and I are now quits and I can get back on the job again.

Yes, I'll have to go to Atlantic City. The dress rehearsal is to be there. Also three performances. I've asked Tyler and he says it's imperative for me to be there. Why do you ask about this so particularly? Is there any chance of your coming down to Point Pleasant and being able to make the show at A.C. from there? It's a great scheme if it can be worked.

Honestly, Agnes, there's no chance I can make out of getting any place here. We have had Mrs. Phillips, the Connors, all our friends on the trail. Mama has also followed up all the newspaper ads. that sounded good. There seems to be nothing under 200 a month—and all, without exception, won't rent unless you lease until Oct. 1st. New York is jammed with people, an unprecedented situation, and every hotel is booking their rooms 3 weeks in advance.

I enclose the check for 450.00. It was delayed in transit by Madden. Shove it in and send me a few blank checks, will you? The ones I had I cashed for a total of sixty-four dollars—not so bad for seven weeks.

I'm unhappy as hell and my whole being is one big ache of loneliness for you. Never again! No more separations, My Own! I've learned my lesson. Life without you is—impossible! Well, one way or another, the trial will soon be over. All my love to you and Shane.   Eugene

    1.   Agnes and Lillian Brennan.

～◡

97. **AB to EO** ALS 2 pp. ([Provincetown, Mass.]) [Harvard]

Saturday / [February 28, 1920]

Dearest Gene— Your long and interesting letter arrived yesterday afternoon, and I was surely glad to get it. I am really awfully sorry about Scotty. Perhaps he is *too* real—makes the others appear too much as stage-sailors. He certainly was corking in your short plays, and it seems very queer he has fallen down in this.

I saw Helen Freeman in *John Ferguson*,[1] and didn't care for her acting—although she was pretty good in the hysterical scene.—she seemed awfully *artificial* to me. She is very very handsome—on the stage, anyway.

Are you "out" yet? Will you answer the following, as it's *quite important to me to know*.

1. Are you going to Atlantic City, and *on what date*?
2. Is *Chris* scheduled definitely for New York, and what date.
3. Will you have to remain for N.Y. opening *(Important)*
4. How long will you have to remain in A.C. if you go?

If *Chris* opens there on the 8th, that is a week from Monday,—quite soon!—and if you are to come back at once, I want to know—or if you are to stay!—so I can arrange accordingly.

We have just enough coke to last till next *Wed.* Then there is neither coal, coke, or wood to be had in town—nothing but kerosene and charcoal. The freight trains are all held up, and they have no idea of when they will get in.

I am feeling all right again—Do be careful of yourself, dear, won't you.

No time for more, if I'm to get the noon mail.

Much love, and a long kiss! A.

1. A drama by St. John Ervine, opened May 13, 1919.

98. **AB to EO** AL 4 pp. ([Provincetown, Mass.]) [Harvard]

Saturday night. / [February 28, 1920]

Dearest Gene— I doubt if I've brains enough to write you a decent letter! And I'm sure I've got good grounds for divorce! Any man that goes off and leaves the income tax to his poor wife—! Well, it's all off now, signed and sworn to—There will be no tax to pay, because, deducting $500 for me, $250 for Shane—and $2,000 for you. (There you have our respective values!) there was a good deal less than nothing left. Honestly, it's awfully complicated! If you've had in cash, during the year, $2,000 or over, you've *got to fill in blank and send*, no matter what you deduct. I deducted $300 expences from your "business" (N.Y. trips 3)—and then the $750, (wife and child).

Well,—*honey*—you found the real cure, did you? Terry and I were wondering if a few good drinks wouldn't help. It surely must have been *fierce* in that hotel, these weeks. The spree will do you more good than anything—just as long as you didn't get worse cold. Did you? You are a wild one, to go off like that—when you're supposed to stay in.

Glad you sent the check, as we are getting *very low*—in fact, I've put off several

bills on that account,—*not counting* your $65, there is about $150.00 in the bank—
which would leave less than $100.—It is appalling, isn't it?—about $200 a month, as
near as I can figure out. And I've been "setting" a "cheap" table too. There's $40. rent,
$72 wages—$46 coal—well, it's all down in the check book. Honestly, Gene, it almost frightens me! I feel awfully blue about it really,—but—well—

$9.00	wages	$5	cash (drugstore, papers, etc.)
5	rent per week	15	table (for 3, $5 each—
6	food	20	
$20.	⟶	20	
		$40.00 a week already!	

There—this has spoiled my letter to you! And I wanted to write a nice one—now
I feel too blue. I didn't know it was so much!)

Am feeling better—but still rather rocky. I guess I better stay right where I am—
so the Doc. says. Will you let me know how soon after the 8th you will be back?
Soon?

Anyway, I wouldn't want to see *Beyond*—even if I were in town. Read the "story"
of it in the *Trib*.—with the curtain going down on "God Damn You!" All that splendid
last scene—all Robert's speech, which meant so much—no, I believe I prefer to read
it! I can't tell you how much I am looking forward to seeing the[1] book—and how
proud—happy—amazed—to think so fine a thing should be dedicated "To Agnes."
There are some things that bring a lasting happiness into one's life—*that* is one of
them—perhaps you cannot see how something that may appear relatively unimportant is so much to me. But it is.

Alice Ullmann wants me to go to a "church-supper" Wednesday night. I have
accepted but—am going to be taken suddenly ill. After coming in *social* contact with
people—I usually find I'm very irritated with myself. And with them.

Shane is getting to look just like Lord Byron. Sometimes I say: "Do you know
you have a *very* wonderful father?"—and he always gives a big grin. He's an imp—
and a delight.

Goodby, darling! I'm glad you *do* miss me—after all. I thought you didn't anymore. But you couldn't as much as I do *you*. *Your Own*—

1. The word "our" was crossed out and replaced by "the."

99. **AB to EO** ALS 2 pp. ([Provincetown, Mass.]) [Harvard]

Monday night / [March 1?, 1920]

Dearest— I was just going to write to you, when Susan came in—and then Mrs.
[Winston?][1]—and so it's too late now for more than a line, if I'm to mail this before

seven. So don't count this as a letter—it's just to let you know everything here is fine, that I went to the Doctor's, & he said, all o.k.—but most of all I guess I'm writing it because I want to say *something* to you somehow. I'm missing you terribly. But I still feel that we are *together*, my own, my darling— *Agnes*—

    1. Possibly Mrs. Norman Winston, wife of a shoe manufacturer who had contributed to the Provincetown Players.

～◞

100. **EO to AB** WIRE, addressed to Provincetown, Mass. (New York) [Yale]

MAR 1ST 1920

EXCUSE NOT WRITING ALL UPSET FATHER HAD STROKE VERY SERIOUS YOUR LETTER WORRIES ME ARE YOU ILL WIRE.   EUGENE

～◞

101. **EO to AB** ALS 2 pp. (Stationery headed: Prince George Hotel, / Fifth Ave. & 28th Street / New York) [Harvard]

Monday / [March 1, 1920]

Own Dearest: Well, we've been having one hell of an awful time at home here for the past forty-eight hours! Not one whit of sleep in all that time for yours truly. Papa's condition, which had seemed to be improving, suddenly took a bad turn for the worse. The night before last he was on the very fringe of death, following another slight stroke. We had Doctor Aspell in at once and he just managed to keep life in Papa. Then he told Mama and me the truth. Papa, it seems, is doomed. He has a growth in the intestines which is bound sooner or later to prove fatal. It ought to be operated on at once but this is impossible in his case as his heart is so bad he would die at the first sniff of ether.

And Mama and I have to go around nursing him, watching his every movement, and pretending to kid him and cheer him up! Can you imagine it? And I've also had to hold sessions with Stanhope on *Chris* every morning, ten to 11.30, as I can't leave the hotel to go to rehearsals. As if I gave a damn about *Chris* or any other play now!

To have this happen just at the time when the Old Man and I were getting to be such good pals!

I'm not going to write any more. I'm all broken up and begin to cry every time the meaning of it all dawns on me.

It can't be more than a little over a week now before I'll see you. I'll send detailed dope on *Chris* as soon as I see Tyler.

Be brave, My Own! This is a bad bit of road for us both but we have our love and we'll soon be together to fight back to back again.

All my love! Gene.

P.S. Sent you wire this noon.

[across top of first page:] P.S. Did you receive special with check?

~⁓

102. **EO to AB** ALS 3 pp. (Stationery headed: Prince George Hotel, / Fifth Ave. & 28th Street / New York) [Harvard]

Tuesday night / [March 2, 1920] / (just before bed)

My Own: Your letter about the income tax reached me when I got home for dinner. The Old Man was much better today seemingly so I went to *Chris* rehearsal. Will say nothing about it because in my present state of depression all things look bad. Your letter was such a cheer-up to read, Old Sweetheart; and how I want to have you with me again!

It may be much sooner than you think, too. I'm trying hard to get out of the A.C. trip. If they don't absolutely hold me to it I may be able to get back to you end of this week. Don't count on it, though; but do believe I'll set sail for P'town the first second I can—and how gladly! I need you so in this sorrowful time which should be so glad.

Papa is all gone. It's horrible to see him fade from day to day. God, it's awful! Of, course, he has a chance of living quite a while yet—to die by inches and in pain all the time!

I'll be back to you to tell you all about everything—to arrange everything for the immediate future with you—the first second I can. Oh, My Own, I love and need you so!

And don't worry about the damn money. We can count on enough in the future to keep us going at present rate for a while, at least.

God! God! How I need you now, and how impossible it is to try and bear up under all this without you! But I'll see you soon again—cry in your arms—so soon now! I've been tempted to desert the ship, to go back to you so many times, but I know I wouldn't be the man you love—and respect—(in some things, anyway)—if I didn't "come clean" with my present obligations.

All my love! Gene.

~⁓

103. **AB to EO** WIRE, addressed to Prince George Hotel, New York (Provincetown, Mass.) [Yale]

MAR 2 1920

TELEGRAM JUST RECEIVED VERY WELL NOW SO SORRY ABOUT YOUR
FATHER MUCH LOVE   AGNES

◦

104. **AB to EO** ALS 4 pp. ([Provincetown, Mass.]) [Harvard]

Tuesday. / [March 2, 1920]

Dearest Gene,   I am so terribly sorry to hear about your father. From what you said in
the wire—(which came this A.M. by the way, although sent yesterday at one o'clock!—)
it sounds very serious. I am so sorry for your poor mother. But I am hoping, as is so
often the case in "strokes" that it isn't nearly as bad as it seems at first. By tomorrow
I hope you'll have written details. If you think I should come down, perhaps you can
get a room at the Hotel Rutledge, right near you. I hear you can—nice ones. I am all
right now—feel very well. I explained in my letters what was wrong. Didn't you get
them?

I wish there was something I could do. But there isn't, is there. Give my very best
love to your mother. All my love to yourself. *Agnes*.

◦

105. **AB to EO** AL 5 pp. ([Provincetown, Mass.]) [Harvard]

Wednes. night— / [March 3?, 1920]

You dear silly Nut!   Where did you get the idea that I am dissatisfied, and think you
are giving me a dirty deal! You must have been delirious—dreaming! Why, I only
wrote that long letter, with the plan for coming to N.Y. because I'd gathered from
your letters that you *wanted* me! And you thought it was dissatisfaction! Shows how
people can misunderstand.

As a matter of fact, I *dreaded* going, and was relieved when you wrote not to try
it. I wanted to see *you*—don't misunderstand *that*—but the idea of dragging Shane—
through those infected stations, and trains, and then all the *fuss* of having him there—
it is *not* my idea of a good time. Of course, I'd like to see the plays, but I will sometime, that's sure.

All I wanted was *you*—you nut!—there, or here! I've really loved P'town this
winter, and from all I hear of N.Y. it is a *very* rotten place to be in.

And as for saying I didn't realize how sick you were! Did you read my *letters*?
Did you get my *wire*? I simply suffered *tortures*—*you* don't know anything about it!
When I realized you were all right—better—I felt ashamed of having been so silly

and cut out the over-solicitous stuff, because I thought maybe it annoyed you—you didn't write, anyway, as if you liked it much. I filled my letters with warnings about not taking cold, etc., and what to do, and with how much I loved you and how worried I was, and as in your replies you ignored all I said, naturally I thought it was nothing to you—probably a bore! But I probably *did* reproach you—not much, however!—about not letting me know about *Beyond*—I know so little Gene dear, and I love the play so; I don't know yet if it's going on evenings has ever been discussed even! Bennett closes in *For the Defense*—*Beyond* moves—I see all this in the papers—and not a whisper from you of what the plans are—though you must know *something*! Also, you've never *breathed a word* about what the author's royalties are adding up to per week (although you must know that, too) and you must realize that I am interested in knowing how soon the $1,000 advance will be paid off. You know, don't you, that you haven't told me any of this?

However, dearest, these weren't reproaches, only inquiries, and I thank you from the bottom of my heart for having so faithfully written—it has made me happy, both for your letters, and because I realized you must really love me to write so faithfully,—and that's all I want—your love.

I'll deposit the $450. It is perfectly appalling how the money goes. I am being as careful as I can, though.

Susan was here today—I think she'd like to hear from you about if T. got her play. She seems awfully anxious about it. I told her how perfectly rotten you were feeling, and how you coughed, etc., and she was saying how nice it would be for you if we could all go to Bermuda after *Chris* got playing good, for a month anyway, and you could lie around on the beach in the sun and get well. Steeles write entrancing letters about it. You really ought to do something to get in good shape again. I'm worried sick about you—the cough and sweats sound so dreadful—and your lungs are *not* strong. You poor, poor dear baby. I wish I could take care of you!

Anyhow, honey-beloved, if the Dr. don't think you are taking a chance, come up as soon as you can, and I'll try for a week to get you better—really nurse you. But for *God's sake*, avoid getting cold on the way up—you usually do—

I'm working—but guess I told you. I think you'll like the last act of *Now I Ask You*—I enclose a letter—it's all right, isn't it to open them when I see they are from a club, or something? I wouldn't open personal ones.

Dearest, do take care of yourself. (There I go again!) But *do*.

All the love in the world, *Your own*.

106. **AB to EO** ALS 2 pp. ([Provincetown, Mass.]) [Harvard]

Thursday, March 4th '20.

Dearest Heart— There is no use my telling you how badly I feel about your father; you know. And believe me, dear, I appreciate fully how you are affected by it—you, and your mother, too. It's something one can't talk about. Some day, my own, I suppose I go through the same thing, and then I will have your understanding, as you have mine, now.

Personally, I am deeply shocked and upset by your father's illness. He seemed such a wonderful, strong, old man—and he was so kind to me—and I had often thought of he and Shane together—ah, dearest, maybe it isn't as bad as they think. Poor old man! We *must* arrange for him to see something of Shane. Shane's such a dear he'd almost make anybody well!

Anyhow—though it's a poor consolation in the face of sickness and suffering—you can certainly boast that you've given your father a *real* happiness—a tremendous gift—in your success, and in that feeling that has grown so between you the last year or so—that you love one another—that you are his *son*, of whom he can be proud as any father in the whole world—and that means so much to him particularly. Love to your mother—and you dearest.   A.

107. **EO to AB** ALS 1 p. (Provincetown, Mass.) [Harvard]

Friday—10 P.M. / [April 23, 1920]

Own Sweetheart: Have just finished typing my stint for tonight[1] and am thinking desolately of the lonely, cold bed that must act as set for the finale of this misbegotten day. Fifine is still messing about in the kitchen. She was just in to tell me how much she misses Shane. I, too, miss him—I do when I'm away from him. I'm like that—and above all I miss you, My Own! The flat is so still. It seems to lack all the life of a home now. The dryad had departed the tree and autumn is here, not spring.

We must swear off petty moods, you and I. They *are* petty—and so stupid! We who love so much—we ought to be ashamed of ourselves! Isn't it so? Last night is a case in point. When the snivelling little irritations were swept away, how glorious and fine and sweet and true it all was! I look back to it now and have a great feeling of gratitude that we got the better of our little tempers and came down to bed rock again. Really, our occasional "spats" should "brighten the corner where we are" instead of throwing shadows. Where is our sense of humor when we take such trifles with so great a long face? If we stopped to think a moment we should laugh whole gales. For we are extremely ridiculous at such moments—aren't we? Confess!

I hope you will be met by Jim. I sent wires to both Edith[2] and my mother. I also hope the trip doesn't prove too much for you. If I had had any idea of how much of a labor it would be I would have howled for you to wait until I could go with you. I didn't realize, honestly, until you turned up at the train with those two heavy bags. Well, we won't let it happen again. I'm sorry if I seemed unfeeling about it. I just simply didn't realize and you seemed so sure of yourself in talking of it. Forgive me, won't you, Dearest! All my love and a good-night kiss to you and Shane! I'm hoping so you're both peacefully asleep on the boat by now.

Eugene O'Neill in Provincetown, early 1920s. Photographer unknown. Yale Collection of American Literature, Beinecke Rare Book and Manuscript Library.

Good-night, My Own, My Own!   Gene.

1.   EO was working on *Gold*, a full-length version of *Where the Cross Is Made*, which itself was adapted from a story AB had sketched, "The Captain's Walk," probably the only instance where her writing was directly used in his.

2.   Either Edith Unger, who is otherwise unidentified, or Edith Adams, a friend who lived in New York City, and on whom (AB says) Hutchins Hapgood modeled his leading character in *The Anarchist Woman*.

~~⌒

108. **AB to EO** ALS 3 pp. (En route [to New York from Provincetown]) [Harvard]

En route—nearly at Newport
April 24th 1920

My dearest— Just a few lines, as I'm too dead tired to write the long letter I'd *like* to,—really, this is just to tell you how much I am *missing you*! Dearest!

Think of me every night before you go to sleep, for a little while, will you? — Perhaps you're thinking of me now!

I won't enjoy myself one bit till you are with me.

Sat.—didn't get this off as I planned. The groundswell was *fierce*, and I got sick as a dog— never had such a rocking. Jim and *Edith* met me—went up to P.G. this afternoon—family were *smitten* with Shane—your father looks very badly, but your mother looks well—I will write you a long letter tonight, but want to get this off now—

Goodby, dearest [own?]—more later. I wired you.   Your *Aggy*.

~~⌒

109. **AB to EO** ALS 3 pp. (36 Commerce St. / New York) [Harvard]

Sunday afternoon. / [April 25, 1920]

Dearest 'Gene: Well—I'm here—and as soon as ever I can make it, I'll *not* be here! Shane, upset by the trip—or what, who knows—is cross, howly, and peevish. I didn't think it best to take him to P.G. today, he seemed so unwell—nervous and fussy, anyhow. If it had not been that I had wired Margery[1] to meet me on Monday, I would have left today. However, I've decided to try and manage until Tuesday A.M. and see *Beyond* with Margery on Monday night.

I'd never have brought Shane here if I'd seen it first.— There's no heat at all, except small gas heaters, which warm the spot they happen to be in, and it's terribly drafty. Also, no way of bathing him except in the kitchen sink.—

Have been awake since four o'clock this morning. I haven't been out today except to 'phone your mother I couldn't bring S. up, as he wasn't well. Won't attempt to go anywhere except to *Beyond* tomorrow night—and when I'm not tending Shane, I am reading—or trying to—the *Dial*—which seems good.

Adele[2] wants me to go to Romany Marie's[3] with her, but I have no ambition to go anywhere—after a four o'clock rising! I did go to Christine's last night to see Susan,—got there before the plays started and stayed to the first—*Where the Cross Is Made*—*very* poorly done—no comparison to last year.

So don't bother about my having a giddy time! I haven't even the desire to buy a hat any more—!

"Booze" seems to be freely flowing—Jim has a line on some "very fine"—at $25 per gal. So cheer up! *You* can have a *real* vacation, anyway.

Always, with much love— *Aggie*

[postscript across top of first page:] Give Mrs. C. my best, and I'll write her.

1. Margery Boulton, also known as Budgie, was AB's sister.
2. Adele Holladay.
3. Greenwich Village restaurant.

～⌒

110. **EO to AB** ALS 1 p. (Provincetown, Mass.) [Harvard]

Sunday 10 P.M. / [April 25, 1920]

Own Sweetheart: Have just finished my union labor typing bit for ye Sabbath—eight hours today!—and feel all in. Damn such a job, anyway! I can understand how machine workers take on the character of their engine in time. I feel as if I had keys myself tonight. But, glorious thought, the job will soon be finished! And then I can rest up a day or so before departing for N.Y.

Sure hope there'll be a letter from you tomorrow morning. I'm lonely as hell and miss you dreadfully. I also miss Shane. Every once in a while I think I hear his college yell, "When do we eat!," from the distant bedroom. And I catch myself tiptoeing into the bathroom so as not to wake him. He has crept into my life much more deeply than I was aware of. It took the want of him to make me realize.

Fifine is lost without him. She keeps repeating what a hole his absence has left in her existence. She is really all broken up about it. You will have to whisper in his ear how popular he is getting.

No news. Haven't paid a call or seen a caller. I hope you'll fill this gap with a lot of happenings in your letter of tomorrow. (You see I am firmly counting on getting one!)

Will make no plans for my own exodus until I hear what yours are.

Timmy and Chris both in the pink and send you their loudest barks and mews.

I trust this letter will get you before you set out for P.P. Remember what you promised yourself you would refrain from down there—the fits of temper! You'll come back in a better state if you obey this rule, and not have that dark brown taste of the morning after a domestic brawl to take back to New York. We must be happy and relax for the few days we'll be there together. Isn't it so?

All my love, My Own! It won't be long now. A kiss to you and Shane!   Gene.

111. **EO to AB** ALS 1 p. (Provincetown, Mass.) [Virginia]

Monday 7 P.M. / [April 26, 1920]

Own Sweetheart: Well, your letter arrived on schedule and I was sure happy when I saw it had come. In fact it so inspired me that I plunged into typing and have got the job done. Now when I go over it, get it bound, etc. I'll be free.

There was also a letter from Madden. *Beyond* played to 7,018 week before last—strike week.[1] M. says there was a general falling off, and I think it's a good sign the play stood up as well as it did and didn't fall below seven thousand.

You'll have to furnish all the news of this correspondence. I have none. Haven't spoken to a soul except Fifine and Terry. She sent the baby's stuff to Point Pleasant today via Parcel P. She's been cleaning up and working quite hard at it, I guess. She talks of Shane incessantly.

I'm enclosing a postal from Dippy Dorothy.[2] If you can make out the last part of it, you're a bear. After a glance at her handwriting, one doesn't have to psyche her to discover a scrambled personality.

I'll say again I'm some lonely person! Today was fine for a change and I went on a long beach walk up to [Bangorville] and back. In my remaining period up here I'm going to try and cram in all the rest, sun, outdoor exercise I can so I can appear in N.Y. blooming.

All my love and a kiss for both of you!   Gene.

P.S. Am sending this to W.P.P. [West Point Pleasant] to make sure. My best to your family. Keep your temper!

    1.   There was a major strike of railroad workers during the first two weeks of April 1920.
    2.   Perhaps Dorothy Day (1897–1978), radical journalist and cofounder of the Catholic Workers movement. She and EO had been close friends in his Hell Hole days.

112. **EO to AB** ALS 1 p. (Provincetown, Mass.) [Harvard]

Tuesday 7 P.M. / [April 27, 1920]

My Own: Didn't get your letter of Sunday until 2 today. I was so damned sorry to hear of poor, little Shane being bunged up. Mrs. C. is in a fearful stew, too. We both hope to hear in your next that he's his old self again. I judge, however, from the fact that your wire doesn't mention it that he must be better.

Am sorry Edith's is so punk a place. Did you hear of or look at any other?

I'm all through with *Gold* now and hate the sight of it. As is usual at this stage, I think it's the punkest thing ever written and have half a mind to toss it in the stove. *Chris*, the new play, is very much in my mind and the plot is now very clear to me so I'm writing a scenario before I forget it.[1] This will help in telling Tyler about it.

Had a very fine letter of thanks from Max B[2]. today. Very interesting, too. Will bring it down to show you. Also heard from my cousin. The man in New London who makes the kayaks has made 3 new ones this winter—beauties, Phil[3] says—which he will sell at 125 apiece. I'm going to write and take one. They last a lifetime, if properly cared for, and I think it's a good investment for me with my particular angle on living.

I'll look for that *long* letter tomorrow, and hope you've kept your promise. The weather is again grey and wintery. I'm lonely as hell and have to keep working at something all the time or I'd go "nuts." The hour in bed each night before I go to sleep is the hardest to take. Your old place just aches for your head to be pillowed there on my shoulder.

Think I will leave here Thursday. There's a lot I still want to do, however, on *Chris* and I may not get started till Friday. Will let you know more definitely tomorrow.

All my lonely love to you both! Gene.

1. EO was probably sketching *The Ole Davil*, the second version of what would become *"Anna Christie"*.
2. Probably Maxwell Bodenheim (1893–1954), poet, playwright, and Greenwich Village bohemian.
3. Philip Sheridan, EO's second cousin.

~⌀

113. **AB to EO** ALS 7 pp. ([Prince George Hotel / New York]) [Harvard]

Tuesday. / [April 27, 1920]

Dearest Eugene:— This paper is an ingenious idea—there is no other to be got this hour of the night, and I'm bound to write to you. This comes from the bureau drawer.[1]

I know if I don't write you now about *Beyond the Horizon* I never will—so here goes: Why does a man who has the intelligence Williams seems to have,—the artistic conscience—allow so many obviously bad things in a production he's in charge of? That's what is puzzling me. I simply don't understand him.

But first of all, the good things. Bennett is great. Without knowing about W. or what you've said of Bennett, simply seeing the performance, I'd say Bennett was the only person with brains connected with the production! Just in the end—in certain speeches Robert makes, I felt, perhaps, that he didn't quite "get" what he was saying—that some of it was just words to him. But apart from that he sure was fine—*particularly* the first two acts.

Andy is good—very good. I liked the Captain, too. Now I'm going on to the things that got my goat. First and foremost, Louise Closser Hale!

Her characterization of the old lady, as a thing *apart from your play*—is great stuff—funny. *In* your play it stands out as something frightfully out of key—damnable. The audience [one word missing] on her words and laugh even before she speaks—which is bad enough, quite, in the second act. — but my God—in the third act—that dim, tragic room, that subdued tone—where, as you wrote it, everything goes on with sombre relentlessness—what happens when the curtain goes up and the audience realizes that one of the two figures by the stove is Grannie Mayo?—Why—the same roars at her slightest word. Is that good production—now is it! CHRIST IN THE MOUNTAINS!

I'll finish with dear Louise by telling you she has added at least one line to her part, in order to hear another of those laughs that are sweet music [to] *her*! I'm positive *you* never wrote it. She has a speech something like "Everything's done wrong on this farm" (implying, "except by me") (not just that—look it up). And as she says [it] she picks up a ball of yarn and threads a needle—Then (after a time) she [looks] at needle threaded with yarn, and says [in] a staccato scream, "Deary me! I've gone and threaded this wrong! Bother!" Everybody roars. Nice cheap stuff, isn't it?

Second, Helen Freeman is rotten as Ruth. [She's] got a Jew hooked nose—I never noticed it and will you believe me when I tell [you] she frequently, during the play—(where she ["acts" most?]) uses the Irish-Scotch [accent?] of the Girl in *John Ferguson*!

Having gotten off my mind these two ladies, proceed act by act, and tell you the things that jarred me.

Act One.— 1. Richard Bennett's pose, à la a tombstone effigy, on top of what is supposed to be a stone wall, (when he lies flat on his back, sticks his legs into the scenery, and reads). Some one should have told him how he looked.

2. R.B.'s get up of a suit evidently well worn, but as evidently costing $125—[illegible] back and boots that look like golf stockings, so he looks as if he just came in from a good time at the country club. Irritating.

Act. 2 Scene 2. When Rob and Andy stand talking—(no action)—for a long time—so:

⌐ xx ○ ⌐ The crosses are them, and the circle is the baby) the [sweet infant?] got the entire attention of the audience by going through a series of the damndest contortions and actings you ever saw. She knows the audience thinks it sweet when she yawns: so yawn she does, looking out at the audience for appreciation she holds the doll high in the air, wriggles, and squirms and pouts. As a consequence, everybody near where I was was saying: "Oh, the dear little thing!" "Do you suppose she's sleepy" "Why, she's only a baby!" etc. etc.—all this while Rob—and Andy, talk—(I suppose a few serious thinkers are listening, perhaps, to *them*.) *Question*—If that child cannot be made to behave, why not let her go down the hill further—out of sight?

Oh yes—I forgot the spot light planted on Andy & Rob, then Rob and Ruth, the first Act. Why do they do that? It's so stupid, because when they take it off, for the last few minutes of that act, it's infinitely better—oh, tremendously.

—And a few other small things—awfully easily seen and remedied. These I have mentioned are the high spots in a production that makes me wonder why Williams makes any pretense at being an artistic producer. And, yet, his letters! And he *took* *Beyond*!—Gee, it's after two o'clock! I must quit! Goodnight, my own! I'm going to Pt. P. tomorrow—couldn't make it today—staying tonight at the P.G. (wouldn't you think they'd have writing paper?) And I have a helluva cold! And Shane is even crosser!—he's just got a tooth!

Goodnight again, belovedest! I certainly do love you!   A.

And when the old father fights with, and curses Andy, why doesn't he keep getting madder and madder, until he works up to the last, instead of howling it all out in the same tone of bull voice, so you simply get tired of hearing him roar? Or let him vary his voice somehow.

All Souls' Eve was a *terrible* failure!

1.   The letter is written on what appears to be drawer-lining paper; some words have been lost on the torn and crumbling pages.

~~つ

114. **AB to EO** ALS 7 pp. (Stationery headed: Prince George Hotel, / Fifth Ave. & 28th Street / New York) [Harvard]

Wednesday / [April 28, 1920][1]

Dearest Gene— I hope you are not on your way, and going to miss this letter. You ought to take at least two days' rest—don't you think so?

I wrote you a long letter last night about *Beyond*. I really think you should sit through one entire performance—and then insist on some changes.

It is pouring again today. I have a fierce cold. Got it the night I went to *Beyond*— I guess. I'm not in any shape to resist the smallest cold germ, evidently. I've been up with Shane every day since I've been here between four and five—besides that, washing all his clothes and didies every day, boiling water all the time for his food, etc.— Edith has no hot water—and then having to cook my own meals and wash up the dishes, why, it's got me pretty tired. I've been out just *twice*— once to the P. Players, getting there about 8:30, and home to Shane at ten. And to *Beyond*.

But the worst of it is not knowing what to do— That is, it's so hard to plan to get Shane even to the P.G. and back, and have everything right for it—so as not to interfere with his nap or something or other-!

I stayed up here last night as Edith expected Bob [illegible] back. She gave *her* room to me, and slept on the sofa, which was uncomfortable. Now this A.M. the thing is, shall I take Shane down there while I pack my trunk, or what shall I do? I can't leave him here very well.

And then, I know so little of what conditions are at Pt. P. I won't know till I get there if I shall stay two days or a week. One thing is sure. I can't bring Shane back to N.Y. to stop over. We've got to beat it straight home! I've had quite enough of the gentle pastime of taking care of him in New York—!

The only possible way—and I knew it all along, you remember I wrote you about it when you were in New York—would have been to have brought Mrs. Clark along. It *wouldn't* have cost so much. However, I let myself be deluded into thinking I might manage alone—well, in the future I stay home, and become a Yogi!

If it wasn't that it means so much to Cecil,[2] I'd come right home now! I feel so rotten with this dreadful cold—and no sleep. There was so much I wanted to do, too. Oh, hell, I *could* have had an awfully good time, if it hadn't been for Shane-! Everybody's so nice to me now—and asking me to go.

Susan and Jig accidentally got seats Monday night too—but nowhere near ours— we were up front. I think I saw Joe Williams, dark, and short, very nice looking? The house was *very* good—and Monday night, too.

The P'town Players have got a big new impetus, and everybody according to Susan, is quite wildly enthusiastic—Jig wants to do it along the line you were speaking of—bigger, long plays; more attention to acting and scenery, etc.—and on a basis to enable them to *pay* good people to devote their time to it. They are counting very much on *you*. I think—oh, well, it's all tremendously exciting. I think it would be a wonderful thing to do, don't you?

Teddy Ballantine told me Barrymore was dreadfully sorry now he hadn't done *Beyond*.— I'm glad.

Your father has some grand whiskey—

Well, you will arrive about the day after I leave, I suppose! I sure wish I was going to see you. Isn't it horrid?

A hug, and *many* kisses!—(One comfort, sending kisses by mail you won't catch my cold!)

Goodby dearest!   Aggie.

1. Marginalia on this letter, in AB's hand, reads, "not mailed—too peevish probably! about Apl. 29–30th 1920." The dating is probably wrong, but there is no way to know whether her memory that the letter was not mailed is accurate.
2. Cecil Boulton, AB's sister.

115. **EO to AB** TLS 1 p. (Provincetown, Mass.) [Harvard]

Wednesday P.M. / [April 28, 1920]

Own Sweetheart: Another beautiful spring day! Raining, blowing like hell from the southeast, rain leaking in the bedroom, cold as the devil, heater going in back of my chair, etc. Your letter, which arrived at two, has done much toward dissipating my gloom, however. Not that your picture of the Old Man is cheerful. God damn it, isn't it hell that such things have to happen in such a way! My poor Mother! It must be terrible for her! I don't see how she stands it.

It was so good, though, to get such a long letter from you. I won't repeat again how lonely I am and how direly I miss you. You must realize all that by this. The weather being so rotten makes things worse. One hasn't much ambition to go out; and so I've been plugging away at this machine, getting a lot of necessary manual labor done if nothing else. Have finished a long scenario of the new *Chris* play. With this done, I'm sitting back dreaming of being with you again and trying to decide when to make a start for N.Y. I wish I could get in one good, complete day of sunshine and open air rest before I go but, from the way things look now, the sun is never going to come out. I may suddenly make up my mind to start tomorrow—if not, Friday sure. It all depends on what kind of a day it is.

Fifine forces a lot of her conversation on me these days and, to tell the truth, I am rather grateful for it. She has handed me a lot of old village tales—one of which don't forget to remind me to tell you. It would make a bear of a story or short play—if it could be done. She is everlastingly wishing Shane were here.

Had a nice note from Don Corley[1] asking me to stay at his place when I arrive in N.Y. This I will probably do—unless you can arrange to leave Shane at P.P. for a couple of days, in which case we could camp together at Edith's. You need a couple of days vacation at least, you know it. I think Shane's peevishness will disappear when he has a rest and fresh air at P.P. It seems such a futile thing, and so unfair to you, to have to just rush through New York with him on the way back. Can't you plan it out better than that? Couldn't Margery stay with you a couple days in N.Y. on the return and work relays with you on Shane—in which case you could go to any hotel there was a room in and not be handicapped by Edith's. Of course, you haven't said whether he is really sick or not. What's best to do would all depend on that. I'll leave it to you—but do try and fix up some way out so we can have a few days in N.Y. together to play in. Honestly, I'm not thinking of myself. With Father the way he is, I don't anticipate anything but sadness from my journey. But I do believe you need to re-lax—and me, too, for that matter—and we might help each other, as in the old days, to do this. I wish we could hire that old room of ours where we lived together, for a couple of days.

All my love to you both! I do hope Shane will be all right by the time you receive this. And for Pete's sake, write Clark! I think she expects it and she'll be terribly hurt if you don't. I'll wire you when I leave here. Sweetheart, I love you so!   Eugene.

1.   Donald Corley (1886–1955), an illustrator, was a member of the Provincetown Players.

116. **AB to EO** ALS 2 pp. ([West Point Pleasant, N.J.], on stationery headed: Prince George Hotel, / Fifth Ave. & 28th Street New York) [Harvard]

Ap[ril] 29, 1920

Dearest Gene,   Just a line. I'm coming back Saturday for a week. Oh, happiness! Mother is *wonderful*. Cecil is *much* better.

Where are you, I do wish I knew. Haven't heard since Monday's letter— Dearest—a thousand kisses— *Agnes*

Write me where we shall stay, Stella, Edith, Don?—

117. **AB to EO** ALS 2 pp. ([West Point Pleasant, N.J.]) [Harvard]

[April 30?, 1920][1]

Dearest Gene— I'm coming up tomorrow A.M. Sat.—will be in town about 11:30, by then *may* have heard where you are—if not, will go to the P.G.—I don't think I can get morning mail here before leaving, so will probably not get your morning letter—

This is another hasty letter—seems I have no time. Oh, how I want to see you again!

Much, much love. *Aggie.*

1. This letter is dated April 23, 1920, in a handwriting resembling Boulton's, but the date is in pencil whereas the letter is in ink, and probably was added by Boulton much later when she and Max Wylie were attempting to organize them.

118. **AB to EO** ALS 4 pp. ([Provincetown, Mass.]) [Harvard]

Tuesday. / July 7th, 1920

Dearest Gene— The Hapgood children, Charles, Miriam and Trixie, are here, and I'm going to take a chance and send this to you at the Crocker House,[1] because I don't know where else to reach you—probably you'll never get it! Have had no word from you—so far—there's probably something waiting at P'town. I started another letter to you.

When are you coming back, dearest? It is awfully lonesome without you. The last two days have been perfect, and I kept thinking how you'd have loved it.

I am feeling all right—things physiological are just the same—no change.

Shane is fine. And Clarkie seems to miss you terribly! Quite blue!

I'll finish up my long letter to you and mail it tomorrow, when I know where you are. This is just on a chance of meeting you.

My love to your mother, and Jim.—I hope—against hope—your father is much better.[2] Your own, *Agnes*.

    1.   A New London inn.

    2.   James O'Neill Sr. was hospitalized in New York on May 14, 1920, then transferred to a New London hospital on June 10.

~∽

119. **AB to EO** ALS 4 pp. (Old Peaked Hill Bar / Provincetown, Mass.) [Harvard]

[July 12?, 1920]

Dearest 'Gene— Everything went O.K.—Ramos took me and all the goods over in style. Edith and Mac[1] were there when I arrived, with Deem[2] and Fisk. They thought the place was wonderful—and Shane a child to be proud of. Of course it rained, and as they had to get the boat, we fixed them up in rain coats, etc., and they managed beautifully. Deem and Fisk stayed over Sunday, and seemed to enjoy themselves.

(Tuesday evening) / [July 13?, 1920]

The Coast-Guard just brought the mail, but nothing from you. Of course I know it must be all right with you, but at the same time, wish you'd written. I have no way of mailing letters here—you have. No wire either. Not terribly thoughtful of you, as you've been gone four days. Also, you left me no address, and I don't know where to write you.

Mrs. Clark goes in tomorrow, and so I'll be alone here. She didn't suggest *not* going, so neither did I, although I don't feel very well—a bad headache.— Nothing has actually happened yet—but seems about on the *point* of happening. Quien sabe?

Well, hope for a letter from you tomorrow. Will have Mrs. Clark mail this. Much love to all. Lovingly, *Agnes*.

    1.   Probably Kenneth Macgowan (1888–1963), dramatic critic and author of studies of the American art theatre and little theatre movements. He and Robert Edmond Jones and EO founded the Experimental Theatre, Inc. in 1923, and within this organization Macgowan acted as producer of several of EO's plays.

    2.   Charles Demuth.

~∽

120. **AB to EO** ALS 4 pp. ([Provincetown, Mass.]) [Harvard]

[July 29?, 1920]

Dearest Gene— This letter will no doubt be perfumed with gasoline and engine-oil.—and if exhaustion, back-ache, and extreme exasperation had an aroma of their own, with that even more strongly.

To be explicit—: Yesterday afternoon the water suddenly turned brown, then ceased. I—remembering Tony's injunctions not to touch any screws or bolts—started up our little engine—It went—for five minutes—then stopped. That catch affair—(spring) was wrong again. I fixed that, but could not get it started again. This A.M. I started it again, after unscrewing the bolt to prime it. (*Some* job!) It went—for one minute—nor will it start again. So here we are—no water. Cecil has just gone up to the C.G.s to get some for Shane's bottles. What little there is in the cold-water spigot is brown.

Why, oh, why, couldn't I have run the engine a few times under your direction—when we *knew* you'd be away!

One thing is sure—we can't be here without water. Neither can Tony come across the dunes every day or so to pump. The only thing I see is to depart with Shane for some oasis until your return.

Of course, turning and turning that crank has about finished me. I feel fit for a sanatorium—or the grave. Also, I have to go in to see Hiebert *right* away, as a new symptom has appeared—an awful burning and soreness, accompanied by a funny, very thick white discharge—what it means I can't imagine.

This isn't a very pleasant picture of your home by the sea,—but that engine is enough to knock all the beauty out of life—particularly if one doesn't feel well.

There's no use asking about your father, I suppose—But how are *you*? I hope the change did cure your hives, give my love to your mother and Jim, Fondly, Agnes.

I miss you terribly.

121. **EO to AB** WIRE, addressed to c/o John A. Francis, Provincetown, Mass. (New London, Conn.) [Yale]

JUL 29TH 1920

FATHER VERY LOW END EXPECTED ANY TIME NOW AM WRITING ALL LOVE. EUGENE

122. **EO to AB** ALS 4 pp. (Lawrence and Memorial / Associated Hospitals / New London) [Harvard]

Thursday, P.M. / [July 29, 1920]

Own Sweetheart: Am writing this at the hospital. Papa is lying in bed watching me, his strange eyes staring at me with a queer, uncanny wonder as if, in that veiled borderland between Life and Death in which his soul drifts suspended, a real living being of his own flesh and blood were an incongruous and puzzling spectacle. I feel as if my health, the sun tan on my face contrasted with the unearthly pallor of his, were a spiritual intrusion, an impudence. And yet how his eyes lighted up with grateful affection when he first saw me! It made me feel so glad, so happy I had come!

The situation is frightful! Papa is alive when he ought to be dead. The disease has eaten through his bowels. Internal decomposition has set in—while he is still living! There is a horrible, nauseating smell in the room, the sickening, overpowering odor of a dead thing. His face, his whole body is that of a corpse. He is unspeakably thin and wasted. Only his eyes are alive—and the light that glimmers through their glaze is remote and alien. He suffers incredible tortures—in spite of all their dope. Just a few moments ago he groaned in anguish and cried pitifully: "Oh God, why don't You take me! Why don't You take me!" And Mama and I silently echoed his prayer. But God seems to be in His omnipotent mood just now and not in His All Merciful.

One very pitiful, cruelly ironic thing: He cannot talk plainly any more. Except when he cries out in pain it is impossible to understand him. And all through life his greatest pride has been in his splendid voice and clear articulation! His lips flutter, he tries so hard to say something, only a mumble comes forth—and then he looks at you so helplessly, so like a dog that has been punished it knows not why.

Death seems to be rubbing it in—to demand that he drink the chalice of gall and vinegar to the last bitter drop before peace is finally his. And, dear God, why? Surely he is a fine man as men go, and can look back to a long life in which he has kept an honorable faith and labored hard to get from nothing to the best attainment he knew. Surely the finest test of that attainment is the great affection and respect that all bear him who knew him. I don't believe he ever hurt a living thing intentionally. And he has certainly been a husband to marvel at, and a good father, according to his lights. I know these are the conventional virtues that are inscribed on tombstones—but he is the one person in a million who deserves them. Perhaps these virtues are so common in cemeteries because they are so rare in life. At any rate, looking at it dispassionately, he seems to me a *good* man—in the best sense of the word—and about the only one I have ever known.

Then why should he suffer so—when murderers are granted the blessing of electric chairs? Mankind—and myself—seem to me meaningless gestures, to be mocked at with gales of dreary laughter. The last illusion—the soft beauty of Death—"gone glimmering through the dream of things that were"—one result of this present visit.

There is a man on the floor above—an automobile accident case—who is howling monotonously & with every expulsion of breath—ticking of the clock of agony. He is dying, too, it seems. Like a wounded jackal he bays uncomprehendingly at the setting moon of Life. These hollow cries reverberate echoingly through the wide, cool halls where the nurses march from room to room—fat, buxom, red-armed wenches, mostly. They walk quietly on their rubber soles—insistently efficient with a too-fleshy indifference.

I'm afraid you'll find this letter a false note of drama. It isn't. It's sincere as hell! Perhaps I'm too keyed up to write convincingly. When the Ultimate plucks you by the sleeve and you stand confronted by a vast enigma—brought home—what more can you do than—stutter! But I hope I've conveyed something.

Later—He was asleep when I was writing the above. Then he woke up and called me over. He made a dreadful effort to speak clearly and I understood a part of what he said, "Glad to go, boy—a better sort of life—another sort—somewhere"—and then he mumbled. He appeared to be trying to tell me what sort—and although I tried my damndest I couldn't understand! (How appropriate! Life is at least consistent!) Then he became clear again: "This sort of life—froth!—rotten!—all of it—no good!" There was a bitter expression on his poor, sunken face. And there you have it—the verdict of a *good* man looking back over seventy-six years: "Froth! Rotten!"

But it's finely consoling to know he believes in a "better sort—somewhere." I could see he did—implicitly! He will die with a sigh of relief. What queer things for him to say, eh? They sound like a dying dialogue in a play I might have written. Yet I swear to you I am quoting verbatim! He didn't mention God, I am sure. His "somewhere" didn't appear to be a Catholic Heaven. He tried to tell me and I couldn't understand! Isn't it ghastly?

Oh My Own, we just mustn't fight and hurt each [other] any more! *We mustn't!* It's the unforgivable sin—a crime against the spirit of our love! I can see that the great thing my father hugs to his heart as a something vital, not froth or rotten, is my mother's love and his for her. He has thrown everything else overboard but that remains—the real thing of the seventy-six years—the only meaning of them—the justification of his life because he knows that, at least, is fine and that it will go with him wherever he is going—the principal reason he is not afraid to go, I believe!

So let us protect our love against ourselves—that we may always have the inner courage, the faith to go on—with it to fall back on. All my love,   Gene

P.S. Am keeping my promise. So don't worry—and *rest!*

P.S. again. They expect Father to go any moment now. It can't be long postponed—and they can't be any more definite. His pulse is almost out. I'll write all developments.

Am staying at my cousin's with my Mother.

123. **AB to EO** ALS 3 pp. (Old Peaked Hill Bar / Provincetown, Mass.) [Harvard]

[July 30?, 1920]

Dearest Gene— Your letter just came, via Mrs. Clark, and I have already read it three times. It is dreadful about your father—it made me weep to read your letter—I pray you or I won't have the torture of watching through a death like that—

My previous letter said little except about the engine.—I had come from too long a siege of amateur engineering to be articulate on anything else—but there was much else I wanted to say about everything—I can't tell you what a frightful sense of hopelessness our quarrel left in me. I'm really not over it yet. The way it dragged out—we made up—embraced—and in the midst of these embraces, broke out at one another again in hatred! Last night the horror of it took form in a dream, where it seemed I discovered you had been more or less unfaithful to me ever since our marriage— every time you'd been away. The hopeless, drained feeling with which I awoke!—I can't tell you—No, you are right—we must *not* fight any more. Because it's so silly— I don't know about you, but as for me, there could really be no living without you. Oh, darling, you don't know how I miss you this minute—(hugs) oooo (kisses) xxx

Only, I wish you hadn't said our marriage was an unhappy one. (Doesn't it look terrible down in black and white?) When you said that, you created the greatest antagonism of all—because it seemed as if you had forgotten all our lovely moments, and remembered only the horrid ones. And I hated you for doing that. It made you seem alien from "us."

Sat. A.M. / [July 31?, 1920]

Dearest: "Cookie" is here—has been running the engine—nothing was the matter with it—except I did not know how to regulate the gas—so I'll give him this letter— and more later—my darling. A.

~⌣

124. **EO to AB** ALS 3 pp. (Lawrence and Memorial / Associated Hospitals / New London, Connecticut) [Harvard]

c/o Mrs. Mary Sheridan,
55 Channing St.[1]
Friday P.M. / [July 30?, 1920]

Own Sweetheart: Again at the hospital. Father is just the same—hanging on by the merest thread. The doctors expect it to happen any moment—but it doesn't. The head one says it is only Papa's *marvelously strong heart* that is keeping him alive! And that fool in New York was afraid to operate on him months ago because he claimed his heart was *weak!* Isn't it all a ghastly joke? Who could ever trust a doctor's word after this revelation of their criminal ignorance.

How long it will keep me here, I can't tell; but now that I am here I'll have to "stay put" until the finish. There's no help for it when they tell me it's liable to happen at any hour. I believe myself it is only a question of hours. If you could know how horribly he has failed since my last trip, you'd realize why I'm so sure of this. There is Death written on his face.

When I'm not enduring the ordeal of the hospital, I'm stupidly watching the hours drag. There's nothing to do but hang about and wait. The town and the people are dead. I despise both. Tried to work on the *Gold* script last night but didn't get much done. Can't concentrate, naturally. Feel better physically, though. My hives seem to have gone, thank God—and Hiebert's medicine which I have been religiously taking.

The Old Man's business affairs are in a hellish tangle and my Mother is worried sick. I'm afraid when the end comes and the tension she is under relaxes, she'll collapse.

Oh, My Own, I miss you so in the long, long hours! I hope you're resting and keeping your promise to me as I'm keeping mine. I love you so, and want so much for you to feel fine and your old self again. And I'm praying that the other thing has come around all right or will very soon.

We've taken a solemn oath in the name of our love that we won't fight any more, haven't we? Remember! It's so silly—and criminal—for us to wound each other in that vicious fashion.

Got my suit—60.00—and low black shoes—Hanan's—14. Still have hat and socks to get.

All my love to you and Shane, Dear Little Wife of Mine! Remember me to Cecil & Mrs. C.   Gene

P.S. I'll be back the first second I can. Burial will be soon after death on account of his condition.

Oh, by the way, if you have to get Cooky to start engine, tell him not to monkey with anything. She works fine as she is. Show him how to hold finger over hole to start her.

I discover I have checkbook. Put it in pocket that day you & I started—so keep track of any checks you write. Again adios—and a long kiss, Sweetheart!

1.   Mary Sheridan was a cousin of Ella O'Neill.

~~⌒

125. **EO to AB** ALS 2 pp. (New London, Conn.) [Harvard]

Saturday. / [July 31, 1920]

Own Sweetheart: The Pater's condition shows no change. The Doc says it's absolutely impossible for him to live longer and that it's practically a miracle the way his heart holds out. So there you are; and there is nothing for me to do under the circumstances but stick the vigil out to the finish. I'm awfully lonely—longing to be with you again—and bored to a frazzle by the stagnant life down here. Jim and I go up to Louis's gambling joint after we return from the hospital in the afternoons and get a flash of interest watching the [boobs buck faro bank?] and waiting for the ticker returns on baseball games and the races. By way of excitement I put up a lone dollar on Jim's "best bet" in the last race yesterday—Thimble. It actually won at 6–1 so I am "in" the price of my mourning hat.[1] Now don't get the idea that I am in the act of adding gambling to my other vices! I'm proof against that, at any rate. But a dollar on a race does give one an interest in something in New London—a very desirable result, cheap at the price.

I've been working a lot, too—at night up at my cousins'. Have the first two acts of *Gold* in fit shape for Boni and Liveright and hope to get more done tonight.[2]

So, confess now, ain't I a model husband to trust so far away from your "riding herd" on me? I drink not at all, I flirt not at all—I even work!

Your letter which I received this morning worried me terribly. Why did you attempt to crank that damned engine yourself? Oh My Own, won't you ever get sense and take care of yourself? What is going to happen to us if you don't? For Shane's sake and mine—if you won't consider your own—you *must* be careful! You could have got Cook from the station to fool with the engine. He understands it pretty well. I can't understand how the water gave out so quick. Clarkie must have let it run when we were away in Truro. It was full the day we left.

I'm glad you're going to see Hiebert right away about the new symptom. For God's sake, do! And I was hoping everything would be all right with you by this time. I should rather say, I was praying! And I'll keep praying that your next letter will contain good news. Dear Sweetheart, please, please rest and take care of yourself! Won't you? You know your promise! I'm so worried about you! And it's hell to be held here, so far away, when I know you're feeling so blue and sick. Let's hope I'll be home soon now. Miracles can't last forever.

All my love to you and Shane—a kiss for him and a long, long kiss for you! Gene.

1. Thimble won the sixth race at Saratoga on July 30, 1920.
2. Boni and Liveright's edition of *Gold* appeared in September 1921.

～

126. **AB to EO** ALS 4 pp. (Old Peaked Hill Bar / Provincetown, Mass.) [Harvard]

Saturday night / [July 31, 1920]

My dearest— You wouldn't believe how I've missed you all day! It's been one of those bright, blue, windy—not too windy—days—and the ocean and the dunes and the sky, seemed—really!—to be waiting for you to come and be with them.

Oh, and I have some good news, too. You know what I was worried about— going to Hiebert—talked of going to New York, etc? Well, it's all right, thank the Gods! A tremendous load off my mind, I can tell you—and I guess off yours, too.

So when you come back, we can *really* start fresh—with no worries. Aren't you glad—my boy?

Six copies of *Beyond* arrived.

There has been no wire, so I suppose your father is still lingering on. It is a dreadful thing—wouldn't it be so much kinder if the nurse would give him an overdose of morphine, and end that cruel suffering.

When you come back I really want to make the rest of the summer a period of rest and peacefulness for you.—for us both.

No one has been over except Fisk, who walked back with Cecil. He seems very moved and touched by her—and she seems so much enhanced when she is with him—so that when the two of them are together something very fine and simple and—intensely young, and pure, and beautiful seems to have been reached. Strange—! But that's very definitely the emotion—it *was* an emotion—they gave me. I think they are really in love.

Mrs. Clark says to tell you she misses you "round the house." She says grimly: "I like Mr. O'Neill!"

Shane is daily becoming more adorable. When I say "mousie!" he puts his head down on my shoulder in the dearest, sweetest way! He crawls all over the beach, and makes "baby-tracks"—which are something like very wide and embroidered snake-tracks. The beach flies have not been so bad. What did your mother think of the pictures?

I am really feeling much better. I think the *worry* had a lot to do with my nervousness and depression, don't you?

Sunday— / [August 1, 1920]

Although I had Cecil drop her a note saying I wasn't well, and I couldn't see anyone for a while, D. Carb[1] conducted a "picnic" over the dunes today, saying that "they weren't going to bother me"—etc. etc. As the party consisted of Susie Street,[2] and MacMullian & Gilmore,[3] also a Miss McClure[4] whom Fisk told us was very talented and amusing, I really had to see them—it would have been horrid not to, as it was Susie's first trip over, also the two girls—But I thought it was awfully inconsiderate of Dorothy, and I told her so—I was really mad.—She burst into tears, etc.—Oh dear, I wish I had that valuable selfishness which hardens one to people like Dorothy! Not that I wasn't glad for them all to come over—they were a nice bunch—but just now!

Monday— Fisk is going over to the mail, or I should say returning to the city. So au revoir dearest.   Your *Agnes*

---

1. David Carb, a playwright whom EO had known since Harvard, was a close friend of the O'Neills and a member of the Provincetown Players.
2. Susan Watts Street was a New York socialite and patron of the arts. She was a close friend of Charles Demuth.

3. Possibly Margalo Gillmore (1897–), who first appeared onstage in 1917 and who played Eileen Carmody in *The Straw*.

4. Hutchins Hapgood mentions a May McClure "who was the only woman, I think, I met who seemed to have all the robust qualities of the bohemian without any unattractive limitations." Hutchins Hapgood, *A Victorian in the Modern World* (New York: Harcourt, Brace, 1939), 572.

127. **EO to AB** ALS 2 pp. (55 Channing St. / New London, Conn.) [Harvard]

Sunday eve. / [August 1, 1920]

Own Little Wife: Have just finished the "once-over" revision of the *Gold* script on which I have been laboring all afternoon. And now I don't know whether to be glad or sorry it's done—because what in hell am I to have now to take up my time and make me forget for a moment or so the intense loneliness which gnaws me. I tried to make today shorter by staying in bed late, but some atrocity-monger has presented the Congregational Church nearby with a new set of chimes—so I had to get up to escape their damn racket. They play five different hymns, the tunes of which I now know by heart—and loathe most mightily.

Father's condition remains exactly the same. He scarcely notices any of us any more—seems sunk in a coma, and tries to speak only at rare intervals. All of those "in the know" at the hospital expect him to depart every night—morning, rather—between two and five, the hours of least resistance. Every morning they seem astonished to find him still alive. His case appears to be unprecedented in their experience, and they have given up any attempt at further prophecy except to remark vaguely that "it may happen any moment, that human flesh and blood cannot hold up much longer,"—which they have been saying for a month!

All of which puts me in a hellish quandary. Shall I continue to stay on, or shall I go back to you as my heart longs to every waking minute? It would be some reconciling satisfaction if I could know my presence here *means* something to Father. I am sure hoping it does; but judging from his actions—or rather, lack of action—I should say he was too far removed from life to value with its values.

On the other hand, what a futile thing for me to return to Peaked Hill Bar if I am liable to be called again immediately! I haven't spoken of the trip before but it is sure a long, tedious ordeal and one I would like to avoid a repetition of. I so much want to be sure that when I get back to you and my work again, I'll be able to devote all my time unreservedly to both of you.

So you see what a perplexing mess I'm in! Try and feel sorry for me a bit. The life, the people I meet, everything in New London—my cousins excepted—bores me to a nervous sweat with the incredible inanity which makes up so large a part of a town of this size. Talk about intellectual stagnation! Oh boy!

I sure hope there'll be a letter tomorrow morning! If there isn't, I don't know

what I'll do! I'm so lonely, Own Little Girl! I want you so, love you so, *need* you so!!!
Life is just simply meaningless without you!

A million kisses, Sweetheart! All my love to you and Shane.   Your lonely Gene

128. **AB to EO** ALS 2 pp. (Provincetown, Mass.) [Harvard]

Tuesday / [August 4, 1920]

My dearest— Two letters from you last evening! I was so happy getting them. It's
awfully hard, you, being away—and not knowing when you'll come back.

Listen—remember your promise! You will, won't you? Going down to Mr.
Montague's[1] the temptation must be there—but don't *forget!*[2] After all, it really isn't
a temptation, when you think of it—when you think of how much you suffer, all the
bad effects, and how very little you get out of it—and then, of course, with your father
dying—However, this is all foolishness, and you'd even have a right to be peeved at
me for writing so—*of course* you won't forget your promise. Dearest!

How are your hives? You never said. I hope so much that they have peacefully
departed.

Give your mother my very dearest love, and try and convey to her some of my
sympathy with what she is going through. If only your father were well enough to
give him a message, I would want you to give him my love too, and tell him Shane
will be brought up to love and honor his grandfather, of whom he has so much reason
to be proud.

I'll meet you in Boston when you come back, if you want me to. Dearest, I wish
I knew when I'd see you!

You've no doubt had my letter by this time telling you the news about myself. It
is wonderful to be free of that worry—and for you, too.

I don't understand about the addresses.—You have some strange return address
on your letters. Where shall I write!

Goodby, beloved one— Always your own, *Agnes.*

Please tell me where the checkbook is?
Mrs. C. sends her love.—and fond wishes for a hasty return.

1. Louis Montague was alleged to have run the town brothel in New London. See Doris
Alexander, *Eugene O'Neill's Creative Struggle* (University Park: Pennsylvania State University Press, 1992), 65.

2. Croswell Bowen writes that EO's boyhood friend Art McGinley recalled that EO and
Jamie "did a good deal of drinking at local bars [in New London] during June and July."
Croswell Bowen, *The Curse of the Misbegotten* (New York: McGraw Hill, 1959), 119.

129. **AB to EO** ALS 3 pp. ([Provincetown, Mass.]) [Harvard]

[August 4, 1920]

My dearest— I mailed a letter yesterday, but didn't write one, as I went into town with Cecil. I didn't hear from you yesterday, and today waited in for the 2:30 mail, but alas, nothing came! I know it is silly, but somehow, not hearing for two days has started me worrying about you. And then—I had a frightful dream last night—You, it seemed, had broken your promise to me—and you came home—oh, quite a ghastly wreck—and worst of all, a person whom it seemed I no longer knew, who no longer meant anything to me. I looked at you—with a sickening pain in my heart—or where ever one gets such pains and thought "But this *isn't* Gene. Where is he?"

And suddenly I seemed to realize that I'd never have *you* in my life again—or that *you* weren't *you*—funny! It—oh, I can't tell you the horror of it! Then, you seemed to go away, but a moment later I heard you calling in agonized tones, "Agnes! Agnes! The house is on fire!" I rushed into the big room, and sure enough, the place was in flames—upon which I woke up, in the middle of the night, my heart pounding, in a cold sweat.

Isn't it silly the way a dream like that will affect you? However, I am hugging to my heart your promise to me. And I *know*, dearest, you'll keep it. The only time I've said—"Gene, *promise!*" Alone here, worrying, upset, I say to myself—"he promised." And something peaceful and beautiful comes over me. Oh, my dearest, if you knew how much it means to me to feel that you are going through this terrible period of suffering, loneliness and *boredom*, dreadful as it must be, with our love as the talisman that will help you! And when you do return at last, dearest, we will have forgotten, won't we, all the unhappy things, and we will start over again—you and I—

No—I shouldn't say "will start"—We have started, haven't we when we said goodby—and told one another to wait for your return.[1] Dearest Gene—I love you so—*so*—much. *Agnes*

1.   About this time, AB joined EO in New London to await the death, which occurred on August 10.

⁓

130. **AB to EO** ALS 2 pp. (Adams House / Boston) [Harvard]

Monday / [October 11?, 1920]

Dearest— Arrived last night after that disgusting trip—too weary—and late—for anything but bed. It is now seven-ten—*A.M.* Did *you* miss *me* last night! I did. In fact, I always do.

Kiss our baby for me. I miss him, too, the darling.

We passed some theatre last night, advertising a musical comedy called "The Tooting Tooties," and featuring Rae Samuels.[1] There were many photos of her, and she *looks* as if she had the well-known "personality." Just for fun Sissie and I are going to see her—and I shall see the eyes that smiled on your mad youth!

Goodby, dearest old thing! I *may* write tonight. I love you.   A.

My best to Clarkie.

1. Vaudeville entertainer (1886–1979). She was performing on the Orpheum circuit in 1911 and possibly then crossed paths with EO, who was traveling with his father's vaudeville version of *Monte Cristo* on the Orpheum circuit early in 1912.

Agnes Boulton and Shane O'Neill, around 1922. Nickolas Muray photographer. Yale Collection of American Literature, Beinecke Rare Book and Manuscript Library.

II.

1921–1926

THERE NEVER WAS AN EXTENDED PERIOD OF QUIET CONTINUITY INTO WHICH O'NEILL AND Boulton could relax with their marriage. Always it seemed that the next move would create, for once and for all, the ideal conditions, but the dream never came true. At first there were the long summers of exposure to the elements at Peaked Hill Bar, a Thoreauvian retreat from the concerns of modern life, but these were more and more complicated by the influx of visitors, each bringing some trace of the social and professional pressures of the outside world. Then, too, the house was not well-suited to life with a toddler, and the stove, the roof, the insects did not conspire to make life easier. During the winter, other accommodations would always have to be found. There were discussions of wintertime traveling abroad—Europe, the Far East—but these ideas always involved "just the two of us—alone," and the opportunity never materialized. As early as 1920 they talked of going to Bermuda, a temperate and beautiful place just outside the reach of U.S. Prohibition laws. In the winter of 1924–25 they made the move, at first staying in an old hotel, then renting a house. Finally in 1926 they purchased Spithead, a magnificent old estate on the shore, with a house and grounds greatly in need of renovation. This was the last of the homes-that-might-have-been for them.

Both continued writing during the first few years of the decade, with O'Neill completing two plays in 1921 (*The First Man* and *The Hairy Ape*) and working on several others. This year also saw three of his plays produced in New York (*The Straw*, *Gold*, and the final version of *"Anna Christie"*). Of these, only *The Hairy Ape* and *"Anna Christie"* had profitable runs. In fact, there were at least as many misses as hits during the 1920s. O'Neill's rapidly growing reputation as the most ambitious, most demanding, and most visionary of American playwrights was not sufficient to carry off some undeveloped and/or stilted scripts. Still, even the least of his plays during this period provided an occasion for journalistic probes. Virtually every book or article that took the measure of American drama, or American arts in general, gave prominent attention to O'Neill's career.

During the mid-1920s Broadway hit its peak in terms of sheer number of productions. Competition for the top talent and also for the audience was fierce. For each play O'Neill continued to seek commercial backing, but for some of his more experimental

161

work he returned to the Provincetown Players. After that organization dissolved, O'Neill, Kenneth Macgowan, and Robert Edmond Jones joined together as "the Triumvirate" of producers behind the Experimental Theatre, Inc., using some of the more capable artists who had been associated with the Provincetown Players.[1] Even with that organization in place, the need for solid financial backing for some of the more large-scale of his plays drove O'Neill to deal with the Theatre Guild, which had its own maddening ways. That organization was too high-brow for the Broadway audience, too European in its taste for the Provincetown Players' artists, too cautious for very experimental work, under-funded for many extravagant or spectacular projects. And they were chronically indecisive. Four new O'Neill plays opened in 1924 *(Welded, All God's Chillun Got Wings, The Ancient Mariner,* and *Desire Under the Elms),* but after that, no plays in 1925, only one in 1926 *(The Great God Brown),* and no plays in 1927. Thus, O'Neill could reasonably alternate between pride in his success and a desperate sense of failure. He could feel both rich and on the verge of poverty.

During the early years of the decade, Boulton too applied herself to writing, suddenly turning her attention to a novel (now lost), two plays (seriously considered by several producers, but never presented), and a couple of articles in *Theatre Arts Monthly* magazine. There were also a few stories published, notably two accepted by H. L. Mencken for *Smart Set* and one published in *Holland's Magazine.* The latter was clearly Boulton's version of *Beyond the Horizon,* a story of the "tragic futility" perceived within the life of a farm woman. One of the plays *(The Guilty One),* written cooperatively by both Boulton and O'Neill, has been interpreted as an early version of the O'Neill family story that would become the substance of *Long Day's Journey into Night.*[2] But the demands of motherhood and maintenance of an increasingly luxurious domestic life took precedence. Her diary from 1925 survives and testifies to the fact that she worked very hard through the winter, just prior to Oona's birth, to finish a play she called *Little Hope.* It interested several producers, but not enough to generate a production. After that, there is no word of her writing until the fall of 1927.

While both Boulton and O'Neill continued to scorn certain aspects of jazz-age society with its assumed sophistication and bourgeois self-indulgence, they were hardly opposed to some of its comforts, such as a custom-made touring car, a Victrola, a handcrafted kayak, and an outfit from Lord & Taylor. Money was suddenly plentiful. Film rights to *"Anna Christie"* had been sold for twenty-five thousand dollars. With a few long runs of his Broadway plays and an active market for amateur rights and book publications, they were suddenly able to afford the finer things. The most coveted possession for O'Neill (and to a lesser extent Boulton) was a home where privacy and quiet and intense concentration on the essentials—work and the marriage— could be obtained. The purchase of Brook Farm, a thirty-acre estate in Connecticut with a fifteen-room house, pond, orchard, and woodlands, gave them a winter residence (the intention was to rent out the house during the summer, when they would go back to Peaked Hill Bar). It was, as in the old George M. Cohan song, "Forty Five Minutes from Broadway," not too distant and yet far enough so they could enjoy their isolation and their work. But the automobile had brought such country houses within easy reach and there are various stories of drunken evenings with several of O'Neill's friends. One evening Eugene returned home to find that Agnes had invited the millionaire arts patron Otto Kahn and several other socialites over for drinks, and he was furious. On the other hand, Eugene invited his old friend Peggy Baird, her husband Malcolm Cowley, and the poet Hart Crane to the house for a weekend, which turned into a "roisterous time" as Crane recalled.[3] Cowley's opinion was that "the O'Neills rattle around in this big country house like the last dried peas in a box—or better, like castaway sailors who have blundered into a deserted palace on the shore. But the sailors would laugh if they found wine in the cellar, where Gene hardly even smiles."[4]

The wine in the cellar, or the cider, or whatever liquor could be obtained was becoming an oppressive problem during these years. The index item with more entries than any other in the first volume of Sheaffer's biography of O'Neill is "drinking and dissipation," and the second volume picks up at nearly the same pace. But O'Neill made serious efforts to control his drinking habits starting in 1922, beginning with visits to the famous psychoanalyst Dr. Smith Ely Jelliffe. There had been episodes of violence in the marriage since the first year, and Agnes began to insist upon his seeking medical help, as had several others of the Provincetown Players group including Robert Edmond Jones and James Light. O'Neill's letters began to contain such repeated phrases as "No need to worry," alluding to his efforts to stay "on the wagon."

It was not just the drinking they wished to address. Eugene was beginning to experience more and more symptoms of the nervous condition that would ultimately bring his writing career to an end. The tremor in his hands, the drinking, the bouts of depression, the tensions in the marriage all seemed related. At the suggestion of Kenneth and Edna Macgowan, Agnes and Eugene filled out a questionnaire administered by Dr. Gilbert Van Tassel Hamilton, a psychoanalyst who was preparing a study that would be published as *A Research in Marriage*. Both Eugene and Agnes returned to Hamilton for individual sessions, concentrating on Eugene's drinking problem. Hamilton was hesitant about offering full-blown psychoanalysis to artistic people due to an uncertainty about whether he might thereby undermine their creative capacities. It is not known just what method of treatment was tried, but it appears that it was Hamilton who gave O'Neill an abbreviated psychoanalysis and in the course somehow enabled O'Neill to stop drinking permanently. In the process Agnes was asked to prepare extensive notes on the patterns of Eugene's drinking. The letters from this period (1926–27) begin to reflect an analytical attitude toward the marriage and their individual psychiatric peculiarities.

Most of what was uncovered in Hamilton's analysis can be read only within the statistics of his cross-sectional study of one hundred couples. There, of course, the marriage of these two distinctive personalities merges with many other marriages that were not all that different. Based on complete case histories, this statistical analysis was notable for showing, well before Kinsey, that the modern marriage entailed a remarkable range of sexual behaviors and a significant amount of dysfunction. Hamilton determined that the one hundred men in the survey had had a total of 681 love affairs. About one third of the men had had affairs while married, and the numbers were nearly as high for women.[5] It was during the summer of 1926 while vacationing in Maine that O'Neill encountered a woman he had not seen since the spring of 1922. Carlotta Monterey had played the role of the genteel woman who visits the stokehole in *The Hairy Ape* and permanently upsets Yank's sense of belonging.

Carlotta was born Hazel Neilson Tharsing, just a couple of months after Eugene O'Neill in 1888, and grew up in Oakland, California. Details about her childhood are obscure, but eventually she went to London to study at the Academy of Dramatic Arts. She was named Miss California in a beauty contest in 1907, then went through a series of marriages and other relationships to men of considerable sophistication. Meanwhile, she played a number of supporting and leading roles in unimportant and mostly unsuccessful shows on Broadway. She was often featured as an "exotic" beauty, but it was probably her sophisticated manner that gained her the role in *The Hairy Ape* in 1922 when the production was moved uptown to Broadway. Four years later, after breaking up with her third husband (*New Yorker* caricaturist Ralph Barton), she had retired from the stage and was vacationing with Elizabeth Marbury, an agent in the same firm as Richard Madden, O'Neill's agent. Marbury's cottage was only a short trip through the woods along the lake from O'Neill's. Soon, Carlotta became a statistic, and within three years she would become his wife.

At first, toward the end of 1926, O'Neill attempted to address his attraction to Carlotta openly with Agnes. After all, a marriage that had been founded on love alone— not shared property or contractual obligation or an imposed sense of duty—ought to be able to adjust to the coexistence of another love. Ultimately this premise would prove untenable, either because it was too modern or because it was contrary to human nature. Hamilton's study showed that even more women than men (41 of the 100) had had extramarital affairs, and he reports that many individuals among the couples he surveyed told him "it may even enrich the lives of a husband and wife if each can have an 'outside' affair about which there shall be no cheating or secrecy."[6] There are various indications that Boulton might have had such affairs herself, but the correspondence shows definitely that deception was involved in O'Neill's affair.

Monterey herself came to seem a kind of refuge to O'Neill. At least at the beginning she represented the peace, the stillness, the security never achieved or found within his turbulent, exploratory years with Agnes. These issues are addressed in some detail in the concluding segment of the correspondence, but in the sketchier middle portion one can glimpse some of the practical troubles which would put stress on the marriage. Doris Alexander has done much to illuminate this period of the marriage by careful analysis of the marriages depicted within O'Neill's plays. She reads aspects of Agnes in Abbie Putnam (*Desire Under the Elms*), Margaret (in *The Great God Brown*), Princess Kukachin (in *Marco Millions*), Pompeia (in *Lazarus Laughed*), Nina Leeds (*Strange Interlude*), both Ada and Amelia (in *Dynamo*), and both Elsa and Lucy (in *Days Without End*). O'Neill's *Welded*, written in 1923 and quickly dismissed by the critics in 1924 as second-rate Strindberg, deserves especially close attention for this reason if no other. It has often been interpreted as a dramatic inquiry into the terms of his marriage with Boulton. The main characters, Michael and Eleanor Cape, match Eugene and Agnes in age and physical description, and after five years of marriage they think of themselves as "an old married couple." Michael is a playwright and Eleanor an actress, yet Michael conceives of the play he is writing (and she will act) as "our" play. Eleanor observes that she is merely an interpreter of a part he has created, but he dismisses this self-deprecation with an assurance that she has taught him how to write parts for women. For Michael, it is crucial to believe that the marriage has been "a consummation demanding and combining the best in each of us." Still, when it comes to the crux, Michael dismisses her as merely an actress, an unequal partner in art, and as an insufficiently dutiful partner in the marriage.

The dramatic conflict in this *Dance of Death*-like play is complicated by a rather contrived jealousy plot; they each pursue other partners—he a prostitute, she a theatrical director—as a way of attacking the other. The expressionistic staging that is prescribed and the heavy-handed language all make for a torturous evening of theatre, but as a self-analysis of the terms of O'Neill's marriage it opens some interesting questions. Was Boulton's work within the popular literary market seen as the equivalent, in some way, of being an actress? What were the consequences and implications of presenting such an explicit representation of the marriage? To what degree were the misogyny of Strindberg and his critique of marriage as servitude adopted or rejected by Boulton and O'Neill? Marriage and the conflicting relations of men and women in general remained a theme to which O'Neill turned often in his career, but with limited success, and eventually the topic itself was kept at a distance. *The Iceman Cometh* seems to be an inquiry into the grounds for human aspiration or despair, the capacities of self-deception, the ambiguous value of truth, but it is just as much a study of failed marriage. However, the wife figures in this play are all dead or imprisoned and the only women present are whores. The wife in *Long Day's Journey into Night* is progressively more and more absent from the world of the male characters. A ghost in the spare room, she returns gradually to that time when the beginning of her marriage coincided with the end of her happy existence. In those late plays, marriage has come to seem a remnant of an old and now unrealistic desire, the ruin of an abandoned romanticism. It is so hard to achieve that moment of stillness or inner peace in oneself, those plays seem to say, that it is absurd even to dream of doing so with another. Such cynical conclusions as O'Neill was to reach about the possibility of an ideal marriage were surely being actively formed during these years with Agnes Boulton, and there are many indications in these letters of the pains felt by both of them upon this discovery. There were recriminations and suspicions and disappointments, as well as numerous signs that they fought—to keep the dream alive. In general, biographers have tended to see Boulton as an unworthy partner for O'Neill, less concerned about the central emotional and spiritual values in marriage than about the lifestyle of a celebrity's wife. These letters suggest that this reading of her is unfair, that her commitment matched his, and that she, as a writer, was equally involved in the fabrication of the story of their marriage, defining its terms, advancing its plot. Indeed, her perspective on the marriage opens an important window on white, middle-class women's experience in this period.

At just the time when *Welded* had its brief run, O'Neill's first mentor, Clayton Hamilton, delivered a series of lectures at Columbia University later published as *Conversations on Contemporary Drama*. Hamilton, a drama critic who lived in New

London, knew James O'Neill Sr. and had advised his son about those very first efforts to write a play, telling O'Neill to write about his experiences at sea. Now, ten years later, he offered some trenchant observations about how O'Neill's career was developing. He observed that O'Neill succeeded in spite of his defiance of the popular market, and the crucial factor in his view was the gendered perspective offered by his plays:

> Mr. O'Neill, as I have said, knows nothing of Times Square. He is seldom in New York. He does not keep track of what is going on in the theatre and never bothers to find out which way the fashion of the season trends. He does not care about what the other fellows are doing; he cares only about what he wants to do himself. He never imitates anybody else, and he never writes a play which at all resembles any other play that has been successful on Broadway. He remains absolutely aloof from those prevailing influences that permeate Times Square which I analyzed last week as being detrimental to the development of the American drama.
>
> One point which sets his work apart from that of any other living dramatist is the fact that—whether consciously or not—he writes primarily for an audience of men and takes little or no account of the women in the audience. The world that interests him, the world he writes about, is a man's world. Several of his one-act plays, including two or three of the very best, are entirely devoid of women characters. In his longer plays, he has not failed to depict his women characters with truthfulness; but it is evident that he is interested in them not so much for their own sake as for the sake of their effect upon the men-folk of the play. He is interested in women because of what they do to men or because of what men do to them. His almost exclusive masculinity of interest would not be so remarkable in a novelist; but it is practically unprecedented in the modern drama. In the present period of the theatre, our matinée audiences are made up entirely of women and our evening audiences are made up mainly of women and the men that they have brought with them. From Ibsen onward, every practical dramatist has recognized this fact and has framed his plays more or less deliberately to appeal to the women in the audience. Every Broadway manager will tell you that, unless you please the women, there can be no hope for your play at the box-office. Yet along comes Mr. O'Neill, writing about a man's world for an audience of men, and upsets all established precedents by finding out that women are just as willing nowadays to see his plays as they are to go to prize-fights![7]

In this assessment of O'Neill's writing Hamilton gives more weight to O'Neill's one-act "sea plays" than a critic of even a year or two later would be likely to do, but it is true that many of O'Neill's plays of the 1920s continued to explore these masculine concerns. Still, in plays like *Welded,* *"Anna Christie,"* *Desire Under the Elms*, and especially *Strange Interlude*, O'Neill gave close study to the experience of female characters, and it is possible to see in these characters aspects of Agnes Boulton both as a person and a writer. These women tend to be seen as relatively free agents in comparison with conventional portrayals of white women in the period, but also in comparison with many of O'Neill's male characters.

The theatre of O'Neill's father had appealed to women in the audience more directly, enlisting sympathy and understanding, and it had won the heart, initially at least, of O'Neill's mother. During the mid-1920s O'Neill was tentatively exploring his personal history in terms of the Oedipus complex. In a diagram he drew in 1926 in conjunction with his sessions with Dr. Hamilton, O'Neill recounted his passage into adolescence in terms of the loss of his love for his mother (due to the discovery of her morphine addiction) and a crystallization of his resentment toward his father into an attitude of hatred and defiance. He records that the world of reality, largely unrealized in childhood due to the abundance of protection and love from his mother and nurse and a heroicized image of his father, becomes visible and known in adolescence. But the proximity of that reality, with its darkness and terror, in his own home, leaves him as an adult with an "inability to belong to reality."[8] The lines in the diagram representing his mother's influence break off completely at adolescence; the lines that continue all come from his father or an otherwise masculine-defined world, beginning with the murder stories told by his nurse, stories of the evil ways of men. O'Neill's marriage to Boulton can be seen as an extended effort to reconnect to the love of a woman, to be married in a real way and not within the fantasy world of his parents' marriage. He found in her such a woman as Clayton Hamilton portrayed as the audience of O'Neill's plays, a woman who takes an interest in the six-day bicycle races and who might go to a prize fight. He attempted to "belong" to her, and in a way that would not collapse her into his mother. His sharing of the tangled circumstances of getting his plays produced and his encouragement of her literary work represent efforts to deal with her as an equal partner.

On the other hand, at times he pleads for her to mother him, losing sight of the fact that she is already a mother of three by 1925, and his place is to be the father, not the child. O'Neill recalled his own father treating his nightmares and terror of the dark with whiskey—"drink of hero father"—but it became essential by the mid-1920s that he recover from his own broken adolescence by putting aside that whiskey and facing reality. The reality was a woman fully engaged with the task of constructing a home in Bermuda and caring for children. O'Neill listened to the second Dempsey-Tunney fight in New York on the radio, but Boulton was in bed in Bermuda by eight. He had lost his audience, both at home and, for a while it seemed, in the theatre. Finally, the availability of another woman who was willing to serve as a mother figure to him proved an irresistible alternative.

After the move to Bermuda, O'Neill and Boulton returned to Brook Farm only for brief periods and less and less often, but they did not sell it and completely move out until late in 1927. The move into Spithead was also prolonged because much work was needed on the house and its grounds. Even at the time when the marriage was ending, work on the "refuge" went on. Not long after they had moved in, Boulton got word that her father was dying of tuberculosis. In a letter written the day after she left, O'Neill tells her of his feeling that Spithead is "Our Home," adding:

> *Our Home!* I feel that very much about Spithead, don't you? That this place is in some strange symbolical fashion our reward, that it is the permanent seat of our family—like some old English family estate. I already feel like entailing it in my will

so that it must always be background for our children! I love Spithead—and not with my old jealous, bitter possessiveness—my old man Cabotism!—but as ours, not mine except as mine is included in ours. The thought of the place is indissolubly inter-mingled with my love for you, with our nine years of marriage that, after much struggle, have finally won to this haven, this ultimate island where we may rest and live toward our dreams with a sense of permanence and security that here we do belong. "And, perhaps, the Hairy Ape at last belongs."[9] (#202)

Already though, the fate of this Home was sealed, and half a year later O'Neill would leave this house never to return.

1. Boulton wrote an article, "An Experimental Theatre: The Provincetown Playhouse," describing this process of reorganization, for *Theatre Arts Monthly* 8, no. 3 (March 1924): 184–88.
2. O'Neill's scenario for this play, entitled "The Reckoning," and Boulton's play, which was written under the name "Elinor Rand," are published in *The Unknown O'Neill: Unpublished or Unfamiliar Writings of Eugene O'Neill*, ed. Travis Bogard (New Haven: Yale University Press, 1988), 76–146. Virginia Floyd has interpreted the autobiographical elements in O'Neill's scenario in *The Plays of Eugene O'Neill: A New Assessment* (New York: Ungar, 1985), 178–79.
3. Quoted in Louis Sheaffer, *O'Neill: Son and Artist* (Boston: Little, Brown, 1973), 121.
4. Ibid., 122.
5. G. V. Hamilton, *A Research in Marriage* (New York: Albert & Charles Boni, 1929), 210, 225.
6. Ibid., 225.
7. Clayton Hamilton, *Conversations on Contemporary Drama* (New York: Macmillan, 1924), 211–12.
8. Reproduced in Sheaffer, *O'Neill: Son and Playwright*, 506.
9. This is the final stage direction in *The Hairy Ape* (1922).

∼◯

131. **EO to AB** ALS 1 p. (Stationery headed: 529 Mercantile Bldg. / Rochester, N.Y.) [Harvard]

Thursday—noon / [April 21, 1921]

Own Little Wife: Arrived O.K. after a sneezy night on the "rattler" during which I thought I was acquiring a bad cold—but guess I didn't as no real symptoms have appeared as yet.

Have been out to Saxe's house and met his mother and father—fine, lovable old people. Then down to his office where I am now after having a bum wisdom tooth pulled.[1] It was some difficult job, Saxe declares, although I felt little pain but do feel a bit "woozy" now that the ordeal is half an hour over. He says he can bridge work me all the rest—no need of plates—which will please you, I know—and me, too! No need for further extractions, he says.

This is just a line, Dear One. I do feel a bit "off my oats" as you can imagine, but want to get this off to you. I miss you horribly. I want to lay my head on your breast for comfort, as always when in trouble or pain—but I'm glad for your sake you're away. I wouldn't be a very pleasant companion—(worse than my usual breakfast grouch!)

A kiss to Shane! My life to you! I'll write in full when I'm normal. Sweetheart, I love you so!   Gene

[postscript across top of first page:] (Send letters—and forwarded mail—here. Saxe says it's quicker delivery)

1.   Saxe Commins (1892–1958), later EO's close friend and editor at Liveright and Random House, was at this time a dentist in Rochester. His sister was Stella Ballantine.

132. **AB to EO** ALS 3 pp. (Peaked Hill Bar / Provincetown, Mass.) [Harvard]

[April 22?, 1921]

Dearest—   It was so fine to get your letter—even though it did say you were already undergoing the beginnings of the torture. Suppose you got my wire—and card. It seems as if there hadn't been one moment to write to you in. For one thing, I went up to Susan's this A.M. and aired the place and got the two fires going (Edith & I) so that when Jig & she arrived this noon, there'd be some little semblance of comfort for them. (The girl didn't materialize, so I'm going to let them have Philomena.) Then I had to see Ramos—but why bore you?

The little boat is a beauteous thing![1] I'll let Ramos take it over, crate and all, and leave it in the barn until you come. I have seen—in my mind's eye—a picture of you, tanned, red-tighted, in that slender white boat against a blue sky and sea—wonderful!

Wasn't I mad though, when I discovered that Terry has rooted out the "turn-handle" of the new stove, and he and Edith had used it—gotten it out of order—had Jennings out—according to Edith, it's running all right now, but "doesn't give much heat." It is just what I expected.

Saw Clara Beranger[2] today. She's a little subdued—perhaps a little tired—funny! I saw the letters—but not to read of course—that John Williams has been writing her. One every day. And John, she says, is casting *Gold*. Rehearsals begin *today*! I asked her who played the leading part—she says she promised not to say. What do *you* know about it? One part of John's letter she *did* show us—he said—"remember you'll be in a nest of gossip up there." What do you suppose he meant—*us*? You? Me? All I can figure out is that *he'll* know *I'll* know about his having been so much with Edna[3] & having been so drunk—and may say something to her, and *I* think he's been carrying on with the fair Clara! and doesn't want her to know he's been seeing Edna. Do let me know immediately you hear anything about *Gold*. She says he just won $12,000 in a suit against H. B. Warner for breaking his contract. But *wasn't* it funny about the "nest of gossip" up there?

Buehler[4] painted today. Your portrait looks fine. I got so lonesome when I looked at it! Shane skipped around, past Buehler, and said "Da-*da!* Da-*da!*" He's *some* kid! Well, heart o' mine, do you know what time it is! Eleven-thirty. So I'll go to my lonesome bed-dy-by, and dream of you. I sure *do* miss you! How long did Saxe seem to think it would take to get finished?

A good-night kiss, sweetheart! *Agnes.*

    1. EO had bought a kayak.
    2. Beranger (1886–1956) was a screenwriter for Famous Players. She adapted *Dr. Jekyll and Mr. Hyde* and *Miss Lulu Bett*, among other projects.
    3. Possibly Edna Kenton (1876–1954), journalist, historian, and leading member of the Provincetown Players.
    4. Lytton Buehler (1888–?), New York portraitist.

⁓͜ʃ

133. **EO to AB** ALS 2 pp. (Stationery headed: 529 Mercantile Bldg. / Rochester, N.Y.) [Harvard]

c/o Doctor Commins

Friday. 1 P.M. / [April 22, 1921]

Own Little Wife: I was so happy when your wire came this A.M. It seemed such long lonely ages since we were together, and the few words from you made me feel your nearness—that although you were miles away your thoughts were with me. The latter part of yesterday, after I wrote you, was far from pleasant. The extraction of that confounded tooth hit me hard in the after effects. Saxe says it sure was a bad one. The roots had grown together into a bunch making the tooth much larger at bottom than anywhere else—hence Saxe had almost to call in the derrick squad before he could budge it. The pain was pretty bad last night and only with the help of aspirin did I get any sleep. Altogether, it wasn't a pretty experience just after a sleeper jump on the R.R. Of course, Saxe would never have put me through it if he had known what he was up against. It looked like an easy job—and once started, he had to finish. There is some satisfaction in knowing that the worst is over with and that the filling and bridge work to come will be comparatively painless.

It doesn't look much as if I'd be able to get anything done on the *Jones* scenario up here.[1] I have to come down to this office every morning and I'm afraid I'll be too done up at the end of the torture session every day to have much left to give to "Art."

But enough of me and my durn molars. I sound like a dental clinic.

Saxe's people are fine folks. It is rather a trying time for them to have a visitor thrust on them. The morning I arrived they got a wire from Los Angeles saying Saxe's brother's little girl had died as the result of a tonsil operation. They are all very grief-stricken. I will tell you all about the family, etc., when I see you—or in more leisurely letters later. Stella has a young sister, Ruth, about 16 or 17, I should say, who is a fine—not pretty—very intelligent young person. They are all as kind to me as they can be.

I'm glad to know the ship has arrived. Better have it taken out as soon as possible. It's probably very much in Francis's way just at this time.

It was a relief to know you made a good connection at Boston. All day yesterday I kept worrying about that, wondering if you had.

I hate to make ill wishes about you but I sure hope you are feeling as unhappily lost without me as I am without you. I have a poignant pain of emptiness inside as if I'd lost the vital spiritual organ without which the rest of the machine is a mere whirring of wheels and a futile noise. Well, well, the days will pass somehow, I suppose, and it won't be long until we're Us—One & Indivisible—again. But in the meantime, God, how I wish you were here! I love you so! It truly is a love that passeth all bounds, beyond which there is nothing. I am You. So take care of the real me whilst this poor ghost is haunting dental parlors.

Remember! A honeymoon when I return—a dune & sea one for just us. And the "light-winged dryad of the trees," as Mr. Keats called him, sings out that same message to his mistress.[2] So tell her!

A long kiss, My Own! All love to Shane from his "da-*DA*." Gene.

1. *The Emperor Jones* was performed by the Provincetown Players on November 1, 1920, and was first published in January 1921. Possibly EO was working on a screen adaptation, although this would seem to contradict the advice he is about to give AB.

2. The coy allusion here is to the creature named in the title of Keats's "Ode to a Nightingale."

134. **EO to AB** ALS 2 pp. (c/o Doctor S. Commins / 529 Mercantile Building / Rochester, N.Y.) [Harvard]

Saturday, P.M. / [April 23, 1921]

My Own: It has been a long, hard morning with Saxe drilling away at my teeth preparing for the bridge he is to put in on the right side. To add to the general discomfort, I had a note from Stella with a clipping from the *Tribune* stating that Williams is to open up *Gold* at the Frazee Theatre on May 23rd with the famous Willard Mack, erstwhile playwright of melodramas and hubby of Pauline Frederick, as the lead. I cannot believe this, it is so outrageously inept—and yet, damn it, I have a sneaking suspicion that it's a fact. It's just the sort of thing that Williams would play as a desperate last card. And if he does, he will pretty well have my hands tied as far as objections that would hold good in the eyes of the law are concerned. The clause in the contract which refers to the quality of production states: "To produce and represent in first-class theatres and in a first class manner, with a competent cast to be approved by the author, *as all these terms are generally understood in the theatrical profession*"—etc. Now the Frazee is undeniably a new, first-class theatre, and Mack a well known and excellent actor according to current standards. However, you can rest assured I will fight this production tooth and nail—if the story turns out to be true. I have wired Madden to let me know at once if there's anything in it. It'll sure be a hell of a mess if it's true, what? God damn Williams, anyway!

Received a letter from Warren[1] that Mrs. Clark had sent on—but none from you so far. I guess it takes quite a while longer to reach P'town from this burg—and vice-versa—than we usually count on with N.Y. letters. Please send me Warren's address when you write next. His former letters are in my letter case. He does not give it in this last letter and I ought to write him.

With but little intermission, it has been raining ever since I arrived here. Today is especially wet and I am twiddling my thumbs out at the Commins' home without ambition to work or read or do anything but lie on the bed and dream of you and count the days until I can feel your sleep-walking feet reach out and scratch at mine again. (Yes, they do too!). I feel quite intolerably lonely and I miss you in every atom of me. It is only my iron resolve to get this teeth business done thoroughly for once in a way that keeps me from buying a ticket and grabbing the first train back to you. I simply can't live—really live—without you any more. I'm lost. And yet you say at times that you feel as if I no longer needed you! Dear Foolish One, if you only realized how much I do—more every minute I breathe!

I hope you're not having the weather we are. It's hardly the right variety for moving day.[2] We're practically house-bound. Saxe and I have had a couple of walks but that's all. We read. He took me to the Athletic Club but I don't dare risk swimming when I'd have to come out into the wet afterwards. So you see life is hardly exciting. How I long for this to be over and be back at Peaked Hill with you once more!

Answer all the letters for me you can, will you? It would be a great help to me. That one you got for an interview from the *Musical Review*, for example. Tell them I can't. There's a true and valid excuse this time. Saxe's machine is a Remington and I can't manage it. Also my face is still swollen and pains and I'm in no mood to write letters except to you. If you'll help me this way, I'll be ever so grateful, Dear One.

All my love to you, Own Little Wife! I love you more than man ever loved a woman, I know I do! You are everything! Think of me once in a while, kiss Shane for me, *and do write*. I'm so utterly lonely!   Gene

1. James C. Warren, the attorney who represented EO's first wife, Kathleen Jenkins, in her divorce action in 1912. She had appealed to EO for help in paying for the education of their son, Eugene O'Neill Jr. AB writes of how she first came to hear about this earlier marriage, several months after she had married EO, in *Part of a Long Story* (193–206).
2. AB was arranging the move from winter accommodations in Provincetown to the Peaked Hill Bar house.

135. **EO to AB** ALS 1 p. (c/o Doctor S. Commins / 529 Mercantile Bldg. / Rochester, N.Y.) [Harvard]

Sunday noon. / [April 24, 1921]
(Fountain pen gave out)

Own Sweetheart: Well, Saxe did his bit on me this morning in spite of it being the Sabbath. This P.M.—if the Lord will hold off on his gentle rain—Saxe and I are to motor about a bit in his brother-in-law's car and look over Rochester & environs. This will be the first real shot at enjoyable recreation in the open that has been possible since my arrival.

Madden did not reply to my wire of inquiry concerning the newspaper dope on the Willard Mack-*Gold* stuff. Let us hope no news in this case is good news and that the whole idea is merely another Williams dream which fades away when facts are demanded.

I got your postal last evening and, even though it was just a line, you cannot know how happy merely the sight of your handwriting made me. I love you so! and I mean no reproach by my "just a line." I know how "up to your ears" you must be with so much to attend to. I only wish I could be there to help with the dirty work.

It's good to know the boat looks wonderful to you. I knew you'd be tickled when you saw it. What fun we'll get out of it, just you & I, when the glad, warm days come and we're free for each other again! If wishing could do anything, they'd start in about five minutes!

Did Susan and Jig appear as scheduled? I wonder what the latest dope on the Gilpin-London matter is.[1] I feel isolated from all the theatrical trade stuff up here—quite comfortably so after all the tiresome bickering—but being isolated from you is something else again which I care for no, not at all, as Pepys would put it. If we could only get away together where all these damn worries about plays could be left behind! My idea of heaven! Let's try to make Peaked Hill Bar as much that as possible this summer, will you? And you can work, and I can work, and we can have each other—and help each other—and love each other—and tell the world to go to—and be happy.

Saxe's folks are fine to me—can't do enough. But my real need is you and they can't do that for me. So I am bitterly lonely.

All my love and life to you, Dearest Wife! Kiss Shane for me. Gene.

1. The Provincetown Players had been planning a London tour of *The Emperor Jones* on a double bill with Susan Glaspell's *Suppressed Desires*, but Gilpin fell ill, and the tour had to be cancelled. Meanwhile, casting controversies had created divisions within the group.

136. **AB to EO** ALS 4 pp. (Provincetown, Mass.) [Harvard]

Sunday night— / [April 24, 1921]

Gene, dearest! You darling to 'phone me! But it seemed too awful to hear you, and—
that's all! Only, I didn't *really* hear you. It was very funny. Jig and Susan came up to
dinner, and after dinner—unexpectedly—Buehler, accompanied by Clara Beranger,
came in. We got on the subject of *Gold*, and John W. Mrs. B. said: "John's got a
theatre—and a good man—and really means business!" I laughingly tried to get her
to tell who, and where—"Well, is he well-known—is he a good actor?" etc. She
wouldn't tell but said how it happened, she & John were at a play, and saw this man,
and she said "Wouldn't he be great in *Gold*?"—which made John meditate, and from
that, matters developed. *Then* the phone rang—just at that point in the conversation.
(Of course, I felt this was just another of John's bluffs.)

Well, darling, I couldn't hear anything you said about it, only, "John Williams is
going to do *Gold* at . . . . theatre . . . . with . . . . . . sounded like W. L. Lang." Simply
couldn't hear. Then I thought you said something about my coming to N.Y.—in about
ten days—but had to guess at that. And dearest—was what you said: "I love you"?
Darling, sweetest, angel!

Well, it seemed too terrible to hear your dear old voice, and not talk! And of
course, I had to yell, and they were all listening. Dearest, I do miss you so! Well, then
I went in the room, and they all thought it was such a funny coincidence—so Clara
Beranger supplied the missing info: Willard Mack opens May 23rd,—and name of
theatre, which I have forgotten now, but she said it *was* called the Hudson, and is on
42nd, between 7 & 8th—right off Broadway. Then she said rehearsals had started
Friday—She said Mack was simply *mad* over the play—said he felt it was his real
chance to make good as a fine actor, said he felt it was a great play—and she seems to
feel it is going to be a tremendous success! She said the theatre is good-sized, not
tremendous, and has just been done over very beautifully.

What I kept asking you and what I could not hear your reply to was: are you glad
or sorry? Well, damnit, what an unexpected, uncertain life the playwright's is, what?
I suppose it means all of May in town. Or does it? I wish I knew if you asked me if I
would come down. But you'il write. Meantime, how about your teeth? You are not
going to quit on that, are you, dearest? Oh darling Gene, you don't know how I do
miss you! It's now 12:30 and I feel like sitting up all night and writing to you. It was
so fine to get your letter. You should have had mine by this time.

Mrs. Beranger is corking, really awfully sincere and nice—and you know I wasn't
prepared to like her.

I must tell you about Shane. Whenever Buehler's portrait is in the room, he runs
up to it, looks up at you, and goes "Da-DA, uh,-uh-uh-" you know the noise he makes
when he wants something. Then he pokes his fingers in it—(it's dry) and holds out his
hand, and gets more & more upset because he can't make it talk. "Da DA-uh-uh? uh?
Da DA" Yesterday A.M. I said—"where's Da da?" and he began going through the

same performance, running to the foot of the stairs and getting into a perfect panic. So you see we *both* miss you!

I am sending all mail, none very important. There is a letter from Mabel Dodge, Taos: The book from the [illegible] Society arrived, so you'd better write them—it's very interesting.

Now dearest, write me in detail, won't you?

Good night my own dearest thing I love you so—and miss you so! Your, Agnes

I was so glad you phoned—it was so wonderful just to hear the sound of your voice—even if I couldn't talk to you!

~~

137. **EO to AB** ALS 1 p. (Stationery headed: 529 Mercantile Bldg. / Rochester, N.Y.) [Harvard]

Wednesday. / [April 27, 1921]

My Own: A million thanks for your long letter received yesterday. I was feeling completely all in—much pain—and it cheered me up a lot. Saxe extracted some old abscessed roots on Monday and we both had a frightful ordeal of it. They had grown in under the next tooth and simply refused to be yanked out—had to be cut out bit by bit—and the anaesthetic didn't work right and—well, it was hell on wheels, believe me. Poor Saxe! He honestly suffered more than I did about it. I'm a fine sight—jaw all swollen—and glad you can't see me. No woman could love this face.

That was the principal reason I only wired yesterday and didn't write. I was done up and my nerves all gone. Also things in the Commins family have been rather hectic. Saxe's brother & wife arrived from Los Angeles. I wrote you about their child dying a week ago. It is terribly tragic. Saxe and I have moved out to his sister Miriam's place in the country on the outskirts of town. Very nice out there. I like it better than the town place.

Williams has written me two long letters. His dope doesn't sound so bad. At any rate, there's nothing to be done but let him go ahead and gamble with him. His cast sounds very good—especially Teddy[1] who will be able to keep me posted from the inside.

Saxe expects to be finished with me in about a week—with good luck. My idea is then to set forth for N.Y.—and for you to meet me there, Sweetest One—or as near that time as you can make it. Let me know what you think of this as a general plan and any suggestion you have to make.

This is a short letter but I'm feeling "mighty low." So forgive me this time, Own Little Wife. All love to Shane & you.   Gene

1. Edward J. Ballantine played Nat Bartlett in *Gold*.

138. **AB to EO** ALS 3 pp. (Stationery headed: Peaked Hill Bar / Provincetown, Mass.)
[Harvard]

10.30 A.M. / [April 27, 1921]

Dearest— If you knew the absolute difficulty of getting a chance to really write to you. Firstly: it's Wednesday. Since Saturday we have been in the throes of moving— half in, half out—each day we'd get ready, and then half an hour before the team came, it would rain!

Monday, I got Cookie, and a load out: Saturday, I'd sent the boat. I stayed out Monday, came in yesterday, got the team—it rained! Had to put it off until this A.M. The team has just left with a load, but I didn't dare send Shane & Clarkie, as there is a chill east wind and it is drizzling.—There! I wrote the above, had to go up to Francis after team—but am back. It's 11:20—my god, what rushing! Unless it really pours, I'm going to try & get Shane & Clarkie out this afternoon. Then I'll come in tomorrow . . . Edith had to leave, you see—at the crucial time. Her spouse wired!

You'll think this letter is all my troubles—but I just want you to know why it is I haven't written more. I sent you a day letter yesterday—50 words = 75¢, and your wire arrived today. Also letter about John D. I think your dope on him is right. Clara Beranger shows me his letters to her—he sure is mad about *Gold*. She says there is no doubt it will make a fine picture, too. She's awful nice—very kind and really friendly. She is urging me to write for the movies—wants to *make* me do it—has it all doped out. Says she will give me some of her orders to do—she gets more than she can manage. She says I might not get more than $1,000 (!!!) for my first scenario, but real prices when I had done a few. She wants to take me over to meet the Famous Players[1] heads,—one of them, you see, was editor of *Munsey's*[2] when I used to sell them stuff— and then she will give them my stuff when I do it—also offered to help me do the first. What do you think?

Gee, I miss you! Darling, I'll come to N.Y. or anywhere—don't worry. I'll arrange it all. But listen—this is important—let me know *when* you think you will leave Rochester for N.Y.—the exact date, if possible—and if you will stay till the 23rd. You see, I may try & get mother for a couple of weeks—if you can dope out some real dates. By the way, the Quinns[3] have offered us their apt.—or house—for Aug. & Sept—if we want it. Awfully sweet of them, don't you think. Dearest, I don't care if it did cost $5.50, I'm glad you phoned me. Shane misses you so—it's queer in such a little kid! Dearest, forgive the scrawl.

I'm trying to get [this in?] for noon mail. Will send Warren's address tomorrow. Don't see *Times*—no subscription. A million kisses dear heart of mine. *Agnes.*

1. Film production company formed in 1912 by Adolph Zukor.
2. *Munsey's Magazine*, founded in 1889, was one of the more prominent magazines of popular literature—short stories and articles. AB never published in this magazine, but her

writing did appear in some of the other magazines owned by Frank Munsey. The editor she is referring to was probably Sonja Levien.

    3.   Edmond T. Quinn, a sculptor and friend of AB's father, and his wife, Emily. His bust of EO is in the Beinecke Library at Yale University. Max Wylie reports that Quinn's bust of AB was in her house when he first visited her in 1956.

---

139. **EO to AB** ALS 1 p. (Rochester, New York) [Harvard]

Thursday A.M. / [April 28, 1921]

Own Little Wife: This is written out at the half-farm, half suburban villa, establishment of Saxe's brother-in-law. It is sure nice and quiet out here—woods nearby— reminds me quite a bit of West P.P. although the country is more fertile and has the aspect of comfortable prosperity—big orchards, etc.

    I hope there will be a letter from you when I go in to the office. There was nothing yesterday but the forwarded stuff you sent.

    Saxe is to extract another root today—and, gosh, how I dread it! Thank God this will mark the end of the yanking. He put the bridge on the right upper side in yesterday—temporarily, not cemented yet. It fits and looks very well.

    (Saxe just phoned (11 A.M.) from the office to say there is no letter from you there yet. I don't want to reproach but I do think you could be a little more considerate at this time without straining yourself. Even if you are out at Peaked Hill Bar, there is a C.G. going in every day.)

    All my love to you and Shane.   Gene.

---

140. **EO to AB** ALS 2 pp. (Stationery headed: Five Twenty Nine Mercantile Bldg. / Rochester, N.Y.) [Harvard]

Thursday (late P.M.) / [April 28, 1921]

Own Sweetheart: I wrote you rather a hurt little note this morning because no letter had come from you. Later—about 2 P.M. it arrived—must have been delayed. I'm awfully sorry for being so hasty. Your letters mean so much when I'm down in the mouth—("In the mouth" is right!)—and I was so disappointed at not hearing. Your letter was lovely. Poor little girl, to have so much damn moving work thrust on you. Wish I were there.

    Just had another extraction. Didn't hurt as bad as others—but bad enough. Feel a bit groggy. I'll let you know by wire or letter the exact date and hour of my departure hence just as soon as Saxe can tell me.

    For Christ sake, don't think of the movie writing. My God, you have a soul to express which will create beauty in your novel, etc. if you will only work hard and give it a chance. The films would ruin all that chance—and what for? A mess of garbage! For God's sake, be your beautiful self and live out your life in the light. You may think you can trifle with the film and still do your real work but you can't. The experience of everyone else is against it. Let the Clara Bs of the world do their contemptible scribbling. They can't do any better and they'd like everyone else to "get that way."

Be yourself! God stiffen it, you're not a movie writer! I'll hate you if you go in for it, honestly!

If the above sounds rather excited, pardon me! I just have a tooth pulled and then your letter comes hinting you'd like to become a movie writer! These are grey days. Where is your novel? All my love, Sweetheart Gene

~⌐

141. **AB to EO** ALS 1 p. (Stationery headed: Peaked Hill Bar / Provincetown, Mass.) [Harvard]

[April 28?, 1921]

Darling— Enclose letter from Lucy H.[1] Susan wants you to see—I've written once today. Shane & Clark are off. The house is most ready to leave. I'll walk out tonight, come in tomorrow & finish up here.

Much, much love my ownest, dearest Your *Agnes*

1. Probably Lucy Huffaker, a close friend of Susan Glaspell. She was the wife of Edward Goodman, a critic and director, and closely involved with some of the power struggles going on within the Provincetown Players.

~⌐

142. **AB to EO** ALS 3 pp. (Stationery headed: Peaked Hill Bar / Provincetown, Mass.) [Harvard]

Friday, 5 P.M. / [April 29, 1921]

Dear Gene: I started out to walk to Peaked Hill about an hour ago, after an orgy of tending to things—Tony, carting, closing up the house, etc. etc.—and when I got to the end of Bradford Street, where we turn into the woods, I suddenly felt too all in to attempt it, so I walked back and am staying at Susan's tonight. It seems as if this is the first chance I've had to write you a letter.

I'm certainly sorry you are having such trouble with your teeth. However, dear, it will be more than worth it in the end—it will be *joy* to have something to chew with again! I am so glad you have resolved to stick until it's through. I do wish you had a real definite idea about where you would [land?] in N.Y. I think you'd enjoy it more at the Harvard Club, do you know it? You might go there for a few days before I come down—Wait a second while I look up a calendar—next Sat. is May 7th—a week from tomorrow. Suppose I got in town the 9th, or 10th. (Mon. or Tuesday). Then we could go to a hotel—

Things seem to be all right out at the house. The stove works fine.—

Next morning / [April 30, 1921]

Well, dear, I didn't get this off last night—Again it rains—rains—rains! So melancholy! But I did get a laugh out of your letter this morning—apropos of movies. Don't worry, honey dear, I'm not going to lose my soul—Anyway, I don't suppose I *could* do it. It just seemed a way to make some money—not for *me*, but I've always felt that if I ever could, it would really be *up* to me to make some. And somehow, I feel I could be more successful at the writing out of movie ideas—you see, you *don't* even write the scenario—mail just arrived—Jig & Sue are reading theirs from P. Players. All arranged to go to London, Gilpin signed at $500 per week.[1] Cochran[2] cables, he has mailed contracts, SO THAT IS SETTLED! Also, rec. letter from Tyler says he had my wire, & thanking me, had not heard from you. Write me what you told Tyler.

I'm so sorry about your teeth—dear heart! And don't be afraid I'm going to become "movieized." I am longing to see you— Your own   Agnes.

I enclose a lot of clippings.

1.   Charles Gilpin (1872–1930), who originated the role of Brutus Jones in *The Emperor Jones* (1920), and in doing so became the first black actor to play a leading role in a Broadway production, was going to play the part in London, but later Paul Robeson was given the role for that revival.
2.   Possibly Clifford Cochran, who later coproduced the film of *The Emperor Jones*, or Charles B. Cochran, Broadway producer.

143. **AB to EO** ALS 2 pp. (Stationery headed: Eugene O'Neill / Provincetown, Mass.) [Harvard]

[April 30?, 1921]

Dearest Gene— Enclosed is Tyler's letter. I wired him "Eugene in Rochester am forwarding letter. He will wire." I also enclose clipping sent from the Tyler office three days ago—I hadn't intended sending it—I think Tyler sent it in order to show you *The Straw* was a big risk for him, & what *popular* opinion might be—but any man who could take any stock (or want *you* to see!) such an utterly stupid, cheap write-up—well! I send it *now* because I want you to see what he is trying to do—work on you to cut out the "grewsome stuff," etc.—I think his letter shows up that he won't—or, doubtless can't—open in N.Y. unless it is a big hit on Road—which—it hardly will be—now, certainly within a year or so, you will have gained enough of a *financial* rep. also, that you *can* get a theatre in town—for *The Straw*, even? Why not wait for that? As for his slam on *Gold*, I believe *your* plays have a better chance opening in town in July than on the road in Oct.

A million kisses, onliest! I'll manage somehow to meet you in town. Hastily,   A.

⁓〇

144. **EO to AB** ALS 1 p. (Stationery headed: Five Twenty Nine Mercantile Bldg. / Rochester, N.Y.) [Harvard]

Saturday P.M. / [April 30, 1921]

Own Sweetheart: Received your enclosed letter from Tyler, the clippings, etc. this afternoon when I arrived at the office for my daily session. The end of my dental ordeal is now in sight. Two bridges are made—in addition to the one already in place—and ready to go in as soon as I heal up sufficiently. Five or six small fillings are still in store—and then, release! The work Saxe has done has been fine and should prove lasting. It has *not* been painless—but I expected the worst anyway.

I won't be sorry to leave Rochester. I'm a bit fed up with life up here—although, under the circumstances, I'd have been just as miserable anywhere else. I miss you more and more every day. It seems as if I couldn't wait to see you, Dear Heart of Mine! How I'll love to feel your arms about me again! It will be home, home!!

It has occurred to me that I might run up to P'town from here for a couple of days rest and then we could both go down to N.Y. together. This is only a notion. Write or wire me what you think. I honestly need a rest before facing rehearsals—a rest from pain and ennui. I'm all in—nervously fagged out. And Teddy writes me everything is going fine with *Gold*. Williams is on the job sober every second—and he is good when he's good, you know.

Madden writes that Tyler has agreed to Dec. 1st, N.Y. So that's that! There is no other news to relate.

All my love, Darling!! Soon, now! Kiss our heir for me!   Gene.

⁓〇

145. **AB to EO** ALS 10 pp. (Stationery headed: Peaked Hill Bar / Provincetown, Mass.) [Harvard]

[April 30?, 1921]

Gene dear: I wondered, after I wrote it, if you would think heartless my remark about laughing at what you said about my writing for the movies. It wasn't that: I felt, when I read it, that what you said was the greatest compliment I would ever get about myself—and also a very fine protest against what is all wrong with most of life. But you wrote it in such a dear, funny, mad way! And winding up—"I just have a tooth pulled and then your letter comes hinting you'd like to become a movie writer! These are grey days!" Dear old thing!

As a matter of fact, every time I *allow* myself to think of the novel, I get awfully excited and wrought up. But I *won't* think of it until I *can* write it—because I'd just let everything else drop, I know.

A lot of clippings have come, some of which I have sent on. There is a long article clipped from *Munsey's* magazine, on American playwrights—the very first paragraph mentions you, and there is a lot about you, but they left out the middle of the article! There are almost a dozen photos of almost every playwright in America! Was yours in, I wonder. Also, *Shadowland*, although it announces in its index an interview with you, does *not* include it.[1] I wonder if Muray[2] is not on the job? I thought Mary Dale Clark "had ought to" have some of hers used. (Say, it's the damndest thing about Anna! She is in heat! Jones is not here—the people across the way are keeping him—and it is simply *terrible* the way Anna acts! She crawls along the ground, uttering the most piteous and beseeching cry, and wiggling her behind in the most inviting way! Then she rolls on the floor and bites herself, still crying, then she backs, rear end to up against the wall, and rubs her "hinie" against it, and all the time uttering those terrible sounds! But the worst of it is she does not let up for *one damn second*! If you touch her she goes almost crazy. We have to keep her locked up in the little room and believe me if she has not got over it by tomorrow I am going to walk in and bring Jonesy out! Believe me, it makes me nervous!)

Bill Dunbar[3] sent a wire that he was coming up Wednesday, but did not appear. Then he wrote. I will answer him saying you are away. Several letters have come, which I answered. Wasn't it funny—the one from Mabel Dodge? You got it?

Am sending cheque to you, as I can't deposit it until endorsed. Wish you'd said if you had received it or not.

(Anna kept howling so pitifully, I just took her & dipped her into a basin of cold water, from the waist down! It *may* calm her, and at least will keep her busy drying herself—yes she has stopped! and has retired under the stove!)

Am anxious to talk to you about the New Provincetown Player[4] plays, about which a great deal has been told me by Jig. They are forming a stock company for $150,000.00—you, Susan, Jig, Fitzie, & Harry Weinberger[5] are the heads—I am wondering if it involves you in a financial responsibility? However, the thing that rather got my goat was—well:

Agnes: But Jig, will you stick to your plan, American plays only?

Jig: Certainly—decidedly.

A.   But *do* you think, Jig, that you can get *enough* good American plays to keep a theatre like this going. Remember, after all, this has been an exceptional year.

J.   Why yes. Why not? There are three of us who have proved that we *can* write successful plays (I suppose he, Sue, & you). Then, I think Floyd Dell[6] will do us a long play, and Lucian Cary[7] will do one, and Alice Rostetter[8] has done *one* good play—

A.   Well, it seems to me rather foolish to rely on *them*. They had chances all along to write those fine plays they tell you they have up their sleeves. After all, I think your *new* good plays, with a theatre like this, will be more likely to come from people outside—new people, who'll feel encouraged to try plays, instead of turning to some other form.

J.   Well, perhaps; but at least we have as I said before, three people on whose work we can count—Gene, & Susan & I.

A.   Of course, a good deal of Gene's work is done uptown . . .

J.   —Well, but if we have this Theatre, will Gene want *any* of his work done uptown? I think Gene sees by this time that the uptown commercial game is no good. They won't give him a theatre—(he referred to John W. having to wait til May in order to get a theatre for *Gold*—) I think Gene *will* want us to do *all* his plays—

The End.

Now, do you, or don't you, think it rather presumptuous on Jig's part to feel that when they have this new theatre, which will seat 299 people, that they can count on the pick of your work?

I felt it was. But I tactfully said no more—

Well, this is a long letter. Hope you read it all. I wrote you in town today and mailed it. Then I walked out here—in a pouring rain, by the way. I arrived about 5:30, had supper, and wrote a lot of letters—just answers to stuff that had accumulated and finished up with this. It's now 10:30—so I go up to my lonesome couch.

Honey dear, it *will* be good to see you again! I'm so sorry about your toofies! Goodnight, my sweetest lover,   Your Agnes.

Shane still loves his DaDA!

1. *Shadowland* published "A Colloquy between Eugene O'Neill and Oliver M. Sayler" exactly one year later, in April 1922, p. 66. See Estrin, *Conversations with Eugene O'Neill*, 21–25.

2. Probably refers to Nickolas Muray (1892?–1965), a Greenwich Village photographer who had recently made portraits of both EO and AB.

3. William Dunbar played Major Andrews in the Provincetown Players production of *Exorcism* in March 1920.

4. The story of the reorganization of the amateur Provincetown Players as a fully professional theater is told by Sarlós in chapter 8 of *Jig Cook*.

5. Attorney (1888–1938) for the Provincetown Players and later EO's personal attorney.

6. Floyd Dell (1887–1969), journalist, playwright, and associate editor of *The Masses*.

7. Lucian Cary (1886–1971), journalist and short-story writer.

8. Alice Rostetter had written and acted in *The Widow's Veil* for the Provincetown Players.

146. **AB to EO** ALS 3 pp. (Stationery headed: Peaked Hill Bar / Provincetown, Mass.) [Harvard]

May 1st [1921]. Sunday

The above date is a jest, my dear! We are in the midst of a howling, raining, cold nor'easter. No wood—relying on the new oil heater—suddenly, unexplainably, *that* goes out— nothing will make it go. We begin to freeze. Shane begins to look blue about the mouth. Finally—as a last desperate remedy, we take the wrench, unscrew the "feedpipe" and, finding it clogged, clean it. Then, glory be, the thing works again.

Good thing it did! I was so utterly wretched and furious and tired out when this happened that I was vowing, between clenched teeth, that I'd sit right down and write you that I was *through* with the struggle of trying to live out here with a family! And that we'd better get a place in town; and you could come out here to write! But honestly it is discouraging! I've been after & after Tony—Somehow, I feel now as if the exhausting struggles of running this place spoiled the pleasure of it—that it is all right for two people alone when they can live simply as you & I did that first summer—but that when it comes to a family—! And all the time, Clark's loud strident voice talking, talking—if not to me, then to Shane. No peace—no quiet. "Shane! Shane! Ain't he cute! Shane, leave that alone!" etc. How she shouts! Like a woman used to talking in an uproar of people!

I wrote you a long letter last night. For God's sake, let's go abroad or somewhere, until Shane is four or five and we can come out here without anyone but ourselves!

Evidently this is likely to happen to the *stove* at any moment. And you know about the pump—next thing the pipes will rust through, and we will need a new plumbing system.

Another thing—I find out through perfectly unintentional chatter of Cookie's that while I was away, Mrs. Clark got her to go and play with Shane in his crib—in the morning. Shane wearing only his nightgown, in that cold room and standing up!— while *she remained in bed*! Then I find Shane has a cold, and cough! No wonder! At least I thought I could trust her with Shane—that was the big excuse for her.

Just looked up Warren's address, it is 1475 Broadway. James C. Warren, Attorney.

Much love, my dearest, forgive this cross letter—but I *am* blue! *Agnes.*

147. **EO to AB** ALS 1 p. (529 Mercantile Bldg. / Rochester, N.Y.) [Harvard]

Monday P.M. / [May 2, 1921]

Own Sweetheart: Two letters from you this forenoon. I am just as happy as can be! But I feel guilty because I failed to get one off to you yesterday. It was a case of too much Jewish family—crowds and crowds of them, seven or eight children running and shouting about—Talk, Talk, Talk!—a general pandemonium at the Commins home all yesterday afternoon and evening. Twelve or more sitting at dinner! I nearly went "nuts," and writing was out of the question. But I was sort of guest of honor and had to stick it out.

I am wiring you to expect a letter with definite dope. I can't give it in this but will write later on—this eve—when I have had a chance to look up train connections. I think, unless a hurry call comes from N.Y. in the meantime, that I will come to Provincetown—if any sort of connections can be made—leaving here either Wednesday or Thursday night, this depending on Saxe. Then I will stay there—with YOU!!—until Monday or Tuesday when we can go down together to N.Y.

Damn your suggestion of Harvard Club! Is there a wife Agnes there? What I need is a few days rest and quiet in the open air—and you, you, YOU!!! My Own Love, My Little Sweetheart Wife, the thought of seeing you so soon again just drives me foolish with joy! I've missed you so horribly all these long, painful, rainy days.

I'll wire or write exact data later! A million kisses! Gene

~⌒

148. **AB to EO** ALS 2 pp. ([Provincetown, Mass.]) [Harvard]

[May 2, 1921]

Dearest— Just a line to send my love.—Gee, how I wish I could talk to you!

I haven't got today's mail yet. S'pose you got my letter—& wire. All over at dunes now, and everything going fine—stove, etc.—but still rotten weather—

There now! I wrote this letter this morning, & waited over instead of going to the "backside" first because I wanted that daily letter that has meant so much. And no letter! This is scribbled at Susan's. I'm awful lonely—there's so much I want to say—gee. I feel like jumping a train to Rochester. Much love, *Agnes.*

~⌒

149. **EO to AB** ALS 1 p. (529 Mercantile Bldg. / Rochester, N.Y.) [Harvard]

Monday night. / [May 2, 1921]

Own Love of Mine: Saxe seems so confident of having me all fixed by Wednesday that I have made a definite plan on that score. Will leave here for Provincetown Wednesday at 6:30 P.M.—arrive in Boston 6:30 A.M.—have time for breakfast and catch 7:30 for P'town—and be with you at noon Thursday—go to N.Y. Monday or Tues.

The above will be carried out to the letter unless the unforeseen occurs—in which case I will wire you at once.

I'm so lonely! I miss you so, want you so, need you so, love you so!!!! I've simply got to come back to you before facing this *Gold* gamble. And New York would be a bum place for our first reunion. In our home, Darling Girl, where I can lie safe in your arms. Wouldn't you rather it to be this way and then us go down together? I know you would, Sweetheart, if you love me half as much as I do you.

I kiss your dear lips, Sweetest Wife! I love you above everything! I'm dying without you. It seems as if all the world were strange and ugly when you're not with me.

Oh, I just love you! That's all I can say to express it. Kiss Shane for me.   Gene.

150. **AB to EO** ALS 3 pp. (Stationery headed: Peaked Hill Bar / Provincetown, Mass.) [Harvard]

May 2nd [1921]

Gene Dearest— I suppose the letter I wrote you yesterday *was* rather gloomy. But don't mind it. Only I do hope you don't sit down and write me a cross reply, and say that when you are suffering and need cheering up, I fail you!

The weather has cleared considerably—however, I don't rely on it. Rain is liable to come upon me again tomorrow—rain and wind and gloom! I was much cheered this afternoon, however, on walking up to the s.q. station, to receive your two letters. As for your coming up here, I really don't advise it. Think of the trip—coming and going—and for a couple of days—and of course it would be *bound* to rain then! I really do think under the circumstances that it would be a foolish thing to do. Once you really get through with your teeth, you will find you'll get over the nervous exhaustion. Write ahead to the Harvard Club that you want a room. Then stay around the club all you can—and if you don't feel like it, I *wouldn't go to rehearsals the first two days you are in town.* And just see the people you would enjoy seeing—make appointments later on—(there'll be lots of time)—with the others. Then find time to try the pool every day—tell the telephone operator not to give you any calls until after 10:30—eat—and I believe you'd get more of a rest than if you rushed up here and back.

I will try and get in town by Monday—a week from today. *I* need a rest, too—really. I do believe that I've lost weight—running across the dunes so much, etc.

I have not heard from Mother yet—hope she can make it.

Am sending by this mail a number of more or less important letters—including one from Ralph Block.[1] I wrote Dunbar a note, saying you were in Rochester, and wouldn't be here 'til the end of May. I fear he is a pest!

What do you think? Today Shane saw your outing coat—the one you wear so much with the corduroy collar—and he grabbed it and tried to pull it down and look inside it, and began whining and crying Dada DaDA—That sounds as if it was invented, but it's every word true!

Gee, this paper seems pretty blotty, what? I must get some *black* ink.

Dearest, I had the awfullest dream about you last night! Well, it won't be long now, dear darling old thing! Your own,   Agnes

1.   Ralph Block (1889?–1974), movie producer, writer, critic. EO's belated reply to Block's letter is in *Selected Letters of Eugene O'Neill*, ed. Bogard and Bryer, 155.

~~)

151. **AB to EO** AL 3 pp. (Stationery headed: Peaked Hill Bar / Provincetown, Mass.) [Harvard]

May 4th, [1921]

Dearest Gene,   I'm trying to get a letter off to you every day—you say you appreciate them!

Started this out at the house, but had to come in—found a letter from mother—she can't come, as Barbara and Walter,[1] who it seems have been married nearly a year but keeping it quiet on account of his mother, are going to have an addition to the family in June. As Barbara has no woman around and is not at all well, Mother does not dare leave her—the house is far away from any neighbors. I guess something like this is about the only thing that would keep mother, she is usually so willing to do anything. Of course it puts me in a pickle. I am hoping there may be a letter from you this afternoon, with some definite plans, and will wait for the mail before closing this.

I don't like to leave Shane with Clark for 2 weeks—out there—even with Terry—Edith will be here, but I don't know that she makes so much difference!

Suppose the best thing would be for me to stay here—you come up for a day or so—what do you think?[2]

Am at Jig & Sue's. There are high rows going on as to who shall, and who shan't go to London with *Suppressed Desires*![3] Susan is sick—in bed.

Poor dear, how very awful you must feel. After all that work how much will Saxe charge? Stella kept saying: "It won't cost Gene anything," but you'll have to insist on an account—it would probably come to about $300 or even more with most dentists.

It is cloudy again today—ain't it awful?

1.   Barbara Boulton, AB's younger sister.
2.   Sheaffer reports that EO did return to Peaked Hill for a few days before going to New York for rehearsals of *Gold*, perhaps accompanied by AB. After EO fled back to Provincetown in despair over the impending disaster of the production, AB took his place in New York to report on preparations for the production. The opening of *Gold* was postponed once, from May 23 to June 1, when it finally opened and ran for thirteen performances.
3.   Cook and Glaspell cowrote *Suppressed Desires* in 1914; the London tour was eventually cancelled.

〜◯

152. **AB to EO** ALS 3 pp. (Stationery headed: Prince George Hotel, / Fifth Ave. &
28th Street New York) [Harvard]

[May 31?, 1921][1]

Dearest— It's early—we got to the hotel at 8—so, although there is naught to tell you
but that we made connections and I love you, I can't resist this opportunity to drop
you a few lines.

Got an upper on the 10:45—ate at a quick lunch, and Cookie and I wandered the
remaining hours about Boston, looking in the shop windows, and reflecting on the
utter lack of joy in a Boston holiday mob.[2] For believe me, we were in the worst of it!
The trip down was O.K. with the exception of the conductor rousing me out of my
slumbers because he said *he* couldn't find any ticket for me—after I had given it to him.

They greeted me here with apparent joy, and gave me a room for $4.00, which, to
my surprise, besides being very light and airy, *has a bath!* (for 2, $4.00! and remem-
ber what we got at the Brevoort for that price!

Well, dear, if you knew how much I missed you, you'd be overjoyed! Only hope
you do, too. But I'll be back very soon, and then we will plan our really wonderful
summer.

I'm going to take a bath and then start 'phoning. Goodby my onliest, sweetest
own! *Agnes.*

   1. Assigning this letter to late May, the period of AB's trip to New York in EO's place to
observe the opening of *Gold*, is purely conjectural.
   2. Presumably she is referring to Decoration Day.

〜◯

153. **AB to EO** ALS 9 pp. (Stationery headed: Prince George Hotel, / Fifth Ave. &
28th Street New York) [Harvard]

Tuesday. / [May 31, 1921]

Dearest Gene— This letter, I hope, won't get to you until after I have wired that
Gold is a famous success! But, should my wire be otherwise, it will perhaps explain
much—anyway, old dear, it's been a harrowing day!

I called up Stella very soon after writing you this A.M. She asked "of course,
you've heard the big news?" I said, another postponement? "No," quoth she "Mack is
out of it, and Geo. Marion[1] is going to play the Captain."—Mack, it seems, quit on
Sunday. I told this to Nathan over the 'phone, and Nathan though it was a great piece
of good luck, so did Teddy—said Marion was much better, said Mack improvised the
lines, etc. Well, then Teddy said no reason had been given to the company for Mack

not being there, also said no announcement had been made.—He feared Mack might show up and open in it. Said I should go to rehearsal. Went, saw Saint-Gaudens[2] (stayed only 2 minutes) who seemed completely worried and who told me Mack was back! Well, *he* seemed to think it was an outrage to let Mack do it, but said it was "up to John." Suggested that I see Williams, and that perhaps Williams would be glad to use *you* as an excuse for getting Mack out of cast. I had an appointment with Madden, and of course when I told Madden about this, he thought it was fierce, thought you should and could get out an injunction against Mack appearing in it. Then *he* grabbed the phone and got Williams, said I was there and that he thought Williams should come up or we go down—Well, Williams just did the frigid squelch to Mr. Madden, and got away with it. Told Madden that of course he rehearsed Marion—that he always insisted his understudy be letter perfect—that the show would open as per announcement! Goodby!

Well, Madden was like a little licked dog—said to W. "Oh, it's just rumors, then? sorry, Good luck"—Then said to me "Williams says it's nothing but a lot of talk. . . ." Madden didn't realize that what Williams said did not alter situation one iota—that is, that Mack, after *never* learning his lines—Teddy says he has completely re-written & transposed some of his speeches in the last act—and after quitting the show cold for 4 days—comes sneaking back for the dress rehearsal and the opening! Even St. G. doesn't want him!

As Williams had made an appointment to phone him, I called the office. He was exceedingly disagreeable—that is, maintained a freezing silence!—sort of "Well? Yes?" I told him about being informed that Mack was out etc. (I had to say so, as he knew I wanted to see him about that)—whereupon he tried the same stuff on me—"I always rehearse my understudies, etc. . . . " Whereupon I got a bit sore—and very much to the point I said "I feel, Mr. Williams, that Eugene, or anyone else, would consider it an extraordinary thing for the man who plays the leading part in the play to absent himself for the last week of rehearsals, and then turn up for the opening;—and besides, Mr. Ballantine wrote Eugene that Mack did *not* know his lines." Then I told him that I had understood from Mr. St. Gaudens' [attitude?] that Marion was the better bet, and that it would be of advantage to the play to have Marion instead of Mack; and that I had thought, if he, Williams, could not, as manager—(or friend) get rid of Mack, that it might be wise to wire you to give your consent to have all the blame for Mack's dismissal on *your* shoulders. Then I added: if Eugene were here, I am sure he would consider it an outrage to allow Mack to open in it—(All this in a *very icy* tone!) Well, he suddenly got very nice, said he'd like to talk it over with me, could he call me up & see me? Said he wanted to *open* with Mack, as per *ads* (of course it *would* have been a shame to spoil those ads!) but might do the other later.

Well, suppose I had wired as I intended. "Thurs. A.M. Mack out, Marion's very fine as Bartlett. Think it is wonderful. Good luck." Then later: "Mack returns at dress rehearsal, insists on opening in play."—Damn it, why aren't you here? I wanted to wire you about Mack, but Madden thought it useless, as you could not easily get injunction to stop him without seeing him.[3] Again, wire might not reach Peaked Hill until say late Tuesday, then you would have felt fine!

Dearest, dearest, dearest—how I miss you! Remember—you and I!   A.

1.   George Marion (1860–1945) played Butler in *Gold* and understudied Willard Mack as the Captain. He later played the role of Chris Christopherson in *"Anna Christie"* (November 1921).

2.   Homer Saint-Gaudens, the director.

3.   In the end, *Gold* opened on June 1 with Mack in the lead and his performance was generally praised, while the play was generally condemned as bad melodrama. It closed after thirteen performances.

154. **EO to AB** ALS 1 p. ([Provincetown, Mass.]) [Harvard]

Outside.
Wednesday A.M. / [June 1, 1921]

Own Little Wife: Just a line which I hope will greet you on your arrival at the farm. No wire yesterday. I've been worried to death wondering how you made the trip. Hope you got a berth that night. Yesterday was so hot it would have been awful taking that six hour train trip. Today is much cooler out here—wind from the north. Hope this is true of New York—for *Gold*'s sake.

Jimmy is still out here—goes back to Truro today. They want me to go over there tonight but I don't know—think I'd rather spend the opening out here alone with just your memory, Sweetheart. I've missed you so! Come back to me the very first second you can, won't you? Whether *Gold* is success or failure, I'll need you to share it. I always need you to share everything—or it isn't real. That's my secret.

Jimmy and I have tried out the boat. She is a beautiful success! You must christen her when you return. Names suggested so far have been the "Sarah Allen" (if *Gold* goes)[1]—the "Spanish Willy"[2]—and the "Rider to the Sea."

All my love! A million kisses everywhere! I'll look forward to your wire after the ordeal.   Gene.

1.   Name of the ghost ship that returns in *Gold*.

2.   EO eventually decided to name the kayak after his favorite bootlegger, Willie Fernandez, known as Spanish Willie.

155. **AB to EO** ALS 1 p. ([Biltmore Hotel, New York]) [Harvard]

Sat. A.M. 7 / [June 4?, 1921][3]

Spent the night in the Biltmore, grand style—$4.50 with bath for the two of us— in bed by 9, a mistake, as slept too early—and dreamt vividly all the rest of the night.

Shane bird thinks it's great as it's just across from the station, and he can look down into the train yard.

Leave here at 8:45. 83 miles to *Hartford*.

A million kisses, 500,000 hugs, four thousand squeezes. *Aggie*.

1. The dating of this letter is based solely on EO's allusion in the previous letter to AB's visit to "the farm," presumably her mother and father's farm near Litchfield, Connecticut. This would account for her traveling to Hartford.

~~⌒

156. **EO to AB** ALS 1 p. (Stationery headed: Eugene O'Neill / Provincetown, Mass.) [Harvard]

Monday P.M. / [August 8?, 1921]

Own Little Wife: Well, here is the picture of Shane—the right one, I think. After I left the train, went for the stove wire but they couldn't find one so I lost time and thereby missed the C.G. wagon. Walked back, gave the "Spanish Willie" its second coat, took our heir with me for a dip—and here I am.

Hope the trip to New London was not too dreadful and that my wire got Jim down to the train to meet you—also that you will enjoy your short stay there.

I'm going to work hard while you are away, you can bet. I already feel pangs of loneliness and the house seems empty without you. Work will help take my mind off my aloneness.

I hope you'll find the right apartment in N.Y. and arrange everything just as you would have it. Your happiness means mine. This because I love you and not from any selfish motive. Our lives & love ought to mean that—doing our best to make each other happy, to help each other work and grow. A good-night kiss, Own Sweetheart. Gene.

~~⌒

157. **EO to AB** ALS 1 p. (Stationery headed: Eugene O'Neill / Provincetown, Mass.) [Harvard]

Tuesday P.M. / [August 9, 1921]

Own Sweetheart: A gorgeous day—wind northwest—no flies, no "skeets," water wonderful. I labored hard at *The Fountain* this morning, also for a while this P.M. This is the crucial point, this vision scene, and requires some writing to make its mysticism breathe. It must be done with a bit of white flame. I'm hoping I can.[1]

Shane was in the water with me this P.M. As usual, it meant ecstasy for him and he performed no end of antics and extemporized dances in honor of the sun and sea. You and Mrs. Clark seemed to think he might be sick on account of his being so peevish yesterday. No chance! If he is sick, so is Jack Dempsey.

I forgot to tell you yesterday that I brought Terry over with me when I came back. Met him at Francis' and he looked so done-up and sick that I thought I ought to come to the rescue. He has been tortured to death by the mosquitos in his swamp villa. (No, no beer party. I have told him it won't be ready for two weeks.)

Am enclosing a letter from Bobby[2] which I opened, knowing it would be for us both. You will note that he says Hopkins plans to start on *"Anna Christie"* about Sept. 20th. I hope he makes it Oct. 1st instead. I want that full month of Sept. up here with you so much. As Bobby says, "It is a very rare thing that you and Gene and the place make all together"—even if at times *you* don't think so.

I hope you'll get good news from Dave[3]. Find the place you want. I'll say again, I want you to be happy! Everything is secondary to that.

All love, My Own! I miss you! Come back as soon as you can make it.

A long lovely kiss! Gene

P.S. My best to all your family.

1. *The Fountain* was finished early in 1922 but not produced until December 1925, when it ran for twenty-five performances.
2. Robert Edmond Jones (1887–1954) was theatrical designer and director for the Provincetown Players, the Experimental Theatre, Inc., and many other producing organizations. He designed and/or directed many O'Neill plays, beginning with *"Anna Christie"* (1921) and *The Hairy Ape* (1922).
3. Dave Carb.

158. **EO to AB** ALS 1 p. (Stationery headed: Eugene O'Neill / Provincetown, Mass.) [Harvard]

Aug. 11, 1921

Own Little Wife: Only a postcard so far but am hoping for more attention from you via today's mail. It is getting quite lonely out here without no letters nor nothin'.

Not that we lack company. Two beautiful young ladies are with us—Viola and the bank president, Young's, daughter. The latter popped into the studio by mistake this noon and caught me stark naked. She gave a shriek and fled. It must have made quite a moment in her 17 year old life. Viola brought me out a box of fudge. They are nice girls and it's rather refreshing—the chatter of youth about the place—when one is lonely.

The Beautiful (?) Blond was also out. She finally got me cornered and asked for advice about going on the stage. I told her to try out for a part with the P.P.—which "passes the buck" very adroitly, I think.

Terry went back to his shack yesterday. I wanted him to stick around but I guess

Eugene O'Neill, mid-1920s. Photographer unknown. Yale Collection of American Literature, Beinecke Rare Book and Manuscript Library.

he pined to return to his brewing. I'm regretful. It's comforting to have him about when you're not here. He has a quality all his own.

No sunbath today. Flies frightful again. Worked hard at my scrivening and got a deal done.

Suppose you will be leaving Litchfield tomorrow for N.Y. and P.P. Hope you are having a good time there and that you will write me all about it—how Eddie & Cecil are coming along, etc.

Well, bye-bye for this time. There is no news to tell. We are all fine.

A long kiss! I love you so! Love us & Peaked Hill and come home soon!   Gene.

159. **AB to EO** ALS 3 pp. (Milton, [Connecticut]) [Harvard]

Thursday / [August 11, 1921]

Dearest Gene: I really feel wicked not having written you at New London—but the truth is I didn't get a chance. Your mother and Jim met me, and of course we sat a while up in her room and talked. The next morning I sat with her, then we spent the afternoon going to "the Beach." Seeing N.L. in all its glory of bathing suits and bronze flesh; then dinner without even returning to hotel, then up to Sheridans, then from Sheridans back to the 9:30 movie from which we didn't get out until eleven. Your mother had persuaded me to stay over night: the only connection for Waterbury left at 7:55 A.M.— and I left at that hour the next day—traveled until nearly four before getting here last night. And had to pay, besides $4.something railway, $5.00 for car to get from Torrington to Milton. During all this time, I was faithfully taking the pills, and this A.M. had the cramp & back-ache—but didn't mind them, as all was O.K. Then I discovered that my arm, from which I hadn't removed the bandage, was badly festered, a big hole in it full of pus, and this has made me feel very rotten—sort of sick at my stomach, etc.[1]

This is a stupid letter, dear, but I will write you a real one when I feel a little better—your mother & Jim seem fine, and were delighted to see me. The house we thought of is *unfurnished*— & besides, your mother has an idea of going to Cal. if she can manage it.[2] I leave here for Pt. P. Monday—Cecil and Eddy[3] and all send their love. How are you, my dearest? I *do* miss you so, and look forward to being back— All my love, every bit, to you.   Agnes.

You won't have to wait so long between letters again. Kiss Shane, & my best to Mrs. C.

1.   AB indicated to Max Wylie that she had a two-month series of boils and abscesses requiring draining and dressing during this period.
2.   EO had thought they might spend the winter in one of the O'Neill properties in New London (Louis Sheaffer, undated interview of AB, Connecticut College Collection).
3.   Cecil Boulton and Edward Fisk.

∽

160. **EO to AB** ALS 1 p. (Stationery headed: Eugene O'Neill / Provincetown, Mass.)
[Harvard]

Friday, Aug. 12, '21

Own Sweetheart: Still no word from you—no letter yesterday, that is. You are writing "occasionally," as you put it at the train, with a vengeance. But I will heap coals of fire on your head by writing this, my fifth, and hoping today's mail will bring the long-awaited. If I don't hear from you this eve., I'll feel quite sure you've eloped with some farmer lad.

Still laboring on my vision scene but it draws near the end and I ought to finish it tomorrow. Whether it is what it ought to be or not, I can't tell at this juncture. It is much too close now for me to see it. I sure hope it's right. I've sweat some blood over it.

A letter from Margaret Steele[1] came for you yesterday. I opened it. There is nothing of interest in it or I would forward. She simply says she has been sick but is O.K. again—wants to know when we are coming over. I sat down last night and wrote a long letter to Wilbur for both of us and told him all the news, what our plans were, etc.

Also received word from the London Everyman Theatre yesterday. MacDermott[2] says *In The Zone* convinced his finance committee that other plays could pay beside Shaw's, and he would like to go ahead with more of mine besides the two he has. He wants to contract for *Ile*, *The Rope*, and *Beyond The Horizon*—wants to read *Gold & Diff'rent*. I've written Madden to arrange for *Ile & The Rope* but to hold back the long plays for the present.

A note from Bobby enclosing the snaps he took of me in the kayak—both very good. He said the films of Louis[3] as Christ got light-struck and were worthless. You should have seen Louis when I told him! He was utterly prostrated!

Mrs. C. urges me to confide to you that Shane's bowels are in grand form. So that's that.

Here's luck to your apartment-talk with Dave. Hope he has found something. Suppose you will see him today or tomorrow. Get the one that will make you happy.

All my love, own Darling. Gene.

1. Margaret and Wilbur Daniel Steele (1886–1970) were instrumental in the founding of the Provincetown Players. He became well-known as a writer of short stories and novels.
2. Norman MacDermott, founder of Everyman Theatre. See his *Everymania: The History of the Everyman Theatre, Hampstead, 1920–1926*, published in 1975.
3. Louis Kantor (1900-1961), Provincetown bohemian and writer (using the pen name Louis Kalonyme).

∽

161. **EO to AB**[1] ALS 2 pp. ([Provincetown, Mass.]) [Harvard]

Saturday evening. / [August 13?, 1921]

Own Darling: I can't tell you how it bucked me up when your wire came—a little thing but big in meaning to my loneliness. There was some warmth to the sun after that. I spent the day—or most of it—on the beach and in the water. Tried to swim myself out of this accursed lethargy—must have done over a mile altogether. And it was a good cure as far as my body is concerned. Tonight it feels healthily tired and has lost its abnormal tension. Now if my mind will only return from those dim regions in which it seems to wander, a haunted thing, I may be able to greet you on your return my old self again, able to help and not hinder you in deciding our future whereabouts, etc.

"Here's to September!" You're right! We'll make it and the rest of our stay here *our* time, won't we, Dearest? And we'll be happy! I know it! We always are with each other. It will really be our first chance this season. So far, when you come to think of it, we've always either had someone or been preparing to have someone. We've earned a rest—the right kind of rest—together. And you must come back in this frame of mind. You've promised, remember! And we'll start again to *help* each other.

Your dancing snapshot is in a frame on my desk. It looks beautiful—you—luring and enchanting—my Love forever!

The cricket has left our hearth—honest! He won't come back until you do. He knows there is no home without you.

Shane has been with me a lot of today. We get on wonderfully together. Mrs. C. has been super-industrious—cleaned up Jim's room, Margery's, Big Room, Studio—was all over the place.

Good-night, My Own Wife! I love you with every bit of worth in me! You are my Everything! A long kiss!   Gene.

P.S. No one has been over yet.

1. Marginal note, probably by Max Wylie, reads, "His most honest letter."

~⌒

162. **AB to EO** ALS 3 pp. ([Litchfield, Connecticut]) [Harvard]

Sunday / Aug. 15 [14], 1921

Dearest Gene—   Tomorrow, at seven, I'll be leaving here, for Pt. P., and as I'll probably be traveling all day, won't get a letter off, so this letter now is for tomorrow.

I hope you got my wire Saturday. I didn't mention it in my first letter, as I didn't want to worry you, but I was feeling pretty rotten, probably on account of that strong medicine, and had quite a fever. I'm all right now—and have the "11th" marked down as a Red-letter day. The joke of it is, I came sick on the day which was O.K. according to my *second* set of calculations—so there wasn't much chance of anything being wrong. Hereafter, let's hang a calendar in the bed-room! (*You'd* enjoy that!)[1]

Eddy and Cecil are so happy, and so nice. Cecil is really doing *wonders* with her drawings—those humorous, slightly obscene ones? And Eddy is urging her to go on and helping her—you ought to hear him praise her—but they are worth it—I think they will make a rep. for her some day. They get along like two young angels, and Eddy is looking very handsome. My father is getting a lot of painting done also, and seems well & happy.

The moon is shining in through the window—not quite a full moon—and it makes me feel happy, and a little strange to think that at Provincetown she is sailing along somewhere up over the house—and that perhaps you too will gaze at her this evening. It has become suddenly *very* cool today—almost like autumn. Isn't it wonderful at Peaked Hill in the autumn?

We ought to be happy this winter together, dearest one. You know that beneath it all we do deeply, and eternally love one another—so let's forget and forgive the silly bickering, and irritations, and start again. I think (in spite of *your* doubts) that the change will be good for us both, and that we'll grow even closer in new interests, not apart. Only—we *mustn't do any partying in N.Y.* If we want to, we'll take a trip somewhere, and have some *real* fun—together. But I don't see why we should need that, either. Kiss Shane. Your own, *Agnes*

1. AB told Louis Sheaffer that she thought she was pregnant at this time and "took medicine to prevent it" (undated interview, Connecticut College Collection).

~~⌒◝

163. **AB to EO** ALS 3 pp. ([West Point Pleasant, N.J.]) [Harvard]

[August 16?, 1921]

Dearest Gene— The four letters awaited me—dear sweet own thing, to have written one every day! I read them all over twice—and it really seemed as though *you* were there—and that meant more than anything else in the world.

I'm at Pt. P.—just got here yesterday. And I'm blue—the house seems in *such* bad shape. Then there is the problem of—your having to go down early to rehearsals—*I'd* like to be with you then. But what ho, I guess we can get along somehow. Wait 'til I've seen Dave. Maybe it *would* be better to get a home outside of N.Y. Write when you get there, what you think.

Your P.P. party sounds fine. You really didn't open up the beer? You should have, for them. But then I *do* suppose Jig would have drunk it all up. Honey dear I wish you were here, I love you so much.

If this is to get off by tonight's mail, I'll have to stop. Goodby my own love. Fondly as Always, *Agnes.*

~⌒

164. **AB to EO** ALS 7 pp. (Harvard Club / 27 West 44th Street / [New York]) [Harvard]

[August 18?, 1921]

Dearest Gene— Got into N.Y. yesterday from Pt. P. and called up the Macgowans, but they were in for some opening, and I couldn't get in touch with them. So Dave suggested I stay in the apt. he has—there is an extra bedroom—and was going up to the Harvard Club, but I told him I didn't believe the world would be too scandalized if he didn't, so he didn't. It is a charming place, and I only wish we could get one like it.

As Dave had nothing on hand last night, we sported around a bit,—dinner at the Brevoort—then to a *terrible* movie,—but then on to the real event—a mid-night performance of the negro musical comedy, *Shuffle Along*.[1] It was *great*. And so wonderful to be in a lobby full of *dark* faces—I am so sick and disgusted with all the mean, petty, tired, horrible *white* faces, that I had a feeling, among those negros, of being in a better, more real world. I think I am sorry I am not a negro. I'll tell you about the play, later—

A little later.
Called up Edna,[2] and am going right over there this afternoon,—then Edna will come in tomorrow & we'll look for apts. Dave, by the way, *didn't* have any on a string—hadn't done anything about it—not even an agent's address—but then I don't suppose there is much he *could* do. He suggested that we get an apt. with extra bedroom and rent it to him— He has gone off to his various engagements—he seems to have dozens,—and said to call him at the Club if he could do anything. I *did* think he was going to help me get one! He is a queer and funny thing. I think he doesn't like it because I didn't immediately jump at the chance of having him with us this fall.

Honey, my arm is *awful*, there is an area of about 5 sq. inches covered with red lumps full of pus, and I have to keep a wet and disinfectant compress on it all the time. Nice to have, just now! Otherwise, I feel pretty good.

I'm so glad about the mysticism book. You know my theory—things come to you when you really need them. But it was really Bobby's doing.— Dave said Bobby told him to ask me to call him up at the Bergdoff Studios; but I hardly like to.

Just talked to Geo. Tyler over 'phone, he says thinks *Straw* will open sometime in Oct.—but it's all a case of getting the theatre. He gave me two seats for *Dulcy*[3]— it's a *big* success—for tomorrow night. I didn't want to accept them for Friday, he said it is sold out every night anyhow. If Westly[4] is in 'phone-book, I'll call him up later.

I'll really try and get a letter off to you every day now.—and—keep you info. about apt. etc. Wish you would write me c/o Macgowan's, 155 Leen Lane. P.M.[5] I miss there being no letter from you this A.M.—maybe there is, some where.

Goodby my own, sweetest darling. Kiss Shane-bird for me. Your loving, *Agnes*. *My best to Mrs. Clark.*

1. Musical by Eubie Blake and Noble Sissle, opened May 1921.
2. Probably Edna Behre Macgowan, wife of Kenneth Macgowan.
3. Comedy (1921) by George S. Kaufman and Marc Connelly.
4. Possibly John Westley (1878–1948), actor, who was then appearing in *Dulcy*.
5. This should be 155 Spruce Lane, Pelham Manor.

~~❧~~

165. AB to EO ALS 3 pp. ([Pelham Manor, New York]) [Harvard]

[August 19?, 1921]

Gene dear— This is a scrawl, as my arm is *much* worse. Am at Macgowans, will see *their* Dr. Don't think I'll have any trouble about apts, lots of them for rent of kind we want. I did wire Hutch[1] about Dobbs Ferry house, but now *don't* think you'd care about commuting life, anyhow, so think I can get house with furnace at Pt. P. for 25 a month for Clarkie, the two kids, & my father, & you & I be in town,—I'm sure we can make it as cheap as one house for us in suburbs. Am seeing some apts this afternoon. I may not get back quite as soon as I expected, on account of this arm but, dearest, will as soon as I can—must get things all settled though, so we can move, if necessary, on Oct. 1st—

I hardly slept all night for pain in my damn arm. Lovingly, *Agnes.*

Write the Macgowans

1. Hutchins Hapgood.

~~❧~~

166. AB to EO ALS 4 pp. ([New York]) [Yale]

[August 20?, 1921]

Dearest Gene— Am at present in bed—yesterday I felt *awfully* sick, all over, had to stay in bed, and had a fever of 101. I'm sure I don't know what it is—taking all that strong medicine, & the infection in my arm—which is better—& the traveling I guess. I have very little fever today, and feel better. Will leave here & arrive at Point Pleasant on Monday.

Bobby's letter was nice, wasn't it? I wonder how definite that is about *Chris*?

Cecil & Eddy seem so very happy here, and are accomplishing lots of work.

Your letter meant a lot to me. I am looking forward to Sept., too. Take care of Shane-bird and *don't* let Terry drink up the beer. It made me feel rather funny to think you had him back with you just as soon as I left, anyway. It must be like the good old days. It's wonderful you are getting on so well with *The Fountain*. Will it be done when I get back?

I hope I get better. Just writing this letter has made me feel worse again. Excuse its shortness. Lovingly *Agnes*

~~~

167. **EO to AB** TLS 1 p. (Peaked Hill Bar / Provincetown, Mass.) [Harvard]

Sunday. / [August 21?, 1921]

Own Darling: This dashed off between melodious (?) lines of *The Fountain*. My letter of last night must have sounded awfully down in the mouth. Well, I felt that way. The ordeal of the conflagration had me quite as much of a wreck as the charred remains of the barge.[1] Then, added to that, I had been expecting you—with what great yearning you would not believe—tomorrow sure and when your letter sort of dashed my hopes of that, why I felt all bogged down in a morass of despond. I've been terribly lonely and lost for the past few days. It seemed as if the fire was a disruption of mood that knocked me off the creative heights where I had been clawing for a foothold for the past two months and let me down physically and mentally into a melancholy backwash where the world looked grey indeed. Probably my regular August attack of melancholy was about due to hit me, anyway, and the worry of the barge opened a way for it. Your being away was the worst blow. I had no one to go to for comfort. How I was longing to lay my head on your shoulder and weep a few tears of frustration just to hear you say you loved me and to find in your love the life-solace it always is to me!

Well, I feel more alive today, but still low in spirit. The sun shines but it's a remote and lonely sun and its warmth doesn't reach to my heart. I want you and need you so and wish so intensely that you were here—or at least that I could be sure you were coming soon. Please do!

If I really believed that *The Fountain* were as rotten as it seems to me now I'd hang the script out on the hook in the toilet. Either it is a dead thing or I am. I can't get up enough interest to go on with it.

Come home and bring my life back! These days crawl sufferingly like futile purgatories.

My best to the Macgowans. All love. Come home soon! Gene.

P.S. Remember Saxe is due this week and Mrs. Clark hasn't had a chance at town in two weeks now.

I love you so! A long kiss! Hope you've seen the Doc. and that your arm is now much better.

[On the back of this letter appear the following words in AB's handwriting: "Arm better & Got apt. W 35th share with Bobby very {fine?}."]

1. A coal barge that was beached near Peaked Hill had recently burned.

~⌒◡

168. **EO to AB** ALS 1 p. (Stationery headed: Eugene O'Neill / Provincetown, Mass.)
[Harvard]

Tuesday eve— / [August 23?, 1921]

Own Little Wife: The C.G. failed to bring out any mail today, darn 'em, and so I
don't know whether there is any letter from you or not. If I were sure there was I'd
hop out over the dunes myself to get it, but it's a frightfully hot day and I'd perish sure
if I got there and found there was nothing.

What do you mean—Terry drink all the beer up? You're very unkind at times. As
a matter of fact, he hasn't even seen it and isn't much on beer, anyway. And as for my
bringing him over here as soon as you were gone, that, as I thought I explained, was
the mere accident of my meeting him at Francis'. You must have been in a gloomy
mood to let your thoughts run off on such a tangent.

I'm so damned sorry to learn how badly you've felt, Dear! My only consolation
is that I know you must be all right by this or you would have wired. Damn that
medicine and the soreness in your arm—and any ill in the world that makes you
suffer! I wish to God He would visit me with them in your stead.

Don't worry about your Shane-bird. He couldn't be in better shape.

Come back soon, won't you, Darling! I miss you more and more keenly as each
day without you goes by. I want you and need you—for I love you!

A long kiss, My Own. Think of me sometimes.   Gene.

~⌒◡

169. **AB to EO** ALS 4 pp. (New York, on stationery headed: Peaked Hill Bar / Provincetown, Mass.) [Harvard]

Aug. 25, 1921

Dearest Honey:—   (Seems queer to be writing on Peaked Hill paper!) Sent you (Kenneth & I) long wire this afternoon. I *must* rush back to Pt. P. for 24 hours to see about
place there. Then home! by *God—how glad I'll be to be back!* It has been simply
awful! I had to finally go and pay $15 and get my arm operated on—[*14 places*]
opened, scraped, cleaned out w/ the iodine-covered probe—it nearly killed me—I
wept—but I'm glad, as for the first time in two weeks I've been without pain, also,
last night was the first time in five nights I have slept without triple bromide—Dr.'s
orders!—*to* take them, I mean.

The apartment arrangement I think will be fine. I was having a time getting what
we wanted, when this A.M. Kenneth had an inspiration that Bobby might like to come
in with us—he spent all day trying to get hold of him, finally did tonight, and Bobby
was only too willing—I didn't see him, but he told me over the phone, he wouldn't do

such a thing with anyone but us—Ken explained apt. (room, location etc.) arrangement to him, & he will pay $70 a month, we $100—so, although the whole affair is
arranged via Kenneth, I'm going ahead. Bobby is really so very busy he can't attend
to anything but work, but he does want to do this, and later, as soon as one or two
plays are on, will tend to opening the apt.—I only saw him one afternoon with K. at
the Bergman studios for an hour. I think it will be quiet, don't you? (His bedroom has
separate entrance.)

Darling, I'm so sorry you've been blue—and lonely. *So have I!*

A million kisses, —until I see you—and can *give* you a million. Your own *Agnes.*

~~◡

170. **EO to AB** AL 1 p. ([New York]) [Harvard]

[October? 1921][1]

[Page 2 only of letter:] He says he doesn't know what theatre yet—but I suspect he
simply is holding back. It won't be the Plymouth, more's the pity. *Daddy*[2] is picking
up. *The Claw*[3] is a big financial hit, from all I hear. Which is fine for Hopkins. Jack B.
is due from Europe a week from today. Hoppy will rush *The Fountain* to him at once,
he hinted. I had a long talk with Ben-Ami.[4] He is still eager to play it—promises that
his English will be fine in a few months. He is to open in *Idle Inn.*[5] He is going to do
a short extra season in Yiddish each year—wants to translate and play *Beyond.* Phoned
Madden. He has received notices from London[6]—says all are extraordinary. I didn't
have time to go to his office.

Bobby is in the dumps at having to do sets for *Idle Inn* which he hates. Our
apartment is all fitted up in Mrs. F's most engaging manner—atrocious but comfortable enough. She phoned this A.M. but had so much to say I can't think of one thing
she said. Bobby is letting her arrangement of our house stand until you arrive. He is
pretty blue over the theatrical trade. He & Pauline L.[7] & I lunched together at the
Rotisserie.

Asked about dog for Shane. All say wise bet is to wait for dog show next month
where good bargains can be had. Jamie knows several dog men well from old drunken
Garden days. They will tip us off—

1. EO and AB were living in New York this fall. Possibly at this time AB was away
because her sister Barbara had given birth.
2. Probably *Daddy's Gone A-Hunting* by Zoë Akins, which opened at the Plymouth
Theatre in September 1921.
3. Play by Henri Bernstein, adapted by Edward Delaney Dunn and Louis Wolheim, produced by Arthur Hopkins, opened October 18, 1921, with Lionel Barrymore, Charles Kennedy,
and Edward J. Ballantine.
4. Jacob Ben-Ami (1890–1977), actor, who later played Michael Cape in *Welded.*
5. Folk tale by Peretz Hershbein, adapted by Isaac Goldberg and Louis Wolheim, opened
December 1921, with Jacob Ben-Ami in the cast and sets by Robert Edmond Jones. Alexander

Woollcott in the *New York Times* called it "preposterously mounted" and one of Jones's "rare lapses" (December 21, 1921).

6. *Diff'rent* opened at the Everyman Theatre in Hampstead early in October 1921.

7. Pauline Lord (1890–1950), actress who played the title role in *"Anna Christie"* and later Nina Leeds in *Strange Interlude*.

～○

171. **EO to AB** WIRE, addressed to Bradford St., Provincetown, Mass. (New York) [Yale]

OCT 27 1921

ANNA CHRISTIE WILL OPEN AT VANDERBILT THEATRE NEXT WEDNES-DAY *THE STRAW* OPENS IN NEW LONDON FRIDAY OF SAME WEEK NEW YORK FOLLOWING MONDAY WIRE WHEN TO EXPECT YOU LOVE   EU-GENE

～○

172. **AB to EO** ALS 2 pp. (On the train to New York) [Yale]

[December 16?, 1921] / en route

Dearest Gene— *Now*, who wrote first? Why I haven't been out of P'town an hour yet. I will mail this at Middleboro. Got the *Smart Set* & *Vanity Fair* at the paper store & enclose Nathan's few remarks. Ha ha! I will mail both magazines up. Geo. certainly tells them where they get off. And it's *true*.

I never saw anything quite so gorgeous as the vivid afternoon sunlight on the hills of the Truros. Wish you could see it. I feel awful going away. I love our home and you, my own precious dear—darling—⊗⊗⊗ (Three kisses.)

I'll write tomorrow, night or afternoon, & send it special so you'll get it Sat. night or Sunday; will try to have all the info. you want. Kiss Shane—love to Cookie, Teddy, Gaga, [illegible] & your dear old self—your own   *Agnes*.

～○

173. **EO to AB** TLS, 1 p. (Provincetown, Mass.) [Yale]

Friday eve. / [December 16? 1921]

Own Sweetheart: I am writing this on the machine because I seem to have caught more cold last night and have acquired the damndest stiff neck ever. At that, it is just as well it is my neck because I can do something for that, even though you are absent, while if it were — but I will whisper the rest when I see you. Loneliness makes me Rabelaisian.

Well, you did beat me to it with your letter, you sweet old thing, you. And beyond the joy your note brought me for itself, it was fine to get the Nathan and Broun[1] articles. George certainly takes up the cudgels, doesn't he? And what he says is right as rain. He has sure been the best friend I have had where my work was concerned. I owe him a lot. But his article is due to make the critics sorer at him than ever—and they will try to hit back at him through me, being too wise to have it out with him directly. Well, what ho! To hell with them.

Broun has very graciously changed his tune, what? But his reasons for it remain as mistaken as the former contrary. But I feel almost conscience-stricken at the Boy on the B.D.[2] slam in my article. I judge, however, that that bit of writing will never see the light.

Several clippings arrived today—one very interesting of Rob Parker's in the *Independent*.[3] Get it if you can. I also saw the one of Hackett's in the *New Republic*[4]— quite favorable but with that superciliously superior air of condescension that makes me loathe the little group of serious thinkers on that weekly. It will get your goat, I know.

I have made a revolutionary decision. Walking this P.M. my legs were frozen. So will you get me at Lord and Taylors six pairs of long drawers, three medium and three heavy? I will need heavy ones for going out in dory—am firmly set on renting one now—think lack of exercise is my principal trouble and walking gets boring.

Worked hard today on fourth scene—hope to finish it tomorrow. All love to you, Own Dear Little Wife! I am lonely. I need you. Gene.

X X ×
Mine Cookies Shane's

1. Heywood Broun, "More Moral Victories," *Vanity Fair*, January 1922.
2. On December 18, 1921, EO published a letter to the editor in the *New York Times* (sec. 6, p. 1) in which he wrote: "But how about those sentimental [critics] to whom the Boy on the Burning Deck represents the last word in the heroic spirit our drama should strive to express— the American Oedipus Rex? Surely they must read something into my ending besides mere eternal happiness."
3. Robert Allerton Parker, "An American Dramatist Developing," *Independent & Weekly Review* 107 (December 3, 1921): 235.
4. Francis Hackett, "After the Play," *New Republic* 29 (November 30, 1921): 20.

174. **AB to EO**[1] ALS 4 pp. ([New York]) [Harvard]

Fri / Dec. 17 [16], 1921

Dearest Gene— I got Madden on the phone; he says *Anna* is still doing remarkably well—he asked me to call him up tomorrow A.M. and he will give me the latest dope about *Jones*, etc. Has not heard from the Guild.[2] Also, Williams has not returned the plays yet, although he has promised to—

Marge, Cecil & I went down to the P. Players, had lunch with Fitzi, Susan & Pauline, also Chas. Kennedy,[3] who I tried to pump about *The Fountain*—about all he could say was that *Lionel*[4] was crazy about it. He seems to feel that *The Fountain* may wait until next fall for production— that is what he hinted at—I really think he was pretending that he knew inside dope which he would or could not divulge—Then we went to see *The Verge*[5] as today is its last appearance. It wasn't as good as when Susan read it. Then Oliver,[6] who informed me he would stop in about five to discuss your affairs, appeared at that hour with his wife, his mother, and a middle-aged house-frau from Indiana—so practically nothing was discussed—except he said there is now talk of *Anna* running on 'til May. I am going out to dinner with Cecil & Eddie—so more later, dearest heart. (I want this to go off before 8.) I miss you *dreadfully*. Your own loving Aggie

Love to all———

Dearest Gene— Of course, after hurrying up to write it, my letter didn't get mailed. I'll put a special delivery on, so you can get it Sunday. Saw Bobby this A.M.—he is coming up *after* Xmas—has an opening Dec. 26th[7]—He seems fine. Margery & Cis & Ted and I are going to the Metropolitan Museum this afternoon; and to a concert tonight—very highbrow, what? Just called Madden—he says *Jones* goes split week between Norfolk & Richmond just to see what reaction it gets, then one night stands in Pennsy. working back to week stands in larger cities, Detroit, etc. They played 5,000 in Wash.—due to performance at University[8]—does not go to Boston for a number of weeks—this is good news, don't you think? *Anna Christie* played more last week than week before & more this than last—isn't that fine?—One 800 Wed. mat. this week, one of the worst days in the year Madden says—no news of Shaw[9]— forgot to ask Bobby about Jack B.[10] but will tonight & write—gee, my wisdom tooth is aching all the time—dearest! I just got your letter—darling, I am so glad you miss me—a million hugs—I love you so— More tonight— Aggie

1. Marginal note, probably by Max Wylie, reads: "Takes adversity & pain much better than he does."
2. The Theatre Guild was considering—and would reject—EO's *The First Man*, which was then produced by Augustus Duncan at the Neighborhood Playhouse and opened March 4, 1922, for twenty-seven performances.
3. Charles O'Brien Kennedy (1879–1958), actor, director, and playwright. For the Provincetown Players he directed *Diff'rent* (December 1920), which moved to various Broadway theatres and played for a total of one hundred performances.
4. Lionel Barrymore rejected the script.
5. Play by Susan Glaspell, produced by the Provincetown Players in November 1921.
6. Oliver Sayler, press agent for Arthur Hopkins.
7. *Idle Inn*.
8. The play had a special series of performances at Howard University.

9. The Theatre Guild was then planning for a production of Shaw's *Back to Methuselah*, which opened February 27, 1922.

10. John Barrymore, whom EO seems to have been trying to interest in *The Fountain*.

175. **AB to EO** ALS 2 pp. ([New York]) [Harvard]

[December 19, 1921]

Dearest honey darling—(how's that for a salutation?)   I got your second letter—it cheered me up a lot. You have no idea how *much* I have to do—I didn't realize. Yesterday, Sunday, we lay abed 'til 11. Then had lunch, met Cis & Eddy at the Metropolitan Museum & saw Art. Then the 4 of us had tea at the Brevoort—not a soul there—then Budgie & I went over to Stella's where we had dinner, also Fitzi—There seems to be no definite thing about John Barrymore, beyond that his wife[1] has said he will never act again as she feels the theatre is too cheap & bad for an artist to bother with, also *she* will not write for it again for the same reason.

It is now 9 A.M. & we are going out to shop—lunch with Chas. Kennedy's wife (both last night & this engagement I *can't* say I enjoy)—Bobby has got us seats for *Idle Inn* this Tues. What did you think of that skunk publishing your article as a *letter?*[2]

I'll get the drawers—good idea—but six are too many—don't you think—you act like a grand duke! Love to Shane & Cookie & Teddy & Gaga—Tell Teddy I bought a lovely Cézanne book—full of prints— All my love, sweetest—I adore you— *Agnes.*

1. Barrymore had recently married Blanche Oelrichs, a poet who published under the name Michael Strange.

2. EO's letter to the *New York Times* concerning the supposed "happy ending" of *"Anna Christie."*

176. **AB to EO** ALS 2 pp. ([New York]) [Harvard]

Tues. A.M.— / [December 20, 1921]

Dearest—   This will be just a line, as I am certainly "going it" in an attempt to get everything done—I haven't called up L'Engle[1] or Quinns.[2] [I was?] unwell yesterday—that's bad—last night Budgie & I went to *A.C.* and went back as you suggested to see Polly[3]—she was fine—I'll tell you all about it—says Hopkins has his heart set on—lifting the entire production to London—after the run here—The house was *awfully* good last night—Monday—& everyone crazy about it—

Got coats, etc., bring them in my trunk. Shoes & pants are coming C.O.D.—very fine shoes—got a few toys for the kids—*tell Gaga to get Xmas tree things in P'town.* Got $50 Victrola,—& will bring the Spanish Willy[4] etc.—Will try to get Jig & Sue up—called up P.G. yesterday & today. Your mother not there—isn't it funny[5]—Love to you my dearest—I'll tell you how much when I see you— A.

1. Bill L'Engle, Cape Cod painter, or his wife Lucy.
2. Edmond T. and Emily Quinn.
3. Pauline Lord, who played Anna.
4. Probably meaning the muscatel made by Spanish Willie.
5. Ella O'Neill was soon to leave on a trip to California with Jamie. The purpose was to sell some properties, but they intended to remain in California till the spring. In Los Angeles she suffered a series of strokes and died February 28, 1922.

~⌒

177. **AB to EO** ALS 4 pp. (Stationery headed: Prince George Hotel, / Fifth Ave. & 28th Street New York) [Harvard]

[September 2, 1922]

Dearest Gene— I wanted to write to you on the boat, but after looking on every deck I discovered there was no place to write, no ink, paper, or desk, and alas, I hadn't a pencil or paper along! We went to see *Shuffle Along* in Boston. I didn't sleep at all hardly on the train. I felt uneasy, somehow. I wish you were along sweetheart.

When we got here we were dumbfounded & damn mad to find that *every* store & shop was closed—might as well have been Sunday—nothing to do—went up to [Weylie's?] & got some books which are coming up . . . (*he* was open). Called Bobby— Arthur away—*Hamlet*[1] *is* going on first. So we will have October, sweetest—I am going to work hard—Nothing definite about when rehearsals start. I will try and see Arthur on my way back—Bobby is coming here to dinner tonight with me and Budge. I am going to see the school tomorrow.[2] How are you sweetheart?

I have been thinking of you so much—do stop being blue—everything will be wonderful I am sure, now. Love, and a big hug, dearest, *Aggie*

1. Hopkins produced John Barrymore's *Hamlet* in December 1922.
2. AB was seeking a school for her daughter Barbara..

~⌒

178. **AB to EO** ALS 4 pp. (Stationery headed: Prince George Hotel, / Fifth Ave. & 28th Street New York) [Harvard]

[September 3, 1922]

Dearest Gene— Went up to Tarrytown this afternoon to see school. Guess it will do—anyway, have no time to look around. The children seem fine, and a very "homey" spirit prevails—the only objection I have is that it all *looks* so dismal—perhaps all schools do! $85 a month, payable monthly. Leave tonight for Pt. P. Isn't it the *damndest* thing that I didn't have sense enough to realize that I hit on *three* holidays running! When I can do practically nothing! Bobby came to dinner last night, looked well, talked Taos, and read a letter from Mabel. Says *Old Soak* big hit of season.[1] Very blue about how cheap and shallow life is here. It *is* sickening, too. I hate N.Y.! Haven't seen one other soul, P. Players deserted, even phone cut off. No one at [Jugros?]. Fitzi in Conn. I hardly slept a bit last night either—kept waking up—Tomorrow (Monday Labor Day) will be spent in Pt. P. without being able to accomplish much I am afraid, as a holiday—I wish to God I was back at Peaked Hill. I miss you & Shane so much— Did you meet Williams?

I will leave on the boat Thursday night, rain or shine or hell let loose! I *may* take sleeper and P'town Boat—you let me know if it will be running.

Goodbye my darling child—that's what you are! Budgie sends her love. Kiss Shane, & tell him I'll bring him a boat.   A.

1.   Comedy by Don Marquis, produced by Hopkins, opened August 22, 1922.

179. **EO to AB** TLS 1 p. (Peaked Hill [Bar / Provincetown, Mass.]) [Harvard]

Monday A.M. / [September 4, 1922]

Dearest Own: I didn't get a chance to write to you last night because both Eben[1] and Wilbur[2] turned up during the afternoon and stayed the night. Eben goes back today but Wilbur, of course, will remain. I have given him the little house and he is out there now working. I'm a bit drowsy today and you can expect this to be a very stupid note. Didn't sleep hardly at all. A terrific thunder storm came up just as we were going to bed—the worst I have ever experienced out here—and it kept booming back and forth for hours, never letting up until four this morning—and needless to state, I didn't get to sleep until then. Shane was frightened badly—Mrs. Clark had to take him up and hold him until the storm was over and he cried most of the time. It was a bear, and when we hear the news from town I'm sure we'll find out that there were a lot of hits made. I thought we had received a bullseye a couple of times.

I'm eagerly awaiting your letter which I hope the Coast Guards will bring out— otherwise shall have to walk to town. I wonder if you got any definite news of any- thing from Bobby, or if you were able to get in touch with Hoppy.

By the way, bring back the *Memoirs of Vidocq*[3] with you if they are still at the house. Don't forget! I have a hunch something sometime can come out of them.

When I was lying on the beach yesterday dreaming of you there suddenly came out of memory a verse of "The Blessed Damozel"[4]—a poem I haven't read or thought of for years. Perhaps I remember it wrong but with a "she" substituted for a "he" here it is:

> Yea, verily, when she is come
> We will do thus and thus:
> Till this my vigil seems quite strange
> And almost fabulous
> We two will live at once, one life;
> And peace shall be with us.

Only let's do it here on earth and not wait for "the gold bar of heaven." You wouldn't want to find me waiting for you at a bar even a heavenly one, would you?

All my love and a long kiss, Sweetheart. Here's to Friday and a new beginning! Gene.

1. Eben Given, a Provincetown painter.
2. Possibly Wilbur Daniel Steele.
3. Eugène François Vidocq (1775–1857) was a famous French detective whose four volumes of memoirs were first published in 1828–29.
4. Poem (1850) by Dante Gabriel Rossetti (1828–82), with "seems" substituted for "seem."

~⌒

180. **AB to EO** ALS 1 p. (Stationery headed: Prince George Hotel, / Fifth Ave. & 28th Street / [New York]) [Harvard]

[September 7, 1922]

Dearest— Just to see if this letter will get home first! I do miss you so! And love you so much!

Always your devoted Aggie.

Thurs. A.M. before going off to see Hoppy, etc.

~⌒

181. **AB to EO** ALS 2 pp. ([Brook Farm / Ridgefield, Conn.]) [Harvard]

[November? 1922][1]

Dearest Gene— Arrived O.K. What time did you wake up? You were so sleepy, poor dear, when I left!

The house seems so nice & I can hardly wait till we move in.[2] Those beastly people have carried off a number of things, including the carpet sweeper, wait till I see them!

Are you feeling better? If you managed to sleep all day, you should be. "Take keer you'self!"

Much love, & excuse this short note. I can't think of any of the dozen things I'd like to say.

Goodby, my darling *Agnes*.

Mencken sent the novelette back—same old stuff about liking to "see more"[3]— Will probably be up about eleven o'clock A.M. Thursday—

1. The date May 30, 1921 is written in block letters at the top of this letter, probably added at a later date and probably wrong.
2. The O'Neills bought Brook Farm in Ridgefield, Connecticut, in October 1922.
3. AB's "Memorial Day" was rejected by Mencken in a letter dated November 12 (no year). Mencken called the story "very ingenious," but added, "I fear the Comstocks would give thanks to God if we printed it—and I hesitate to suggest bowdlerizing it, which would probably spoil it" (a copy of this letter is in the Wylie papers at Boston University). Three pages of a piece called "Memorial Day" were among the manuscripts AB left to her daughter.

182. **AB to EO** ALS 2 pp. (R.R. Station / [New York?]) [Harvard]

3 P.M. / [Autumn 1922?][1]

Have more time than I expected here, and it suddenly occurred to me you might not understand my leaving bag, so "am writing." Well, I felt too tired to lug that heavy old bag, and anyhow, there was nothing to take—you've the T-shirt—and [Cowperthwaite?] wants to see me Friday at 3. So I'm coming back tomorrow. I have a heartache all the time I am away from you, which is the real reason I'm coming back so soon,—because it hurts me too much to stay away—

My dear dearest, I want to write my soul out for you, telling the way I feel about you, but there's no use; all I can do is beg you to please be careful that nothing happens to you, because I am tormented with a horrible fear every second. God only knows why—because I love you so much, I suppose. Love has its hellish phases. And to think you won't miss me—you won't now.

Goodby, my own, own dear. A.

1. A later hand has dated this letter May 30, 1921, which is almost certainly wrong, but internal evidence is lacking for a definite dating. I have assigned this date based solely on the possible reference to Cowperthwaite's furniture store, with the idea that AB and EO were seeking furniture for Brook Farm.

183. **EO to AB** ALS 2 pp. [Virginia]

[1922?][1]

To Agnes from Gene— With all his love!

This will help you to remember that there is a time to eat, and a time to sleep, *and a time to work,* and a time to rest, *and a time to play*—in sooth, all matter of different times; but let each second slipping into the other mark for you that Duration, which, like God, always was and will be, and which, being boundless, is the only fit measure of my love for you. And let each tick at your wrist remind you of this until Time be lost in a Bigger Dream.

    1. This dating is purely guesswork. AB's birthday was September 19.

184. **EO to AB** WIRE, addressed to c/o Provincetown Playhouse, 133 Macdougal St., New York (Baltimore, Md.) [Yale]

MAR 6 1924

STILL HELD UP PLAY[1] BETTER HOPE TO GET AWAY TOMORROW EVENING TOLD MADDEN TO PHONE YOU THIS NOON IF STILL IN TOWN WIRE ME TONIGHT WILL WIRE TOMORROW DEFINITE ARRIVAL IF POSSIBLE ALL MY LOVE   JENE [*sic*].

    1. *Welded* opened in New York on March 17, 1924, and ran for twenty-four performances.

185. **AB to EO** WIRE, addressed to Hotel Belvedere, Baltimore, Md. (New York) [Yale]

MAR 6 1924

JUST RECEIVED YOUR WIRE TEN THIRTY THOUGHT YOU WOULD BE HERE TONIGHT TRY TO WIRE YOUR PLANS BEFORE THREE TOMORROW GLAD PLAY IS GOING BETTER ALL MY LOVE   AGNES

186. **AB to EO** WIRE, addressed to Hotel Belvedere, Baltimore, Md. (New York) [Yale]

MAR 6 1924

WIRED YOU THIS AFTERNOON WAS PLANNING GOING RIDGEFIELD TO-MORROW AT SUSIES[1] TONIGHT HADNT YOU BETTER STAY UNTIL PLAY IN GOOD SHAPE WIRE TOMORROW MORNING SO I KNOW IF TO WAIT IN TOWN MISS YOU TERRIBLE LOVE   AGNES.

    1. Probably Susan Glaspell. After the death of George Cram Cook in Greece on January 14, 1924, Glaspell returned to New York and resumed her career as a writer.

187. **EO to AB** WIRE, addressed to c/o Wilbur Daniel Steele, Nantucket, Mass. (New York) [Yale]

JUL 9 1925[1]

WROTE YOU LAST NIGHT BUT IT DID NOT GO OUT UNTIL MORNING NO NEWS CAR[2] IS AT LARKINS AND AM TO SEE HIM TOMORROW MISS YOU TERRIBLY ALL LOVE TO SHANE IONA[3] [*sic*] AND YOURSELF WILL WRITE TOMORROW   GENE

    1. The O'Neills had just returned to the United States from Bermuda, with AB going on to Nantucket and EO remaining in New York. The date of this telegram conflicts with information contained in EO's "Work Diary," transcribed by Donald Gallup, where the day of their arrival in New York is given as July 11. Eugene O'Neill, *Work Diary: 1924–1943* (New Haven: Yale University Press, 1981), 1:18. EO's "Scribbling Diary" indicates they arrived June 29 (2:489).
    2. EO kept a custom-made touring car at his Ridgefield house.
    3. Oona O'Neill was born May 14, 1925, in Bermuda.

188. **EO to AB** WIRE, addressed to c/o Wilbur Steele, Nantucket, Mass. (Brewster, New York) [Yale]

JUL 15 1925

SET OUT THIS AFTERNOON WITH KENNETH[1] PLANNING TO STAY PROB-ABLY TAKING STEAMER FOR NANTUCKET HOTEL FORWARD YOUR TELE-PHONE MESSAGE TO BREWSTER DID NOT RECEIVE IT SHALL LOOK OVER RIDGEFIELD HOUSE BREWSTER TELEPHONE TWO FIVE ONE FOUR ALL LOVE   GENE

    1. EO spent some time with the Macgowans during July, sobering up after a period of drinking.

~◠

189. **EO to AB** WIRE, addressed to c/o Wilbur Daniel Steele, Nantucket, Mass. (Brewster, NY) [Yale]

JUL 18 1925

KENNETH HAS ATTENDED TO BEDINI[1] DELAY ON CAR OWING TO FACT I
THOUGHT COULD TURN IT IN TO DEPONT [*sic*] AND GET NEW CAR[2] FOR
LESS MONEY EVENTUALLY HAVING GRAND TIME[3] BUT WILL BE IN NEW
YORK SUNDAY AND TAKE BOAT MONDAY ALL MY LOVE TO YOU DAR-
LING AND CHILDREN   GENE

    1.   Vincent Bedini did the outside work at Brook Farm.
    2.   EO bought a new DuPont automobile.
    3.   EO's "Scribbling Diary" indicates that he had been up all night in Harlem with Paul
Robeson and Harold McGee, a director of the Experimental Theatre, Inc., arriving home at 10
A.M. EO's comment: "Disaster" (2:489).

~◠

190. **EO to AB** ALS 2 pp. (Stationery headed: Hotel Lafayette / University Place /
New York) [Harvard]

Wednesday night / [July 22, 1925]

My Own Aggie: Just got your wire on my return with Bobby from a long session
with Belasco. The Old Master is very long-winded when he starts reminiscing over
his past but sharp and direct enough when it comes to practical present details. He
certainly admires *Marco*, God bless him! He showed us over his place—a truly amazing museum and packed with wonderful stuff he's collected.[1]

I tried to write you last night but the flesh was weak. It was the hottest ever! My
hand stuck to the paper and I gave it up.

I got a nice wire from John Barrymore today saying he'd look forward to reading
the play.[2]

Had lunch with Walter Huston.[3] I like him better every time I see him. Bobby and
I now agree we ought to try him on the part in *Fountain*. Atwill[4] has been acting like
a true "ham"— demanding all sorts of impossible money, comparing himself to Irving & Mansfield[5] & Barrymore—in short, playing the jackass—and we all feel "off
him." He just doesn't belong with us and Huston does. But whether Jones & Green[6]
can be made to see this is another matter. I hope so.

So much for news.

I'm damn lonely! Every second I spend alone in the room I miss you like the
devil—and I miss Oona over on the couch. I really love her! Never thought I could a

baby! And I love you, my dear wife and pal, more than I have power to say! When you leave me I really feel a sensation of having had some vital part of me removed— my heart, probably—it's with you in Nantucket![7]

Good night, Darling! My love to Shane & Oona and kisses for all of you! Gene

1. In January 1925, David Belasco took an option to produce *Marco Millions* and EO revised the play according to his requests, but ultimately Belasco dropped his plans. The play was finally produced by the Theatre Guild in January 1928, directed by Rouben Mamoulian. Belasco lived in private rooms at the Belasco Theatre.
2. EO was trying to interest Barrymore in the double role of Dion Anthony/William Brown in *The Great God Brown*.
3. Actor (1884–1950) who played Ephraim Cabot in *Desire under the Elms* (1924) and Ponce de Léon in *The Fountain* (1925).
4. Lionel Atwill, English actor (1885–1946).
5. Henry Irving (1838–1905) and Richard Mansfield (1854–1907), two of the foremost late-Victorian actors.
6. Robert Edmond Jones directed *The Fountain* and also coproduced along with EO, Macgowan, A. L. Jones, and Morris Green.
7. The O'Neills spent most of July–October in Nantucket.

191. **EO to AB** COPY of WIRE[1] (New London, Conn.) [Connecticut College]

October 5, 1925

We have terrible trip.[2] Never arrived here till six this morning. Transmission locked in neutral way out of reach of any town. Took us three hours to get it working again and then we lost road in fog and rain. Both of us all in today. Will get sleep tonight and leave early tomorrow. No more night driving. Was Rotten experience. All love. Eugene

1. Sent to AB at the Hotel Shelton, New York City.
2. Upon returning from Nantucket, EO had gone to New London to attend to business affairs relating to the estate he had inherited from his parents. He was also visiting his old friend Ed Keefe.

192. **AB to EO** ALS 1 p. (c/o Boulton[1], / New Preston, Conn. / Merryall R.F.D.) [Yale]

[mid-October?, 1926?]

Dearest Gene— The cheque and statement came from Moran,[2] but I think it better to bring them in when I come, which will probably be next Monday.

I will have to go to the Shelton for overnight anyway, as I had my wardrobe trunk sent there. I try to get in about noon, and will telephone you at the Harvard Club at that time Monday, anyhow.

I'm hoping there will be a letter from you on today's mail. Much love, and be good. *Agnes.*

1. AB was visiting her parents on their farm.
2. Julian Moran, a New London lawyer who was handling matters related to the O'Neill estate.

~⌒

193. **EO to AB** ALS 2 pp. (Harvard Club / 27 West 44th Street / [New York]) [Harvard]

Thursday A.M. / [October 14, 1926]

Dearest: Hello, old Sweetheart! Just got here and up to my room after a Godawful night on the train—couldn't sleep a wink—I'm no longer a "good trooper"—the choochoos bother me—I kept smelling the coal gas and every time I dozed off the engineer stopped with a jerk that was worth two alarm clocks. I finally gave it up and got dressed again at six. At that I don't feel so bad—yet! Probably about four this P.M. I'll be going asleep on my feet. Am going to try and get in a nap and retire early tonight.

Kenneth is coming here soon. Am going to call up Hamilton[1] & Nathan.

Don't forget—send me the photos of the house to give to Ross.

All best love, Own Little Wife! Kiss Oona & Shane for me. I certainly wish you were here. I feel most lonely for you, knowing you are so far away. It's different from your being in R'field where I know I could reach you by phone anytime.

I'll write soon again, Dear—as soon as I've some news of some sort.[2]

I just remembered I forgot all about the island option.[3] Better send it to me to sign. Kisses!   Gene.

1. Dr. Gilbert V. Hamilton, psychoanalyst, was counseling EO concerning his alcoholism. He was also doing research on married couples which resulted in *A Research on Marriage* (1929). The O'Neills and Macgowans were part of Hamilton's survey, and Kenneth Macgowan coauthored with Hamilton a version of this study for the general public, *What Is Wrong with Marriage* (1929).
2. EO was seeking backers for *Marco Millions* and *Lazarus Laughed.*
3. EO was in the process of purchasing Spithead, a twenty-five-acre estate in Paget Parish, Bermuda.

~⌒

194. **EO to AB** ALS 4 pp. (Harvard Club / 27 West 44th Street / [New York]) [Harvard]

Friday A.M. / [October 15, 1926]

Dearest: Well, yesterday was a long hard day, and I didn't get time for any nap, but somehow managed to pull through without passing out although my eyes were a bit glued together toward the finale.

First, Kenneth came over and we had lunch together and much talk. Nothing definite on *Beyond T.H.* yet.[1] All the people we wanted for cast seem to have other jobs. And just at this moment Kenneth is having his troubles with their opening production, a good many now having broken out. We had lunch here with McAvoy,[2] the author, a nice fellow and very amusing.

I called up Doc. Hamilton. He's going out of town over the week-end and couldn't see me yesterday but I'm to see him Monday.

Then we all three went over to the Comedy and dropped in backstage to see Paul Robeson[3] for a moment. He was very nice—is discouraged at play and again wants to quit stage for singing.

There is nothing new on *Lazarus*. I'm to see Kommer today about the Reinhardt thing. Chaliapin is due in a few days. [Hurok?], the singer's agent, is still evasive and hedging to Kenneth. I'm going to see him. There's nothing new from the Russian, Dantchenko.[4]

As for the Tiffany[5] movie thing I went to see the American Play Co. folk in the P.M. and Ramsey is going out himself to see if Tiffany means money. He advised me to demand a hundred thousand down. Marbury[6] wasn't there. I'm going to call her up today.

Then went to Nathan's. He is fine as ever. Lillian Gish won't be on here until Christmas.[7] That's that! He took me over to Gilbert Miller's office at the Empire.[8] Met Sid Howard there, also Holbrook Blinn, also Judith Anderson.[9] Some amusing incidents but will wait until I can tell you.

I liked Miller very much but he won't get definite on *Marco* until he has right actor for it. Hunter is out.[10] He gushed about play but showed Miller he didn't know what it was about—the satire—he wanted his Marco to be the romantic, handsome hero! Dear actors, what! So *Marco* is hung up again.

Nothing much more. Dinner here with Kenneth. Saw Dave Carb. Jimmy Light came up at nine & we talked till eleven. He has been "on wagon" ever since his illness last April. What did I tell you? He looks fine.

The things from Park & Tilford came. Gawd bless you, Delicate Attending Nymph! They are very welcome. All love, Sweetheart, to you & ours. I won't get any chance to write tomorrow, don't suppose. We leave early, lunch with Baker before game.[11]

I love you—and miss you. There's no one to confide in now.[12]

Adios, Darling! Gene.

P.S. Feel much better today. Had good sleep. So don't worry.

1. EO, Macgowan, and Jones were planning a revival of *Beyond the Horizon* for the Experimental Theatre, Inc. It opened November 30.
2. Probably EO's misspelling of Joseph Patrick McEvoy, screenwriter.
3. Robeson (1898–1976) was appearing in *Black Boy* by Jim Tully and Frank Dazey,

based on the story of Jack Johnson. He had played Brutus Jones in the 1925 revival of *The Emperor Jones.*

4. EO and Macgowan were pursuing various alternatives for getting *Lazarus Laughed* produced. Rudolph K. Kommer, Austrian journalist and translator, was Max Reinhardt's representative in the United States, and EO had hopes of a production on the scale of Reinhardt's *The Miracle.* EO was also intrigued by the idea of the Russian singer and actor Feodor Chaliapin (1873–1938) performing the role of Lazarus. The Russian-born impresario Sol Hurok (1888–1974) later planned to create an O'Neill repertory company. Vladimir Nemirovich-Danchenko (1858-1943) had broken away from the Moscow Art Theatre (of which he had been a cofounder with Stanislavsky). He had interest in directing a Russian production. The play, which had been written in 1925, was not produced until 1928, when the Pasadena Community Players presented it.

5. EO asks Macgowan about "Tiffany films" in an October 1926 letter, but it is not stated just which play is under discussion. *The Theatre We Worked For: The Letters of Eugene O'Neill to Kenneth Macgowan,* ed. Jackson R. Bryer (New Haven: Yale University Press, 1982), 136.

6. Elizabeth Marbury was a partner of Richard Madden in the American Play Company. She spent her summers in Belgrade Lakes, Maine, and EO and AB had rented a house next to hers during the preceding summer. Carlotta Monterey was Marbury's house guest at that time.

7. Gish (1899–1993) was a close friend of George Jean Nathan.

8. Miller (1884–1969), New York producer, was considering *Marco Millions* for production.

9. Playwright Sidney Howard (1891–1939); actor Holbrook Blinn (1872-1928); actress Judith Anderson (1898–1992) later succeeded Lynn Fontanne as Nina Leeds in *Strange Interlude.*

10. Actor Glenn Hunter (1896–1945).

11. EO and Macgowan went to the Yale-Dartmouth football game on 16 October (his thirty-eighth birthday). They joined George Pierce Baker, who had been EO's playwriting teacher at Harvard and had since moved to Yale where he started the School of Drama. He was considering *Marco Millions* as the inaugural production of the new Harkness Theatre.

12. EO's "Work Diary" mentions that he saw Carlotta Monterey on the 17th and two other times during October.

～つ

195. **AB to EO** WIRE, addressed to Harvard Club, 27 West 44th St., [New York] (Augusta, Me.) [Yale]

OCT 16 1926

MANY HAPPY RETURNS OF THE DAY AND LOVE FROM US ALL INCLUDING GAGA　AGNES

～つ

196. **AB to EO** TLS 1 p. ([probably Belgrade Lakes, Maine]) [Harvard]

Saturday. / [October 16, 1926]

Dearest Gene: As I wired you I was sick, so wasn't able to write before. I am up to the neck now in trying to get things all packed and sent off. Oh, dear dear, I do think we must never leave Bermuda once we are there, I *hate* this more than poison, and it is dreadful with the kids. And all the letters and the bills and the this and that! And to think it will be like this more or less for another three or four weeks. Gee, I'll be glad to get there and *stay* there!

Another futile letter from Hill[1]—too stupid. No info. at all. He *is* an ass.

A letter from Harold,[2] which I truly opened by mistake—took it for granted it was for me. I am writing him soon that we are too *cash-short* to buy now in Lovell. Think this is a very wise thing to tell him.

I go through N.Y. Wed. A.M. if all is well, and may call you on the phone at the Harvard Club about ten or so. So be in a good temper!

I do hope that you went to the game and had a fine time and all's well. Hope to get a letter hearing about it. By the way Keeler says he thinks the people leave on the 25th.

Am forwarding what little mail there was for you. I'm freezing just at this moment, it's gotten very cold. Much love dear old thing, be a good boy, and don't forget me.   A.

1. Contractor who was responsible for renovating Spithead, the O'Neills' house in Bermuda.
2. Harold DePolo.

197. **AB to EO** ALS 8 pp. ([Hamilton, Bermuda] on stationery headed: Furness Bermuda Line) [Yale (first four pages); Harvard (last four pages)]

Sunday. [November 21?, 1926]

Dearest Gene,   Sunday on a boat seems about as dull as Sundays elsewhere. Fortunately, the sea is calm—a very smooth trip so far. And it is warm—almost like Bermuda. I do wish you were along—it seems a very meaningless trip without you, also Bermuda without you along would be a very flat place, I'm afraid. Gaga said suddenly today: "I seem to miss Mr. O'Neill—I really do."

Barlow saw us off, and will reserve a ticket for you for next Saturday. I think our last dope on the subject of your coming is the best—if you still feel low and uninterested in life, come: if you've picked up, and can get something out of a longer stay, then stay.

Yesterday a little square man with an odd face presented himself to me very formally as Mr. Azzimonti: bootmaker to the great. He, it seems, made your father's shoes for years, at the price (so he says) of $59 per pair. He's an amusing character—a temperamental artist in shoes, who talks of the foot as though it were a lyric poem.

He knew your father & all his friends intimately it seems. I will have him come to Spithead sometimes to see you. He & his wife live in St. George.

Harold met a young man on board who has charge of the bath houses at Southshore, who has given him a lot of dope about places. Harold Frith is running the hotel himself now, which I was glad to hear of, as I didn't care so much for Mr. Johnson. Bill the Barkeep is back, it seems, after having gone to South America.

All's gone well with Oona and Shane so far.

Tuesday [November 23?], very early A.M.

Am sending this off by the *George*.[1] Saw Spithead yesterday afternoon with Hill. The cottage is simply charming, and they are getting well along with the other work. Stayed one day at Elbow Beach, go to Bel-more today. Tried hard to interest the De Polos in that house & South Cote, but Helen insisted that Harold would drink himself to death from loneliness there. They are looking today at a house near Salt Kettle, which won't be so bad. H. has already formed several acquaintances. I don't like Bermuda without you. Do you know, I think when it's finished, we'll have the ideal home at Spithead. I'm telling them today to go ahead with the tennis court.

If you will be well there, I suppose it won't be so bad for you to stay on for a while in N.Y. But, just the same, I hope like *hell* you decide to take the next boat down.

Have had an interesting time reading the H.D. book.[2] There's a re-creation of Greek & Roman life and characters in it—treating them like moderns—that will interest you.

Love to you, dearest— A.

1. S.S. *Fort George*.
2. Hilda Doolittle (1886–1961), expatriate poet, associated with the Imagists, published her most well-known novel *Palimpsest* in 1926.

～৹

198. **EO to AB** WIRE, addressed to Hamilton, Bermuda (New York) [Yale]

NOV 25TH 1926

WORRIED NO WORD PLEASE CABLE AM SAILING SATURDAY SURE LOVE[1]
GENE

1. On his return trip, he wrote an impassioned letter to Carlotta saying that he would tell Agnes the truth about how he felt upon leaving Carlotta, although without declaring that he intended to end the marriage. In fact, he did tell Agnes about his feelings, declaring that he felt love for both of them.

Agnes Boulton and Oona O'Neill, around 1927. Photographer unknown. Yale Collection of American Literature, Beinecke Rare Book and Manuscript Library.

III.

1927–1928

THE SUMMER OF 1927 WAS SPENT AT SPITHEAD. THE HOUSE AND GROUNDS STILL REQUIRED extensive work, but a guest house became an effective working retreat for Eugene. There he could enjoy quiet and solitude apart from an increasingly lively main house. Three household servants helped manage the estate, and there were numerous other repairmen and gardeners to maintain and alter the property. Oona was just two, Shane was approaching eight, and they were visited this summer by Eugene Jr., who was on the verge of entering Yale University, and Agnes's teenage daughter. The O'Neills were also visited by several friends and neighbors, although it was the "slack" season, and the social atmosphere of their lives was changed significantly by the fact that Eugene had ceased drinking. This newly attained self-control came not with any surge of confidence or sense of health but with a deepened sense of gloominess, a pervasive uncertainty about how he might achieve happiness.

He felt disconnected from society, from his children, and from Agnes. That she continued to drink (moderately, she says) began to seem to him a betrayal and an assault upon him, as did any instance where she acted for herself or for another, even sometimes for the children. When she traveled to New York to visit her dying father, he spoke loudly of his own needs and took the occasion of her departure to make an elaborate case for her to dismiss all memory of what had happened with Carlotta as "my one amusing (yes it is!) gesture of a virginal Casanova." Perhaps he was preparing her for the gossip she would be likely to hear in New York, but he asks her to understand this as a moment of maturation: "I let you into my deepest secrets! This is a bad policy even with a wife one loves! One should keep one's posing before the mirror of oneself in decent obscurity. It is an awfully adolescent, undeveloped naked-ness I am revealing to you!" (#202). Max Wylie drew attention to this letter in one of the notes he wrote about this correspondence: "Right here, one feels that Agnes could have saved her marriage; that she could have, had she truly wanted to; that she could have, had she been equipped with some of Carlotta's hardness. O'Neill was a man who had to be managed. Until Carlotta came along, no one had ever managed him. Agnes let him flounder; let him live as he always had, taking his lashings and thrashings with light complaint, quick forgiveness. (There was enough masochism in her own machinery to make this possible.)"[1] The proximity to the sea, the abundance of comforts

221

in the Bermudan utopia, and the new habit of sobriety might have made this summer a time when he could connect once again with his family, but instead, perhaps because the managing hand was not felt, he grew more and more isolated.

He channeled his energy into writing, first completing cuts on the nine acts of *Strange Interlude*, then revising *Lazarus Laughed* for publication, and finally in August attempting to write an introduction to the volume in which *Lazarus Laughed* would be published. This last project caused him enormous difficulty. The aim was to come up with a statement that would "set for[th] all my long-cherished ideas & ideals about the theatre," and he labored on this for over a week before deciding that it entailed too many ideas, was too long, and would require a book some day.[2] O'Neill never would manage to write such an extended treatment of his ideas, but at this time he partly attributed his failure to Bermuda, complaining that "one rarely gets the chance . . . to say a word to a human being above the intellectual and spiritual level of a land crab and this solitude gets damned oppressive at times."[3] The heat also became oppressive to him at this time, and after a bad attack of influenza in July he developed some sort of infection late in August. Then too the chronic problem of his "nerves" seemed to flare up, and the idea of his escaping from the domestic sphere for a time seemed suddenly attractive, both to Eugene and to Agnes.

The idea was that he would go to New York, see his doctors, and try to spur the Theatre Guild into making a decision about producing *Strange Interlude*. At the same time he could help plan the production of *Marco Millions* and continue efforts to find a producer for *Lazarus Laughed*. A visit to a hydroelectric plant would help give form to his ideas for a new play, *Dynamo*. But above all he could call up friends like George Jean Nathan and Benjamin De Casseres and enjoy the intellectual companionship he missed in Bermuda without all the distractions of domestic life. He could enjoy his well-earned prosperity at the race track or the six-day bicycle races, take weekends in the country with wealthy friends, exercise the liberty of his status. Agnes urged him to find ways of enjoying himself to take the place of the alcohol.

Soon after he departed, though, he discovered that New York would not answer his needs. He had never enjoyed the crowded, noisy, dirty, expensive conditions of the city, but now, compounded by the late-summer heat and his various ailments, the city seemed a miserable nightmare. The pleasures of intellectual companionship proved difficult to find during the vacation season, and little progress was made toward resolving the uncertainties surrounding productions. From the start his letters express bitter resentment toward Agnes for urging him to take this trip, and she can do little more than encourage him to take whatever steps are necessary to make life easier. The letters from this period are long and numerous and exhibit some of the same rhythms as the Provincetown-New York correspondence from the early years of the marriage, but now with an undercurrent of deep hostility. There are constant calls for response, thwarted by the several days' delay for each letter to make the voyage, then the accusations when letters do not arrive, and the alternating periods of recrimination and conciliation. The tone of his letters changes somewhat when he makes contact with Carlotta once again. She had just returned from Europe and at first they met as old friends. He acknowledges as much to Agnes. But his Work Diary shows that their meetings became more and more frequent during the weeks when he alludes to business meetings and medical appointments as the hindrance to his return to Spithead.

Agnes' letters from this period are also filled with complaint—about the boredom and isolation of island life, about the frustrations of managing the work on Spithead and dealing with the needs of the children. At a certain point, perhaps projecting, he charges that she must have urged him to go to New York because she had a lover. Her response is vehement:

> God damn it, if you knew how damned bored & lonely I was here—never mind, I think I'll pack up & arrive in N.Y. next boat, kids & all—then we'll see how that will work. I see through—of course you intended me to—your remarks about taking to drink—or *love*. Well, do it. (Love, not drink.) Remember your conversation with me, in which you told me you wanted to divorce me—remember the days & days of silent dislike & hatred on your part—remember the things you've said & done—Do you think I can forget all that— You love me & need me now, yes, because you're bored and lonely—but that love speedily deteriorates into an intense irritation as soon as we've been together two weeks. (#236)

When he takes back his accusations a couple days later and again declares his compelling need for her the words seem sincere, but it is also unmistakable in retrospect that he sees the need to say anything to prevent her from encroaching upon his reawakening relationship with Carlotta. "Darling, I do wish you were here! But don't come!" (#243).

It seems significant that they both look to *her* return to writing as a crucial matter. There are several references in these letters to some sort of article she was composing, something that would have to be "personal, & yet not personal!" (#233). But a couple of weeks later she admits that her progress has been slow and that "I have not by any means gotten to the stage where it has again become an absorbing interest in life" (#248). She later recalled that by this time she had lost her conviction that he was a great writer, and yet it was obvious that in his work O'Neill had found some access to that "deep inner peace" that was so essential to him and that he had formerly associated with his marriage itself. Boulton sought to recover that same sense of clear purpose in her own writing. There are signs in these letters from both of them of an awareness that their lives have become too attached to the grandiose and superficial—supervising the myriad details of increasingly vast plays, engineering a visionary dialogue between such disparate entities as Max Reinhardt, the Theatre Guild, Lillian Gish, and a hydroelectric plant in Connecticut, meanwhile selling one "white elephant" mansion (Brook Farm) to pay the bills on another (Spithead). Agnes later told Louis Sheaffer: "I think where he made his big mistake was in getting so involved in production, the business end. They would talk for hours about who to cast and how it should be put on and all that business stuff. Was he an artist or a businessman? It seems to me that a real artist can't be bothered with business."[4]

With Carlotta in New York, Eugene sought to reestablish his life on an intimate, elemental basis. Perhaps Agnes was attempting the same in the details of reconstructing the house. If only she had enough cash to finish rebuilding a wall or refinish the floors perhaps the house would become the space for that simpler, quieter life, the deep inner peace. At one point she tells Eugene that she has acquired an old horse to help cut down on the expenses of going to town. For her there seems to be in this action a turn to simpler ways, perhaps even to her own rural past. But for him the measures taken by Agnes seemed so many distractions, if not threats, to his happiness, a happiness that seemed to exist only at a distance from his house and family. The horse was soon sold back.

Finally he returned to Bermuda on October 19 to await the final casting and beginning of rehearsals of *Marco Millions* in late November. His letters to Carlotta begin almost from the moment of his arrival and are filled with declarations of his loneliness, his need for her, his love. Still, the decisive break with Agnes had not occurred by the time of his return, although he did mention to Carlotta that certain attitudes had changed and she could write freely to him without fear of being read. Perhaps it was at this point that the turning point was reached, a moment she later described to Louis Sheaffer: "I let Carlotta have him. I was bored with him, and I found him sexually unsatisfactory."[5]

After his return to New York, the correspondence with Agnes resumed with much recounting of the circumstances of production. But the letters come less frequently and seem more and more distant, and here all the replies of Agnes have been lost, so it is only from his perspective that we can glimpse the breaking point. It came about Christmastime. He sent her a letter, probably on December 20, along with some presents for the children. For Agnes herself, he declares, he has been unable to find a suitable gift, and so instead he offers a check for one hundred dollars, which he then seems to forget to enclose. But the real gift comes in the second half of the letter: "So my Christmas present to you is really to give you back your absolute liberty in any way, by any method, you may desire." The letter combines the gesture of attack ("You've tortured your last torture as far as I'm concerned") with an attitude of resignation ("Something in me is so damn utterly dead that I don't care about anything any more—except doing my work"). He is insistent that no one is to blame for this situation ("It is simply the curse of the soul's solitude, the grinding, disintegrating pressure of time, that has destroyed Us"), and in particular that no "outside circumstance," meaning Carlotta, "has anything to do with it" (#274). This letter and the ones that followed refer her to the implied contract of the marriage they chose to make with one another, a marriage founded solely on love. If that love did not exist, then the marriage could not and should not exist. His letters seem to anticipate her fighting for the marriage as a right and a possession, a power to be used, the motivating force for high Strindbergian drama.

Agnes's recollection of this breaking point was somewhat different. She told Sheaffer that at about this time she received a cablegram from him saying he had fallen in love and wanted to be free: "I wired back that was all right, and he had my best wishes. He wired back that I didn't understand, that he wanted a divorce. I wired him, I do understand, dear, and it's all right, I understand completely."[6] On another occasion she told Sheaffer: "How did I feel when we split up? Was I bitter? No, because I didn't feel elated at being Mrs. Eugene O'Neill, as he expected. Frankly, my chief feeling is that I was bored with him."[7] Shortly after the cablegrams were sent he wrote her a long letter definitively breaking the marriage, asking her to divorce him, and giving as the reason his deep love for someone else. In this letter he portrays the recent years of marriage in frightening Strindbergian terms as a strenuous exercise ("too many torturing scenes") of possessiveness and jealousy, an entrapment of the soul: "What has bound us together for the past few years has been deep down a fine affection and friendship, and this I shall always feel for you. There have been moments when our old love flared into life again, but you must acknowledge that these have grown steadily rarer. On the other side of the ledger moments of a very horrible hate have been more and more apparent, a poisonous bitterness and resentment, a cruel desire to wound, rage and frustration and revenge" (#275). He asks her to look upon the break as a liberation, as the opening of an opportunity for each to find, separately, a future happiness.

As to the arrangement of property matters, provision for the children, and so on he promised to be generous, but specifically asked her to defer a visit to him until after his plays *Marco Millions* and *Strange Interlude* had opened in January and early February. Nevertheless she arrived in New York soon afterward and stayed in the same hotel, different room, as Eugene. There were some stormy scenes. She told Louis Sheaffer: "I don't think it was because I was drinking, I wasn't drinking much in those days."[8] It seems she had a cold and one day borrowed from the hotel or from O'Neill a sunlamp. She was taking a sunbath naked when a knock came at the door. Believing it was her sister, Agnes opened the door only to find Eugene. They made love, and it felt to Agnes as if it were "between two ghosts"—"it was kind of sad."[9]

Agnes returned to Spithead early in January and probably never saw Eugene again. He set to work with his lawyer, Harry Weinberger, to figure out an acceptable property settlement as well as how and where the divorce could be obtained with as much speed and little publicity as possible. It is instructive to read O'Neill's letters to Weinberger alongside his letters to Boulton.[10] From the first in plotting his legal strategy, he takes an adversarial tone toward Agnes, openly expressing his fears that she will play this as a high stakes celebrity divorce case. He refers several times to the just-concluded divorce of Sinclair Lewis, whom he and Agnes both knew slightly. His situation was awkward during these first few months of negotiation because, while it is true that his income had been flat for quite some time, first one and then the other of his new plays opened to critical acclaim and proved to be commercial hits. Shortly after *Strange Interlude* opened, he and Carlotta escaped to Europe, eluding the newspaper reporters who were scenting marital scandal, and without even informing Agnes. He never did give her an exact address where he was in France, so all communication had to pass through Weinberger.

The deal he was offering included a minimum payment of six thousand dollars a year, going up as high as ten thousand in years when his income met or exceeded forty thousand dollars. Also, she would be permitted to remain at Spithead. But Agnes found many uncertainties in this arrangement. Who would pay for the children's schooling? What if she preferred not to live at Spithead? What if O'Neill decided to sell

Spithead? O'Neill and Weinberger urged her to take this settlement, trusting in good-will to take care of such details. If she did not, then let it be known that he might abandon work on his new plays, and then what income would there be? Finally in the springtime she hired a lawyer. The rift between them, however, came not so much from the financial details as from another source. She wrote him that their moment beneath the sun lamp had resulted in her pregnancy, and evidently in her letter she included some information about how many months pregnant she was, except she apparently slipped in her calculations. O'Neill reasoned that he could not be the fa-ther and that therefore she must be having some sort of affair in Bermuda. He claims to have heard rumors about her loose behavior. After another letter from Boulton, presumably a correction of her dates and a reassertion that O'Neill was father of the unborn child, he backed away from these accusations but the damage had been done. His pledges of eternal friendship to her now seemed a facade behind which his offen-sive, manipulative impulses showed through. He made minimal inquiry and expressed no sympathy when she had an abortion that spring. Instead, O'Neill was equipping Weinberger with information—suspicions really—about Agnes's past in an effort to find some damaging fact with which to thwart what he now viewed as her attack upon him. Weinberger, who had been friends with both O'Neills, found himself in a very awkward position.

   Eugene had two wishes for Agnes's future. One was that she would find someone else to love, and the other that she would return to her writing. Of the latter he wrote: "You know as well as I that that is what you deeply need—and I'll be so damned happy when I know you're on the job again because I feel so strongly that that means peace for you and a new life all your own" (#277). Clearly he wants her experience to match his own because, as he writes repeatedly from France, he has found happiness, has been writing well, and has discovered the liberation of a clean break from the past: "I feel reborn. *I am sure!* At last I 'belong'! There is only one thing lacking to my complete happiness and that will come when you write me that you are working again, that you have readjusted your life and begin to see in your new freedom a chance for new life and happiness—and new love!" (#285).[11] For a time, though, all he hears from her is about her loneliness, the distress of the children, and matters of property, especially how to cover the unpaid bills for Spithead. On the latter subject O'Neill becomes resistant, accusing her of running up the bills. At last in early April, not long after the abortion, he hears from her that she is writing and declares his joy that now she is free of his presence and can come into her own as a writer. What she set out to write at this time is unknown. He alludes to a "script" she described to him at one point and adds a puzzling comment on how he has always "done my best to encourage you to do your best and not to attempt easy things, or unimportant themes, or junk for money" (#289).[12] At the time of the divorce in 1929, Boulton was writing a series of stories, portraits of fiercely independent New England women. She pro-posed this book to Horace Liveright and received encouragement, but just about this time his publishing company collapsed.[13]

   One story, however, had to be told, and that was to answer once and for all re-porters' questions about rumors of divorce. She had up to this time supplied a series of lies to the press, denying the rumors and privately expressing to O'Neill her resentment at having to do so. At last in late April he asked her to make a statement to the newspapers, a simple statement that they "couldn't hit it off any longer," with no mention of a third party and so on. The announcement was made in June and was discussed throughout the summer in such stories as one that came out in the *New York Evening Journal:* "Our Love Problem Dramatist Fights to Solve His Own." Accompanied by a sidebar of apposite quotations from O'Neill's plays (*Strange Interlude* and *Welded*) came a mostly factual story which concluded with a statement Boulton made to the press. This reported that O'Neill had written her how he was "free at last" in Europe and gave this response:

> I had attempted the experiment of giving an artist-husband the freedom he said was necessary for his dramatic success. Perhaps from the standpoint of dramatic art and the American theatre, my decision may be a success; matrimonially, it has already proved a failure. This illusion of freedom—so long maintained by the male sex, particularly by the artistic male—is very much an illusion. Now I know that the only way to give a man the freedom he wants is to open the door to captivity.[14]

The history of O'Neill's marriage to Carlotta Monterey suggests strongly that captivity was not to be escaped for either of them, and unfortunately the dream of rebirth was not to come true for Agnes Boulton either. She later told Louis Sheaffer that she felt sorry for Carlotta and did not blame her. Agnes did find other loves, a former newspaper editor in the 1930s and a fisherman in the 1940s and 1950s. Both men were writers and there were many cowritten projects, though none were published or produced.

Agnes Boulton also stayed close to her children, unlike O'Neill, who eventually broke ties with them all. She preferred the entangled, engaged life, and to the end, living on in "Old House" in West Point Pleasant, she used language for conversation rather than consecration. And perhaps in the end she knew why.

1. In 1927 file, Wylie Papers, Boston University.
2. Eugene O'Neill, *Work Diary: 1924-1943*, vol. 1, *1924–33,* transcribed by Donald Gallup (New Haven: Yale University Library, 1981), 44.
3. Letter to Benjamin De Casseres, in *Selected Letters of Eugene O'Neill,* ed. Bogard and Bryer, 245.
4. Louis Sheaffer interview of Agnes Boulton, July 15–20, 1959 (Connecticut College).
5. Ibid.
6. Louis Sheaffer interview of Agnes Boulton, April 16, 1962 (Connecticut College).
7. Louis Sheaffer interview of Agnes Boulton, July 24, 1958 (Connecticut College).
8. Louis Sheaffer interview of Agnes Boulton, n.d. (Connecticut College).
9. Ibid.
10. The O'Neill-Weinberger correspondence is located in the O'Neill collection at Yale.
11. There were distinct limits to his wishes for her writing, as the clause in the divorce agreement specifying what she will not write about indicates. In the final stages of negotiation O'Neill wrote Weinberger: "I think you should have brought more pressure to bear, what with all the muck we have on her—and as far as the writing clause goes you can tell her for me before Driscoll that if she ever dares write a line about me, either outright or as thinly disguised

autobiography, I will write the play—a damned good play it would make, too!—about her past and her family's that will blast them off the map!" (February 8, 1929, Beinecke Library).

12. Indeed, early in the marriage in 1921, when she told him of an invitation she had received to write scenarios for Hollywood at more than a thousand dollars apiece, he declared he would hate for her to do so: "My God, you have a soul to express which will create beauty in your novel, etc. if you will only work hard and give it a chance. . . . You may think you can trifle with the film and still do your real work but you can't" (#140).

13. See manuscript of "A New England Woman" and associated correspondence in the Liveright Collection, University of Pennsylvania.

14. *New York Evening Journal*, August 11, 1928.

~~⌒)

199. **EO to AB** ALS 1 p. ([Hamilton, Bermuda]) [Yale]

Friday evening / [April 15?, 1927]

Own, Own Wife: God, how I miss you![1] And how horribly alone I have felt ever since returning here! I actually broke down on the bed in our room in a fit of hysterical crying when I first went up there. I know this is unreasonable, a bit absurd when you are only going to be gone a week, but my whole control seems gone and my inner being is in pretty shattered shape. *I need you, need you, need you!*—intensely more now than ever before in our married life. I feel—it's so hard to attempt to explain—as if this were a crucial period in my life, an ordeal, a test on which everything I have built depended—God knows what!—and our lives were in the balance. And it's so bitterly hard to be alone—although I know your love is here with me and in that faith I can come through.

This sounds incoherent. Well, I feel that way. But don't be frightened. There's no danger of anything you might fear. I'm just alone and miserable, and will be until your return.

Because I love you! Remember and think over our talk last night.

I kiss your dear lips and body. Your Lover always   Gene

1. AB had gone to New Preston, Connecticut, to visit her father, who was dying of tuberculosis.

~~⌒)

200. **AB to EO** WIRE, addressed to Bermuda (S.S. *Fort Victoria*) [Yale]

APR 16th [1927]

NEVER AGAIN   AGNES.

~~⌒)

201. **EO to AB** WIRE, addressed to S.S. *Fort Victoria* (Bermuda) [Yale]

[April 16, 1927]

CHEER UP DEAREST ALL LOVE   GENE

~~✑~~

202. **EO to AB** ALS 6 pp. (Spithead / [Hamilton, Bermuda]) [Harvard]

Saturday night / 4/16/27

My Own Aggie: Well, I've certainly been feeling lost since that moment when your dear familiar beautiful face blurred out into the background of the receding *Fort Victoria* and I about faced and took up my burden of a wifeless life for a spell. There was nothing of the slightest interest in the remaining mail at the post office—and it wouldn't have interested me any if there had been. So, after finding the Grays office closed, I drove right back to Our Home. *Our Home!* I feel that very much about Spithead, don't you? That this place is in some strange symbolical fashion our reward, that it is the permanent seat of our family—like some old English family estate. I already feel like entailing it in my will so that it must always be background for our children! I love Spithead—and not with my old jealous, bitter possessiveness—my old man Cabotism![1]—but as ours, not mine except as mine is included in ours. The thought of the place is indissolubly intermingled with my love for you, with our nine years of marriage that, after much struggle, have finally won to this haven, this ultimate island where we may rest and live toward our dreams with a sense of permanence and security that here we do belong. "And, perhaps, the Hairy Ape at last belongs."[2] I have, as you know, never felt this deep peace of permanence about any place where we have lived before. Perhaps, a lot of this feeling is due to the change in me. In the old—and how really far distant and improbable those days seem to me now! alcoholic times there could be no confidence in the security of anything. Perhaps we should rechristen Spithead Water Wagon Manor! It is certainly connected in my mind with sobriety and sane living.

But what I started out to say was that it is a very lonely home right now. I miss you so much, Dearest! It isn't a keen stabbing pain, because I can keep telling myself that, after all, ten days are not so horribly long, but a dull aching longing as if the Familiar Spirit of our home whose presence alone gives it meaning and makes it *my* home, were gone from it. It is now just a large empty house in which I sit alone at my desk and am desolately conscious that I am alone, that no matter how late I stay up there will be no sound of your coming along the empty rooms to my room, that when I go to bed there will be no other half of me lying beside me and spiritually completing me—without the necessity of saying a word or making a movement, the sound of your breath, sleeping, is enough, it is my breath too, without it my heart stifles and beats laboriously as if it were only hitting on one lung! And it is! We are the two lungs that give one life its life—our life which we have slowly created out of our separate lives.

You seem to think I never have such thoughts any more. But I do! Many, many times. Perhaps I should tell you of them more than I do, as I used to do in more hectic shifting days, but the reason I don't is that I have come to accept them as a recognized part of my being, that I seem to feel them in you too and that I expect you to feel them in me, that they are of the soul and sound bald and shallow when forced into words, that here silence, the silence of a love that knows itself loved in return, is the only eloquent speech.

I love you! For over nine years I have loved you and you alone, loved you with my whole being, without reservation given you my life, with joy in that giving even at times when everything else in the world was joyless. That is all I can say to you, now or ever, in that utterance all is uttered, it is the deep whole from which all my emotions flow, from you out to the world and back to you at last.

I seem to hear a single doubt, an exception, a sorrowful suspicion creeping into your mind to destroy its peace. You will think of Carlotta. Don't. Dear One! Please! If you could only look into my heart and mind and see how little trace is left there of that incident, you would never give it a thought, much less an apprehensive thought, again! You would find in me only an amused—yes, ironically amused!—memory of an outcrop of childish vanity by that Playboy part of me. Also, an astonishment—an amazement at myself for my utter lack of a sense of humor at that time! You would be amused too! Honestly you would! For I was never in love with her. That was nonsense. I was simply dramatizing a gratifying shot in the arm of my vanity! As for your fear that there could ever, under any circumstances, be a recurrence of the symptoms, I swear to you that's ridiculous. When you begin to smile at the ghosts in yourself they never materialize again. Mine don't, I know. You give the lady credit for too much intriguiness—and ability at it. After all, am I an ass? Or an innocent, with my life behind me? One hair of your head is more to me than the whole body and soul, liver and lights, of any other woman! If I lost your love, I'd go mad with grief! Am I liable to long for any such exchanges of peace and fulfillment with you for torture and frustration? No, thanks! I love you and only you, now and always. You should forgive my one amusing (yes, it is!) gesture of a virginal Casanova—as you would forgive Shane kissing Peggy Ann to show what a little man he was!—and then banish it from your mind, except when you want a laugh!

I let you into my deepest inner secrets! This is a bad policy even with a wife one loves! One should keep one's posing before the mirror of oneself in decent obscurity. It is an awfully adolescent, undeveloped nakedness I am revealing to you! But I do want you to laugh at that incident, to see it clearly for what it was. *Was!* "Dead for a ducat, dead!," as Hamlet says.

All this about C.—which I write because I so earnestly and with justice want to relieve your mind of the slightest consideration about it—again makes me think to warn you that if, as is most improbable, any malicious person, alleged friend or otherwise, should bring to your ears any tattle about it, that you shut them up at the first word. For I told you the whole inside truth of it, all there is to be told, when I came down. And I know there are so many people, mostly "friends," who would get a mean satisfaction out of "getting your goat" by some innuendo or other, that it's just as well to be ready for them. After all, we've got to remember I'm in the "show business" and a good subject to hang any rag of scandal upon for the multitude of the failures and the envious ones. And she did come to rehearsals twice!

When I write the above, I feel bitterly ashamed of myself, ashamed of having been such an ass as, even innocently, to have ever allowed myself to do anything that could lay you open to being wounded. It was rotten of me! It was stupid and meaningless! Forgive me again! It will never happen again, I assure you!

But enough of that! I certainly never intended to speak of it when I sat down to write you. All I want to do is get it out of your mind when it is so entirely forgotten and out of mine! The fact that you recur to it so often has made me feel guilty toward you even yet.

Well, the bold Dan hasn't showed on the lot yet. I had a solitary day—swam, took a nap, practiced tennis strokes, played with Oona for a while and gave her your present. She went to sleep tonight without protest except to call for you wonderingly and beseechingly a few times. She was tired out—but healthily tired, she is in fine shape, don't worry about her. Shane I allowed to go to the matinee of *Rin Tin Tin* with Peggy Ann and their nurse who invited him in Mrs. Huber's[3] name. He returned all steamed up about it. He evidently got a great thrill out of it.

Well, it's bedtime. Good-night, Sweetheart! I love you so damned much! We must get away alone to beaches and places when you return. We don't do enough of that. We ought to have our private life together as well as our life in our family. Kisses & kisses, Dear!

(I'll add some to this tomorrow and let you know anything new.)

Sunday / [April 17, 1927]

Awoke this morning feeling pretty poorly. My detestable hives seem to have come back on me with a bang overnight—in spite of diet and everything. It is ridiculous that this petty ailment should keep on making so many fine days miserable for me. There must surely be something that can be done to stop them altogether, once and for all, if one only knew what that something [is]. You might speak to Hamilton about it—or call up Doctor Eugene Du Bois whose address was 1215 Park Ave.

I have been thinking of Teddy. I feel guilty because I haven't written him—but you know how one keeps postponing from week to week the important things one ought to do. I hope you will tell him, if he is strong enough to care about listening, that my intentions at least have been good—and of how sincerely sorry I am. You know that I have always felt a real affection and respect for Teddy. If there is anything more that can be done to make his lot easier where I can be of help, by all means do it.

Oona & Shane have been looking for Easter eggs that Gaga had hidden about the grounds—and getting a lot of fun out of it. They are both fine.

A depressing bit of news is that our water in the barrels is now all gone. This morning Simons and Johnston began getting some from the tank in buckets but there's very little there and it's hard to get at, so I suppose we had better see about ordering some from Wathington's. There's no sign of rain.

It has seemed horribly lonely here today and I miss you damnably. The fact that I feel so rotten makes it less bearable, of course, but that's only a tiny part of it. Dearest One, I love you so! Maybe it is tonic to have you go away every once in a long time. It makes me realize how much I do love you, how tremendous and deep a part you have in my life, and how beautiful and sweet you are! But one day of that loneliness would be enough! Ten is too much! I'm already counting the days before you get back. What joy your return will mean to me! Please don't let anything keep you one hour more than you planned, if you love me! I should be too horribly disappointed!

Your prognostications about Harold have been wrong so far. He hasn't showed up at all. Hurn was here for a short time this afternoon. This morning I worked at reading the Sagas but didn't find much that works in with my scheme.

I can't understand not having heard from Harry[4] on the Ridgefield mortgage transfer. I hope when you get in touch with all those people in New York it will result in your getting some good news to bring back to me. God knows we need it!

Don't forget Evangeline![5]

Again all my love, Own Sweetheart! I can't tell you how much I long for you to be here again! Kisses! Your Gene

P.S. Don't forget to mail those four letters I gave you, if you have not already done so.

Monday noon / [April 18, 1927]

Can't resist the temptation of dropping you a word more. It's stormy and blowing a gale today, but no rain, worse luck! A new crop of hives sprung out on me during the night in spite of my taking soda and the diet and all. Can't understand it. It's laughable in a way but I can't quite appreciate the joke, so if you get a chance to consult anyone who savvys the secret why and wherefore of this affliction be sure and get all the dope you can. I know this is an imposition when you have so much to do and worry about so if it's too much bother, don't worry about it.

Oona and Shane are fine so there's nothing for you to be anxious about there. I hope you got my Marconigram to the *Victoria* in answer to yours.

If there is any very important mail today I'll get another letter off to you by the supplementary. I'm sending this in this afternoon.

I'm so lonely, Dearest! It's hard to think there's a full week more to wait before you'll be back again! I certainly hope I won't have to go up and leave you for a long, long time. You can explain to Langner[6] how unwilling I am to go unless it's a case of absolute necessity—unless I have absolute guarantees that they're going to do something of mine, not just argue about it.

I hope you had a good passage and were not sick. Good'bye for this time, My Own Sweetheart! I love you! Come back to me soon! I'll cable if I don't get any cables about anything. I kiss your dear lips!   Gene

1. Alluding to Ephraim Cabot, the patriarch in *Desire Under the Elms*.
2. This is the final stage direction in *The Hairy Ape* (1922).
3. The Hubers lived next door to Spithead.
4. Harold Weinberger.
5. Evangeline Adams, New York astrologer.
6. Lawrence Langner (1890–1962), director of the Theatre Guild.

203. **AB to EO** ALS 3 pp. (S.S. *Fort Victoria* [en route to New York]) [Harvard]

[April 17?, 1927]

Dearest— I went to the cabin and cried. Perhaps it's only sentimentality—seeing I'll be back so soon—but it was awful, seeing you fade out—waving. I discovered it's *you* I miss—

Saturday night it started to rain & blow. I've lain in bed, unable to eat, in a sort of doze.

Now we are getting in to N.Y.—and it's very cold & damp, as though snow were in the air. Glad I brought my fur coat. By the way, did it rain hard in Bermuda?

I've been thinking things over lying here. Perhaps this trip away will be good for me—some amount of introspection is certainly good, & God knows I get none of it in my everyday life. (Funny, because I used to be very addicted to it.)

Also, in these 48 hours—for there wasn't much real sleep—I read *Cosmopolitan* (all I could get) from cover to cover, including the ads. There is one *good* baseball story by R. Lardner[1]—you must read it. What a frightful magazine!

Was so glad to get your dear cable. "Never again" meant "never again without you."

Kiss our babies for me.

How I do wish you were here just this minute, so I could tell you how much I love you! Your own, *Agnes.*

1. Ring Lardner (1885–1933), humorist and short-story writer. "Hurry Kane" was published in the May 1927 issue of *Hearst's International-Cosmopolitan*.

204. **EO to AB** WIRE, addressed to c/o Madden,[1] American Play Co., 33 West 42nd St., New York (Bermuda) [Yale]

APR 19 1927

BOBBY[2] AT LAFAYETTE TELL HIM READ HOPKINS[3] SCRIPT *LAZARUS* ASK HIM COME DOWN LOVE   GENE.

1.   Madden typed a note to AB on this telegraph, informing her how and when she could expect to get the script of *Lazarus Laughed* from Hopkins in order to give it to Jones. He also advises her to make an appointment to see Kenneth Ives, a real-estate broker, to discuss another matter, probably having to do with selling Brook Farm.

2.   Robert Edmond Jones.

3.   Arthur Hopkins.

~~

205. **AB to EO** ALS 6 pp. (Stationery headed: Hotel Wentworth / 59 West 46th Street / New York) [Harvard]

[April 21?, 1927]

Dearest—   I've seen nearly everyone now. First Harry: he says there is simply nothing to report on the Ridgefield mortgage—that he told the Bank that Danbury Bank was attending to papers for mortgage—& they have not asked further. Ives seems inclined to think it might be well to let R.field go for 36 or 37—says he could have sold it for 35 cash. He is going out this Sunday to look it over again carefully, & will report to me.

Evangeline Adams says "liquidate"—get all overhead expenses cut down, predicts bad financial slump for next year for the U.S.A. Your financial status will pick up about October. She didn't tell me much—says you should go and see her when you come. Says you should close with Theatre Guild before May 10th.

Langner talked & talked—the gist being you should come & get the "personal touch" with Guild. He hopes that they will decide definitely for *S.I* at the Sunday meeting.

Arthur was as kind & as unperturbable as ever—says he wrote you about *Laz.* "*Impressed—but didn't "get" it.*"

Hamilton was fine—seemed very tired from his work. Only saw me for half an hour—Sergeant was fine also—I didn't see Cornell[1] myself, but Sergeant saw them both & got their reactions—K.[2] had read "most of it" & liked it, but G.[3] hadn't read it, apparently only glanced through it, & feels it is *not* "commercially possible"—couldn't *possibly* get people to pay for two nights to see one play—also thinks "asides" can't well be done . . . etc. etc. Very ordinary reaction of a person interested in the theatre really only from the point of view of if a thing will be a popular success. He is going to read it tonight.

Rumsey is terrifically interested in the "saga" & I will tell you his plan of campaign when I get down. DuPont is *flourishing*, had one of the best exhibits in the automobile show this Jan. especially a new convertible model which made quite a sensation. So you see.

I can't write about Teddy. Budge is going to have a baby in June—I am so damn tired & worn out I would give ten years to go back in an airplane to Bermuda. Believe I lost 10 pounds since I got here. Your wonderful letter was the only bright spot—I think you are right about having more of "our own" life.

I'll add more to this later dearest. Goodnight for now.

Later—

Was awfully upset by your cable. Didn't get it until ten o'clock Friday. Rec. second cable[4] just now—wish I was sailing Sat. Never mind, I won't come away again, dearest. Think it better to mail this on boat, afraid miss mail.

All my love, dearest,

Kiss Oona and Shane. It's awful about water—& your hives. Am trying to get dope on them.   A.

    1. Katherine Cornell.
    2. Probably Kenneth Macgowan.
    3. Possibly George Jean Nathan. EO had specifically planned that Nathan should receive a copy, either from AB or Sergeant.
    4. These cables have not been located.

206. **AB to EO** WIRE, addressed to Bermuda (New York) [Yale]

APR 22ND [1927]

YOUR CABLE UPSETS ME FRIGHTFULLY CERTAIN SITUATION IN CONNECTICUT NOT CONNECTED WITH TEDDY HAS MADE URGENT STAY UNTIL WEDNESDAY ARRANGE CERTAIN MATTERS YOU WILL UNDERSTAND WHEN IN [sic] EXPLAIN SITUATION CANNOT CABLE DETAILS PLEASE BE CONSIDERATE AM NEARLY CRAZY WORRY WILL NOT STAY IN NEW YORK BUT COUNTRY I WILL HAVE TO RETURN WEDNESDAY EVEN IF YOU COME WITH YOUR LETTER MEANT SO MUCH CABLE IMMEDIATELY WENTWORTH   AGNES.

207. **EO to AB** ALS 3 pp. ([Hamilton, Bermuda]) [Harvard]

Friday / [April 22, 1927]

Dearest Aggie: I'm writing this in pencil because I'm laid up in bed with a rotten sore throat—quit smoking abruptly for two days and this is result—or perhaps just a coincidence. I've just answered your second cable in answer to mine of yesterday. I know mine was harsh and unreasonable but I had been counting the days and was frightfully disappointed—and was sick in the bargain and dejected about Ridgefield and financial worry in general—and because I'd heard from Arthur turning down *Lazarus* and it seemed as if our tough luck would never break and, looking ahead, that we're heading for a most frightful cropper unless something turns up soon. So forgive my cable. I need you, that's all.

Your cable of today sounds hectic. I cannot imagine what new trouble your folks can have gotten into. But I feel compelled to say something—and if I'm talking about things that never entered your head, I hope you'll forgive me because I absolutely feel it's necessary to guard against these possibilities right now for the sake of your happiness and peace of mind and my own and my power to work. Firstly, don't bring Budgie or anyone of them back with you. It would be fatal to all concerned. Speaking for myself, I simply couldn't be fair about it. I feel too strong a resentment in the matter. Nothing could be solved by it. It would only be an added complication. And just now I owe it to myself—and you owe it to me—to have comparative peace of mind or I shall go bugs entirely and there will be no work done. Even your going away has thrown me completely out. I haven't written a line on anything, and I see no hope of doing so until you get back and life gets regular again.

Secondly, look out how you involve me financially. You know what our situation is. We simply cannot do it. People have got to help themselves or get help elsewhere. It is morally unfair for anyone to look to us at this juncture beyond what we are doing for your father. And as long as your people own property like Point Pleasant which is salable I cannot help but look upon their holding on to it while they accept gifts from others who are themselves in difficulties as not honorable and an imposition. Even in the case of helping your father, I'll admit I have felt this. It goes against my grain somehow. And you know I am no niggard. But just now my foot is down. It has to be in self-preservation. I'm doing all I can or will do.

Now don't get sore at the above. I think I am speaking within my rights as your husband and for the peace of our relationship. If none of my suppositions have any basis, then all the better, I apologize. They are only inspired in me by your cable. I feel damn resentful and disgusted that in addition to your worry about your father, they should bother you with other matters. It is weak. I think if they did not have a lazy feeling that if the worst comes to the worst they have always you to fall back on, it would be a damn sight better for them and for you. And as far as I am concerned— and in the end it always comes down to me through you—you can be absolutely frank with them about the way I feel—*am compelled to feel*. If I was flush and flourishing it wouldn't matter, any more than it ever has mattered.

Another week to wait! It will be a long one, Dear. I was all pointed to meet you Monday A.M. I miss you terribly.

Oona & Shane are both grand. The shutters are being fitted and painted (first filler coat). You want same final color as shutters to your balcony and the window trim throughout, don't you? You'd better cable yes to this. I'm afraid to let them go ahead on it without your O.K. although that color has proved good and I think the shutters should be same logically. No more news from Smith—no estimate yet—am going to call up.

Don't fail Wednesday or I shall never have faith in anything you ever say again! You will have been gone 2 weeks.

All best love!   Gene

Miss Sergeant[1] was going to give *Interlude*[2] script to Bobby. That is all right. Ask Bobby [to] send it to Nathan at Royalton. Kenneth can get it from Nathan and after reading, give to Hamilton who can give it back to Miss Sergeant. I'll write her whom to send it to—Jimmy Light. He could call and get it and give back to her. That will about use up those I want to read it before it's hawked about. Get this straight!

1. Elizabeth Shepley Sergeant (1881–1965), a writer. Her interview with EO in Maine in 1926 was published as "O'Neill: The Man with a Mask," *New Republic* 50 (March 16, 1927), 91–95. In 1927 she spent six weeks at Spithead recuperating from an accident.
2. EO had just finished a draft of *Strange Interlude*.

208. **EO to AB** WIRE, addressed to Bermuda (S.S. *Fort Victoria*)[1] [Yale]

MAY 14 1927

HAPPY RETURNS TO WONA [*sic*] LOVE   GENE.

1. EO was bringing a revised script of *Strange Interlude* in an effort to persuade the Theatre Guild to produce the play.

209. **EO to AB** ALS 3 pp. (Stationery headed: Furness Bermuda Line [en route to New York]) [Harvard]

Sunday eve. / [May 15, 1927]

Dearest Aggie: In spite of old Doc. Hamilton's infallible bromide remedy I have been teetering on the verge of sea-sickness ever since we lost Bermuda under the horizon, and it hasn't been so terribly rough at that. What a bull of an admission for an old windjammer sailor, what? But so it is. And my dreams of doing a lot of work have come to nothing much. I've sort of doped out a plan for condensing the three travel scenes of *Marco* into one running scene—looks good & workable—but outside of that I've done little. I've really felt punk. Harold has slept in my upper—his own was really pretty bad—but outside of that I've seen little of him as he's always out on deck with Groener. Tonight it's gotten very cold—for me!—and I feel half frozen. I never got the room with bath. The one I have isn't much, and I feel a bit sore about it and am going to mention it to Barlow if I see him. I sent you a Marconigram last night and I hope it reached you O.K. I've been spending most of my time missing you and lamenting that I ever had to leave Bermuda—and you needn't blame it all on my feeling sick either! I hope there may be some sort of cable from you tomorrow at Langner's or Guild. Don't think you have to try the policy of never letting me hear a word from you. Under the circumstances that would be very bad business. I need to hear from you. It was partly your never sending me any word when you went to Bermuda and left me alone in New York that helped me to forget myself.

But word or no word, you can absolutely trust me to keep my word to you. So don't worry, Dearest! I love you and I don't love anyone else and that's all there is to it!

Don't mingle with the actresses too much! They're so startlingly the layman's idea of actress—and you know what Bermuda is—I mean, public stuff—it's all right to have them over to the place—although they're hardly your kind, much, or mine. However, this isn't advice. Do as you like.

Again all love—and good night, Sweetest. Kiss our heirs for me. I'll cable when there's any news. Gene.

P.S. Don't forget about the rowboat and punt.
Give Gaga my love.

~〇

210. **AB to EO** WIRE, addressed to S.S. *Fort Victoria* (Bermuda) [Yale]

[May?] 15th [1927?]

HOPE HAVING A GOOD TRIP ALL LOVE. AGNES

~〇

211. **AB to EO** WIRE, addressed to c/o Langner, 14 West 11th St., New York (Bermuda) [Yale]

MAY 17 [1927?]

TWO EARTHQUAKES TWO DAYS RAIN HOPE LIFE IS AS EXCITING WITH YOU ALL MY LOVE. AGNES.

~〇

212. **AB to EO** WIRE, addressed to Theatre Guild Inc. 245 W 52 St. (Bermuda) [Yale]

MAY 19 1927

THACKFUL [*sic*] CABLE LETTER AWFULLY LONELY CAREFULLY FOLLOW-
ING ADVISE [*sic*] YOUR LETTER ALL LOVE   AGNES.

~⌒

213. **AB to EO** WIRE, addressed to Theatre Guild, 245 W 52nd St., New York (Bermuda) [Yale]

MAY 20TH 1927

ROMICKE [*sic*] *MARCO* REVIEWS[1] ALL ENTHUSIASTIC CONGRATULA-
TIONS LOVE AGNES.

  1. Reviews of the book publication of *Marco Millions*.

~⌒

214. **EO to AB** WIRE, addressed to Bermuda (New York) [Yale]

MAY 23RD [1927]

JUST RECEIVED CABLE ON RETURN WERTHEIMS[1] COUNTRY PLACE STOP
SAILING TUESDAY STOP MEET ME DONT WORRY[2] LOVE   GENE

  1. Maurice Wertheim was a Wall Street banker and board member of the Theatre Guild.
  2. EO's "Work Diary" indicates he had engagements with Carlotta on all but two of the
eight days he was in New York.

~⌒

215. **AB to EO** WIRE, addressed to S.S. Fort Victoria (Bermuda) [Yale]

[May?] 25TH [1927?]

MEET YOU TOMORROW LOVE.   AGNES.

~⌒

216. **EO to AB** WIRE, addressed to Bermuda (S.S. *Fort St. George*) [Yale]

AUG 27TH 1927

REMEMBER FRONT HOME CHAIR LOVE MISS YOU.   GENE

∽

217. **EO to AB** ALS 2 pp. (S.S. *Fort St. George* [en route to New York]) [Harvard]

Sunday A.M. / [August 28, 1927]

Dearest One: Well, the voyage so far has been an exceedingly calm one—and I've spent quite a little time out on deck. Got a chair with the Whitneys and have enjoyed talking with him. He is an interesting and likeable chap and it is a shame that someone with his decidedly above the average qualities and appreciations should have been trapped into the Bermuda rut (which at heart he hates).

Mayor Dall's wife is also on board with a couple of children. The rest of the passengers look to be a dreary lot. They might all come from some New Jersey suburb, but as various of them shriek and applaud viciously when the orchestra plays "Dixie," I judge these are from South Brooklyn.

My report on the infection for this A.M. is that it is no worse—and no better. So I continue to be worried. It is perhaps too early to expect final results from Orton's medicine but I had hopes—. I'll await your message on his second analysis with a good deal of anxiety. I had a grand long sleep last night and feel rested today but even the slight roll of the ship in this fair weather keeps me a bit uneasy in my innards. Truly I am not the doughty sailor man I once was!

I hope you got my Marconigram last evening and that you deciphered the message I intended. I meant "Remember our front of house steamer chair love." I wanted you to have pleasant longing thoughts of me my first night away as you remembered the night before! Did you blush when it came to you over the phone?

Dear One, I do miss you so much and wish so longingly that you were here with me! Everything seems so right in our relationship now after all the nervous bickerings and misunderstandings of the summer. I feel deeply at peace now about you and me, as if we had reached a new understanding of our married life together, a fresh faith to carry us on together through the rest of our lives with a love that will grow tenderer and be freed from all bitterness as the years pass. And this feeling is a great consolation in my loneliness for it keeps you near to me in spirit even though you are so far away in the flesh. Never mind, Dear One! It won't be long before I'll come down or you will come up. And I feel when we see each other again we will love as never before! Is that a promise? In the meantime, don't worry about anything—except hurricanes, and I'm hardly liable to be caught in any emotional storms again!

One request: As I'm going to see Owen Davis,[1] will you send me by return mail the scripts of my movie scenarios of *The Hairy Ape* and *Desire*? It would be a good thing to have him read them, I think, don't you? Show him I *can* write that way. You will find them somewhere in the *top drawer* nearest the door of my cabinet.

Kiss Oona & Shane for me. Don't let them forget me. Love to Gaga & my best to Lily, Johnston, Powell[2] & the rest.

And a million kisses to all of your dear self, Own Wife of Mine!   Gene.

P.S. Get latest *Mercury*.[3] Read first story "We Rob a Bank" written by a bank robber now serving a life sentence in Folsom Prison, California. Read first his life history as given at the back of the magazine. Interesting stuff! True story of a bank robbery written from the bandit's point of view.

Later (Sunday eve)

I'm going to mail this now. Have been reading all day. All love to you again, Darling!

1. Davis (1874–1956) was best known as a playwright (1923 Pulitzer Prize for *Icebound*) but had also written many screenplays.
2. Employees at Spithead.
3. The *American Mercury* was edited by George Jean Nathan and H. L. Mencken.

~⌒

218. **AB to EO** ALS 3 pp. ([Bermuda]) [Yale]

[August 28, 1927]

My dearest— Today went by like a dream. I can't tell you how much I missed you. I feel as though I hated Bermuda now—funny, just as I said to you that morning, everything here seems flat and stale.

Well, I guess that it's a good thing that you are going away for a while. It will give me a good chance to "reform." But I do hate to have you go, & I do miss you.

My sweetest, write to me, & tell me about everything. Remember I Love You!

Your loving wife, *Agnes*.

~⌒

219. **AB to EO** ALS 4 pp. ([Hamilton, Bermuda]) [Harvard]

[August 29?, 1927]

Dearest— Of course I had to do what you did when *I* went away—got a terrible cold, stayed in bed three days, & felt sick all over. I think I was pretty well worn out. Am sitting up in bed now. I don't understand if it is the heat or what, but I feel just completely prostrated, I lie in sort of a comatose state—not asleep, & not awake. It has been *very* hot, no wind, & my whole skin is always wet. Dr. Orton sent me some pills. I had the darnedest time getting the report from him, as I called him several times, then after I got in bed & stayed there, I didn't want Gaga to ask. However I finally heard from him it was neutral. Thank god! But you probably know that by now. I do miss you just terribly. Maybe after I get up & around, & I can do some of the things that need doing, I'll feel less blue. Your loving, *Agnes*.

(P.S.) There is a lot of breakfast over this letter!

～○

220. **AB to EO** WIRE, addressed to Hotel Wentworth, New York (Bermuda) [Yale]

AUG 29 1927

LOVE FROM US ALL   AGNES.

～○

221. **AB to EO** WIRE, addressed to Hotel Wentworth, New York (Bermuda) [Yale]

AUG 30 1927

I MISS YOU   AGNES.

～○

222. **EO to AB** ALS 3 pp. (Hotel Wentworth / [New York]) [Harvard]

Aug 29th, '27

Dearest One: It's now eleven and I've had quite a hectic day of meeting people. Madden (nothing new from his end as to *Laz* or anything) met me at the boat, also Harold who went back to Maine at 6 P.M. Then I saw Liveright[1] and went over everything with him. There is nothing to tell you new because he only repeated what you read in his letter about *S.I.* I guess it is best to let him go ahead and publish. *Lazarus* was given me in proofs and I'll have to get busy and read them. Kenneth had lunch with me, or rather I with him. I called up Wertheim but couldn't reach him. Miss Helburn[2] is ill at home so I couldn't see her. Jimmy was up for a few minutes this A.M. on his way somewhere—said Patti had written you.[3] I've got a small and cheap (4 per day) inside room but light and noiseless (comparatively). Don't like it so much but suppose I'll have to put up with it. Bobby was here to dinner and afterwards we had a long confab. He certainly is stimulating and a fine person. Outside of him the day was flat and I feel very blue. It seems as if now that I'm here there is really no reason for my being here and what the hell I'm going to do[4] with myself most of the time, damned if I know! Read detective tales, I guess. There seems little chance of my being invited anywhere in the country—except Harold's and it's freezing up there. However, I suppose something may develop, although I can't see how. The Wertheims are, I understand, swamped with relatives at Cos Cob, Kenneth is full up with Eddie's folks, there isn't a damn place for me to go. To make everything worse, Doctor Du Bois is away not to be back for months, Doctor Andrew is away also, Jelliffe[5] is in

Europe—there isn't a damn doctor I can go to except Maloney and, on careful thought, I won't go to him no matter what. (And I guess he isn't here anyway.) The infection will simply have to take care of itself. It isn't any better—in fact, after a tiring day, worse tonight.

I insisted I had premonitions against this trip as is. I have them worse now. I wish I owned a home in the country like some lucky people! Of course, I'm due for numerous sessions with the Guild bunch collectively and individually, as soon as Helburn is well and Lawrence returns but what am I going to do with the other 21 or 22 hours a day besides sleeping?

Arthur is rehearsing. Bobby, Kenneth, etc., nearly everybody I know is.[6] But I'm not. It's a lonely, idiotic, costly and unhealthy situation. There isn't even any exercise I can take. The weather is hot and muggy. In fact, I already loathe New York and I feel so disgusted I really don't want to go anywhere or see anyone. What I've done is simply to jump from the frying pan into the fire. And I tell you again you have made a mistake! It is not good to force me to be lonely and homeless under the most unfortunate conditions when I'm sick in the bargain—and this right at the start of a season when I ought to be in the best possible condition, both mental and physical, because of the important work I will have to do.

This may seem like rehashing an old argument but remember that I've never been convinced by your reasoning on this point. Now I'm more than ever certain you have acted wrongly. You have thought of yourself and the inconvenience moving the kids would cause you but you have not considered me or my work—or even my health; and I tell you again it is not fair! I cannot see how, if you really love me, you cannot see this!

It is possible I may come right back to Bermuda since it seems these two alternatives are forced on me—either New York under the conditions as described above or Bermuda at the hurricane time when everyone with sense leaves it. I am phoning to Barlow in the A.M. to have him reserve passage on next Saturday's boat and the following Wednesday's.

I hate to write complaining letters but if you were in my shoes you would appreciate my feelings. And I say again that if you loved me you *would* appreciate them! This homeless situation—which is entirely your choice, please remember, and against my best judgment—is unhealthy and unhappy (for me) and dangerous for our future, if my premonitions don't lie. Are you willing to accept all responsibility for its possible eventualities?

All my love! I miss you like the devil or I wouldn't mind this so much! You *must* realize this.

Not that my love or loneliness can mean much to you, judging by the way you've arranged this all-important fall season for me! By the time rehearsals start I ought to be a fine morbid wreck.   Gene.

P.S. (following (Tuesday) P.M.) Barlow was out. I'm calling again later.

I've just talked with Wertheim—nothing suggested about going out there except over-night—he's practically moved back in town—busy with his new firm. So that's out.

Well, I've just bought three detective stories and between them (and reading proofs in a hotel room) I ought to be able to get through the next thirty-six hours without thinking too much about the happy life, crammed with comforts and pleasures, with which God has blessed me! The alcoholic days were much pleasanter!

1. Horace Liveright was eager to publish *Lazarus Laughed* even though it had not yet been produced. The Boni and Liveright edition came out in November 1927.
2. Theresa Helburn (1867–1959) was a cofounder and executive director of the Theatre Guild.
3. James and Patti Light.
4. Here EO deleted the words "except deliver *S.I.* & talk with Guild."
5. Smith Ely Jelliffe, psychoanalyst and coauthor (with Louise Brink) of *Psychoanalysis and the Drama* (1922).
6. Arthur Hopkins was producing *The House of Women*, adapted from *The Green Bay Tree* by Louis Bromfield. Kenneth Macgowan was producing Noel Coward's *The Marquise* with Billie Burke, and Robert Edmond Jones was designing sets for a revival of *The Ladder* by J. Frank Davis, Murdock Pemberton, and Edgar Stehli.

~~~

223. **EO to AB** WIRE, addressed to Bermuda (New York) [Yale]

SEPT 1ST [1927]

DONT LET YESTERDAYS LETTER WORRY YOU FEEL BETTER NOW BUT MISS YOU LOVE. GENE

~~~

224. **EO to AB** ALS 4 pp. (Stationery headed: Hotel Wentworth / 59 West 46th Street / New York) [Harvard]

Friday A.M. / [September 2, 1927]

Dearest: This will have to be a brief note which I'm dashing off between breakfast and a date with Helburn (who is out of house for first time Today). This is my fault but you'll have to forgive me. Somehow I got my days mixed and thought I had another day in which to write you for this next mail.

There isn't much news of my theatre affairs except a very disappointing bit— Langner doesn't get back until the last week in Sept.! This means the Guild won't be able to have a full Committee meeting until that time to decide on *S.I.* Perhaps I'll hear from Helburn today something definite about the date of *Marco* production. Wertheim is the only one of them I've seen and he didn't know anything. He's been very busy downtown with his business. Simonson[1] is still out of town. Moeller[2] busy directing their road company. And that's all of that.

I've had an evening with Jimmy & Patti. Eugene[3] was in and spent one evening with me. I had a long session with Nathan yesterday and am to have tea with him & Lillian Gish in near future. Hopkins has been busy putting on *Burlesque*[4] which opened last night—haven't seen him. Haven't seen Bobby or Kenneth since I last wrote you. No invitations to go anywhere have been received from anyone. It's a dull and lonely life. I'm reading proof on *Lazarus Laughed*.

The infection seems to have dried up. I finally went to see a Doctor Murray of the Rockefeller Institute—met him two years ago through Bobby—who advised me to take care of myself and have a thorough exam. He is arranging for me to see a Doctor Loeb of the Presbyterian Hospital (son of the famous Jacques Loeb). Murray didn't seem to think there could be anything in my suspicions but thought it might be something else—at any rate, thought I must be run down and ought to be looked into generally. I am frightfully nervous these days.

And that's about all. Oh, yes. I've heard from Moran[5]—says he wrote to Bermuda—(Will you forward all mail at once?)—and it looks as if I'd get that mortgage money (1750). So I'll be able to send you 1000 or more for work on the place. I better hold out some for income tax.

The transfer of mortgage to pay off stock loan is still hanging fire. I've seen Harry.

Madden has told Ives to advertise R'field. I haven't done anything about car yet. No use. No place to go and no one to go with. Let it stay in storage.

I feel as run ragged as if I'd been in N.Y. six months. The weather has been muggy & vile. Rain all day yesterday.

All my love, Sweetheart! I miss you horribly! I am having a poor time of it but suppose I'll be busier with Guild from now on.

Kiss Oona & Shane for me! Love to Gaga. And a million kisses to you! It was wonderful to get your note this morning!   Gene.

P.S. I didn't get invitation from Barlow after all. I've got to stick it out here for a time, like it or not!

P.S. Doc Murray said what I probably needed most was to rest, relax, put on weight, forget work for a time, and forget to worry. Swell chance!

1. Lee Simonson (1888–1967) was the principal set designer for the Theatre Guild and a member of its governing committee.
2. Philip Moeller (1880–1958), most prolific of the Theatre Guild directors. His productions included: *Strange Interlude* (1928), *Dynamo* (1929), *Mourning Becomes Electra* (1931), *Ah Wilderness!* (1933), *Days Without End* (1933).
3. Eugene O'Neill Jr. (1910–50) was just entering Yale University at this time.
4. Comedy by George Manker Watters and Arthur Hopkins.
5. New London lawyer who handled the estates of EO's parents and brother.

225. **AB to EO** WIRE, addressed to Hotel Wentworth, New York (Bermuda) [Yale]

SEPT 2 1927

TELEPHONE MORAN NEW LONDON LOVE   AGNES.

～⌒

226. **AB to EO** ALS 8 pp. ([Hamilton, Bermuda]) [Harvard]

[September 3?, 1927]

Dearest— Just got your two letters—I held up mailing my other until after I had heard from you. I wondered what you meant by your cable. I see now. Your letter was pretty blue, & made me even bluer. I wish I had another letter from you saying you felt really differently. I think it might be best for you to come back for a few weeks anyhow. It still seems a foolish thing for me to bring up the whole family & open Ridgefield, because just about as we got that done you would have to be in N.Y. most of the time.

I sent you a cable, or rather as I thought, a marconigram. They called up later, & said as all marconigrams had first to be *cabled* to N.Y. then marconigramed, they were afraid it would be too late to reach the ship. So I had them change the address to the Wentworth—As for your cable, I *thought* I knew what it meant, but Gaga got it over the phone & she said "What does it mean?" & when I said I didn't know, she said "It sounds as if something must have happened on a chair!" I was embarrassed I can tell you! There's nothing she doesn't know.

This is a bum letter. I'll write a better one next time. I have been feeling *so* rotten, & it's been so warm. It's seemed strange without a soul here, except Gaga & Hilda. Very deserted. I rather miss Powell . . . Oona & Shane are fine. You were mistaken— he did *miss* you, very much.

Goodby, dearest, & be sure & write me all the news. Something must have turned up to make you feel better, I suppose. Lovingly,   A.

～⌒

227. **AB to EO** ALS 6 pp. ([Hamilton, Bermuda]) [Harvard]

[September 4?, 1927]

Dearest Gene— Sunday afternoon—the place is as silent & still as death—I have the feeling of being completely isolated from life. I suppose because so many people have been on the place for so long a time, the contrast is emphasized. I haven't seen one soul to speak to since you left Bermuda a week ago, not one. I don't know where on earth everyone is.

Cut down expenses a lot this week. No Powell, only Scott—who stays on the hill, making the garden, & Usher came one day & put in your bars, etc. & did a few little jobs. Johnston has become too busy to even finish the porch. I'm hoping to get him over some day next week.

You poor dear, I do hope that you are happier now—I honestly don't know what to think about things. It *is* so important to save, and it would be a big expense for us all to go to Ridgefield—I was looking over my clothes the other day, & the children's, & we'd simply have to spend quite a little on clothes—then there'd be the car, & Bedini,[1] and half a dozen other expenses that we don't have here—besides the fare. On the other hand, it seems impossible for the kids to be left here alone—well, perhaps something will turn up—anyway, it's damned lonely for *me* here. I can tell you that.

—Monty[2] stopped in, and interrupted the above. As boring as ever. I did *not* arrange to go to any dances with him! We sat on the wharf & I listened, or pretended to, to his opinions of J. Galsworthy,[3] etc.

Well darling, I'll write again for this boat. I surely do miss you, but I feel that we are very close, even though you are not here.   Agnes.

1.   Vincent Bedini, servant at Brook Farm.
2.   Monteville Morris Hansford, a neighborhood friend. His impressions of O'Neill are given in "O'Neill As the Stage Never Sees Him," *Boston Transcript*, March 22, 1930.
3.   John Galsworthy (1867–1933), English novelist and playwright.

228. **EO to AB** ALS 7 pp. (Hotel Wentworth / [New York]) [Harvard]

Sunday Sept. 4th [1927]

Dearest One: I am writing this in bed at midnight. I've just got back from thirty-six hours in the country—very boring hours! Mary Blair[1] invited me out to Connie's place—a farm he's just got at Redding—and as there was nothing better in sight and it was fearfully hot here in town I accepted. We all motored out yesterday noon in Throck's[2] car—the Throcks, Mary & Connie. I was supposed to stay until tomorrow night—over Labor Day—but I couldn't stick it and made excuses to come back tonight. I don't mean there was any wild party on. There wasn't but there was just enough drinking to make everybody silly and some very boring people came to see Connie besides, and this lousy hotel room finally began to look so good by comparison that I up and beat it.

From which you can imagine what a gala time of it I am having here on this trip! To say I am miserable and blue and disgusted and lonely is putting it mildly! As vacation, change of scene, relaxation, etc. this trip to the States is a wild frost! I feel rotten and I'm so nervous I could scream most of the time.

The principal reason I accepted Mary's invitation is that it would give me a chance to go to Ridgefield and look over the place. Redding, if you'll remember, isn't far away. I got Throck to drive me there this afternoon and I got the keys from Bedini and went all over "our home," even up into the woods where I had cleared out. But more of this later on in this letter.

What I want to tell you about now is very important and I need your advice, Sweetheart, as soon as you can give it and hope you'll get an answer back on the same boat by supplementary mail. Will you please do this? I'll be terribly disappointed if you don't. Briefly, on Friday I saw Theresa Helburn and got the news that *Marco* is not scheduled for production until the middle of January and also that if they take *Interlude* that play could not be done much before then either. This was a bit of a blow to me although I had to acknowledge that Dec. *is* a poor month to produce in, especially a big production. But what it means is this: That no money will be coming in before February and that rehearsals will not start before Dec. 15th—three months and a half from now.

Now what in God's name am I to do in these three months and a half? Of course, I will have to stick in town for some time yet to wait for the *Interlude*-Guild decision, to see if Schwartz[3] is going to do *Laz* at the Jewish Art Theatre (I saw him a couple of days ago, gave him script, but as he is beginning last week of rehearsals for his opening bill I can't hope to hear from him definitely until that is off his chest). Also to see if I can't get an English production for that play. There are certain schemes for that—possibilities—that are developing and may amount to something but I'll write you later about them.

There are two alternatives: I can return to Bermuda before long—that is within three or four weeks. (I'm starting in to see the doctors Doctor Murray is sending me to on Tuesday. That will probably take a while and I think it's important.) But in that case, if you're still determined on coming to New York at the time you planned, I would soon be left alone in Bermuda, and that I positively could not stick! The other alternative is for me to stay on here until you come—but I'm afraid, in that case, that by the time you get here I'll be so fed up with New York and so run down that we will stand a poor chance of having any real vacation together. If you could only be here now, it would be different. There are so many things we could do—a tour in the car, for example—but later on it will be too cold. It is useless for you to go on with your arguments that I need to be away from you now. It just simply isn't true! If you would only give it a little clear thought, you would see that if there ever was a time when I needed you and your love and companionship *it is right now*.

Tuesday. / [September 6, 1927]

The pencilled script is the first section of a letter four pages long I wrote Monday night & Sunday night. I am not sending you the rest of it because its burden was "all blue." In brief, I have been having a poor time of it here so far. I haven't felt well—terribly nervous—and I've missed you like all hell in my loneliness. Also going to Ridgefield made me very sad. The place is so beautiful right now and I couldn't help feeling more keenly than ever that that's where our family ought to be.[4] I have half a mind to open it up myself except that it would be so lonely all by myself—and all of my friends I could get to stay there with me are working now—Bobby, Kenneth, etc.

The house and grounds are in fair shape. Someone tried to break in the porch door to living room but the bolts held. Mrs. B.[5] says the moths have raised hell with the furniture and rugs and stairs carpet and wants to know what she should do. B. advises wrapping in tar paper. Will you write them?

Let me know the agency where you got Kawa.[6] Perhaps I could get him again if I decide to housekeep there alone. It wouldn't be much more expensive than the hotel. I'd like to drive the car a bit—what have we got it for?—but what's the use here in town. There's no chance.

You see this (your) whole arrangement for this fall and early winter may be all right for you but it leaves me flat in the soup in a very unhealthy environment.

Moran is coming down to see me before long to have a talk. I don't want to go to New London, on thinking it over. There's nothing there but the alternative of booze or boredom.

I hope you've forwarded the document he sent. I'm waiting for it. On second consideration, I'd better keep all the money from Moran (1750, I mean) for living expenses. Spithead will have to wait. The prospects until Feb. are nil. *Marco* hasn't sold anything like I hoped—Liveright reports only a little over five thousand copies—and, as you know, I've had a thousand advance already. And Horace's book-of-the-month hunch on *Interlude* seems to have hit a snag. He's too damned cocksure before he gets the true dope on things.

I'm damned sorry to hear you've been sick, poor darling! Too much Spithead! I tell you when the ship gets beyond the influence of the old Gulf Stream on the voyage up it's like a ton of lead off your chest. New York, of course, where most of the air in this weather is motor exhaust, isn't much of an improvement on Bermuda. But the air out at Redding was a pleasure to breathe.

Please write me your advice on return mail. I honestly don't want to go back to Bermuda before the weather down there changes. It had me licked. But I could come down around the end of the month—but what's the use of that unless you were willing to stay there with me—postpone your coming to N.Y.—until I come up for rehearsal the first part of December. Would you want to do this? It seems the one solution since you won't consider the family at Ridgefield. I certainly don't want to come down and then have you leave me at Spithead alone. That would be worse than this is now.

I love you and need you!

There's no new news of any important sort. I'm going to see the doctor I wrote you about tomorrow. The Guild are reading *Interlude*. I got a bit of relaxation yesterday. Jimmy's friend, Rockmore[7]—Jew, of course—took me out to the races at Belmont. I lost ten dollars but had an interesting time. But the trip out and back was pretty bad. No invitations of any other sort.

Thank Shane for his letter. I'll write him by next mail. And Gaga for hers. And I'm so grateful for yours. I was starved for word from you. I miss you so damnably! I feel so much better and cheerier today just because I've heard from you.

A million kisses, Own Wife. Take care of yourself. I love you! Don't worry! Please write often! Gene.

P.S. Be sure forward all mail! There's several things—statements from Day for Aug.—Corn Exchange Bank—Empire Trust receipt for int. on Spithead mortgage that should have arrived there. I need them here.

    1. Actress (1895–1947), played leading roles in *Diff'rent*, *The Hairy Ape*, and *Desire Under the Elms*, and in 1928 *Marco Millions*. During these years she was married to Edmund Wilson. In 1930 she married Constant M. Eakin, a businessman, who is possibly the "Connie" referred to in this letter.
    2. Cleon Throckmorton (1897–1965), set designer, including those of *The Emperor Jones*, *Diff'rent*, *The Hairy Ape*, and *All God's Chillun Got Wings*.
    3. Maurice Schwartz (1890–1960), one of the great actors of the Yiddish stage.
    4. EO deleted the words "right now" at the end of this sentence.
    5. Mrs. Bedini.
    6. Japanese butler who had been employed at Brook Farm.
    7. Robert Rockmore, a New York lawyer who was collaborating with James Light on some theatrical ventures.

~⌒

229. AB to EO ALS 7 pp. (Stationery headed: Spithead / Bermuda) [Harvard]

[September 6?, 1927]

Dearest Gene— Mail day again. I am hoping to hear some sort of good news from you today. Particularly about how you feel. I think your idea of there being no doctor left to whom you could go but Maloney is too silly. You are liable to get yourself into a serious state. You know how important that is, and it is what I have been worrying over the most.

I've got quite a little work done the past few days. It has been cooler, and I find that makes all the difference in one's desire to get something done. Also, have gone over all the bills again, & tried to get everything straightened out. I'm having a general house cleaning also, getting rid of the old trash—and believe me, there's some of it! I want to get the front room fixed up this week so I can have a place to keep everything.

I certainly hope you will be able to send me the New London money, as you said, to use on the house, etc. I am so anxious to get that upper room finished, as I outlined in my plan to you, and get the furniture over there. There is no doubt that that upper living room and gallery are going to be the most attractive part of the place—it's so cool there, & such a lovely view on both sides.

To go back to the bills, I find that the increased expense during July and the first half of August was much more than we counted on. You wouldn't believe it. I'll send you items, later. For instance, the drugstore bill was *double*. Patti got stuff there all the time, for which she said she will have Jimmy send me a check later—then 3 cartons of cigarettes a week—J. & Eugene—@ $1.80 per carton—Also, I didn't tell you, but I lent Jimmy $25. Of course I know he'll return it—and I *offered* to lend it to him as Patti told me they had just $6.00 left to go back on the boat bill [*sic*]—but at the same time it comes out of the present, house money. Also beer & ale at the rate of six or seven bottles a day at twenty-five cents a bottle = 1.50–2.00 a day—besides other booze—though not much, such as the Benedictine. My expenses for living last week were $24.38 = everything except wages.

I have done something which may annoy you, though I hope it won't. Our living bill is very high—just getting to the ferry & back even twice a week is $6.00—Jones won't do it under 6 shillings each way, & I can't ask Gaga to walk—& so when Mrs. Winter came up again & asked me if I wanted to keep the horse on the hill "on grass" and not use him, I thought it over, and decided to take him for a month, anyway, for his keep, and use him. This means I can drive to town, get veg. etc. much cheaper, also drive the kids over to the south shore once in a while. It will cost me just £3.0 a month to feed him, and Scott takes care of him. He is out in the place where Hooper used to put his horse. I had Usher board it up. I am not going to ride him. He has already saved me several dollars, and as he is an old plug—13—he is very quiet.

Don't be cross now, about the above. I'll send him back when you get here.

Scott is the most obstinate old darky. He calmly goes on with all his own plans for doing things his own way. He really should be put into a story, and sold for $200.

Gaga told everyone how you kissed her goodby, said Hilda was standing there with her mouth open, hoping she was going to get one too. Then Gaga, puffed up no doubt by the kiss, told Lily that you said she was a "Wenus" (Venus). I heard Lily & Hilda laughing about how you said Gaga was a "Wenus." My god, what an influence you do have on these women!

Well, dear, this is a very businesslike letter, but perhaps you won't mind. I'll drop you another after I get yours today, & send double postage.   A.

230. **EO to AB** ALS 8 pp. (Stationery headed: Hotel Wentworth / 59 West 46th Street / New York) [Harvard]

Sept. [8?, 1927]

Dearest Aggie: This is to warn you to be on the lookout for a most gawgeous present for your birthday which I purchased today and which they promised would get off to you by this same boat. Perhaps this may seem a bit previous to you but I wanted to be on the safe side and get it there earlier rather than later—and to be guiltily candid I don't remember the exact date, only know it's in the 'teens. You'll have to pay duty on it, which is rather a dirty trick but I don't see how to get around it unless you charge me with it.

As for the present itself, I certainly liked it and I hope you will. Let's hope it won't be damaged in transit—but they will insure it, of course. As for its nature, please regard it as a gentle hint that I miss you and want you and need you and that I'm longing most damnably for the time when you'll be in my arms again. I do love you so much, Own Little Wife! Remember that always and don't worry about anything! Promise?

I've felt much better the past two days because some of my physical worry has been cleared from my mind. Yesterday I saw Doctor Gile,[1] former Princeton wrestler, now a prostate specialist. He reported me O.K. in every way in that respect. Today I got most of a general exam. from a shark called Barach[2] (better than the Loeb I wrote you about, Doctor Murray finally decided) and so far he hasn't found anything the matter although he immediately saw my nerves were all shot. It looks as if I would have to put up with them philosophically as the inevitable paying the piper for my past, and that everything else that is worn with me is all mental and up to Hamilton & Co. However, I'm very much relieved. I also got a real kick out of meeting these three Docs—all young men, college grads, already in the top ranks of their profession. There was something so high grade and genuinely fine and big about their personalities. They're so damned healthy and strong and sane compared to most of the people I know. I wish I could get to know them better—as friends. Murray I could except that he's moving to Boston. He is a former Harvard varsity oarsman.

Yesterday I had tea with Nathan and Lillian Gish. At the Ritz, no less! And let me say right here that I fell for the Ritz (at five P.M. at least). We sat in a room with a fountain and a pool and were the only people there! I liked Lillian and can understand why people make such a fuss about her (Bobby for example). She surprises you by being the exact opposite of all you imagine when you say "movie queen." She's quiet and has real brains and is nothing startling to look at except that she has fine eyes. I talked to her about my Lucretia Borgia movie idea[3] and she was enthusiastic, said she has always wanted to play Lucretia and has read a great deal about her—a lot more than I have! So something may come out of it. At any rate I'm to see her with Nathan again before long. Nathan suggested she play the Princess in *Marco*. She certainly could make up to look it and it seems she wants to do something on the speaking stage. But I suppose there's nothing much in the idea—just one of his notions. The Guild would probably throw a fit at the idea!

Tomorrow I'm going up to get X-rayed at the Presbyterian Hospital—then to Lief's[4] to get my teeth X-rayed. Doctor Barach wants this done. I hope to God my teeth won't show anything! An extraction now would be almost more than my nerves would stand.

Knock on wood before you read the following! It looks as if I might sell Ridgefield right away—through Kelly of the Bessell drugstore who has a rich Jew in tow who seems to mean business. Kelly was in to see me twice today and it looks good. However, it's unlucky to count chickens before they're hatched! But I expect a definite decision within the next few days. Let's pray! I'm holding out for 35 but will sell if I can get the price I paid (32,500) in cash! I've decided I ought to.

Here's a question: Supposing the luck is good and it does sell and he wants immediate possession? I couldn't afford to risk losing the sale by saying he couldn't have it for a month or more (waiting until you could come up, I mean). Do you think I could manage the superintending of the packing of furniture? Better let me have all the dope on who did the packing before, how long they took, etc., etc. That is, if you get (or have gotten by the time you receive this) a cable from me that the sale has gone through. Get this dope back to me by return mail—also any advice, instructions, etc. you have to offer. Is there any inventory around that I could show a packing co. to get an estimate? In the meantime, I'll pull whatever wires I can to find some friend of a friend of some packing place, etc.

I sound hopeful but from what Kelly told me there is reason to be. God I hope this doesn't fall through! It would solve our Spithead fixing up, wouldn't it, and we'd be settled at last!

I sure hope you're feeling "in the pink" again by this time. Please take care of yourself, Dear One! If all our troubles blow over we really must have a wonderful time together either when you come up to join me or when we come up together after I've been down to Bermuda again, however it works out (I discussed the alternatives in my last). But for God's sake let's stick together and try and make it a real honeymoon and be selfish about ourselves and not let any outside worries or family or friends intrude to keep us from being absorbed in each other. What I mean is what we had a ten days' taste of last fall in New York. Those were wonderful days, weren't they? Then let's go after a month or more of those this time! Promise? There are so many things we can do together—(one thing above all, what!)

There's no new news on the plays. Haven't heard from the Guild since I wrote last. They're reading *Marco* but Simonson is still out of town. Helburn is strong against publishing *S.I.* before it is produced—if they do it. Some sort of compromise will have to be reached—by me!—between them and Liveright. I can't afford to lose either of the chances for getting some coin.

Friday / [September 9?, 1927][5]

Just a line. This is another of my bad days—feel like the wrath of God, completely done up and nervous as hell! This feeling punk four or five days per week is no fun. Of course, the answer is simple. New York never did agree with me and I ought to be out in the country, especially in this weather. I never get a bit of exercise now and there's no fresh air. When I got weighed this morning at Dr. Barach's I found I was *almost fifteen pounds underweight*—I only weighed 137 with all my clothes on! This is serious—and yet they can't find anything wrong with me so far but it may be something latent that hasn't made itself apparent as yet.

The Ridgefield deal is hanging fire. The man wants to go out with his wife and look it over again. I'm no longer optimistic about it.

The *Lazarus*-Jewish Art Theatre scheme has come to nothing. They were afraid down there it would offend their Orthodox audience.

No chance of getting any definite decision from the Guild until Lawrence Langner comes back on the 26th, I'm afraid. It is a matter of their discussing whether they can cast and direct and fit it in with their other plans. He'll have to be in on this discussion. In fact, it's wise for me to wait until he is.

So there's no good news to give you—and small prospect of there being any for some time.

You evidently don't read my letters through. I'm sorry if they bore you. Of course I realize how entirely your attention is monopolized by Spithead and perhaps I should be more considerate and not bore you with any letters at all! I wrote you some time ago to send movie scripts of *Hairy Ape* and *Desire*, it was important, but haven't got them yet. They are in left top drawer near door of the cabinet in study.

Oh, hell! I feel rotten about everything! It seems as if we manage things in the exact way to make everything turn out all wrong—and this fall's mess certainly draws the prize! You must have framed it up with the idea of becoming a widow!   Gene

P.S. Forgive this! But I do feel sick and despondent.

1. Dr. Harold H. Gile, a urologist.
2. Dr. Alvan L. Barach, a diagnostician.
3. Perhaps alluding to the sixth play in his projected, but never executed, "Atlantis Series," outlined in EO's 1921–31 Notebook. *Eugene O'Neill at Work*, ed. Virginia Floyd (New York: Frederick Ungar, 1981), 174.
4. Dr. J. O. Lief was EO's dentist.
5. EO's Work Diary for September 9, 1927 reports: "Called up *Carlotta* who has just arrived back from Europe." He records meeting with her every two or three days up until the day before his departure for Bermuda on October 19 (1:46).

231. **AB to EO** ALS 4 pp. (Stationery headed: "Bellevue" / Paget East, Bermuda [crossed out]) [Harvard]

[September 9?, 1927]

Dearest Gene— I was on the point of cabling you two or three times this week—silly cables, such as "I miss you."—but my determination to keep down the weekly expense stopped me, which is no doubt just as well. By the way, find out if the *Wentworth* has a cable address, & let me have it. I have missed you so much. Often sudden memories of something in the past come back to me—like suddenly it seemed that we were walking, as we used to do when we came from Peaked Hill to town—through that stretch of woods between the dunes and the road, & watching those crows who lived in the pine tree, & who flew about whenever they saw us. I think the memories of Peaked Hill—& they are all, all I recall, fine ones—are the only memories that stand out visually & clearly in my mind, and the only memories that I recall with a deep sense of happiness. I think perhaps that is why I was so hurt by your determination to put all that out of your mind as recalling a period that you wanted to forget.

The hurricane has not come yet, but the weather is rather sullen—as though summer had grown tired, and longed for a change, not only longed, but was determined to have it. There has been no one working here this week at all, I decided not to go ahead with anything until I get the check from you. By the way, will you send me the $500 which I paid out of my household money for labor, *if you feel you can*, as that is one reason why I am so far behind in my bills. I won't bother with the bal. over the $250 for the Lights' & Eugene's visit, if you will do the above. As I wrote you, it was a good deal more than $250—including extra wages, etc.

By the way, what about my two white felt hats? Please let me know. I need them very badly.

I will worry about you until I hear what the examination shows. I hope you have been having some sort of a decent time. Please do anything you want to do—anything that will make you happy, or give you pleasure. Remember our talks about that—& remember that it is *necessary for you to try & get some sort of enjoyment out of life that will compensate for drinking.**

Shane and Oona send their love to Daddy. *Shane caught a 10 lb.* porgie off the wharf. Some excitement! First thing, he wanted me to photo it, so he could send the picture to "Daddy." Lovingly Agnes.

* This *does not* mean that I am trying to force you into a love affair!

232. **AB to EO** WIRE, addressed to Hotel Wentworth, New York (Bermuda) [Yale]

SEPT 9 27

RETURN TO BERMUDA WHENEVER CONVENIENT YOU I WILL NOT GO TO NEW YORK MUCH LOVE AGNES.

233. **AB to EO** ALS 7 pp. (Stationery headed: Spithead / Bermuda) [Harvard]

Sept 10th [1927]

Dearest Gene— Your letter came yesterday, too late for me to get a reply off, unless I had gone over alone to town, as there was no one here to take it. So I cabled, instead.

I'm sorry that you have been having such a bum time. It's the time of year, I suppose, nobody around. Connie is a pretty dull bird, especially when he has a few drinks, so I don't wonder you were bored.

The situation, or rather the solving of it, seems simple enough to me. Come back to your home in Bermuda as soon as it suits you. You speak of three or four weeks. Well, by that time the weather will be cool. Today, as a matter of fact, is delightful, and the nights are no longer hot. From what you say I imagine that you will get here about the middle, or first week in October. I will not go up to N.Y. as long as you are here, but I might go back with you for a couple of weeks, or even come up for a week, if the hurricane season is over, & then come back with you. The only important thing I have to attend to in N.Y. is my teeth, & they certainly need attention.

You say you will not let me have the money for Spithead, but I certainly do think you should let me have enough to get the livingroom floor done, and the ceiling painted, so that I can follow out my plan of moving the furniture from the cottage over there. Also, I do think, as I said in my last letter, that you should let me have the money I paid out for you for wages, from my household account.

It will be infinitely more comfortable all around if we can get the living room in the big house fixed up. I am going to have Usher fix a door into the lower front room next week.

As I wrote you, we are living on almost nothing. $20 this week for food and other expenses. I have no one working down here now, so that means no wages, except Scott, who is on the hill fixing the garden all the time. I spoke to Johnston about having him work here regularly, & he seems very willing to do it, but won't be able to start for a couple of weeks, as he is finishing the church & doing the De Polo's house too, besides one or two other jobs. In that way, he can get the necessary remodelling, walls, etc. worked in with the general work.

Have you considered keeping some of that mortgage money out to manage with until Jan.?

I personally think you are damn fortunate to have a place like this to come back to, you know you always disliked Ridgefield in the late fall & early winter.

I am having potatoes planted this week. Also a lot of the garden stall has been put in, so we will have early vegetables. The chickens are looking very fine. I want to get a cow as soon as I can, as that will be a great saving.

Haven't seen one soul, except "Monty," on Sunday, as I wrote you. I go to bed very early, read a while, & go off to sleep. Then get up fairly early. I am struggling with that damn article. . . . Some job. How to be personal, & yet not personal! I am forwarding you a large manilla envelope with *all* mail, & will continue to do so until I hear from you.

I'm so glad you went to Ridgefield, and that things looked fairly well. It seems strange to hear you refer to it affectionately as "our house," after your usual remarks about it, damned hole, etc. Do you yourself, really think it would be sensible to open up the place, that is, take the family there? It would certainly be *most* expensive—no doubt whatever of that. The only thing I regret is the car not being used. But you could manage to use that, I am sure. Listen, why not go out to R'field over week ends? With the car. Mrs. Bedini, I know, would either cook for you, or get you some one. You could take out a cold ham, fruit etc., and get two or three people to go out with you. It seems to me that is the sensible thing to do, and it can be done very easily. Mrs. B. knows where the linen, etc., is. You could arrange about the car all right. I know Jimmy & Patti, for example, would love to go out for a couple of days.

It seems a rotten shame about *Marco*. I don't see why they can't start rehearsals right away. In spite of what you said about the "book of the month," I think that *Interlude* will have a big sale if advertised as Horace was going to do it. Of course, if The Guild don't do it, I suppose that Horace will?

Sunday. / [September 11, 1927]

We had warnings of a gale, so I had Johnson come & nail up where necessary. There is no sign of it yet. Shane & the two Johnson kids—they are very nice by the way—are diving off the spring board, and Shane is having a wonderful time showing them what he can do. Oona is "goin' to fising" in the fishpond, aided by Gaga. Have not been fishing since you left, by the way, but Shane caught a big shark off the wharf. Also a 10 lb. porgie, both of these absolutely on his own, i.e. he got bait (small fish) from the pond, and baited up the lines himself. He was so proud, in a very quiet way, but I think he missed being able to show them to his Daddy most of all.

I'm going to take Shane for a walk later on, & see if I can't get some ideas from old houses about doing our courtyard—

About enclosed letter—I was going to cable you to telephone Elliot, then reflected that the man had to wait until his letter got to Paris, & wife cabled back—but I advise you to telephone Elliot immediately now—the operator will get him for you—and in regard to the furniture, I think we could or should, sell some of it—what was in the house when we came there certainly. I hope something comes of this.

How soon are the De Polos coming down? I'm really awfully disappointed that you cannot send me that money to go ahead. It seems as though we were bound to drag through life with things always upset—

Ever so much love, sweetest. I hope to get a letter from you today with better news of some sort in it.   A.

⌁

234. **EO to AB** ALS 7 pp. (Stationery headed: Hotel Wentworth / 59 West 46th Street / New York) [Harvard]

Sept. 11th [1927] / *eve.*

Dearest Aggie: I have again been feeling vile, physically and mentally, ever since I wrote you Friday, and have had to drag myself around to keep my various dates. This evening I feel much better—for the good reason that I've stayed in all day, seeing no one, resting and reading. What I need is rest in the country but where or how to find that is a problem. So I'll stick on here until the end of the month or later—whenever I get a decision on *Interlude* from Guild. If they don't take it, Liveright will and will start rehearsing as soon as he can cast it. In that case I'll have to stay on. I hope not.

I'm not up to it and it would make *Interlude* open just as *Marco* started rehearsing. In which case, by the time *Marco* opens I can confidently predict that I will exit from the last dress rehearsal to enter some nice quiet sanitarium in the country.

There is very little for me to do here now and time hangs heavy. For every interesting thing I do I get trapped into about five uninteresting ones. It's the same dull old game. Outside of my one meeting with Gish and meeting the doctors (who are only professional acquaintances) I haven't seen a fresh face. Kenneth is out of town writing the golf book,[1] Bobby is head over heels in a new Hopkins production, even Jimmy is all tied up with the de Acosta play.[2] The Guild bunch are swamped with getting 2 road companies out, and new productions rehearsed. I haven't seen one of them in ten days.

Carlotta is back. I saw her yesterday—had lunch with her. The cure at Baden-Baden seems to have done her a lot of good—in appearance and nerves. She remarked on how thin and badly I looked compared to when she saw me last. She's quite right. I wish Hamilton were here. These other medicos are simply going to find that all my organs are intact, and that will be that—except that I'll be just where I was!

Last night I went for dinner and the evening down to Patti's sister's (the musician). About ten people were there—a dreary lot! Paul Robeson sang, but I'm about fed up with negro spirituals. I talked with him about his doing *Lazarus* when he gets back from his tour in Europe. Don't laugh. It's a good hunch. A face (white) of Lazarus could be designed for him and his face built up to fit it. White folks make up to play negroes and there's no reason why the reverse shouldn't be practiced. He's the only actor who can do the laughter, that's the important point. It would be good showmanship, too—no end to the publicity it would attract. I think it's a fine hunch, don't you? Now all we have to do is raise the money!

I *am getting* some things accomplished. Through Rockmore (Jimmy's partner), I got in touch with a real estate shark (pal of R's) and we three went to look over my mansion at 53 Columbus.[3] It is rather a sordid hole but there's a lot of building starting up around it and, as no one can build on the corner without buying my place, ought to be worth real money some day. This real estate guy handles Rockmore's property—gives individual attention to each place he takes hold of. He claims the Joseph Day people have a bad rep. for flimflamming absentee owners with high expenses, etc. I believe him! The check with their last statement was for 20 dollars! I'm going to take it out of their hands the last of this month.

Nothing more on Ridgefield. Harry W. is arguing with the guy's lawyers. Something may still come of it.

I'm having dinner here with Ben de Casseres[4] tonight. Haven't seen him so far but am looking forward to talking with him.

It continues muggy and hot in N.Y. I'd give a lot for a swim and the sun on a beach. I'd let everything slide and hop down to Bermuda right now but the thought of the heat down there stops me. I want sea & country but not that kind. It's staying down there that is responsible for the state I'm in, I'm sure. Never again, no matter how much more it costs to come up here! It's bad dope! Perhaps this year it couldn't be helped—but it's a damned shame that I have paid and am paying and must continue to pay for it with my health! That's not economy. It would be cheaper to buy new clothes for you & the kids than to pay doctors. I suppose my bills to the docs. are already over two hundred and it's costing me at least 150 a week to live here. And supposing I get good and sick and can't work this winter? What will it profit then, this economy?

Well, I hate to go off on that tack again—but somehow it sticks in my gorge and won't down! Every time I sit alone in this stuffy room looking out over the dirty, smelly roofs and streets, feeling low and sick and depressed and lonely, I'm overcome by bitterness and a feeling that something is all wrong when you deliberately sacrifice me for your own designs and convenience. It isn't your work. You could have worked at Ridgefield. It isn't the sale of the place. Even if it were sold while we were there we could have put a limit before a purchaser could take possession. It isn't economy. Between my expenses and yours—two establishments—it's costing more than R'field (or any place we could rent near N.Y.) would. (I haven't counted the extras all over the place in my weekly estimate.) It isn't healthy. You're making our children run the risk of the hurricane down there. Supposing it is a really terrible hurricane like the Florida one? Perhaps you don't worry about this but I do! It's just another worry piled on when I already have enough! I won't feel right about it until I know the hurricane is over and you're safe! Perhaps this is morbid but the point is that you know how liable I am to such fears at this period! And if anything happens to either of the children I swear I will never forgive you! Then there's my health, living in New York, wasting time, sick, doing no work, getting no vacation or enjoyment.

I sit and try to figure out why all this should be happening to me. What have I done to you that I should be treated this way? There's no reason I can figure out except that you must have a lover down there as I suspected before! If so, I wish you'd be fair enough to be honest about it and let us quit! I simply can't imagine, for example, why you should deliberately put me in this lonely and distracted situation where I long for love and care and tenderness (knowing as you did what the particular temptation as it exists now would be) unless you are in love with someone down there and don't care what I do or who I love! It's simply unbelievable that you could have done such a ridiculous thing except for some good reason of your own! You know damn well I'm not interested in little sex affairs for sex's sake alone, that it is love or nothing! Do you want me to love someone else?

Oh hell again! What sort of a game is this you're playing, Agnes? Either I'm crazy or you are! Probably I am, anyway. Or, at any rate, I wish to Christ I could escape from this obscene and snaily creeping tedium of dull days, and empty hours like nervous yawns, into some madness—of love or lust or drink or anything else! This camel's back is beginning to crack and snap under the strain!

Oh, well, I suppose it isn't as desperate as it feels now. I'm simply on edge, that's all. As I said before, coming to N.Y. under these trying circumstances, all alone, was like jumping from the frying pan into the fire! What I needed was a healthy change, a fresh outlook, but this is hardly it. Still perhaps it had to be. You may be right. I can't think straight now. I feel too much like The Hairy Ape: "It's all dark, get me? It's all wrong!"

I dread the thought of that hurricane! Be sure and cable me as soon as it's over. I hope the damn dock holds up!

I'll phone to Barlow soon and reserve passage for the first week of next month or thereabouts. I can always cancel it, if necessary. If Ridgefield sells when could you come up to see about furniture—in case I can hold off the taking possession until Oct 15th or Nov 1st. Or would you want me to do it?

To offer a synopsis of this long story: I'm not well. I'm lonely. I love you. That's the whole case in a nutshell.

Tomorrow will be full of doctors and a dentist.

Kiss the kids for me! Your   Gene

1. Kenneth Macgowan and Charles Blair Macdonald, *Scotland's Gift—Golf* (New York: Charles Scribner's, 1928).

2. *Jacob Slovak* by Mercedes de Acosta opened October 5, 1927 at the Greenwich Village Theatre.

3. A property EO had inherited from his mother.

4. De Casseres (1873–1945), critic, poet, essayist, had written to EO about *Lazarus Laughed* in June 1927. He and his wife Bio, a novelist, became close friends during the next few years.

235. **AB to EO** WIRE, addressed to Hotel Wentworth, New York (Bermuda) [Yale]

SEPT 13 1927

THANKS WONDERFUL LETTER TELEPHONE W L ELLIOT WILTON CONN IMMEDIATELY GOOD PROSPECT RIDGEFIELD THIRTY SEVEN THOUSAND LOVE   AGNES.

236. **AB to EO** ALS 9 pp. ([Hamilton, Bermuda]) [Harvard]

[September 13?, 1927]

Dearest Gene—   Your letter—all but the post script—was so encouraging to me— made me happy—then the fatal addition, in which you seemed again so blue & so hopeless. I am looking forward very anxiously to a letter from you on next boat.

It has been hot here, & I have felt rather low this week. Also rather discouraged about getting anything ever done here.

Shane is writing you a letter. He loved yours. He has had a slight bilious attack, and had to stay in bed for a couple of days.

How did things turn out about Ridgefield? I sent you a cable, saying "telephone W. V. Elliot, Wilton, Conn. has prospect $37,000" as I thought you would want to investigate that before selling to the other man for $35,000.

I am dying to see the birthday present—you have me very excited. I hope it comes on today's boat.

Just got your two letters, and am sending this off on supplementary mail. I feel pretty damn hopeless—you being so *continually* miserable—the way the luck is breaking—everything. To anyone with any practical or common sense, the thing I did, of staying here, is the thing that should have been done—however, it merely gives you an excuse to say that I must have a *lover*,— *you*, who know as well as I do that such an idea, from any angle, is absurd. Who, pray? God damn it, if you knew how damned bored & lonely I was here—never mind, I think I'll pack up & arrive in N.Y. next boat, kids & all—then we'll see how that will work. I see through—of course you intended me to—your remarks about taking to drink—or *love*. Well, do it. (Love, not drink.) Remember your conversation with me, in which you told me you wanted to divorce me—remember the days & days of silent dislike & hatred on your part— remember the things you've said & done—Do you think I can forget all that—You love me & need me now, yes, because you're bored and lonely—but that love speedily deteriorates into an intense irritation as soon as we've been together two weeks. And even now, your letters betray a resentment at me for not doing an absurd thing— leaving here in August with two children & opening up a big place which was likely to be sold any minute—Well, don't worry about Spithead. I've lost all interest in it. It's finished, as far as I am concerned—I really mean that, nothing has been done here, & I'm not interested in doing anything. I wonder how I could have been so interested in "chickens" "cow" "flowers" etc. I have sent the horse back today. I am spending very little money to live on, as I wrote you. . . . you don't mention that in your letter. I've got my little pistol locked up in a drawer, & lost the key, otherwise I think I'd take out the punt & finish it, right now, tonight. Bermuda is so empty & lonely, and then, on top of that one hears again the old mistrust. Honestly, I almost wish there was an interesting man around somewhere. Don't you know that letters like yours are enough to make a woman go out into the "hedges or [illegible]" *looking* for a *lover*? Damn you anyhow 'Gene—something must be all wrong for you to say such things.

Goodby. I'm glad Carlotta's nerves are gone. Do you think she would be interested in taking charge of Spithead? If so, tell her I've given up the job. She is certainly much more beautiful than I am. Yours. *Agnes.*

P.S. The present hasn't come yet!

237. **EO to AB** ALS 6 pp. (Stationery headed: Hotel Wentworth / 59 West 46th Street / New York) [Harvard]

Sept. 13th [1927] / (Tuesday)

Dearest One: First, I want to ask you to forgive me for the letter I mailed you yesterday which you will get by this same boat. As I remember it now, it was too damned
crazy blue—but the truth is I am really on edge and worn to a frazzle and I get fits of
such terrible depression that it seems as if I'd go "off my chump" if I didn't have
someone to pour out all my woes to. I know it's hell to make you the goat for this but
you're all I have to turn to in such black moments. I hope you'll understand, Sweetheart, and make allowances.

**Eugene O'Neill at Spithead, 1927. Photographer unknown. Yale Collection of American
Literature, Beinecke Rare Book and Manuscript Library.**

I'm particularly down in the mouth just now because the Ridgefield deal has
fallen flat. This morning, after the contracts had all been drawn (32,000 cash) and I
was about to send you an hilarious cable, the damned Jew changed his mind—said
after mature consideration he'd decided the place was too far from the station. It was
a blow, believe me! It looked so certain when Harry first phoned me this A.M. There
certainly must be a jinx on us!

The second irritation is that that damned old fool, Mary Vorse O'Brien, hasn't
even paid the interest on the note for five hundred I'm on and the bank is sore and
won't renew but insists she pay it. As she is (of course!) broke and, from the way she

sounds over the phone, in a sodden stupor, this means I will have to make good on it unless she can—but how?—square them some way. Isn't it hell how things are breaking? I feel under a curse! Never again will I sign anyone's note!

So it is a bad time to be asking me to send you an extra five hundred. It will be hard enough to part with the regular five hundred for Sept. at the end of the month. I had to give Harry eight hundred of what I owe him the other day. He had gotten in a bad jam through speculating in an up the Hudson real estate scheme and was really up against it. As my debt to him has been running since the first of 1924 and he's charged damned little and been so nice about everything, I felt it was decidedly up to me to come across. This, with the incidental expenses of transfer, ate up all of the cash over the loan on the stock, that would have been coming to me from the raising of the Columbus Ave. mortgage. Today I have to mail four hundred and fifty to the Income Tax. I ought to pay Larkin's bill too (200). And there's 360 in taxes that are long overdue on Ridgefield and which the real estate men say I ought to pay up because it hurts the sale—when clients find it out they think I'm broke and have to sell for anything I can get, is the dope. And right now we have only a little over 2000 in the Corn Exchange. Out of this your five hundred per month has got to come. I haven't heard from Moran although I wrote and sent him the signed release a week ago. I'm damned afraid that party may have changed his mind too. In which case, no 1750 for anything. There won't be anything from my books until Nov. 1st—by which time we'll probably need it damnably—and, as I explained before, the returns there will be disappointingly small. Until Feb. 1st you can make up your mind that we will be in a bad pickle and unable to go forward with anything unless R'field sells. For there is one thing I have promised myself—and it is a wise thing!—and that is that I won't hock or sell my stocks again unless it is for money to live on. If *Marco* fails and *Interlude* doesn't go on (if the Guild passes it, this is possible. Hopkins won't do it and Liveright is only talking big. The point is he would have to raise backing for it and he failed lamentably in this where *Marco* and *Laz* are concerned. As a producer, he has no standing), we will be forced to do this.

There are a few facts for you to face. They're disagreeable but they can't very well be ignored when you look at the future. Added to them is the reserve (in stocks) in case the Spithead mortgage mix-up breaks wrong. The way the luck is breaking now, I feel as if a run of black were on and we could count on losing every bit! I hope to God I'm wrong.

I'm sorry to have to be continually writing in this vein. God knows it's as hard on you as on me and I don't want to. I had so hoped to send you a glad cable today of R'field sale, and surprise you! I'm blue as hell about it! Well, it's spilt milk and no use crying.

Are you working hard on your article? That would come in handy later on, looks like. I'm very anxious to read it. You'll send me a carbon as soon as it's done, won't you?

My best love to Shane, Oona. Kiss them for me. Did Shane get my letter? Did you get my present? I'm anxious to hear what you thought of it.

I've just got your cable about Elliot at Wilton, Conn. I'll have Harry get in touch with him at once. Let's hope this is a live one!

Doctor Gile, the prostate specialist, has decided that that running pain I got that lays me out (you know) is not, and never has been due to piles, but is a prostate affair. I am now undergoing treatment. However, don't misunderstand. The trouble has no sexual causes or effects of any kind, past or future, and, outside of the pain I get, of no serious moment. So that's that.

Love & a million kisses, Sweetheart. I hope it won't be so damned long now before I can come down and be with you again. I've got to rest and build up somewhere. Your, Gene.

⁓

238. **AB to EO** ALS 9 pp. ([Hamilton, Bermuda]) [Harvard]

[September 14–15?, 1927]

Dearest Gene— I decided after all that there was no use in trying to do what I thought best, & trying to save, etc., after your letter in which you again accuse me of not—or never—having any motive except a selfish one—this time a lover. So I am going to close the place here, & come up. The change will probably do us all good—We will go to R'field, & may as well plan to stay all winter. I will have to get clothes for the children & myself, as Mrs. Eugene O'Neill can't go round in three-year-old things, & of course the kids have completely outgrown all they have, & while they can manage here, they can't make the boat trip—

In regard to expense, I see you have it figured out that it costs more for me to stay here than all going up & running the place in R'field. Of course if you are spending $150 a week in N.Y. it may be so. I have written you what it is costing here—about $20. Your room costs 4.00 a day, didn't you say—$28. a week. If conditions are as bad as you write, I think *you* could manage to cut down a little here. We owe a great many bills here—as I wrote you, you *not only* used— borrowed—$500 of my house money, but the extras for the three people came to nearer 500 than $250, so you see I am *way behind*. I was counting on charging *so* little during Sept. that I could use a lot of the Sept. 500 to pay back bills. I will be able to do this to some extent, but on the other hand there are certain things outside of house which I've had to pay for—manure, a certain amt. of work, plowing, Scott, etc—

However, I am through with trying to do anything here. It has been damn hot & unpleasant for me in more ways than one—& bad for you, too. I really thought it would be a good thing for you to be away from family life for a while, also I thought you would find life more amusing than you have found it.

I have been re-reading Dostoevsky—

I would *insist* Mary borrow that $500 from someone else.

Your present hasn't come yet, but I expect they send it by express instead of mail, so that would account for a small delay. I am crazy to know what it is—

Well, dear, it's hard doing all this by letter, & I will see you & talk to you in a short while now. Like you, I am fed up with Bermuda—my idea of making it a lovely place for you to come back to seems to be out of the question entirely—principally because there isn't ever enough to carry out the simple plans which I outlined to you—

I think Shane misses you a great deal.

Gaga suggested that she & *Shane* go to R'field & open it for your weekend. She said she would love to be out there with Shane. That wouldn't cost much either—

Goodby darling— A.

239. **EO to AB** (Stationery headed: Hotel Wentworth / 59 West 46th Street / New York) [Harvard]

Sept. 15 '27 / Thursday P.M.

Dearest Aggie: Just got back from Wertheim's a few hours ago—went out with him late yesterday afternoon and came back around two today. Very pleasant. Had two swims in his lake and feel greatly set up. He sure has a wonderful place—beautiful horses. You must come out and visit there with me when we're here in town together. I know you'd like it. The cottage he called me about is at present occupied by Arthur Lee's (the sculptor) wife who has been very sick. I'd think seriously about going there if it were vacant, although it's right on the state road and a bit noisy.

Doctor Barach, the diagnostician shark I am being gone over by, has at last found something wrong. After exhaustive tests it turns out I am deficient—subnormal—in thyroid and he has given me thyroid tablets to take. I've now had two doses and, although it may partly be imagination, I certainly have felt extremely bucked up and full of pep yesterday and today by comparison with the half dead & alive way I have been feeling. As New York is at present sweltering in a belated heat wave, and everyone seems all in, this is remarkable. Barach also made a series of tests of my smoking and he found it was all wrong and has given it out cold & clammy that I must stop smoking right away and stay stopped. He says he never saw anyone so nervously sensitive to the effects of cigarettes before. It is going to be a hell of a job, quitting in N.Y. but I've made up my mind to stab at it. This ought to be refreshing news to you, Dearest! At least, you won't have me grouching around the house while I'm breaking my habit!

(Later)

Your letter of the 10th just arrived. As for that extra five hundred for labor, of course I *can* send it to you, if you insist, but I'll wait until you've read the details of the situation in regard to our finances as I outlined it to you in my last letter mailed on Wednesday's boat.

I'm hoping every day to have some startling bit of good news to write or cable you about R'field or something but so far none of the breaks have come my way.

Sept 16 [1927] (Friday)

I had dinner last night with Mary and Bunny[1] and Pat Kearney.[2] Bunny reports everything in Provincetown (Peaked Hill) in good shape but says he never could locate the concealed alcohol you wrote him about. He is only down here for a day or two—is going back tomorrow night.

Ben de Casseres had dinner with me here the other night and stayed all evening. A damned interesting man! We had a good time of it talking together. I have given him *Interlude* to read.

I think the Guild bunch will give me a decision on *Interlude* soon. I've got to read page proof on *Laz* within a few days—sign my name 750 times for the special edition!—and then not long after do this all over again for *Interlude*, two sets of page proofs & all. I'd like to get all this off my hands before I come down. It's work suited to a hotel room in its boring quality and it does keep me busy.

Shane's letter came today along with the envelope of mail. Tell him I will write him soon and that I was tickled to death to hear from him. He is getting to be a grand little dictator! I had to grin when I imagined how elated he must have been over that porgie and that shark! It is a wonder to me how he could have landed them without getting pulled overboard. Did you try eating the shark? I've always wanted to see what they tasted like.

On second thought, I'm enclosing the check for five hundred. You will have received my last letter in which I tell you all about the financial situation and you can act about it as you think best. If you think things warrant it, why use it to repay back labor—if not, consider it as the regular money for this month. I leave it up to you. I don't want you to feel I'm playing "stingy."

I feel much better again today, Dearest. A bit edgy, for I've started in cutting out smoking—it's late afternoon and I've only had three puffs of one cigarette so far!—which is going some for N.Y. It's great to feel better, and I think I can now have a fairly decent time of it the rest of my stay in N.Y. and get a lot more done. And I'll certainly try not to write you any more letters full of my troubles. You must have been worried about some of them, I get such bitter fits on.

I've just had a phone that the Guild will decide about *Strange Interlude* tomorrow. I think they're going to do it—but can't be sure. Will tell you all about it in my next.

Don't worry about me. I'll be all right from now on, I'm sure.

Kisses to Shane and Oona. Give Gaga my love. And all love to you, Darling! I'm looking forward so to being with you again! Your   Gene.

---

1. Mary Blair was married at this time to Edmund Wilson (1895–1972), critic and essayist, known as Bunny. They lived in the Coast Guard station at Peaked Hill Bar occasionally in the years after the O'Neills left.
2. Patrick Kearney was a playwright.

240. **AB to EO** WIRE, addressed to Hotel Wentworth, New York (Bermuda) [Yale]

SEPT 16 1927

MUCH COOLER NOW WHY NOT COME DOWN IMMEDIATELY LOVE AGNES.

241. **AB to EO** WIRE, addressed to Hotel Wentworth, New York (Bermuda) [Yale]

SEPT 17 1927

AFTER REREADING LETTERS DECIDED WILL ALL COME TO NEW YORK PROBABLY SATURDAY WILL CABLE   AGNES.

242. **EO to AB** WIRE, addressed to Bermuda (New York) [Yale]

[September 18, 1927]

GRATEFUL CABLE UNNECESSARY COMING DISREGARD LETTERS CONDITIONS BETTER NOW DETAILS IN LETTER COME BERMUDA SOON LOVE DEAREST   GENE.

243. **EO to AB** ALS 7 pp. (Stationery headed: Hotel Wentworth / 59 West 46th Street / New York) [Harvard]

Monday, Sept. 19th [1927]

Dearest Aggie: I went out to the races at Belmont with the Rockmores on Saturday—it was Futurity Day, the biggest day of the year at the track—and then had dinner with them & Jimmy & Patti, and after that Paul Green[1] came to their place to meet me (he is a nice guy even if he is a playwright), so I didn't get your cable until I got home about one. I sent an answer, deferred rate, yesterday morning. Hope you got it all right and that my last letter which you will get today will explain. I am in much better shape now and there is no need for you to give up all your plans to come up, especially as I'm planning to come back to Bermuda as soon as I possibly can. But I sure am grateful to you, Dearest One, for your willingness to sacrifice your own ideas— which are undoubtedly a good deal wiser than my overwrought, morbid notions of feeling abused have been!—to come to my rescue. Now that I'm healthier I can be fair and see how fair you have been.

I ought to be able to sail home the first week in October—or, at the latest, the second week. Lawrence is due back the 29th and although the Guild definitely decided to do *Strange Interlude* at a meeting they held Friday night without needing his vote—(that's one item of good news for you! It also means five hundred bucks!)—still they must wait for him for a full meeting to decide the where, when, how, the possible casting, etc. and I simply must be in on it. Naturally they won't be able to do it at once—even if they could cast it—but there is the possibility that they'll get it on before *Marco*. At any rate, I'm sure to have enough time before rehearsals start to come to Bermuda for a while, thank God!

Other reasons that would keep me here until the first of next month are that Lief is working on my teeth, Doctor Barach has to have a couple of weeks more to discover by experimenting just how much thyroid is the right dose for me to take each day, and I still have two more prostate treatments (they come a week apart) to get from Doctor Gile. I want to get this all off my slate on this trip so that when I come to Bermuda and come back for rehearsals I will be "in the pink" and have nothing like that to worry about but be free to concentrate on the job. This seems to me essential. With *Marco* & *Interlude* coming close together it is going to be a long hard drive.

I'm having a pleasant time now—nothing hilarious but pleasant enough. The Rockmores have been very kind. I have enjoyed their invites to the races. You certainly must come with me to the track sometime! You'd love it! And if one restrains one's gambling instinct it isn't so expensive. I split even on my little bets (I didn't risk much, naturally!) on Saturday.

Komroff[2] had lunch with me yesterday and spent the afternoon—a damned nice fellow! I like him very much.

I'm due to have dinner with Lillian Gish this week sometime. That will be interesting—all except the dinner part! Why do people always want to meet to eat!

I've seen Carlotta a couple of times. I won't go into that now but wait until I see you. As a matter of fact, there's nothing much to go into—so, whatever you do, don't get to worrying about that. She's been damned nice to me and I've enjoyed being with her—but that's the all of it from both sides.

Another reason I couldn't go down right away is that through Wertheim I have got in touch with the big hydro-electric people and am going to visit one of their plants soon.[3] Unfortunately there isn't one anywhere near New York! They want me to go to Niagara Falls where there is one of the finest in the world. I thought I might get Larkin (if he would do it cheap) to go with me and drive up. It would make a nice four or five day trip through beauiful country there and back. I wish you were here to do it with me! It really isn't 100% American not to do a honeymoon to Niagara Falls! I shall have to advertise for a temporary wife!

But I hope they'll dig up a plant nearer N.Y. I can't afford to be away from town five days now.

I had dinner with Helen MacKellar & George[4] & Sessue Hayakawa,[5] the Jap actor & his wife, at her place a while ago. Perhaps I've already mentioned this. His wife was interesting but he is very much movie-actor.

The *Emperor Jones* road tour has gone blooey—a bad luck item. I thought something might come in from this.

There's not a peep about Ridgefield, damn the luck! Although another hundred and fifty dollars has been wasted advertising it.

Moran was down and spent evening talking over things. He expects to get the 1750 from Packer before long—there's been a delay at the bank of some sort—but the deal for the corner is off (of course!) and there's no other sale in sight. He says things are pretty bad up there. So you can count New London out! An auction wouldn't do at this time, Dillon advised. Everyone there is hard up.

And that's about all the news. I'm sorry there isn't more cash in it!

Darling, I do wish you were here! But don't come! It would break us entirely just now with the bankroll so low, getting the kids up and rigged out and everything. *You were right*! But I'll be down just as soon as I can make it, I promise you! October is less than two weeks off, after all! And then let's really honeymoon! We're always promising ourselves to do this and we never do—except for that ten days last fall!

Kiss Oona & Shane for me. Love to Gaga. All my love to you, Darling.   Gene

P.S. Did my present ever arrive? You haven't said thank you yet. Perhaps you didn't like it?

Later (Monday eve) [September 19, 1927]

Your letter arrived a while ago and it has made me terribly depressed and hopeless again. I feel it most unkind. I acknowledge you have a right to feel peeved at that letter of mine but not to that "God damn" degree. After all, you might have taken into consideration that I have been palpably not myself mentally for the past few months and, as everyone up here noticed as soon as they saw me and as the doctors' diagnosis have proved to be so, physically sick. And why remember the bitter things I said and did? You said and did things just as wounding—more so!—to me and I assure you that I love you enough to have completely forgiven them and not to hold them against you.

My expression of gratitude for your cable in my return cable and in the first part of this letter seem to be misplaced. I thought you wanted to come up to help me but evidently you're merely doing it out of anger and, if you do come, I have only to expect a wife who will hate me! And similarly, what reception can I expect if I return to Bermuda?

It had all become so simple and I was looking forward to the *happiness* of being with you again—but now it's all so hopeless I don't know what to do. Good Christ, why can't we understand each other, why couldn't you see that it was at bottom my loneliness and love for you that made me write as foolishly as I did?

Sweetheart, what the hell is the matter with us, anyway? We act like a couple of children and we ought to be ashamed of ourselves!

Tuesday A.M. / [September 20, 1927]

I've just cabled you again to postpone your decision until you get this letter. The point is I'm planning to sail for Bermuda so soon—want to get something of *Dynamo* done down there— and this will throw all my plans out. It seems to me the logical thing now—considering finances, etc.—for you to wait and then come back up with me when I return for rehearsals. I hope you will see it that way. Otherwise we'll soon go cash broke.

All love, Sweetheart. Forgive that crazy letter and forget it, please do! Remember we both desire so much to start a new life together.   Gene

P.S. Can't understand present not having arrived!

1. Paul Green (1894–1947), playwright, novelist, and short-story writer, best known for his folk plays of African American life..
2. Manuel Komroff, an editor at Boni and Liveright.
3. EO was doing preliminary work on *Dynamo*.
4. George D. MacQuarrie, Helen MacKellar's husband.
5. Sessue Hayakawa (1890–1973) was a well-known film actor, married to the actress Tsura Aoki.

～○

244. **EO to AB** WIRE, addressed to Bermuda (New York) [Yale]

SEP 20 1927

CABLE IF PRESENT RECEIVED ADVISE YOU NOT DECIDE LEAVE BERMUDA UNTIL READ NEXT LETTER GUILD TOOK *INTERLUDE* GOOD NEWS LOVE GENE.

～○

245. **AB to EO** WIRE, addressed to Hotel Wentworth, New York (Bermuda) [Yale]

SEPT 21 1927

PRESENT IS WONDERFUL WROTE YESTERDAY SO HAPPY YOU ARE BETTER DISREGARD LETTERS MUCH LOVE AGNES.

～○

246. **AB to EO** ALS 3 pp. ([Hamilton, Bermuda]) [Harvard]

[September 20?, 1927]

My dearest— How could you have guessed the very thing I wanted more than any-thing else—I've wanted one for years, every time I took a trip & had to fuss around with packing, it's gone through my mind, "if only I had one of those outfitted bags."
     You are a bad person to spend so much money on me, though—
     Please never mind my last two letters. I was really very deeply hurt by what you wrote me—more than you will understand. Yours,   Agnes

     It's so perfect, too—the initials & everything, & the way the trays fold over to make another suit case—

247.**EO to AB** (Stationery headed: Hotel Wentworth / 59 West 46th Street / New York) [Harvard]

Friday—midnight / [September 23, 1927]

Dearest One: You will have to forgive me if this is just a note. I meant to stay home tonight and write you as long a letter as usual but right after dinner Nat Lief (the brother) phoned me and asked me to go to the Ziegfeld Follies and I thought I better take him on as the show is as usual a sell out and I wouldn't see it otherwise. I haven't been to a "gal" show in years and wanted to see how I'd like it. Well, I had a grand time—laughed my head off at Eddie Cantor and enjoyed the semi-nude beauties. Ziegfeld—or his manager—found out who was coming and we got the seats Ziegfeld reserves for himself & friends—two in the center of second row where a good close-up could be had. It was all good fun.
     Last night I heard the fight over the radio.[1] Did you in Bermuda at Ushers? Poor Jack! They did him out of it on a technicality—nearly all today's papers are agreed on that. Tunney was out for thirteen seconds in the seventh round, really. However, it's good business! Now they will probably stage a third fight next year.
     I've found out there is a big hydro-electric station in Conn.—about 15 miles north of Danbury—and so I guess I'll look that over instead of Niagara.
     Saw Terry Helburn & Wertheim yesterday. Nothing new on *Marco* or *S.I.* We're all waiting for Lawrence Langner now.
     Had dinner with Nathan & Lillian Gish night before last. I like her immensely. She seems crazy to have a try at the Princess in *Marco*. I haven't broached that to the Guild yet. I hardly know what to think of the idea myself. In a way it would be an enormous ad but—.
     Pinchot[2] has taken some wonderful photos of me—best ever! He asked me as a

special favor to let him take some of me for the ad. of it. He has left Muray, you know, and is starting on his own. These of me are certainly fine work.

I've reserved passage on the *St. George* on both Oct. 5th & 12th. I'll try to make it on the 5th. It will all depend on how soon Dr. Barach is through with me and on Guild developments following Langner's arrival.

It's late and I'm all worn out. Good-night, Dearest. I'm so tickled you liked my present. I thought it would hit you right.

Tell Shane I've meant to write to him and will soon. Kiss him and Oona for me.

I've also been reading page proofs on *Laz*—made a lot of changes—finished today. So I've really been working hard in spite of all my social excitement! Now I'll have to sign 750 sheets! And then *Interlude* proofs will be coming on me and sheets to be signed for that too! Busy is the word!

I'm feeling better but getting no fatter. I'll be glad to get back home and rest. I miss you like the devil, Dearest! The whirl keeps me from thinking too much about it but I'm very lonely inside.

Any hurricane news? I worry about that.

All love, Sweetheart! Your   Gene.

1. The Jack Dempsey–Gene Tunney fight was on September 22, 1927.
2. Benjamin Pinchot, portrait photographer. EO's Work Diary records that Carlotta accompanied him to the photographer on September 21, and probably it was on that day they were photographed together. See photograph in Gelb, opposite p. 842.

~

248. **AB to EO** (Stationery headed: Spithead / Bermuda) [Harvard]

[September 23?, 1927]

Dearest Gene— I got the lovely suitcase—Gaga brought it over in the carriage with the last mail, although it came by boat, not by mail—and immediately wrote you a short note, & got it off on sup. mail. Then I got your cable the next A.M. asking if I had received it, and sent a cable back to you at once.

It surely is the one thing I would have picked out if I was choosing anything for myself. It is so complete in every detail, & the initials, & the toilet set are so lovely that I can't thank you enough—dearest—

Your letter did sound so much better, & I was so relieved. First of all, I think that the idea of the Dr. discovering that you had a thyroid deficiency is something very important for your future. If you remember, Dr. Bisch had the same idea—but not being a gland specialist, I imagine he did not know the right way to administer it. I have, myself, as I'm sure I've told you, thought there might be something like that. You certainly have what are popularly supposed to be the symptoms—slow heart, etc. Also—this sounds like a real "I told you so letter,"—I have always had a hunch that smoking was very bad for you, and I am glad that it has been definitely decided, once for all, that you are not to do it. With these two things attended to, it seems to me that your nervousness should certainly decrease a whole lot. Honestly, I suppose I should have had better sense than to get mad at your letters, but when you wrote that last one it did seem a little too much. Particularly as I have had a *very* boring, rotten time here, as you can imagine—not only have not seen a soul, or gone anywhere, but I have not even had the satisfaction of going ahead with the work on the place, as you know. As far as writing goes, I am going to confess that I have not made *much* progress—*some*, I admit, but I have not by any means gotten to the stage where it has again become an absorbing interest in life. I honestly think the weather has been against it, for although the days and nights are cooler, there is a horrid sultriness in the air, worse in fact than all summer. Oona and Shane have felt it, too, I believe. Oona's sores don't seem to get very much better, so today I called up Dr. Tucker, who everyone says is a marvel with kids, & I'm going to see if I can't get him to give me some satisfaction. The damned Bermudans are so afraid of giving their Island a bad name that they refuse to recognize, or investigate these sores, simply saying, "Oh, too much sun," while as a matter of fact I imagine they must be an infection from something or other in the water. Gaga now is getting some, & she never goes in in the middle of the day. The barber, Williams, says a great many kids get them.

What on earth did you mean in that part of your cable which said "advise don't decide leave Bermuda until after getting next letter"? I thought you had already cabled me *not* to leave. The whole cable was rather ambiguous, I thought, except about *Strange Interlude*. Well, that sounds fine. I only hope there are not a lot of strings tied to the acceptance which will tie it up. You'll tell me all about it in your next letter, won't you?

It's close as hell today. I envy you your trip to Wertheim's. Do you think they'll ask us to go out there together some time? I'd love to go.

How about the Elliot Wilton deal.

X PLEASE ANSWER THESE IN YOUR NEXT LETTER. X

(1) *How about my two white hats?*

(2) *Where did you say you put your gun? I can't find it.*

Do you know, Shane caught a 4 1/2 pound rock fish off the wharf last evening. Isn't it great? He *does* miss you a whole lot—

Later—I'll close this up, then send you a sup. letter after I get yours today. I miss you *awfully* dear—it seems like years, rather than a month since I've seen you. Lovingly, *Agnes*

249. **AB to EO**[1] ALS 2 pp. (Stationery headed: Spithead / Bermuda) [Harvard]

[September 24?, 1927]

Darling— I got one letter off to you today, but as I said, I waited for the mail & will try & get this off supplementary. Your letter which came today seemed to be divided into two parts—a nice & a nasty—the nasty written after you had rec. mine, and saying that I was coming up "out of anger," etc.

Well, dear, perhaps my letter sounded that way, but I *wasn't* coming up "out of anger," but because I thought you wanted me. However, as you write that you will be down very soon, there is no need of going into that. I surely hope you can manage it by Oct. 15th, anyway. I will plan to go back with you, as I absolutely *must* go to the dentist. I look a sight as far as teeth go, as that filling has come out again.

I haven't cashed the check. I certainly can use it for back bills, as I explained, but will wait for your decision.

Did you bet on the fight? It sounded from here as though J.D. was the better man. (I am speaking from the "Colonel's" report, as I was in bed the night of the fight at 8 o'clock.)

Lovingly,   A.

1. The stamps on the envelope containing this letter were not canceled, perhaps indicating it was not sent.

250. **AB to EO** (Stationery headed: Spithead / Bermuda) [Harvard]

[September 25?, 1927]

Dearest Gene— Just got your letter, & will get this off by sup. mail—I'm so glad, dear, that you are better—& having some sort of a good time. Don't pay any attention to my letters—I *was* sore at your thinking I never did anything but for a selfish motive—but that's all over now, & when you come down we'll have forgotten all about it. I'm glad you do feel that it was wiser & cheaper for me to stay here, particularly, as I said, because it has been very lonely for me.

It will be wonderful to have you back again, dear, but *don't* make the mistake you made last spring, of leaving just when you are really enjoying yourself, & when you can attend to things, just because you feel I want you to come here—I want to go back to N.Y. with you for a while when you go, & get my teeth in shape, & it would be better for me to leave not earlier than the first part of November, & then the hurricane season would be absolutely over, so even if you came down in late Oct. we could go up together. Anyhow, the point is I feel you should (now that at last after *all* these months of wretchedness you are feeling well & capable of enjoying life) do just what you feel you really want to do.

I only do wish there was a *little* money to put into this place, dear, just enough so I could get the floor & ceiling of the living room done, & that furniture brought over from the other house. I think it would be so much nicer on your return if we had that done. Johnston is still on his other jobs, but I have "Jack Tiny" working about the place, getting things cleaned up, etc. & of course Scott is still up on the hill—

If you feel you can, send me the Oct. 1st money, otherwise will use the $500 for

Oct. but I certainly ought to pay up some of those bills. I just paid the electric light co. £18 last month (back) then £12 this month—well, anyway, we've spent little on living since you left. The horse was a *great* saving when we had him here, but I let him go.

Well, darling, I'll write a long letter for Monday. I miss you—dearest—but I want you to be happy.   A.

I felt that the Carlotta thing would turn out as you said.

Listen—be *sure* & write Shane, he waits so eagerly for every mail & is so *disappointed.*

251. **AB to EO** ALS 3 pp. ([Hamilton, Bermuda]) [Harvard]

Monday 5:15 / [September 26?, 1927]

Dearest— Just got your note. You sound so resigned, I think there must be a beautiful blonde or something, met at Nathan's? It's not like you to be so forbearing—Joking aside, I do feel damn sorry—Listen, why not run down here for 2 weeks? I wish to god I could come up—

Honey, I miss you! I wish I could spend a quiet evening in the W'worth with you. More on next boat.—have to hurry this for Hilda to take to [illegible]. Love   A.

252. **AB to EO** ALS 3 pp. (Stationery headed: Spithead / Bermuda) [Harvard]

[late September, 1927]

Dearest Gene— The weather has changed, a real rough cold wind from the north, and you don't know [how] much better I feel. As though I had a little real ambition for a change.

I am going to try my damndest now to get that article done, and go ahead & work hard on other things too. I suddenly feel that I *must* be self-supporting!

Do you see Elizabeth Sergeant? Give her my love. Also, you say you saw Bunny. *Did* you get the extra hundred, or shall I write him about it? We need it. I could get the floors done for that.

Got letter from Jarboe, enclose copy![1] What did I say? Do you know, it seems to me that the horoscope for last winter said something about it being a bad time to build. Read the enclosed letter to E. Adams, put a $20 check in it, and mail it for me, will you? Why don't you go & see her. The experience of meeting her is quite worth it, even if you don't believe.

Do you ever see Eugene? Give him my love, and tell him I prize his letter. What is his address now?

I have been going over the bills. If I could have about 3 months living as we have lived the last month, I'd be all caught up. Meantime you will have received my last letter on the subject. [illegible name] bill for Sept is about £6 instead of £40. Some difference, what?

I enclose some small bills in large envelope, will you make out American checks for me for them, & mail them? They are:

Hanna Stone[2]	$5.50
Wanamaker	11.55
Fowler	30.42.

You can look in the envelopes.

God, I wish Ridgefield would sell! How about the Elliot prospect? Do you know, I have a hunch *Evangeline* might sell it to some one! She knows everybody—go and see her—Follow up this hunch . . .

By the way, do be sure and write Shane whenever you can, he waits so anxiously for every boat to hear from you. Gaga also said to be sure and send her love (from Wenus).

Darling I miss you an *awful lot*. Lovingly,   *Agnes*.

1. The enclosed typed copy of a note from Jarboe reads: "Dear friends. Thank you for your kind invitation to call and see you if I should ever come back to Bermuda, which I hardly think likely, particularly with G?H? [*sic*] Burland. For I had my fill long before I left. Partnership is not always the best thing in the world, and more especially with someone who has no knowledge of the business. Trusting these few lines find your family all well as it leaves us at present. Sincerely, etc. H.S? [*sic*] Jarboe."

2. Probably Dr. Hannah Stone of the Hannah Stone Planned Parenthood Center, which AB is reported to have visited.

~～〇

253. **EO to AB** (Stationery headed: Hotel Wentworth / 59 West 46th Street / New York) [Harvard]

Monday night / [September 26, 1927]

Dearest One: I found your two letters here on my return from Joseph W. Krutch's[1] place where I had dinner with him and his wife and spent the evening—pleasantly, for he is a damned brainy fellow and we had much chat about this and that in and out of the theatre. His wife is also good company. You must meet them both when we come up together. I know you will like them.

It's now quite late and I am all tired out, running around all day—to the dentist's and then down to Wall Street to meet a big bug in the Bankers Trust who is arranging my visit to the hydro-electric plant which they control. It's 15 miles from Danbury and I'm going to drive out in the car—which I haven't used yet—on Friday.

I saw Harold for a while too. He hit town this morning from Maine—says the weather up there has been frightfully cold. But you'll see him soon and hear all about it.

I'm lying in bed—I wish you were here, Darling, for one or two good reasons which you may guess although I'll say one of them is that I love you!—writing this, hence the pencil. I've not been feeling so good the past few days. I've gotten insomnia pretty badly—don't get to sleep until all hours and wake up early. I imagine it may be I'm taking too much thyroid. It jags you up a bit but leaves you fagged out in the day time. The Doc will probably cut down my dose.

As for your two questions—I must confess I've forgotten all about the hats. I'll make inquiries but I doubt if you'll ever see them again. All the staff here and the entire management have been changed. The gun is in the very top of the bureau in the compartment under the lid.

No hurricane yet? I'm anxiously waiting news that that has come and gone and all is well.

I'm enclosing the check for five hundred. The advance on *S.I.* will take care of it, I guess.

There's nothing new on Ridgefield.

Saturday Winston,[2] a friend of Rockmore's, drove me up the Hudson in his car in the P.M. and we had tea at a place above Yonkers—"Long View." A charming spot, much frequented by lovers. We'll have to go out there sometime.

Last evening I visited Carlotta. She's got her apartment all done over again and has made a very pleasant place of it. She has a bug for furnishing places and getting fed up with them as soon as they're finished, I believe.

There's no Guild news. Lawrence is due now in a couple of days.

There's a letter for Shane in this same mail. I hope he will like it. He wrote me that Oona's sores had all gone, but you say they haven't. They certainly should have by this time, I should think. I'm glad you're having the doctor for them.

In spite of the Doc's orders I don't seem to get the smoking cut out although I have cut down on it. It's too damn hard for me to make it in New York, I guess—have to wait until I reach Bermuda.

I've still got passage reserved on both the 5th & 12th. I'm going to try damn hard to get away on the 5th but I doubt very much I'll be able to, the way things shape up. It will all depend on the Guild and Doctor Barach.

I haven't seen Katharine Cornell.[3] It seems like a waste of time until one knows what's going to happen to *The Letter*.[4] From the one notice I've seen it seems to be a big hit in which case, she's out of the reckoning.

I miss you so much, Dearest One! There are so many things I do that I find myself longing for you to be along with me. It will sure be wonderful to have you in my arms again. Not long away now in any case, thank God! A little over two weeks, at most.

Kiss Oona & Shane for me. I'll give Harold any extra news I happen to think of to tell you. All my love, Dear!   Gene.

1. Drama critic (1893–1970) for the *Nation* and literary and cultural critic.
2. Norman Winston.
3. The Theatre Guild hoped Cornell would play the role of Nina Leeds in *Strange Interlude*.

4. Play (1925) by W. Somerset Maugham (1874–1965), which opened on September 26, 1927.

~~⌒

254. **AB to EO** ALS 3 pp. ([Hamilton, Bermuda]) [Harvard]

[September 28–29?, 1927]

Dearest Gene— Am expecting a cable from you any day now. I am feeling blue over the fact that when you return things will be in about the same old shape—well, I suppose it will be a change from N.Y. anyway.

I lost the check, put it in my smock pocket with some letters, it must have blown overboard, on the wharf.

The De Polos arrived, Harold stinko, but they seem to have calmed down. I am *avoiding* them as much as I can, had them to lunch the day I came, but have refused flat to go to the Belmont, or to parties at their house, *if* they have any.

I wish I didn't feel so darned blue about things. I feel we made an awful mistake getting a place as big as this. God knows when it will be livable.

Harold seems to think you will leave on the fifth. He said you looked well, but a little thin. And I hear you've bought some *very* fancy drawers. *This* looks suspicious!

Ever so much love from us all—see you *soon* now. Lovingly *Agnes*

~~⌒

255. **EO to AB** ALS 6 pp. (Stationery headed: Hotel Wentworth / 59 West 46th Street / New York) [Virginia]

Thursday— / [September 29, 1927]

Dearest Wife: I've just got your letter with the enclosures and I'll send the check as you direct.

Sweetheart, I do long for you so much these days! Now that time is growing shorter and I know I'll see you in two weeks, I'm simply eaten up by impatience and actually counting the days! How's that for a nine years husband amid the wiles and glamours of N.Y.? I think I'm pretty close to being a model! It will be so marvelous to take you in my arms and kiss you again! As I write this an image of your beautiful face comes close to mine and I seem to feel and smell your body touching mine and I get goose flesh all over—not to mention other things which I won't make you blush by mentioning! Two weeks becomes a hellish long ordeal, and all the supposedly useful activities that keep me here appear as most frightful bores. I only hope you are half as anxious to have me back as I am to get there! Please answer this, if only by one line, by supplementary mail and tell me you are! I do want you and love you so!

Tomorrow I go out by car—with Larkin—to the hydro-electric plant in Conn.— an all day affair. It will be fun to drive the car again.

Speaking of cars I had a ride yesterday in an Hispano-Suiza. Some boat! And whose do you think it was? Arthur Hopkins! He's had it three years, he says—*What Price Glory*[1] money, I suppose. I had lunch with him yesterday at the Lotus Club. He's the same old Arthur—a bit more beaming because his *Burlesque* is the biggest hit in town (28,000 a week!) and he also has another play that is a big out-of-town hit but hasn't come to N.Y. yet.

I'll try and see Evangeline A. next week.

The note from Jarboe was amusing. So that's how it was! Have you had any word from Burland or from Hill? I suppose not. I wonder what Hill has got up his sleeve to spring on us—if anything.

This morning I went up to Barach's for one of those long before breakfast gland tests. My thyroid remains subnormal in spite of my having taken 1/2 a grain daily for the past two weeks, so he started me today on a full grain. It's a tiresome business— takes so long for them to determine exact reactions—but another two weeks ought to show what my right dose is.

A word about finances. Liveright again has strong hopes of the "book-of-the-month" for December for *S.I.* He ought to know definitely before I leave. If *S.I.* gets it then that means we can count on so much money from it without fail, and then you can go ahead with your plans on the house. As it is, I think we perhaps ought to make ourselves afford the work of painting and fixing up big room, etc. At least, we could go ahead to the tune of one thousand and trust to luck. What do you think? Do you think it may be better to wait until I get down and we've talked it over? Let me know. God, I sure wish I was coming in a week but I don't see how I can possibly make it? How I wish you were here now, Dearest!

(If this letter sounds a bit fleshly desirous—well—I am!—of you! I feel like turning out the lights and taking your picture to bed! Maybe I will!)

Langner arrived this A.M. I hope to see him tonight. Now that he's back I ought to get a little more exact forecasts out of the Committee—(casting of *S.I.*, etc.). Alice Brady[2] is reading it.

Cornell opened in *The Letter*. It didn't do her rep. so much good. No one thought anything of the play except as cheap melodrama but it will probably make money. She's a damn fool! She'll ruin herself.

Bunny is to see me again. He said something about paying me when I saw him but haven't heard from him since.

Elsie Sergeant is still up at Peterboro, I believe.

I'm glad the weather down there has changed and that you're able to work again. I'm awfully keen to see what you've done with the article.

I've seen Eugene twice.

When are the Hubers coming down, do you know? I happened to think it would be fine if they were sailing the 12th—company down.

I've been going to call up Delphine D.[3] but can't locate her in phone book. Do you know her address? I'd like to have a peek at that apartment—might need it for my work sometime.

Don't let the arrival of Harold and Helen get you flustered or off work? Be firm about writing when you feel like it, and not being disturbed by anyone. It's the only way.

Not so long now, Darling—(but much too long!)—and then—! Adios for this time, Dearest. I have a date with your picture! Your lover, Gene.
(Later)

P.S. Just remembered this—

The Gish—*Marco* thing is developing and may happen! I'm to see her again soon. She is genuinely excited—offers to work on voice with Carrington[4] and says she will come to Bermuda, get house with her mother (who is ill) and work on the part with me if I will help her before actual rehearsals start. That would be good stuff. She is a "real guy." You'd like her immensely. She & Nathan seem to be very amoured of each other, if I'm any judge, so he'd probably make a trip down too while she was there.

But this will probably all blow up. I can't believe she's serious about *M*—or brave enough to take such a chance!

    1. Play (1924) by Maxwell Anderson and Lawrence Stallings.

    2. Actress (1892–1939), later played Lavinia in *Mourning Becomes Electra*. She also later admitted it had been a mistake to decline the role of Nina Leeds in *Strange Interlude*.

    3. Delphine Dodge, daughter of one of the owners of Dodge Motorcars. She was a high-speed boat racer.

    4. Margaret Carrington, voice teacher, who had coached John Barrymore and other famous actors, including her brother, Walter Huston, when he acted in *The Fountain*.

256. **AB to EO** ALS 4 pp. (Stationery headed: Spithead / Bermuda) [Harvard]

[October 3?, 1927]

Dearest Gene— Just got your sweet letter. I hope my picture had a happy night of it! Yes, I *do* want to see you again, dear. I have missed you a lot. It's been very very lonely here. Do you know who has missed you terribly—Shane? He really loves you deeply.

I was very encouraged at your saying we could go ahead with the rooms: on the other hand, I doubt if I could get it all done before you come now, the time is so short, and so I think it would be as well to wait until after you get here, & we can talk it over. I think I *will* get Johnston to go ahead & finish up the wharf (wall) as that is what looks so miserable & depressing about Spithead now. I told you he agreed to come & work here regularly, to start middle of Sept., but he has not come yet. Still working on other jobs, & has not even finished the fish pond, or the roofs of the outhouses. However he has promised solemnly (I told him I would have to get some one else otherwise) to start work here this Wednesday. In that case I will have him start right in & finish up the wharf, & try and get it done before you come.

The work on the rooms in the big house wouldn't begin to come to a thousand. I imagine $300 would cover it.

I wish you were here right now, dear, so we could sit out in the moonlight & have a real talk. Gaga wants to know if you will stock up with Zonite, Listerine & Enos Fruit Salts before coming down—two or three bottles of each.

The Lillian Gish thing sounds grand. Wish she would come down—& I do believe she'll do *Marco*, too.

Oona's sores are all right now. Say, by the way, ask Elsie Sergeant if she knows of some nice athletic young girl *(Christian!)* who wants a job with us—do this, now.

You don't know how much I enjoyed your long letter—thanks so much for writing me all the news. *Do* get that thyroid thing straightened out, won't you, before you come down.

Ever so much love, my dear, from us all. Your   Agnes

Don't forget my dress.

257. **AB to EO** AL 6 pp. ([Hamilton, Bermuda]) [Harvard]

Spithead. / [early October, 1927]

Dearest Gene— I'm writing this lying out in a deck chair on the wharf, trying to get rid of my cold by a little sunning. It was much better, then yesterday I must have exposed my throat, for I woke up last night with a frightful cold on my chest. I could hardly breathe, & today the upper part of my chest & neck are very sore & I cannot talk above a whisper. First time I have had a cold like this for years. When I woke up last night I coughed up a great lot of stuff, with streaks of blood in it, but I guess it was just from my throat being sore.

I hope you will decide to get that inoculation this year.

Oona has had a bad cold, also Lily. I expect by the time you arrive we will be all right, though. I was terribly disappointed, & have missed you an awful lot lately.

A letter was returned on this mail, sent by you to Bill Clarke[1] at Bellevue. "Party not there."

I expect I'll get the letter from you on today's boat. I hated to wire you about it, but you see where you wrote me recently that we could go ahead a little on the house, I started Johnston on the completion of the wharf (wall, & washing outbuildings, etc.) & he has been here with three other men, as I asked him to get it finished before you came, as a surprise to you, so I have to pay them this Sat. besides material. This can't come out of the house check, of course, but I can put off paying some of the bills &

use the 500 check until you come. Well, I'm just pleased to death with the wall, it will finish up Spithead beautifully I do think—you don't know how bare & bleak it was getting to look. I was really getting sick of looking at it.

Mrs. Robinson asked me twice to go over there for tea, so yesterday I went. On the way home we passed a negro who was supporting an old white man, whom he had just knocked down with his bicycle. He hailed us, & I took the old guy, who was unconscious, into the back seat with me. He was covered with blood. He was very frail & sickly looking, very thin, & as I discovered afterwards, 84 years old. Finally he came to enough to mutter the name of his house & they took him there.

This A.M. a police constable arrived & required a statement from me of what I had seen of the accident. He told me that the old man was a Scottish minister by the name of Harper, said he had been around the world *4* times since he retired from preaching, was planning to stay here for the winter (with his wife) then in the spring was going to visit a son in the West Indies, then in the summer was going to the North West of Canada where he had another son who owned a ranch, then was going out to Australia or New Zealand, where he has two married daughters. Some exciting life for an old man!

You better wash your hands after you read this letter, as there might possibly be some germs on it.

7. P.M. It was lucky you did not get down this boat, the weather [end of letter missing]

1.   Probably Bill Clarke ("Clarkie"), former circus stunt rider ("Volo the Volitant"), whom EO had met in Greenwich Village in 1915–16 and whom he helped financially for years.

～⊃

258. **EO to AB** ALS 5 pp. (Stationery headed: Hotel Wentworth / 59 West 46th Street / New York) [Harvard]

Tuesday. / [October 4, 1927]

Dearest: I feel extremely hurt at not receiving any word from you by this last mail. If you knew how I looked forward to your letters you wouldn't fail to write, I'm sure. Certainly if here in New York, where the very notion of writing a line is a job, I still manage to write you every mail, you might do the same for me!

I got the cable about the check, of course, and I've written the bank to stop payment on it. Cable me if it turns up and I'll notify them to take off the stop. If you don't find it by the time you receive this then I'll send you another "pronto." But I'm sure you've simply mislaid it and it will bob up again.

I had a wonderful drive out to the hydro-electric plant on Friday. It was in an isolated spot on the Housatonic—dirt roads for 5 miles nearest it—I was taken all over and shown everything from roof to cellar. Quite an experience! I got much more stuff out of it than I had hoped for. Tell you all about it soon. I wish you could have been along.

Sunday the Winstons took me out on a motor cruiser they hire over week-ends and we sailed out in the Sound and I managed to stay in a bathing suit all day and get in some swimming. It bucked me up a lot. The weather has been stifling in N.Y.— hottest this time of year ever known. These Winstons (he is one of heads of Kahler Shoe Co.) have been very kind to me. Later Sunday P.M. he drove me out to Curtis field. We were going flying for a couple of hours but the pilot he wanted was away. (Winston, by the way, has a flying license himself.)

Lawrence Langner is back and I've had one session with him and the Committee. The Gish *Marco* is off. The Guild are afraid it would wreck their company with jealousy and dissension to have her in it. They're having a lot of trouble with their people as it is. Too bad—financially speaking, at least—but I see their point and they're right. They're getting a fine actor from England especially to do the Khan.[1] Nothing new on *Interlude*. Alice Brady is much discussed for it. *Porgy*,[2] their first production, opens in a few days. It's too involved to explain but a lot of their immediate plans have to depend on what happens to that. (*Porgy* has all-negro cast and so can't be made to fit in with their repertoire co. plans and this has them backed up). But I'm forgetting myself and writing you too much. You don't deserve it. You're a bad girl, not writing me! I certainly did miss hearing from you, Darling! It gets me worried that there's been a hurricane or something is all wrong.

The gland experiments progress. I seem to stand a grain a day all right. Now it will be a question whether that's enough. This week ought to decide it.

A week from tomorrow I'll be sailing—surely, unless something more vital than anything I can imagine turns up. So count on me being home for my birthday. (No hint, don't mind getting me anything!) God, I'll be glad to be with you again! I've been having an interesting time enough here—but that isn't you, and I've never stopped missing you!

Kiss Shane & Oona. All love, Dearest.   Gene.

P.S. I saw the lousiest musical show ever written—or part of it—last night, *Sidewalks of N.Y.*[3] God, how rotten! I sat in the seat behind Governor Smith[4] with Walker,[5] the Mayor, three seats away in same row. The papers wrote this up. Illustrious company—all Tammany was there!

P.S. II (later)

On second thought I'm enclosing a new check for five hundred herewith in case you may need it for immediate use and the other hasn't been found yet.

Good-night, Dearest! Don't forget me!

1. Baliol Holloway.
2. Play by Dubose Heyward (1885–1940) and Dorothy Heyward (1890–1961), later adapted into the opera *Porgy and Bess* (1935).
3. Musical comedy by Eddie Dowling and Jimmy Hanley, opened October 4.
4. Alfred Emanuel Smith (1873–1944) was in his third term as governor.
5. James John Walker (1881–1946).

259. **AB to EO** WIRE, addressed to Hotel Wentworth, New York (Bermuda) [Yale]

OCT 5 1927

LETTER MUST MISCARRIED ALL WELL DID YOU GET CABLE CONCERN-
ING CHECK LETTER THURSDAY LOVE   AGNES.

～つ

260. **AB to EO** ALS 2 pp. (Stationery headed: Spithead / Bermuda) [Harvard]

[early October 1927]

Dearest Gene— Seems like an *awful* long time since I've seen you! You didn't
definitely say you were coming the 12th, instead of the 5th, but I suppose you are, as
I have not heard yet that you were coming the 5th. I think you will find Bermuda
weather more to your liking than when you left.

You don't know how *much* I miss you. It's been very lonely without you. Still, I
think that the separation may have done us both good.

You don't know how much it means to me now that you are not drinking. And
how much I admire your firmness in holding out even under the trying circumstances
of the last few weeks in N.Y.—or I really should say the *first* few weeks of your visit.

Well, honey, it won't be long now. Ever so many kisses & much love, dear. *Agnes*

Better order some *square* envelopes.

～つ

261. **EO to AB** (Stationery headed: Hotel Wentworth / 59 West 46th Street / New
York) [Harvard]

Friday night / [October 7, 1927]

Dearest, It's very late and this is going to be just a line or two. Just found your cable
on my return from seeing a musical comedy *Good News*[1] with the Langners and
Hortense Alden, the actress. A good show! I enjoyed it a lot. We must see it together.

I discovered I had forgotten to put the check in my last the next day. Damn fool!
I put it in a special corner of desk so I wouldn't forget it and then went and did! I'm
enclosing it now.

Won't regale you with any news of my doings this time because I'll be seeing you so
soon. We went to restaurant after show and it's now 1:30 and I'm dead to the world.

Kiss Shane & Oona. All love, Sweetheart. See you Friday. Gene.

1. Musical comedy by Laurence Schwab and B. G. DeSylva.

﹌

262. **AB to EO** ALS 1 p. (Stationery headed: Spithead / Bermuda) [Harvard]

Oct. 7th [1927]

Dearest Gene— Just a line—I got your awfully nice letter, glad you miss me but also glad you are having such a nice time. The check *wasn't* in the letter. I *do* need it, because as I said in my last, I am having them go ahead with the wall.

Well honey dear, it'll soon be the 14th—

Love to you dearest. A.

﹌

263. **AB to EO** WIRE, addressed to Hotel Wentworth, New York (Bermuda) [Yale]

OCT 10 1927

NO LETTERS TODAY WHEN DO YOU ARRIVE FAMILY HAVE EPIDEMIC COLDS USE YOUR JUDGEMENT IF BETTER DELAY RETURN NEXT WEEK LOVE   AGNES.

﹌

264. **EO to AB** WIRE, addressed to Bermuda (New York) [Yale]

OCT 11 1927

GUILD URGENT STAY ANOTHER WEEK WORK SIMONSON *MARCO* AND CAST *INTERLUDE* FEEL THIS NECESSARY BITTERLY DISAPPOINTED WANT RETURN HOME YOUR CABLE STRANGE COINCIDENCE EVAN-GELINE WARNED NOT TAKE TRIP AFTER SIXTEENTH POSITIVELY SAIL WEEK LETTER SHOULD REACHED YOU   GENE

﹌

265. **EO to AB** ALS 4 pp. (Hotel Wentworth / 59 West 46th Street / New York) [Harvard]

Oct. 11, '27

Dearest Aggie: I sent you a cable today about the necessity of my staying a week longer—(and, believe me, Guild or no Guild I would not have sent it if it had not been for your generous cable to me to use my own judgment. Thank you for that, Dearest

One!) In fact yesterday before your cable came, when the Committee asked me to stay I told them I couldn't. And I do hate to stay, too! I'm fed up with N.Y. and worn a bit ragged by my numerous goings here and there. But these goings are really doing me a lot of good—getting rid of my self-consciousness—and you'll find the net result will be that I'll be a much better husband in future and take you around everywhere when we're here together. But, as I say, I was all set for Bermuda and you again and it was a bit of a wrench to make up my mind to stay another week.

Evangeline Adams also helped me to decide. I went to see her yesterday. I won't go into all she told or predicted (mostly good) but she did very decidedly warn me against taking any trip before the sixteenth and when I told her I was going to B. said I better postpone it. I didn't pay much attention at the time but the Guild insistence and your cable made me feel a queer hunch that perhaps I better stay here.

The case with the Guild is this: Their first play went on last night and seems to be a success.[1] This puts them in a position (not the success especially but the freeing of their energies & time) to get hot on definite plans for casting *Interlude* and getting *Marco* set. So far, although they have kept me sticking around, and I have seen them one by one, I have had no chance of getting together with them as an acting unit. Simonson, for example, I have seen hardly at all because he has been kept so busy.

Also, final page proofs on *Laz* have arrived and I'll get them off my hands quicker by going after them here than by taking them down and mailing them back. This applies to the 750 sheets to be signed, too. A busy week ahead.

My thyroid continues below par (but I feel well but tired out). It will take some time to get back to normal, they say. There are certain sexual connotations about this that I will confide in you as soon as we meet. Nothing alarming but affecting us slightly in a certain direction.

I saw Hamilton for a while today. He's just back from Cal. looking hale and full of pep. I told him Barach's findings and he felt they helped toward a better understanding of my condition in general.

Thank Shane for his letter. I'm going to bring him a present.

All love, Dearest! I hope all the colds get well quick and I do wish to Christ I was sailing tomorrow A.M.! I certainly do miss you! Kisses!   Gene.

P.S. Met Zelma O'Neal, musical comedy queen who has made a great hit in *Good News*, last night after show. They asked me to go around backstage and see her. A real character! You must meet her. *Good News* is a fine show. I've seen it twice! What d'you know about that? And I'm not stuck on any of the gals in it, either!

P.S. Can't understand your not having gotten letter. I mailed one last Friday eve.

1. *Porgy* opened October 11, 1927.

266. **AB to EO** WIRE, addressed to Hotel Wentworth, New York (Bermuda) [Yale]

OCT 12 1927

TERRIBLY DISAPPOINTED PERHAPS DELAY BETTER HOWEVER STOP
ABSOLUTELY MUST HAVE CHECK SATURDAY AS HAVE MEN WORKING
PLEASE CABLE BANK BERMUDA ALL CAN SPARE LOVE　AGNES.

267. **EO to AB** WIRE, addressed to Bermuda (New York) [Yale]

OCT 12TH [1927]

MAILED CHECK FRIDAY MUST MISSED BOAT CABLE FRIDAY IF DONT
RECEIVE MESSAGE WILL CABLE MONEY IMMEDIATELY LOVE.　GENE

268. **EO to AB** COPY[1] 3 pp. (New York]) [Harvard]

[November 28?, 1927]

　　My only social diversions have been more or less connected with my business—
that is, with the exception of a philharmonic concert Carlotta took me to last Thursday, and even that was, in a sense, because I was told to hear Debussy as being the
kind of note needed for the first scene (Prologue—Music of the Leaves)[2] and they
played Debussy and Stravinsky that night. I was up at the Wertheim's for dinner one
night, met Stieglitz[3] and Georgia O'Keeffe[4] there and liked them both immensely. At
Langner's for dinner another night to meet Alice Brady who was then being considered for *Interlude*. She is a good scout but rather a rough neck, a real daughter of her
eminent father, Bill.[5] Then I went to the opening of Shaw's *Doctor's Dilemma*[6] at the
Guild, to see the same cast in it as there will be in *Marco*, and also Lynn Fontanne. I
think she will give a very adequate performance in *Interlude* but she will be far from
being my "Nina." However, who would be? I've simply got to be philosophical about
it and make the best of the material at hand. The men, at least—Powers, Anders, and
Larimore[7]—should be splendid. And Lunt[8] should make a remarkable "Marco." He is
a fine actor. So the cloud has its bits of silver lining. One can't have everything in our
American theatre. The Guild is our best and they are certainly doing their best by me.
　　Last night I had dinner with Elizabeth Sergeant and Bobby and spent the evening.
Bobby will probably do the sets for *Interlude*.[9] It is only a question of their paying his
price. Both Sergeant and Bobby again concentrated on urging me to go to Taos, that I
simply *must* go. I was a great deal impressed this time. After all they told me I really

feel I ought to go, as if there was something down there I needed and that would give me something. Perhaps I might be able to go down for a few weeks after the plays get on. I've been thinking of this and it seems like a good plan to me. I certainly won't feel in any mood to start writing a new one for some weeks after this ordeal is over, my nerves and vitality will undoubtedly be shot, and some weeks in the desert might prove a wonderful reviver. What do you think?

I'm sending this check to Gaga. I'm also enclosing the check for five hundred to you herewith.

A few reviews of *Lazarus Laughed* have appeared, one in *Tribune* a week ago today, very fine, by Lewis Mumford—one in *Times* today, one in last evening's *Sun*— all fine.[10] So that's hopeful.

I've got to end this—date with Phil M.[11] for dinner and work with him afterward. Much love, dearest, kiss Oona and Shane for me.   Gene

P.S. Just got your cable about house a few minutes ago. I'll have Harry get in touch with Crane tomorrow.

Tuesday A.M. / [November 29?, 1927]

Just got your two letters and am writing a line before going to the Guild. I'll send the check to Bedini. I'm going to sell R'field for 30,000—get rid of the damn place even at a loss. Got your cable about Denton—had Harry phone Winstead to find out what it was about. Later I got this telegram from Winstead: "Have accepted Mrs. O'Neill's offer for two puppies." Signed "Denton." What the hell does that mean? You're not buying more dogs are you, at this time?

I'm so damn busy I'm nearly off my nut, but feeling not so bad, considering the pressure. I'm sorry about no letter on last mail. I'll try and do better after this.

Must run now. Love—   Gene

1. This is a typed copy, probably made by Max Wylie, of a letter for which the original has not been found. A note at the top says, "Page 1 missing."
2. Music for the prologue of *Marco Millions*.
3. Alfred Stieglitz (1864–1946), photographer and art exhibitor.
4. Painter (1887–1986) and wife of Stieglitz.
5. William A. Brady (1863–1950), Broadway producer.
6. Opened November 21, directed by Philip Moeller.
7. Tom Powers (Charles Marsden), Glenn Anders (Edmund Darrell), and Earle Larimore (Sam Evans). Anders also appeared in *Dynamo*. Larimore also later acted in *Marco Millions*, *Mourning Becomes Electra*, *Days Without End*, *The Iceman Cometh*, and *A Moon for the Misbegotten*.
8. Alfred Lunt (1892–1980) played Marco Polo in *Marco Millions*, which opened on January 9, 1928.
9. The sets were by Jo Mielziner (1901–76).
10. Reviews of the Boni and Liveright edition: Lewis Mumford, "Lazarus Laughs Last," *New York Herald-Tribune Books*, November 20, 1927, pp. 1, 6; Brooks Atkinson, "Man's Chal-

lenge to Death in Lazarus Laughed," *New York Times Book Review*, November 27, 1927, p. 5; Edwin Bjorkman, "A Dramatist of Moods," *New York Sun*, November 26, 1927, p. 11.

11. Philip Moeller.

~⌒﹢

269. **EO to AB** WIRE, addressed to Bermuda (New York) [Yale]

NOV 28 1927

WROTE LONG LETTER FORGOT TO MAIL NEXT BOAT TERRIBLY BUSY LOVE   GENE.

~⌒﹢

270. **EO to AB** ALS 4 pp. ([New York] on stationery headed: "Bellevue" / Paget East, Bermuda) [Harvard]

Friday evening / [December 2?, 1927]

Dearest Aggie: I've had no time to really sit down and write until now—and I guess it's too late to catch the mail if I mail it from here so I'll send it over to Gray, the purser, by messenger and have him mail it the first thing when they land.

This week has been spent mostly in hearing people read for all the innumerable small parts in *Marco*. You would think they would be easy to cast but they're not—or else the available brand of actor and actress is particularly poor. It has been a long boring business and the opening has been postponed until the 9th of Jan. instead of 6th, so that the *real* rehearsals start next Monday instead of last. But I feel as if I'd already had a full week of them! I haven't met either Lunt or Fontanne yet. From what I hear they are both pretty dull in the old bean—but that hardly astonishes me. At any rate, they both *can* act. I've also been doing a lot on *Interlude* with Phil. Bobby finally backed out of doing the sets of *Interlude*—had a fit of arty temperament and decided he couldn't work with the Guild people. I suppose he asked Arthur's advice![1] Well, it's his own funeral.

And now about the house in Ridgefield. I sold it, as I cabled you, for 30000 less an agent's commission of 1000 (Harry jewed Crane down to that)—which means that all I will get is 14000 out of the deal—which means, considering the money I've put in out there plus the price paid, a loss of at least ten thousand! Not a bright business deal! But I thought it best to sell and get the white elephant off my conscience. I hope you felt properly relieved when you got my cable. All of this money I'm going to put back into stocks to pay back into my capital what we've used of the cash from the sale of New London stuff in fixing up Spithead—which, as you know, was to be considered as a loan until Ridgefield was sold. I'm sure you will agree that this is the sensible thing to do. Until we're sure what the fate of the plays is going to be, we really mustn't be so foolish as to put any more money into Spithead than what we've already agreed upon—the sum from the stocks I sold for that purpose. We have, counting the 10000 paid in the sale, already got 35000 sunk in Spithead and that's aplenty for an artist who is trying to stick to being an artist. So please, if you think anything of my peace of mind, don't go making plans for Spithead beyond what we've already agreed on, just because Ridgefield is sold. Later on, it may be a lot different but for the present the only sensible thing to do is to stand pat and have a good reserve for me to work on in peace in case the plays flop.

The time limit before the buyer gets possession is until February 1st and he says we can leave the furniture there later than that if we like as he isn't going to start any work on the place (he plans a lot of renovating) until the winter is all over and the weather right. So you know where you stand on that and can plan accordingly. In this connection let me say that you mustn't think I will be horribly hurt if you can't arrange it to come up in time for the opening of the plays. I understand your feelings about first nights. They are the bunk! And at least with Guild productions you can be sure, even if the worst happens, that you'll be able to see both plays for six weeks after they open! And it's your seeing them that is the important thing and not the opening night fiesta, at which I certainly shall not be present, anyway. So do what you think best about this according to your own inclination.

What plans are you making about coming up? You don't say in your letters. Is your Mother going down?

Now here is something that is *very very important* and that I wish you would attend to *without fail* as soon as possible. Liveright has spoken to Rosenbach,[2] the big dealer, about my original scripts and Rosenbach is very much interested and wants to see what he can do about them *but* he must first see them and make sure that I really have a complete set—also their condition, etc. etc. It is no question of an immediate sale but, given the time, he thinks he can work them up to a big price. The point about your sending them immediately is that he is going away in two weeks—to Coast or Europe, I forget which—and I want him to see them before he goes. Now will you find out what is the best possible way—safest—to send them? Perhaps giving them to the purser to lock up for the voyage and for me to call for—or to insure them *very* heavily and send by mail—or maybe there will be someone coming up whom you can trust. (But it must be someone you *can absolutely trust!*) You will find them all in the second drawer from top of the cabinet nearest the door. If not in this drawer, then in one below it—at any rate, in the drawer the steel box with most of them in it is in. And please send *all the contents* of that drawer so there can be no mistake! But do please take the greatest care about all this. Remember this may be a big "ace in the hole" for us and the kids. I really ought to have them in a safe deposit box—fire-proof—up here anyway so they'd be absolutely safe.

And here's another thing I wish you would do—in connection with the R'field sale. I must get all the insurance policies to Harry at once. Will you go through my contract drawer (top drawer in the middle, I think) and get any insurance thing relating to R'field? They must be there, if I have them.

Be careful in packing those scripts! Better ask the Furness people the safest way to send them. And be sure to send everything you find. I've got to convince R. the set is complete.

I've been trying to write Shane—will find time soon—tell him to forgive a busy Daddy—and have him dictate to me. Kiss Oona for me. Bye bye for this time, Dearest, and much love! I know my letters must sound like a stock broker's to his frau but I'm really so damn up to my neck in business that that's all I've got to write about. Kisses! Gene

P.S. I'm sending this by boy down to General P.O.—it can be in time for mail there.

1. Arthur Hopkins.
2. A. S. W. Rosenbach, rare books and autograph dealer.

271. **EO to AB** ALS 3 pp. (Hotel Wentworth / 59 West 46th Street / New York) [Harvard]

Friday A.M. / [December 9?, 1927]

Dearest Aggie: Just got your letter—left downstairs by Mrs. Shepherd—and am dashing off a few words before going to rehearsal—am late as it is.

I couldn't see Shepherd—wasn't dressed when she called.

Let Hill wait a while for his money. I can't afford to pay him now, anyway—until I get the jack from R'field sale, not just the advance.

I took an hour off yesterday to go shopping for Shane & Oona at Schwartz's. Got two toys which may get off on this boat, they said. So watch out for them and hide until Christmas. I'm also looking out for something for you. In case I can't find anything good, I'll send check and you can do what you like with it.

I don't think much of your idea of bringing Shane up here. If he were entered in a school at this time of year, he'd be at a great disadvantage—and that's no way to start a boy off at school. Also the weather would get him, I'm afraid. It's been particularly hellish—freezing one day, rainy & hot the next. I've had a bad cold hanging on all the past week but got some vaccine shot in my arm and managed to beat it.

(That is, it was either the vaccine or the bad air at the bike race. I've been every night so far. Great sport.)

Rehearsals are coming along fine. Good cast. *Interlude* will open 2 weeks after *Marco* instead of one.

Don't forget to send those scripts! Important I get them soon.

I mailed a check to you some time ago for the five hundred. I see by my stubs that it's dated the 27th. Hope you got it O.K. by this time.

Why don't you go out and enjoy yourself? Please don't think that I would have any objections. You are the boss of your own life, to live it in whatever freedom you desire, as I am with mine, and this must be the basis of our new understanding. You have been tied up too long and you deserve any happiness you can get. I feel that very deeply now that I have been able to get a real objective perspective on things.

Bye bye for this time, Dearest. Kiss Shane & Oona for me. Much love to you. Gene.

∽

272. **EO to AB** WIRE, addressed to Bermuda (New York) [Yale]

DEC 17TH 1927

PLEASE CABLE FULLY HOW YOU SENT SCRIPTS STEEL BOX URGENT AM WORRIED MUST GET POLICE HERE BERMUDA AFTER THEM AT ONCE IF STOLEN CANT UNDERSTAND YOUR NOT WRITING OR CABLING ABOUT MATTER SO IMPORTANT LOVE.   GENE.

∽

273. **EO to AB** WIRE, addressed to Bermuda (New York) [Yale]

DEC 19 1927

FIRST PACKAGE ARRIVED ALL RIGHT BE SURE SEND BOX TUESDAY LOVE GENE.

∽

274. **EO to AB** ALS 6 pp. (Hotel Wentworth / 59 West 46th Street / New York) [Harvard]

Tuesday / [December 20?, 1927]

Dearest Aggie: Some lines before going to rehearsal. I have been working like hell the past few days trying to cut some time out of *Interlude*. It turned out to be much longer than I thought and I've simply got to get it down. But it isn't easy. Nor grateful work. Added to everything else, it's almost too much. I've had a hell of a cold and am worn out and depressed. Still this cutting must be done—otherwise the play couldn't be done in one afternoon-evening and that would be fatal. And, at that, I think the cutting will help it as a playing play. The book is a different matter.

Rehearsals of *S.I.* are coming along fine. Real enthusiasm among the company. *Marco* is also blooming—except for the man who is playing the Kaan.[1] So far he is pretty poor but we hope he will finally get it. Otherwise it will be a mess.

Excuse me for speaking so much about my plays. I realize that it's tactless on my part. It's quite evident to me that you're not interested since you never mention them.

I hope the scripts in the steel box will arrive by the next boat. I was terribly worried when one package came and the box didn't. I thought my letter had been very explicit and that you must have sent them and they must have gotten lost or stolen. A pretty appalling thought for me! If they were lost, I'd go off my nut!

I'm enclosing a check for one hundred for you for Christmas. I've honestly tried damn hard to get you a present—gone to stores when I should have been at rehearsal. But I couldn't see or think of anything. Mrs. Winston sent me down to a Chinese importing house. I thought I'd get you a jade necklace, but the only decent ones were five hundred and up and that's out of present reach. They had cheaper ones but I didn't like them and was pretty sure you wouldn't. I explain all this because I don't want you to believe that the check is only a lazy man's easy gift. But you'll probably believe that anyway.

You never say a word about your plans. Are you coming up—and, if so, when? I don't mean for the openings—or one of them. Leave them as entirely out of your considerations as, if you are frank, you must acknowledge they are out of your mind. Think of your own pleasure in making this trip or not making it. If you'd rather stay where you are with the children, if you're having a fairly amusing time down there, don't feel there's any obligation to come. N.Y. is far from pleasant these days, I warn you. The weather has been hellish. In short, what I mean by all this talk is, please feel free to do as you wish without any compunction about hurting my feelings. I honestly don't care. You can't hurt me any more, thank God! You've tortured your last torture as far as I'm concerned. Something in me is so damn utterly dead that I don't care about anything any more—except doing my work. I am so damn tired with the bitterness and futility of all my dead dreams that, as the Senator says in *Laz*, "I could welcome my own death as an excuse for sleeping."[2]

A gloomy letter for Christmas? Well, it really shouldn't be for you. You are still young and beautiful and, with any sort of an even break from fate, you should have every chance for a real happiness before you, a happiness that it has become indubitably evident I never did and never can give you. And I certainly wish you to be happy, Agnes—from the bottom of my heart—remembering our years of struggle and the deep friendship that ought, no matter what, if we are decent human beings, to exist between us for the rest of our lives. For what has happened is neither your fault nor mine. It is simply the curse of the soul's solitude, the grinding, disintegrating pressure of time, that has destroyed Us. If we are not vicious and mean, we can only sadly pity each other. We both tried—and tried hard!

So my Christmas present to you is really to give you back your absolute liberty in any way, by any method, you may desire. I will always do anything you wish to make you happy. I will always be your friend—your very best friend, I hope! I can be that—in fact, as a friend I can be "the works" while as a husband I'm afraid I've been a miserable misfit.

Please believe that everything I have written is an explanation of something that has happened in me. No outside circumstance has anything to do with it. And no one is to blame. Any other supposition would be shallow and absurd. You know well enough that, when it comes to profound inner convictions I am not swayed by anything but my own searching of my own life. And this is a time when, in justice to us both and our children, I have searched deeply. And you are free!

Look into your own heart and face the truth! You don't love me any more. You haven't for a long time. Perhaps you feel a real affection, as I do for you, but marriage, as I wanted it and can live with it, cannot go on on that.

But there's no use going into it. It is. We don't love each other. That's evident to anyone. So, as friends who wish each other happiness, what are we going to do about it? As far as I'm concerned, anything you wish. It doesn't matter to me. Nothing matters. I'll work someplace or other—California, New Mexico, Florida, it doesn't matter a damn. I can rely on myself to do my stuff and outside of that life is meaningless to me anyway.

Kiss the children for me. I hope they like their presents. I love them more than you give me credit for. But what do you understand of me or I of you? And for their future happiness I am sure it's better for me to be more a friend and less a father than the reverse. God bless you and give you happiness!   Gene

1. Baliol Holloway.
2. The Third Senator actually says, "I could welcome my own murder as an excuse for sleeping!" Eugene O'Neill, *Complete Plays, 1920–1931* (New York: Library of America, 1988), 2:577.

～⌒

275. **EO to AB** ALS 6 pp. (Hotel Wentworth / 59 West 46th Street / New York) [Harvard]

Monday eve. / [December 26?, 1927]

Dearest Agnes: I just got your cable a while ago, saying you understand. I wonder if you really do. Well, I will not beat about the bush but come to the point at once. I love someone else. Most deeply. There is no possible doubt of this. And the someone loves me. Of that I am as deeply certain. And under these circumstance I feel it is impossible for me to live with you, even if you were willing I should do so—which I am sure that you are not, as it would be even a greater degradation to your finer feelings than it would to mine to attempt, for whatever consideration there may be, to keep up the pretense of being husband and wife.

We have often promised each other that if one ever came to the other and said they loved someone else that we would understand, that we would know that love is something which cannot be denied or argued with, that it must be faced. And that is what I am asking you to understand and know now. I am sure that I could accept the inevitable in that spirit if our roles were reversed. And I know that you, if for nothing else than that you must remember with kindness our years of struggle together and that I have tried to make you happy and to be happy with you, will act with the same friendship toward me. After all, you know that I have always been faithful to you, that I have never gone seeking love, that if my love for you had not died no new love would have come to me. And, as I believe I said in my last letter, if you are frank and look into your own heart you will find no real love left for me in it. What has bound us together for the past few years has been deep down a fine affection and friendship, and this I shall always feel for you. There have been moments when our old love flared into life again but you must acknowledge that these have grown steadily rarer. On the other side of the ledger moments of a very horrible hate have been more and more apparent, a poisonous bitterness and resentment, a cruel desire to wound, rage and frustration and revenge. This has killed our chance for happiness together. There have been too many insults to pride and self-respect, too many torturing scenes that one may forgive but which something in one cannot forget and which no love, however strong, can continue to endure and live.

I am not blaming you. I have been as much as you, perhaps more so. Or rather, neither or us is to blame. It is life which made us what we are.

My last letter did not mention being in love because, even if I were not so deeply and entirely in love with someone else, I think we ought to end our marriage in order to give us both a chance, while we are both at an age when there still is a chance, to find happiness either alone or in another relationship. Soon it would be too late. And if[1] we have failed to give happiness to each other, then all the more reason why each of us owes the other another chance for it.

Looking at it objectively, I am sure freedom to do as you please will mean a lot to you. You can go to Europe, for instance, as you have always wished—live there or anywhere else you like. You can have the use of Spithead exclusively for the rest of your life as a permanent home. I will never go to Bermuda again. You can be reasonably sure, unless catastrophe beans me, that you will always have enough income from me to live in dignity and comfort. You know I am hardly a stingy person, that I will do anything that is fair, that I will want to do all I can for you. And, above all, you will have your chance of marrying someone else who will love you and bring you happiness. I am happy in my new love. I am certain that a similar happiness is waiting for you. It seems obvious to me that it must be.

When I say I am happy now, it is deeply true. My only unhappiness is what I expressed in my last letter—a bitter feeling of sadness when I think over all our years together and what the passage of time has done to us. At such moments I feel life-disgusted and hopeless. It gives me the intolerable feeling that it is perhaps not in the nature of living life itself that fine beautiful things may exist for any great length of time, that human beings are fated to destroy just that in each other which constitutes their mutual happiness. Fits of cosmic Irish melancholia, I guess! Otherwise I am strangely happy. Something new in me has been born. I tell you this in the trust that your friendship may understand and be glad and wish me luck—and set me free to live with that happiness.

I mean, divorce me. That is what we agreed we would do if the present situation ever occurred, isn't it? It is the only fair thing—fair to you as to me in that it gives us both freedom. A separation is only for people with religious scruples. It is a ruinous thing because it divides and keeps joined at the same time. It forces each party into all sorts of sneaking love affairs. It turns a possible friendship of people who have agreed to disagree into the hatred and revenge of bitter enemies.

But I don't want to go into what should be done in this letter—I mean, arrangements about this and that and the other. As for the children, what I said in my last letter is true and need not be repeated. When you come up all this can be talked over.

This letter is merely to say that you *must* realize this decision is final, that we can never live together again, that I am never coming to Bermuda again, that when you come up we must live separately, that we must try to meet as friends who want to help each other, that we must avoid scenes and gossip and cheap publicity, that we must keep our mouths shut and make the world mind its business and not use our unhappiness for slimy[2] copy, that we must remember our children will forgive us parting and understand it but won't forgive or understand—and they would be right—if we let ourselves get dragged in the dirt. In short, we must act like decent human beings, realizing that we are both hot-tempered and sensitive to take offense at each other's words or looks or whatever, that we can and must, for our own and our children's sake, remain friends who wish each other happiness. I know how I would act if I were in your place—how I would force myself to act even if I loved you and your decision crushed me. I confidently expect you to do the same by me. You don't love me and it should not be hard.

If you can see your way to it, I'd be eternally grateful if you postponed coming up until after my openings. It isn't going to be easy for us, what we've got to do, and for me it would make it terrifically difficult even to think of my plays just when they need my thought most. But if you feel you must come up now, why come along. I don't want to be selfish about it.

This is a long letter! It is horribly hard for me to write these things to you—it is horrible to face the end of anything one has hugged to one's heart for years—but the truth is the truth and it must be told in justice to both of us, to give us both a chance to live our lives again.

Kiss Shane and Oona for me. My deep affection to you!   Gene

1. The words "in the end" are deleted here.
2. Bogard and Bryer read "shiny," which is certainly possible.

～✑

276. **EO to AB** ALS 4 pp. (Hotel Wentworth / 59 West 46th Street / New York) [Harvard]

Thursday / [January 19?, 1928]

Dearest Agnes: As I cabled you, your cable didn't reach me until afternoon yesterday—after the boat had sailed. I went out the afternoon before with Winston and stayed overnight at the place of a friend of his near Greenwich—when I got back next morning went directly to rehearsal without coming to the hotel. I'm awfully sorry. I'm enclosing the check for five hundred plus the Christmas present herewith. Meant to give it to you before you left. Why didn't you remind me then? I'm also enclosing the trunk key.

Also enclosed—if I get it in time tomorrow—will be the draft of an agreement between us that Harry has drawn up. I think we ought to get something of the sort signed and sealed before I go away, for God knows just when I will come back, once I've started off. It is really principally for your protection that this ought to be done. Once this agreement is signed you will know that you can absolutely depend on at least five hundred a month, that it is legally your right. It goes, as per our verbal agreement, from a minimum of six thousand a year to a maximum of ten thousand, depending on what I can afford. When I leave I will give Harry my power of attorney and he will see that you get this the first of every month so there will be no need for you to worry. When you come up in April or May, Harry will have full authority from me to provide for the trip you plan. So you see that I am really trying to arrange everything so you will not have to fret. But I do beg of you, in fairness to me, to arrange your life on a five hundred a month budget. Anything I can afford beyond that you will get. You know I have never been tight on money matters and that you can trust me to do my best by you and the children. But you must look the facts in the face. Six thousand a year three years ago was over one-half my income, the next year it was one-fourth (that was a good year), last income tax year (I mean 1926) it was a good deal more than one-third of my income (if you leave out the sale of property— capital asset—the money from which went into Spithead) and for 1927 (a bad year with only a few weeks of *Beyond The Horizon* from production) you will find that it was also a good deal over one-third. So you see. I doubt on the basis of the above facts that any court would allow you as much as five hundred a month (especially considering I have Eugene to support) if you should sue for it. So does Harry. I merely explain the above to you to point out that it is wise for you to be economical, but that I am not trying to stint you. You talked a lot about my fine position to grow rich now with the Guild but, even if *Interlude* goes well, you must remember that it's late in the season, that both plays will be off by the end of June, that *Marco* plays only two weeks out of every four (on a low royalty scale too), that probably neither play can be taken on the road, that *Interlude* will have only 6 performances a week (no matinees). You must also remember that for almost a whole year now we have been living, with the exception of what came in from books, almost entirely upon my capital and my children's, from the sale of property from my estate.

I know you hate talk about money but for my sake and your own and our children's, you've got to face these facts. Remember, if I don't write a play between now and fall there won't be any money coming in next year for you or anyone else—and I've got to have peace of mind and a chance for happiness in order to do my stuff. So don't let fools advise you to be as hard on me as you can. It's to your advantage in the long run to respect my desires—provided they're not obviously unfair, which you know me well enough to know they won't be. And don't run up outside bills—or I will have to take drastic measures to protect myself! Do you know what your hotel bill was for the last *two days* you were here? 122.00!—85 of it cash! Now I ask you! If that's playing fair, then I must be all wrong!

I'm going to New Mexico and California, I guess. Thought of Europe for a few days but changed my mind. *Lazarus Laughed* is to be done for a week at Pasadena around April 1st[1] and I'd like to be there for some rehearsals—can live near there and still be on the ocean and doing my writing.

Will you send up my father's *Monte Cristo* script for the museum[2] (middle drawer, middle row) and the scripts of the scenarios for *The Hairy Ape* and *Desire*—top drawer nearest door—to show Reinhardt? You remember I spoke about this. Please send right away—also all the letter files in my desk—lower drawer on right—and in the filing cabinet. I'll need these to refer to in case anything turns up. I also wish you'd pack and send me the complete set of all my books ever published that is on the shelf on the beam in what was my study. Please take good care of everything in that room, will you, and don't let worms get into the books, etc. It would be the best thing, especially as you will probably want to use the room for something else, if you will pack everything in it and send it up as soon as possible—especially all the books in there—to the Manhattan Storage people to be stored there in my name. Will you do this?

Speaking of the Manhattan Storage people, I'll pay them as soon as my first *Marco* money comes in—may get the Guild to advance me some. Last week's royalty disappeared in the 1000 advance I had had. And I'm practically broke, now that I've sent this check to you, until I get money from the R'field sale. Did you sell any of the furniture?

So have a care with the bankroll, Mrs. O'Neill! There isn't much of it and you can't get blood out of a stone, by process of law or any other way.

I hope you will soon write me that you are really at work again on your real stuff. This isn't a mercenary wish—it's a wish for your happiness!

I am tired out but I have peace of mind and certainty again—and I feel confident that nothing will disturb my deep feeling of calm and security. So you can plan accordingly. I know you wish my happiness as much as I do yours. We can be friends and we will be. Remember what I said that last night whenever you feel yourself getting bitter against me. That was the truth of my feeling toward you, now & ever after.

Kiss Shane & Oona for me. I love them both dearly—and I will prove it in all the years to come. Good luck & happiness, Old Pal!   Gene

1. *Lazarus Laughed* opened April 9 at the Pasadena Community Playhouse.
2. The Museum of the City of New York.

⁓〇

277. **EO to AB** ALS 4 pp. (Hotel Wentworth / 59 West 46th Street / New York) [Harvard]

Monday night. / [January 23?, 1928]

Dearest Agnes: Just a line before hitting the hay. Harry has been all tied up on some case or other and hasn't had a chance to draw up the agreement yet. He promises to get at it in a few days.

I sent you a cable today about the buyer of Ridgefield wanting to know where all the keys are located. He also wants to know very much what has become of the and-irons, etc. from the fireplace. It seems the deed of sale gives them to him with the house. I didn't remember to tell you that. I never thought you'd want them. As I remember they were ugly. Did you have them packed? If so, better send them right back to him when you get the stuff, or else I'll have to buy him new ones at some outlandish price. Please don't forget this.

I won't be able to give the Manhattan Storage people a check until the royalties for this week of *Marco* are in the bank. It would leave me flat. And I don't want to go borrowing money just to save such a short delay.

Strange Interlude rehearsals have been coming along well. I sure hope it goes over but I have my doubts.

I've been feeling much better—but very tired. I sure need a good rest. My present plans are not to leave for California until the latter part of February. Will probably go to a place called Del Monte[1] on the ocean. *Lazarus* goes on at Pasadena the first week in April and I'll be able to be at some rehearsals and see what they do with it.

I feel very confident these days that I am going to be happy. In fact, I am fairly happy right now in spite of the rather difficult situation and if you keep your promise as scheduled I am sure it will mean eventual happiness for all concerned.

Have you started to work yet? Please do, Agnes! You know as well as I that that is what you deeply need—and I'll be so damned happy when I know you're on your job again because I feel so strongly that that means peace for you and a new life all your own. But we talked enough about that for you to realize how sincerely I believe this. Don't let yourself get back in the old rut!

Write me about what you're doing and how Shane and Oona are. Kiss them for me. Tell Shane I'll surely write to him before long.

Please remember the things I've asked in this letter and the last—sending the stuff up, etc.—and attend to it as soon as you can.

Good luck and happiness! All my loving friendship to you! Gene.

Tuesday A.M. / [January 24?, 1928]
(just going to rehearsal)

Your letter just came. I was so glad to get news of you and the children. It hurts me to know you have such spells of loneliness—and the thought of the children carries a deep pang too. All this is not easy for me, either. You know that. But one must live according to the truth inside one or life is nothing. And I do feel tremendously that, once we go through with this and readjust ourselves to the new life, that it will mean happiness for both of us.   Gene.

1.   Del Monte is on the Monterey peninsula several hundred miles from Pasadena.

278. **EO to AB** ALS 4 pp. (Hotel Wentworth / 59 West 46th Street / New York) [Harvard]

Tuesday / [January 31?, 1928]

Dearest Agnes: This ought to be a long letter because I have a devil of a lot to talk over with you which I can only outline here (I'm so dead tired and nervous and all in) but which I'll give you more in detail in my next in answer to what you say in your two letters.

First and foremost, I'm dead set against your Conn. idea.[1] I've talked it over with Harry and he says it would take a long time and would surely involve a lot of publicity. It is not easy there. Besides I really think, from your standpoint, that the other trip would do you a world of good, help to get you into a new life of your own. And for heaven's sake, after all has been agreed upon, let's not start all over at the beginning again. It is sure to arouse bad feelings on both our parts and we do want to remain friends. And now that I am so absolutely sure, what is the good of dragging out the inevitable over a long stretch of time? It would not be fair either to me or to you.

I'm enclosing a check for February for you, also one to Hill's lawyer.

Your cable about the *Graphic* and the *American* did not surprise me.[2] They have been after me too but I denied the report and nothing has appeared except a "it is rumored" story that we were separating (in the *Graphic*).

The Cal. idea involves my spending a terribly long time out there. Now I may not like it there at all or be able to work there—and then where would I be? No, I think you ought to do exactly as you said and the sooner you want to do it the better for all concerned. The present situation is a rotten one for all of us.

Harry has made a rough draft of the agreement embodying all we talked over. I have also had him put in that if you want Spithead you get all that too except for the interest on the mortgage (600). (This to apply in years to come—no deductions in Kearney case.) This should practically insure you a couple of thousand more a year anytime you feel you need it. You also get 1/2 net if the place is sold.

Now I feel this is being damn fair. You can hardly say that for an artist to guaranty a possible 8000 to 12000 a year is stingy! It will probably have me broke most of the years trying to live up to it. So please try to fulfill your end of it as scheduled.

Interlude was a great artistic success and I feel extremely proud of the reactions it called forth. Whether it will also go commercially remains to be seen.

If you rent the small house to Kearney you can keep that money for yourself.

Kiss Oona & Shane for me. Tell Shane I will write to him soon.
As always, all loving friendship to you.   Gene.

P.S. I'll pay the Manhattan Storage people this week. You can rely on that.
P.S. Harry is having a clean copy of the agreement made and I'll send it on to you
next mail.

   1. AB had proposed filing for divorce in Connecticut. EO and Weinberger were advising
her to go to Reno, Nevada.
   2. Reporters from these and other publications were seeking comment on the rumors of
impending divorce.

279. **AB to EO** AL 4 pp. ([Hamilton, Bermuda]) [Yale]

[early February 1928]

Dearest Gene,   Just a line. The *Araquega* leaves today. I did not get your letter, with
checks, until this A.M.

   Yes, the situation *is* a rotten one—rotten for you and Carlotta to have to wait a
year, & *rotten* for me to have to go to Reno, & get an immediate divorce. In the first
place I am far from well. Then there are other reasons—social, and on account of the
children, why it would be better not to go this spring. I'll explain in longer letter. As
you two are getting all the best of it, and as I am being asked to vacate, with my two
children, I think that my wishes—remember, I am giving you the divorce—might be
considered. However, this note was not to say that, but to say that I think Harry is
wrong about the Conn. divorce. I am going into it immediately. There would be no
more publicity than in Reno, certainly, & one would hardly have to wait. However, I
can let you know in detail next boat as perhaps I'm wrong. Also, some other things
must be talked over—chiefly about the children—before I sign *any* agreement. It is
not fair to me to ask me to sign any agreement now. That is always done when the
divorce goes through. I hate to say so, but it seems to me you are in a hell of a hurry
to get me put safely out of the way. Remember, Gene, what I said—I'll *never* expect
you to give more than you easily can—you know that.

280. **EO to AB** WIRE, addressed to Bermuda (New York) [Yale]

FEB 2 1928

WHAT DO YOU WANT DONE WITH FURNITURE LEFT AT RIDGEFIELD
URGENT PLEASE CABLE   GENE.

~~◯

281. **EO to AB** ALS 4 pp. (Hotel Wentworth / 59 West 46th Street / New York)
[Harvard]

Friday / [February 3, 1928]

Dearest Agnes: I sent a check to the Manhattan Storage people yesterday—so you
ought to get the furniture before long now.

Your cable in answer to mine about the furniture & trunks left out at Ridgefield
came last night. I will wire Bedini. The man who bought it has been after me to get the
stuff out of his way now, if I will do him the favor, as he wants to start making repairs
soon.

*Now the following is important so please get me straight on it and do what must
be done!* The fire place andirons *were* (rightly or wrongly doesn't count now!) included in the deed and as soon as you get the stuff unpacked (I couldn't do anything
about it here as the Man. Storage people had it all packed) you must have these articles repacked and sent back to Ridgefield! Otherwise I will have to buy him all new
ones and you know how much that will cost! Will you please attend to this at once? I
promised the man I would have you do so. He is a very decent chap and we don't want
to pull anything that looks tricky on him.

I've asked Jimmy L. all about his Conn. affair. The time business was easy for
him to get by but would be absolutely impossible for you for two years & a half yet.
So count that out. The best plan is absolutely the one you proposed and we agreed on.

A strange story has reached me via one of your dear-friends-to-your-face. It is
that you said you had been advised to hang on, promise in a friendly way to do everything I desired for my happiness but never really do anything—that you said this
course of action would upset my new life so that I couldn't work and would then give
up and come back—and that you said this was what you were going to do. Naturally,
I can't believe this. It would be hardly an act consistent with honor or the friendship
we swore to each other. And it wouldn't be practical, either—for your own sake or the
children's. For it would undoubtedly make it impossible for me to work—and then
there would be no new plays and no income for anyone to live on—until you decided
to keep your faith with me. And, as far as our personal relations are concerned, if you
did such a thing deliberately to try to ruin what I know is now so surely my future
happiness, I would hate you as bitterly as you would deserve—and who would blame
me?

I am very happy now—deeply happy—at peace in a deep fashion I have never
known before! You must realize this! I know I have found what I so horribly needed
in order to live and move on. *I know now!* It is unthinkable that, knowing this, you
should not keep faith. After all, I've been fair to you, Agnes.

I don't believe the story but I'll admit it has disturbed me. Hence, the above.

Marco is beginning to fall off a bit on advance sales for next week—which is not
a good sign. *Interlude* is playing to practically subscribers only (at 2.50 a seat). There

will be hardly anyone able to see it but subscribers—the Golden is so small—for six weeks yet. So out of my two successes I'm not liable to become rich. Working with the Guild has its advantages—but also its financial disadvantages. When you get a real hit you can't realize on it. The trouble with *Interlude* is that as soon as spring and balmy afternoons arrive no one will want to go into a theatre at 5:15—and I don't blame them. It's too bad the plays didn't get started earlier. My good luck always has a capper on it somewhere.

I have read and reread both your letters. I know that all this is pretty hard for you right now—this period of readjustment—and I am damned sorry. But it simply had to be. We were not happy, we were torturing each other into hatred, there was none of the old love left, and I know that in the long run, for you as well as me, we will look back and find it fortunate that we faced this fact while there was still a chance for both of us to begin again. I am certain that soon you will begin to see the vision of a new life stretching out before you, a life in which you will gain the things you really need to make you happy, which I could not give you.

But the first step in your readjustment must be a complete acceptance of the truth that the old life is absolutely, definitely and completely dead, and to banish its ghost from your memory. Only then can our new relationship of old close friends who wish to help each other really begin. From my end at least, I speak as one who is absolutely sure. Since you left N.Y. I have realized how absolutely sure I am with enormous conviction. Many things have happened inside me. *I know!*

Kiss Shane and Oona for me. I wish I could see them. Don't let them forget me. I love them a lot more than you have ever given me credit for. It is only that I am a bit inexpressive about what I feel toward them.

Goodbye for this time. All my loving friendship. *Start on your work as soon as you can!* Gene.

~⌒

282. **EO to AB** ALS 4 pp. (Hotel Wentworth / 59 West 46th Street / New York) [Harvard]

Tuesday / [February 7, 1928]

Dearest Agnes: Your letters and Shane's keep arriving in installments—some last night and another this A.M. I had already mailed a long letter to Shane. You had better explain to him that it was written before I received his.

I'm sorry you feel that way about my not having sent the notices of *S.I.* As a matter of fact, I never thought of it. I didn't get the papers the next day any more than I did with *Marco*. I simply phoned to Terry Helburn and asked how the press was and she told me it was grand in general and that was that. Later I looked them over in the Guild press books. I haven't got them from the clipping bureau yet because they're holding them pending a check from me, as I already owe them for 100 and have forgotten to send a check. So you see. But *S.I.* was a triumph. The trouble with my triumphs is that there's always so much of my own living on my mind at the time I haven't got any interest left for plays. Do you remember *The Hairy Ape* opening night with my Mother's body in the undertaking parlor? "So ist das Leben," I guess. Or at least my "leben." "The power & the glory" always pass over—or under—my head. I was too busy worrying about what you were going to do—or not do—to help or hurt me in my present situation to be much interested in the fate of *S.I.* You see, there have been so many ugly rumors about what you said to this one and that about how you were going to "wait me out"—rumors not coming from any source supposedly hostile to you, either!—that I have felt anything but secure. It isn't that I don't trust you to keep your word—when you're yourself, the fine, honorable woman you are at bottom. But when you've had even a few drinks you are neither fine nor honorable—and I would be a fool if I didn't take into consideration that under such circumstances, with the foxy (?) advice of some of your lousy friends to egg you on (they meanwhile sneering behind your back and only too delighted to start a mess for all of us!), you might very well do—or not do—something that would burn me up with hatred and keep me from working—I naturally cannot work if I am constantly forced to buck society and live in an atmosphere of suspicion and concealment, of being legally one woman's and emotionally another's.

I repeat again: I trust you, the real you—but I don't trust your—our—alleged friends—and God knows I would be an ass indeed if I trusted John Barleycorn!

You must know that your proposal for me to come down for a week would be a bad thing! It can't be did! It would not be kind to you, or me, or the children. By the end of the week you and I might be hating each other again—look at your stay in N.Y.! No, Agnes, we must not see each other again for a long time—not until the "possessive" stuff has died out in each of us and we are able to meet as real friends and parents of our children. Please realize that! You know damn well it is true. We've got to bury our dead—to wipe out and pass on—before our real friendship can begin. The old destructive habits of thought and feeling have got to be erased from our reactions to one another. I would be doing you a great wrong—retarding the growth of your independent personality—if I came down. I'd like to see Shane & Oona but— this is better in the long run for them too.

I've got a lot more to write you and tell you of my future plans but it will have to wait for my next.

Kiss Shane & Oona for me! I'm damned sorry you are finding things so difficult—but I really can't believe you love me (except as a friend as I still love you) or have ever loved me for years. You could not possibly have done the things you did. You could never have touched a drink, for example. It would have choked you to death—if you really loved me. And now I am really loved I see only too damned clearly by contrast all you failed to give me. I am not blaming you. It was true of me, too. It is what life does to love—unless you watch and care for it. This time I am going to watch and care. And when you fall in love—as I am sure you soon will—you better bear that in mind, too. All my loving friendship always!   Gene

283. **AB to EO** COPY 1 p. ([Hamilton, Bermuda]) [Boston U.]

[February 11?, 1928]

Dear Gene, I am very much in the dark. I received a cable from the N.Y. *Times* saying you had just left for Europe.[1] In reply to a cable sent you at the Wentworth, I receive a cable ambiguously worded. I know nothing.

If you have left suddenly, without letting me know, leaving everything in this unsettled state, I certainly think it unfair. If my only communication with you is to be through a lawyer, I assure you I shall engage counsel to treat with that lawyer. And I assure you I shall get a good one. You can't do things quite like this, you know! If you had any common decency you would have left me a sum of money on which I could draw, instead of having your lawyer send me monthly a cheque which is not enough to pay current expenses, let alone back bills. And which leaves me nothing on which to draw in case of an emergency.

Also kindly cut out your references to "John Barleycorn." They are obviously an attempt at justification of what you are doing. I don't, and haven't, drunk as much as most of your female friends. That's too easily proved. We're not living in the mid-Victorian era, remember. Lots of other men—though few who were such drunkards as you, I admit—have cut out drinking without selfishly insisting that their wives, to whom it did no harm, cut it out absolutely too. Agnes

   1. EO and Carlotta Monterey had in fact sailed at midnight on February 10.

284. **AB to EO** Carbon of TL[1] 1 p. ([Hamilton, Bermuda]) [Harvard]

Feb. 13th, '28.

Dear Gene: I have been trying to write this letter for a long time. It is on the subject of money.

First, you absolutely must realize that our living expenses come—or I should say, have come—to much more than five hundred per month. There is no getting away from this. By "living expenses," I mean running our home, and buying myself and the two children's clothes. Perhaps you may think that I am not a good manager—however, I think that you will find few who know anything about the subject, particularly in Bermuda where living expenses are high, but will agree that trying to run Spithead on five hundred a month, counting, as I say, clothes, is practically impossible. I have been juggling along with the bills until after your plays went on, as I know how you worry about money. Now that both plays are on and apparently fairly successful, I think we'd better face the situation. We owe a lot of money down here, and I think, considering the situation, that is, that everyone is wondering and guessing, that some of them at least should be paid.

I am sending you separately a list of my checks for the past three months under headings of food, clothes, etc. You will notice that a great part of the five hundred you sent me has been paid out for things for which it was not supposed to be paid
—cow, trip to N.Y. etc. Also, I do not know if you remember that when you went away you promised to pay the wages of the two men whom we considered necessary to get the place in shape outside. We figured that this would come to about two hundred a month extra. As I say, however, I did not bother to remind you when you sent me the check for only $500.

In regard to the $2000 which you placed in the bank of butterfiel [*sic*] for continuing the work on the house: I overdrew it eighteen pounds last week and had to take that money from your five hundred to replace it. I am sending you also just what that has been spent for. We still owe the painter, plumber, also have not paid the bill for the electric heater. The carpenter's bill as you will note is for over five hundred dollars. That bath cost 375, counting cess pit.

In looking over the bills it is obvious that some of them are big because things for the completion of the house have had to be continually purchased.

1. This is an unsigned and perhaps unfinished carbon copy of a typed letter from AB to EO. The typing of the original is erratic, with many typographical errors, especially in the latter part of the letter. These have been silently corrected. Half a line of 3s followed the sentence about the cost of the bath. It is possible this letter was never sent.

~~

285. **EO to AB** ALS 2 pp. (c/o Guaranty Trust Co. / Pall Mall, London) [Virginia]

[mid-February, 1928]

Dear Agnes: This is just a line to let you know that I'm still living. The passage over was a bit rough but I didn't get sick—in fact, enjoyed it. The few days I've been in London so far have been wonderful ones. I love the feel of this city. On first impression I feel more at home here than in any city I've ever been. But, of course, I am deeply happy now—happier than I have ever dreamed I could be—and everything seems rather wonderful. I feel reborn. *I am sure*! At last I "belong"! There is only one thing lacking to my complete happiness and that will come when you write me that you are working again, that you have readjusted your life and begin to see in your new freedom a chance for new life and happiness—and new love!

I haven't decided yet where I shall settle. Cooks and others are making all sorts of inquiries for me and I'm waiting to hear the full returns. Every place looks good. I'm feeling fine—no nerves to speak of—peace! I did some work on *Dynamo* on the voyage over—and lots of new ideas and expansions of ones already hatched have come to me. I'm eager to work.

This love of mine and the love that is given me is what I have longed for. It is honestly a dream fulfillment! There need be no indecisions on that score.

Try and sell "Spithead"—for the sake of your own happiness. It will help you so much to make a clean break with the past.

Kiss Shane and Oona for me. I hope you will make it possible for me to see them again— in freedom—by next fall. But I can never see them or you or America again until you do.

But I trust in you—in your honor—in your wish to be fair to me and my work— in your friendship. As ever in friendship. Gene.

~⌒

286. **AB to EO** COPY 1 p.[1] ([Hamilton, Bermuda]) [Boston U.]

[February 17, 1928]

So you are going to Europe. That seems strange. London, Paris, Spain. . . . No, you are there now. It seems queer.

You would have saved me a lot of embarrassment by writing,[2]

But it doesn't matter. Nothing does. Life goes on. We live a little while I suppose, and die. I wish you happiness. Think of me sometimes when you see the Europe I so longed, once, for us to see together. Goodby, Agnes.

1. Annotations on this transcript (Max Wylie's) read: "Agnes letter to Gene, Feb. 17, 1928 (ink, pink paper) only self-pitying moment in Agnes letters; Sneaky—slipped out—Never cared how painfully he left anyone hung. Mrs Boulton's lovely phrase: 'When the smooth hinges turn a wisp of infinity' That is what Agnes did. That is what Agnes was in this marriage."

2. The following passage was deleted: "or mailing, your letter sooner. Even Captain Gregg of the sport shop knew you had sailed before I did . . . and I kept on the story we had agreed on. . . . that you were going to California on business. A cable to paper here, asking for *my* story, reported you 'sailed for Europe today.' I denied it, saying you were going to California. A pleasant position you put me in. Hardly playing fair."

~⌒

287. **EO to AB** ALS 4 pp. (c/o Guaranty Trust Co. / Pall Mall, London) [Harvard]

March 10th [1928]

Dear Agnes: I just received the first letter I have gotten from you since leaving N.Y. four weeks ago. It was forwarded to the Guaranty Trust in London and by them to France. It seems to have been written without any knowledge that I had sailed from N.Y. I can't understand this as I wrote you a long letter the day before I left explaining the why and wherefore of my change of plans—why I'd decided not to go to California, etc. But I can't tell when your letter was mailed as the postmark is blurred out. It would help to make matters clearer if you would date your letters.

Two cables from you to the Wentworth also reached me—somewhat late!—by this same mail. The *Daily News* was after me before I left but I denied everything as usual. The notice they printed was a pretty snotty one from my end with its rot about our starving in the early days and our "frail" son, etc. but it certainly gives you all the sympathy as the pathetic deserted wife which I hope makes you as furious as it does me. But I suppose that's the yellow journal way of looking at it and it can't be helped. But to say you were nearly forty was the crowning insult of all.[1]

I've been enjoying my visit to France, going from place to place looking for the right one to settle down in which I haven't found yet. But I'm in no hurry because I feel that if anyone had ever earned the right to a vacation I have. I'm quite happy just living and looking at things for a change. I'm now in Biarritz for a couple of days. It's a delightful place at this time of the year out of the season. Later on, I hear it's expensive and jammed with society but now it's quiet and peaceful. I've had no permanent address to which to have mail forwarded until I told the Guaranty people to send stuff here for a few days. I came down from Paris slowly through the château district in Lorraine along the Loire and visited a number of the old châteaus and went through them. Wonderful places—and especially interesting to me because I happen to know French history so well.

Harry writes (forwarded from London by same mail) that a lawyer came to him saying you had cabled him but that he didn't seem to know what you wanted to know and so nothing happened. I think you can safely wait until you come up in April or May and then see Harry with your lawyer. I mean there's nothing for you to get excited or worried over as I left a separate account with plenty of money in it to take care of all your expenses, at the usual rate for the next six months, including your trip West. Of course, if you should be influenced to change your mind, why that will create an entirely new situation.

I have sent postals to Shane and Oona several times. Hope you got my letter from London. I'll let you know where I settle down—probably on the Mediterranean coast or in Majorca—as soon as I get put.

Your letter sounds happier. I'm glad. I hope you've started work. Of course, I won't sell Spithead as long as you want to live there. What do you think I am? Please have confidence in me. As long as you act like a friend toward me I will do anything you wish that I can afford. Everything will be taken care of. Send me my Trimingham and Smith bills, etc. Only be economical. I assure you my expenses over here are amazingly small. It will be wise to let me save some money out of this year's luck. As you know from the past, there are bad years that must be anticipated. With four children to support I have a right to save money. Yes, I include Barbara. After all I've done all that has been done in that line.

Kiss Shane & Oona for me. I miss them horribly at times. Don't let them forget me.

I am happy and quite sure of the lasting fundamental value of what I am doing. All deepest friendship always, dear!   Gene

    1.   AB was thirty-six.

~~∽

288. **EO to AB** ALS 4 pp. (c/o Guaranty Trust Co., / 50 Pall Mall, London) [Harvard]

[late March 1928]

Dear Agnes: I have just received, forwarded from London, your two letters to Harry about financial matters. After reading them I feel pretty hopeless about our reaching any friendly agreement since you seem to have determined on the policy of getting all you can out of me, regardless of my welfare or that of our children's future which depends, if you would only have foresight enough to see it, so much on my ability to save money in good years for the lean ones that inevitably have followed in the past when there have been no productions or the plays have been failures. I want to save money this year—(I am living very cheaply over here, thanks to a fifty-fifty basis and the big advantage of dollars in francs)—but if you are crying that you *"must"* have *2500*.00 no less for back bills after I've just paid a thousand in back bills in New York I can see little hope of saving a cent at that rate. Moreover, if you keep this up on me, I'm not going to try to save. It would be too futile. Also, your attitude puts me in no right frame of mind to write any new plays. And if my work stops, my income won't be enough to keep one of us going, let alone four or five! I advise you to give this matter a little careful thought before you try "taking me for all I've got." Then if you want to sue, go ahead. Perhaps that's the best way—and the cheapest for me—for I have a pretty good side to my case to present to any court and, thank God, I'm now out of reach of all the cheap publicity that will be called forth by your action—and I can, if necessary, stay out of reach of it indefinitely over here. So don't think you can frighten me by threatening to sue. Outside of the fact that I should hate you for dragging such a nasty mess of notoriety around our children's ears, when, if you weren't so eager to get all you can, everything could be arranged quietly on a decent human basis, I don't care whether you sue or not. But I've cabled Harry to go down and see you and go over the back bills you've run up[1] and do everything for you that is fair. But you've simply got to cut out running up bills regardless in the future. And you must not ask me to put any more money into Spithead. I can't and won't. I've already put too much into it. It's been the most expensive place that ever was built by any-one—and that's absolutely your fault since it was all left up to you. If I did what I want to do I'd advertise it for sale tomorrow. The only reason I don't is for your sake and the children's. You know that. And if you don't stop running up more bills for other than living necessities down there you'll force me to cable a notice to the Ber-muda papers saying I won't be held responsible for such debts. If you're determined to act like an enemy, you can't expect me to take it lying down. I've got to put up a battle for some sort of financial security for myself in order to do my work.

I suspect that what may be in back of your head—thanks to the advice you seem to be following, for I cannot imagine you acting so unfairly on your own and going back on all you'd agreed on as to your expenses in your talk with me!—is that you think you can make me buy you into keeping your word as to what you promised you would do. Well, you can't. I don't give a damn now whether you go ahead with that or not. It will make no difference in my life over here—except to keep me in a state of mind where no new plays will be forthcoming to earn royalties for you to throw away.

I have received a letter by this same mail from a recent visitor to Bermuda who shall be nameless saying that she had heard the gossip down there that you had "gone to pieces," were drinking, and at least on the verge of becoming a bit promiscuous with your favors, if you hadn't already fallen. "Such a shame for my poor dear little children," the writer went on—and blamed me as much as you. Now, of course, I appreciate the malice in such letters beneath the ostensible friendliness and I don't believe this one—although if you're drinking I know that nothing is impossible! I simply pass it on to you to warn you that there must be such gossip and you would do well, whatever you choose to do, to keep it dark. I have no right to tell you not to have lovers, or not to drink—except in our children's names—nevertheless such letters, even when I discount them, give me a turn. For no matter what our differences are and have been, I still love and respect you as my partner of ten long years in which we both managed to remain fairly clean. And that I fell in love I cannot regard as any breach of good faith since, as long as you let me be, I was quite honest with you about it.

I'm sorry this letter sounds so bitter. I can't help it. I especially resent in the last letter I received from you over here—I've only got two so far—your implication that you are doing all the suffering. For Christ's sake, don't you think I suffer too? If you don't, Agnes, you're a damn fool! Sometimes—and often!—when I think of Shane and Oona I suffer like hell from a sense of guilt toward them, and a deep sense of guilt[2] because I've made you suffer. You know damn well that I am a man who shrinks from the very notion of deliberately causing anyone sorrow. (Rages & fights and what one bitterly says then don't count.) It is in every line of my work. But what could I do? I did my damndest and fairest while I could. And I think, by God, that when you said "forgive me" that day at the hotel you saw the truth that you seem to be getting far away from now, the truth that at bottom you were a great deal more to blame than I was! I gave you every chance a man of honor could give, I fought and was willing to sacrifice myself, all I needed was understanding, sympathy and help in a time of deep emotional and spiritual turmoil. You were deaf and blind and dumb—(until it was too late and the irrevocable was an accomplished fact)—because you didn't want to hear or see or speak.

Think that over once in a while when you take to hating me and wishing me unhappiness!

Oh hell, I'll be fair about bills or anything else. You know that. I always have been generous enough to you and yours—even at times when I couldn't afford it. As for your plans for the future, do what and when you like. It doesn't matter. Life has become so complicated on all sides for me—I don't mean I'm unhappy but that I have to give up so much—all the past—for my happiness—that the one major complication is merely a symbol. And over here where Eugene O'Neill luckily has no news value, what's the difference? So go ahead at your own convenience. You will be fair, I know. Gene

P.S. Kiss Shane & Oona for me. I wrote him yesterday and sent her a postal.

1. The words "you've run up" have been underlined by a later hand, and in the margin someone has written: "Gene ran them up, & repudiated them (e.g. boat)."
2. The words in this paragraph, through "a deep sense of guilt," have been bracketed by a later hand, and in the margin someone has written "Puke."

289. **EO to AB**[1] ALS 5 pp. (c/o Guaranty Trust Co., / Pall Mall, London) [Harvard]

[c. April 8, 1928]

Dearest Agnes: Your two letters reached me yesterday and I was certainly damned happy to know that you've gotten down to work on a thing that deeply interests you. It gives me more satisfaction than I can tell you to hear that you are writing again and confident and happy about it. That was the news that I have been looking forward to hearing. Now you are all right and on your own feet in your own life! That is exactly what you needed! If you had had that in the past few years we might have won out to final happiness together—but I realize it was exactly the fact of my being around that made it impossible for you! The irony of our fate, what? Well, when you come into your own as a writer—and I am absolutely sure you will if you hew to the line!—you can look back and bless the day I got out and left you free to do your stuff!

I shall look forward with the keenest interest to reading your script. It was rather a dirty dig you give me about my "fatal criticisms" of "write something else"? After all, you must acknowledge, if you are honest, that I have always done my best to encourage you to do your best and not to attempt easy things, or unimportant themes, or junk for money. I have always felt that was not only the artistically right thing but also, in the long run, the practical commercial thing. But that is all "old hat." You know what my beliefs are.

As for my own writing, I am now settled down temporarily (for the next month or so, that is—perhaps longer) here on the Mediterranean in a nice quiet little village and I'm hard at work on *Dynamo*. The play has developed a lot in my unconscious (or whatever it is) since I worked out the scenario and it looks grand to me and ought to evolve into a real "big one." I'm going to work slowly on it and try to avoid by careful writing the enormous amount of going over and condensing I had to do on *Interlude*, as I sure hate that end of the job and it takes too much out of me.

It's fine news about Shane and the school.[2] As you say, that's what he needs. I sent him a bushel of postcards while I was still on the move. Hope he got them all right. What I write on them I'm careful to compose so that the P.O. people will have nothing to gossip about, if they read it. I miss him and Oona like hell at times. Don't sneer! I love them as much as you do—perhaps more—in my oblique, inexpressive fashion. At any rate, they will find out I have been a good father—(as Eugene did)—when they are old enough to understand all that has happened and when they really come to know me and about me.

This reminds me: won't you please write to Gaga and give her some definite information about where she stands and what you want her to do?[3] I've just had a letter from her and she seems in a terrible state about our breaking-up and her own future. She writes that she's heart-broken because she knows she'll never see the children again, etc. It almost made me cry, honestly. She said she hadn't heard from you in a long time. I've sent her a hundred but it isn't money she needs. God damn it, Agnes, whatever her faults, we've both loved her, our children have loved her, and she's loved all of us, and stuck to us since Shane was born through thick and thin, and you can't hold her idiotic gossip against her when it's a case of wounding an old woman who has been a good friend to us, if there ever was one. You can't throw her aside as if she were an old rag that you'd used up and wanted to get rid of. Won't you please do something about this? If you think I've ever done anything for you, then I ask this as a favor! I'll pay whatever added expense she cost you. You know I can't do anything for her. It's being near the children she loves in what for eight years has been her home. For Christ sake, please write her. It's on my conscience and I feel like hell about it.

It sounds strange to hear you talk of all the interesting folk in Bermuda. "It was not like that in the olden days," what? I always miss the good breaks socially, eh? And I'll bet you are a good hostess, now that I'm not around to spoil the fun. In fact, when I remember the 2500 you "*must* have" for back bills (in your letter to Harry) I cannot doubt that you are a grand hostess. Also you must consider—and the guests must agree with you—that I am a grand "sugar daddy" to have in the background!

But let's avoid finances. As always, your tendency to be utterly careless with money, tends to fill me with bitterness. As the wife of an artist, in that respect at least, you have always been a grand mate for a rich broker. My only prayer now is, may the broker appear—and soon! In the name of auld lang syne can't you find it in your heart to fall in love with a rich broker? I really think you owe it to me, Agnes—if not to the man, at least to the w.k. hard-working dramatist!

Joking aside, I hope you talked over everything with Harry—that he got down all right on the 26th and that we'll soon be able to finally sign up and both feel put. As for "Spithead," I will do anything agreeable to you about it provided you are agreeable to me on other things and don't crucify me. That is, I will neither rent it nor sell it but give you entire use of it for as long as you reasonably wish provided I have permission to visit the children there. (I mean it might be arranged that when you wanted to come to N.Y. for a few weeks I might go down in your stead.)

Your plans for your trip in May and for the summer sound excellent to me. I think that country out there will be exciting and interesting for you—as much so as England and France and Spain have been for me. You love riding for one thing and you ought to get all you want of it there.

I'm sorry my letter from London in which I said I was happy sounded like "protesting too much" to you. As a matter of fact, I am as happy as I can be, being the sort of brooding person I am, and I feel growth inside me. I have had my bad hours and days, naturally, but they are due to myself alone and to my obsession with the past which it will take me years to shake off. And there are memories I never want to shake off, no matter how much pain of regret for what might have been they cause me—for example, the other day I had a sudden clear vision of the day at the Happy Home when Shane was born, of my holding your hand, remember? And the early days at Peaked Hill come back. These sort I want to remember. It is only the poison and the hate I must forget—in justice to both of us and the nine years in which, speaking in general, we did our best.

How far we have come from Happy Home! How far, indeed! As far as the "indiscretion" and its results you write about. I hate to write about it and what I am saying I say without bitterness, only with sadness—but, for your own good, *mark well what I do say!* You have piled an indiscretion upon an indiscretion! Don't you know that your letter—you always have had such an unfortunate vague memory for certain things!—gives me proof positive of adultery in your own handwriting? If you don't believe this, then kindly remember exactly what you wrote and the light will break on you. You have made the matter so brilliantly clear against yourself that no Judge would hesitate for an instant. Not that I ever intend to use it. I'm not threatening you. I'm your friend as long as you are mine. And it is your privilege to have had a lover or lovers. Certainly it would be ridiculous for me to object. But I do object and most emphatically and to the last ditch when, (notwithstanding that your own statement of the case proves the utter and entire impossibility of it!) (Remember what you wrote, please, and you'll see!) you have the unscrupulous effrontery to attempt to lay this thing at my door! You must have changed, by God, and hardly for the better spiritually—when you can do such a thing! But you might have remembered your dates—which you give explicitly!—better! Why, I wasn't even in the same country with you when this must have happened! Or did you write it deliberately to taunt me? If so, it misses its mark. I'm way beyond that point.[4]

But enough of that! I swore I wasn't going to get bitter in this letter—and I'm not. Naturally, you're free to do as you please—but kindly count me out of the responsibility because I—just as naturally—won't accept it. After all, there is a limit to what you can expect of me! I'm not an utter ass!

Kiss the children for me. I hope it can be arranged so that I can see them before too terribly long. It all depends on you. I can't—and won't—come back to the U.S. until you've carried out your plan, even if I have to give up the idea of having any new play produced next season. Work! Be happy! Gene

P.S. I'm enclosing this to Harry to mail—quicker and safer.

1. In the top margin, someone (probably Max Wylie) has written: "Whole character of O'Neill is in this letter."

2. AB was planning to send Shane to a boarding school in Lenox, Massachusetts.

3. Mrs. Clark's health had failed in the fall of 1927 and she had reluctantly returned to Provincetown. After AB moved from Bermuda to West Point Pleasant, Mrs. Clark rejoined the family there and resumed her care of the children sporadically when her health permitted. She died on July 6, 1929. In the margin opposite this paragraph, someone (probably Max Wylie) has written: "Always gets A to take care of *his* conscience at his convenience. He did nothing for Gaga—ever!"

4. Since AB's letter explaining this "indiscretion" has not been found, it is difficult to speculate on this matter. AB told Louis Sheaffer that she and EO had sex one final time in her hotel room in December 1927. AB was unclothed, using a sunlamp, when EO came unexpectedly to the room. During the winter she discovered she was pregnant. When she informed EO of this fact, she made a mistake in her dates, and EO used this slip to accuse her of unfaithfulness, as above. She eventually had an abortion in the apartment of Mary Blair (undated interview). Harold De Polo confirmed the story of the abortion and stated his belief that the father was one of the workers at Spithead (Louis Sheaffer interview, May 1959).

~~∽~~

290. **EO to AB** ALS 3 pp. (c/o Guaranty Trust Co., Pall Mall, London) [Virginia]

[late April 1928]

Dear Agnes: Perhaps my last letter—the latter part—was a bit strained. But you must acknowledge I had reason. However, let's forget it. I don't want there to be any bitterness between us.

I've taken a motor trip—invitation—to Prague since I last saw you.[1] It's a wonderful town—and I'm going to stick on and do some work here—not in the city but in a remote suburb in a home on the river—a quiet, lovely spot. Will probably remain for the next month or so—then back to the Mediterranean which didn't interest me much as it was too cold for swimming—rotten weather all over Europe—but will be warm in a month.

What I'm really writing about is this, that I feel the time for newspaper secrecy about our estrangement is over and is now doing both of us a lot of harm. I feel Harry is all wrong in his dope. It's simply because we've been so secret that the story keeps hot and they pestering you and all my friends in N.Y. Secrecy makes them suspect that there are all sorts of dirty scandalous charges coming out from one or both of us. What I've written to Harry is why hide when there's nothing to hide, why keep the boys het up expecting scandal? The Sinclair Lewis case[2] is much to the point. It was carried out with dignity and quiet in spite of the fact that it's well known he has been living with a woman in Berlin. Once they get it from your lips that we're definitely separated for good because we simply couldn't get along any longer, but that there's no question of any third party having anything to do with it, and that you've decided to go West and sue for a divorce, they'll lay off of us for good. There's no news value to a simple divorce without correspondent, as you know, no matter how notorious the people. Divorces are too common.

So I wish, for your own sake (they'll bother hell out of you when you go up) and mine (I have to keep ducking recognition over here) you'd give out a simple statement of the facts the next time any paper cables you, or any reporter meets you—or let Harry give it out, as I've requested to him. I was thinking myself of sending out one, ostensibly as a quote from a letter, to be given out via the Guild bunch—to cover simply the separation because, with the best of friendly intentions, we simply couldn't hit it off any longer, and that *I thought* it was your intention to sue for divorce. But when I considered, it seemed better—and your right!—that you should take the initiative—or Harry would be all right as representing both of us and what you say should go. Am I not a perfect gent?

But I do believe that it ought to be put over as soon as possible, don't you? If you do it before you go to N.Y. then they probably won't bother you when you're there at all. It's really stupid to hold back any more but I surely appreciate your consideration for me in having done so so long. They must have pestered you to death. But I'm beginning to be worried about our not saying anything because, judging from some clippings I've received lately, the boys sniff so much dirt under this that they're beginning to improvise pretty impudently. One Coast paper had you about to divorce me "it is rumored" for habitual drunkenness, another somewhere had it "rumored" that you were to divorce me because "according to close friends of the couple" I could not "keep my eyes off my leading ladies." Laughable, eh—but irritating. And an Illinois one had it all scrambled—I was to divorce you—what for, not stated. A mad world! But time we did something, don't you think, or God knows what it'll be next.

Speaking of the Sinclair Lewis case, I hope you read what she got—and you know damn well she bled him for every cent she could, being that kind. She got 1/4 of his net income up to 48,000 but no more after that. She wasn't guaranteed anything per year. Quite a difference from what I'm offering you in our separation agreement! And his income per year for the past ten years has been at least three times mine. Think it over! Better grab mine before I change my mind! Joking aside, I think anyone will acknowledge I have been generous. Will you try to be in your turn?

One thing about Spithead—have you ever figured that I have 45,000 tied up there, that that in preferred stocks would mean an income of well over 3000 a year I'm losing, plus 600 int. on mortgage & insurance, etc. All that really has to be added to what I'm offering you—as long as I hold back from selling it, which I'm certainly willing to do for a period of five years from the time you keep your promise and after that, provided I don't need the money. Of course, anytime I did go broke, you'd have to agree to let me sell, in any event, or else I couldn't support you. After all, I'm homeless, you know. I have no place to work and I've got a right to part of the money from it to try a place.

Why don't you have Shane write me? You might. It isn't cricket for you to try and make him forget me, you know—and he won't thank you for it when he's old enough to judge you!

Kiss them both for me. I miss them. And all friendly best to you. I hope you're happy. I am (but you'll accuse me of boasting). Let me hear about your work.   Gene.

1. EO never made this trip to Prague, although he used the same story with other people, apparently to throw journalists and friends off his track. He even arranged to have postcards sent at various stops to prove he was there.

2. Lewis (1885–1951) was arguably the most famous and successful American writer in the world in 1927 when he was invited to dinner by a well-known foreign correspondent in Berlin, Dorothy Thompson. They were both married at the time, but they fell instantly in love and he proposed marriage that very evening. Grace Hegger Lewis obtained a divorce in Reno, but EO underestimates the amount of publicity it received.

~~

291. **EO to AB** ALS 2 pp. ([Villa Marguerite, Guéthary, B.P., France]) [Virginia]

[early May 1928]

Dear Agnes: Your letter came today. I'm sorry you gave the interview.[1] I think a simple divorce announcement would have been better, done the trick and killed their hope for a scandal. As it is, the mystery still remains to intrigue them—for they know damn well you're lying and they wonder what for.

But don't think I'm blaming you! I know you hadn't received my last letter about this same matter. Also I realize how you've been hounded. I'm damn sorry, Agnes, to have brought you into all this! But what could I do—or can I do? It was fate. But as soon as they know they're making all this fuss about just another Reno divorce, without correspondent or filth, they'll leave us all alone. Believe me, it is not nice for me to have to "hide out" on them, either! It's on my mind continually and I find it hard to get any work done. So for all our sakes, let's get all this settled at the earliest possible moment.

I'm sorry I wrote that severe last part of that letter about your "indiscretion." You shouldn't have given me such exact proof in the dates you gave me. But no matter. I suppose you've gone ahead with what you planned to do—and that ends the matter. I'll forget it. I don't want to have any bitterness in my memory of you. I want always to have your image in my mind as the Agnes I loved so entirely over so many years.

I object to your amendments to my agreement. I still feel the agreement is damned generous as I offered it and that your added demands (with the exception of the [illegible] for [back bills?]) are unjust and unnecessary. Surely you can trust me in the matter of Shane & Oona. Anybody else in question is financially independent and wants nothing from me. What are you afraid of? That I'll sell Spithead? I never will as long as you want to live there—(although I again say you're foolish. You [could?] live like a queen in France on 500 a month—or live in Czechoslovakia—and send Shane to school in Switzerland—unless I go broke—and simply have to have money to live on myself and support you & Eugene & Shane & Barbara & Oona. After all, 45,000 is tied up in Spithead and that represents 1/2 my worldly wealth and I don't get a cent of income from it! Please think of these things, if you want to be fair to me & yourself & the kids! My future, you realize, is yours, and theirs too, and you do no good in making my burden too heavy—for then I'll simply quit.)

Get a lawyer, if you like. But please accept what I've offered you. I'll be generous in addition whenever I can. But don't try to force me. If I had wanted to be foxy with you—as you seem to want to be with me with your added demands—I'd have offered a good deal less in the first place and let you bargain up to what I wanted. But I didn't. I treated you honestly. I offered *more* than I felt I could afford!

But enough of finances. I hope you start on your trip soon. The sooner the better for both of us. They'll never let you alone around N.Y.

I sent via Harry a present for Oona's birthday. Hope she got it and enjoyed it.

What have you done about Gaga? Please at least write her! Don't be so damn cruel to that poor old woman who was our friend for so many years! It isn't like you! She writes me & I her but I'm no good for her. Have Shane write her! If he forgets her so easily, by God he's no real son of mine and I'm not going to write him again until I hear he has done so! I mean this! And he'll get nothing from me either. There is such a thing as being an ingrate—even when you're only eight!

All is well with me. I like Czechoslovakia. And I hope to get really down to work once this present mess of publicity clears away and you're on your way. However, if it keeps up much longer and you keep fighting for more money there isn't much chance of any *Dynamo* for the Guild next year. I can't perform miracles and I can only concentrate on one thing at a time.

And won't you be just too tickled to death to feel that you can—for the present anyway—hurt my work! A grand revenge! But maybe I wrong you. If so, I apologize. If we could talk together—our children's future, money agreements, etc.—everything would be all right and settled in half an hour, but as we can't, hence bitterness.

One last word—and one sincerely for your good! Don't over-drink in N.Y. and then vilify a certain lady! It only harms you. The very people you do it to are the first to sneer at you for a bum sport and yellow loser when your back is turned. This is *friendly* advice.

All good wishes! Find happiness! And work! Gene.

1. "O'Neill Divorce Rumors Scouted," *New York World*, April 27, 1928, p. 3. In the interview AB denied any plans for divorce; she declared that EO was traveling with friends in France and that she planned to join him soon in London: "She refused to say that her failure to leave for Europe with him constituted what other celebrities have referred to as a 'marital vacation.' Nevertheless, she believes in an occasional change of air—'for the man' she added quickly. There could be no misunderstanding."

292. **AB to EO** ALS 2 pp. (New Preston, Conn.) [Harvard]

June 22nd [1928]

Dear Gene: Harry is sending you on the terms to which he and Driscoll[1] have agreed. I had a hard time getting Driscoll to see my point of view, that is, that I did not want to ask for "what any court would give me" etc. He wanted me to ask for house out right, etc.

I would rather you would not think I have been influenced by anyone. I want really nothing for myself, once I become self-supporting again, or marry. I feel that the terms of the settlement now being sent on to you for agreement are absolutely fair. I went over the thing very carefully with Harry: he said that he would personally be behind the agreement as now sent on to you, and asked me to cut out one or two things which Driscoll wanted—which I did.

I asked for the $2,000, as you know that this moving about costs a great deal, & the children and I both need clothes. However, that's up to you. I won't stick out for it. The rest of the agreement I will absolutely stick out for.

I have not heard from you in regard to my operation. Probably Harry advises you not to write.

It is a shame we cannot talk this over personally. I am sure it could be settled. Agnes.

Was at the [Iselins?] for a week, raced twice in Adrian's new 8. meter. Great sport.

1. AB had hired Charles Driscoll of O'Brian, Malevinsky, and Driscoll.

～⌒

293. **AB to EO**[1] ALS 2 pp. (New Preston, Conn.) [Harvard]

[Summer 1928]

My dear Gene: Oona asked me to send you these letters. She writes to you frequently, & today she got quite excited over seeing it was properly mailed & stamped and sealed. She drew a picture of "Oona" on the back for you.

Tonight after she got to bed I said I was going to take her down to N.Y. and she immediately said, can I take my trunk so I can show my toys to daddy? I said you weren't in N.Y. "Where is he?" In Europe. "Is he coming back? Why doesn't he come back, I want him Mummie." (This is literal.) I said he will come back dear & see you. Daddie loves you. *Then* she said "Will he come back & live with us Mummie," and *then she began to cry*. It almost broke my heart. I think it is the most peculiar thing I have ever heard of for a child of three to remember like that. She must be a very strange little kid, and I think somehow that you did always occupy a very important in [*sic*] her small life, and that she cannot get used to life without you. She recognized newspaper pictures of you immediately—

I write you this only because I think you might like to know. I would, in your place. Also, because I do think it's unusual. Why don't you write her anyway, if you don't see her. Or, perhaps it would be kinder all around for her to be allowed to forget. She surely is a strange, emotional kid. *Agnes.*

1. Louis Sheaffer states that this letter was never mailed. Sheaffer, *Son and Artist*, 311.

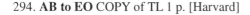

294. **AB to EO** COPY of TL 1 p. [Harvard]

[Beginning and ending of this carbon copy of a typed letter are missing. This page is numbered 5.]

[Summer-fall? 1928]

[. . .] if you still have them, that they were very friendly and showed no antagonism at all. I still hoped—though differently—for a friendship with you—because of the children, too. Meantime your letters showed increasing bitterness—unnecessary, it seemed to me, as you were happy—had what you wanted—and *honestly* had no cause to complain of me, for I was not doing any of the things you had feared I might do. You write me saying someone—*why didn't you say who?*—had written you the children were neglected, I was drunk all the time, "and becoming promiscuous in my favours". You said you understood the malice underneath the friendliness, but for the sake of the past—decency, etc.—why did I give people a chance to say such things? In other words you *did* believe a malicious liar in a lie so totally unfounded and without basis that if I did not know you I would have said you had made it up! This letter I considered beneath me to refer to at the time. I showed it to Harold, who had come up that evening, the first time (except what [*sic*] I had them for dinner) that I had seen either him or Helen since Xmas. (He only came to borrow six pounds to help him get back to New York.) He seemed really indignant and said he would write you. He showed me later a letter he had written you which was quite O.K. except that he had failed to mention that the time I went out with them was before Xmas, not after my return from New York and our agreement. The only person who I could possibly *think* would write anything was Lou Bradley. She came down before Xmas, and as she was running around with Harold and a hard boozing crowd, I did not ask her to the house or go to see her, except the day before she sailed. Harold however said he did not think it was she. My feeling about such a report reaching you was one of perfect security, as *I* knew how I was living, and that time would show *you*. But I could not understand why in that letter you had not made some reference to the financial mess in which I was left (as I felt you must have by that time received my long letter sent to you in London). I had explained to you in that letter that I wanted for your sake as well as my own, to get the past all straightened out, so I *could* start fresh.

In the meantime Harry was planning to come down, and I was thinking very seriously over the agreement which I was to sign. You had said in one or two of your letters that you would certainly not be mean, that you would let me stay in Spithead,[1] and in another you said you would *not sell it* as long as I wanted to live there. I am sure you meant this—but my dear Gene, you must realize as well as I do how time and circumstances change things—and people. It might easily be that in five years you might decide to sell Spithead—no matter what my wishes.

Now suppose in the meantime I had grown to love it even more than I do now?

Part of my plans for the future were to get it into wonderful shape, make a real home of it. In order to do this, for as you know, it is not really finished, I would have to spend some of my own money on it. By my own, I mean money I earned. I would never feel like doing this as long as there was always the chance of losing it. I don't mind doing it if the benefit of my work and interest will go to the children. I felt then that you were honestly interested in me as a person, and in my future life being one we could both be proud of (I feel you are still, if you will get rid of your bitterness) and that you would understand why the security of Spithead would be a *real anchor*. I realized something else also: that you, in all fairness, should make some sort of settlement on Shane and Oona. That is always done, particularly when the wife has no money. You may say you did not do it for Eugene, but you had no money then: and [. . .]

1. The words "until it was sold" have been deleted here.

～⌒つ

295. **EO to AB** Postcard (postmarked: Biarritz B ses Pirénées 1640 10–3 28, addressed to Mrs. Eugene O'Neill, Box 457, Hamilton, Bermuda (via New York)) [Virginia]

[The postcard depicts a tomb, capped by a reclining sculptural figure. The caption reads: *"Loches (I{ndre}-et-L{oire})—Château Royal (mon{ument} hist{orique}) Tombeau d'Agnès Sorel érigé au XV s{iècle}, relevé en 1809."*]

[October 3, 1928]

Dear Agnes: This is a marvelous château! You must visit it when you come to France. Kiss Shane & Oona for me.
    Love. Gene.[1]

1.   Louis Sheaffer observes that it may be significant that this postcard shows the tomb of a woman named Agnes, "especially since he told Macgowan that Agnes was 'dead' to him." Sheaffer, *Son and Artist*, p. 295.

Index